AKANSHA PUBLISHING HOUSE
4649-B/21, Ansari Road
Darya Ganj
New Delhi - 110 002
Ph. : 23263193 / 9811582579
Email: ektabooks@yahoo.com

ENTREPRENEURSHIP AND SMALL SCALE INDUSTRIES

First Published 2006
Edition : 2026
ISBN 81-8370-015-2

[The responsibility for the facts stated, conclusions reached etc. is entirely that of the Author. The publisher and editor is not responsible for them, whatsoever.]

PRINTED IN INDIA

Published by M.P. Misra for Akansha Publishing House, New Delhi and Printed at Tarun Offset Press, Delhi.

ENTREPRENEURSHIP
AND
SMALL SCALE INDUSTRIES

ENTREPRENEURSHIP
AND
SMALL SCALE
INDUSTRIES

Editor
G.P. PRASAIN

AKANSHA PUBLISHING HOUSE
NEW DELHI-110002 (INDIA)

DEDICATED

to

My Elder Sister

MRS. GOMA DEVI SHARMA

who encouraged and guided
my early endeavours

MANIPUR UNIVERSITY,
CANCHIPUR
IMPHAL-795003
MANIPUR. INDIA

Vice-Chancellor

FOREWORD

Entrepreneurship is an important dominant of industrial growth of a society. History of economic development of all societies-developed or underdeveloped bears evidence to the fact that the entrepreneurs have made significant contribution in this respect. Entrepreneurs contribute more in a society which has free economy and provide security and prestige to the entrepreneurs than the one which has regulated economy and less security.

This book entitled Entrepreneurship and Small Scale Industries, edited by Dr. G.P. Prasian, is an outcome of the National Seminar on Entrepreneurship Development organised by the Department of Commerce, Manipur University in collaboration with the Indian Council of Social Science Research, New Delhi.

The main objective of the industrial policy pursued by any Government is to active massive increase in employment by promoting Small Scale Industries and Rural Industries. The Governments are of the firm belief that given the magnitude of unemployment and the number of persons living below the poverty line, the touch stone of all industrial schemes and investments ought to be their employment potential.

For this purpose a thrust has to be given to establish, promote and develop the rural industries which are also called the cottage industries and village industries or small industries including tiny and household sectors, particularly in backward areas where it is essentially needed. All out efforts should be made to provide self-employment opportunity in urban and rural areas. The information technology sector is a viable option for Manipur.

The seminar papers presented here discuss various aspects of entrepreneurship development in Manipur, the Northeastern Region, the IT-industries and Women's Entrepreneurship. This book could provide motivation and can create desire among the population to choose self-employment opportunity and also tap the potential of women's entrepreneurial skills for self-employment.

I am sure that the recommendations made by the seminar would be given due attention by the respective governments, cooperative movements, non-governmental organisations and general public and bring about qualitative development in entrepreneurship.

16 August 2005

N. BIJOY SINGH
Vice-Chancellor

PREFACE

An essential ingredient in the economic growth of any region is the enterprises promoted by the individuals, called entrepreneurs. Entrepreneurship development is viewed as an important determinant in the process of industrialisation. It is believed that an economy is the effect for which entrepreneurship is the cause. Entrepreneurs do not come into existence spontaneously on their own. There are certain factors, which stimulate them to start an enterprise. The environment play a very significant role in promoting entrepreneurship and it is not limited to any class, community or religion. The economic progress of any country or state can be achieved only through a systematic industrial development. In the present era of liberalisation, privatisation and globalisation, where the world economic scenario is changing very fast, people cannot remain economically backward forever. Therefore, to uplift the people the Government machinery should provide entrepreneurial training through IT and banks and financial institutions should come forward to provide liberal loans to them in order to establish new enterprises.

The students are the potential source of entrepreneurs. But most often students are unaware about the opportunities for self-employment and entrepreneurial career. As a result, after completion of their education they search for opportunities for salaried employment. But scope is very limited. Thus unemployment is one of the major problems in India and more so in North East Region among the educated youth. Problems of unemployment have led to many social evils. Again job opportunities being limited, students can be made aware about opportunities for self-employment and entrepreneurship career when they are still students. Keeping in view the relevance of the subject and to develop the interest and importance of entrepreneurship education among the students and public of the region, the Department of Commerce, Manipur University organised a two days National Seminar on Entrepreneurship Development in Manipur with references to Small Scale and IT Industries on April 6-7, 2005. Indian Council of Social Science Research (ICSSR), New

Delhi sponsored the Seminar. A galaxy of social scientists, representatives from training agencies, All Manipur Entrepreneurs Association, All Manipur Trained Entrepreneurs Union, consultancy organizations and faculty members from colleges and universities from Manipur and other places of North East Region attended the Seminar.

The Seminar was formally inaugurated by Prof. N. Bijoy Singh, The Vice-Chancellor, Manipur University. Dr D.D. Mali, former Director, Indian Institute of Entrepreneurship, Guwahati delivered the keynote address. The seminar was spread over two days and divided into five technical sessions besides the inaugural session and valedictory session. The technical sessions were chaired by Prof. N. Joykumar Singh, Dean, School of Social Sciences, Manipur University, Prof. N.Lokendra Singh, Director, College Development Council, Manipur University, Dr D.D. Mali, Prof. Ksh. Bimola Devi and Prof. E. Bijoykumar Singh, Head, Department of Economics.

In the seminar, thirty-one highly interesting, thought provoking, inspiring, informative, educative and research papers, dealing with different aspects of entrepreneurship, including women entrepreneurship and IT industries were presented and discussed. This volume contains the papers presented in the seminar and one additional paper on entrepreneurship development of the North East Region. In addition, the keynote address is also included.

The seminar aimed, at creating awareness about the need for entrepreneurial development with reference to small scale and IT Industries and its impact on the economic development of the region. The book, therefore, present a very authentic, data based, first hand analysis of the pace of entrepreneurial development in North-East while comparing it with other states of the country. The papers have been slightly edited to suit the objectives of the book.

I acknowledge with a deep sense of gratitude and appreciation, all the great encouragement and invaluable assistance, guidance, help and counselling received from Prof. N. Bijoy Singh, Vice-Chancellor, Manipur University at different stages of organising the National Seminar and in bringing out this publication. I am also very much indebted to Prof. N. Joykumar Singh, Dean, School of Social Sciences, Manipur University for all the encouragement and inspiration he has provided to me in bringing out this book. I am very much grateful to all the contributors who have graciously permitted me to include their contributions in this book.

I am very thankful to ICSSR, New Delhi for the financial support extended by them for organising the National Seminar on Entrepreneurship Development at Manipur University. I also take this opportunity to thank my colleagues, Dr N. Tejmani Singh, Dr Rajmani Singha, Dr Robita Sorokhaibam and Dr Kh. Dhiren Meetei who have always given cooperation to me in conducting various academic programmes in the Department.

The academic encouragement received from Dr R.K. Ranjan Singh, Registrar, Manipur University, Prof. N. Lokendra Singh, Director, College Development Council, Manipur University, Prof. R.P. Singh, Department of Geography, Manipur University, Prof. Ksh. Bimola Devi, former Dean, School of Social Sciences, Manipur University, Prof. E. Bijoykumar Singh, Head, Department of Economics, Manipur University, Prof. S.S. Khanka, Dean, School of Management Sciences, Tezpur University, Prof. H.C. Gautam, Gauhati University, Dr. J.C. Kalita, Gauhati University, Prof. A.R.M. Rahman , Dibrugarh University, Prof. M.N. Mishra, Banaras Hindu University, Prof. C.S. Mishra, and Prof. A.K. Mishra of Nagaland University, Prof. P.K. Haldar, Tripura University, Prof. N.B. Dey, Assam University and Dr Kh. Tomba Singh of Assam University is acknowledged with great encomiums.

I am very much grateful to my mother Mrs. Januka Devi and my brother Mr. Kharga Prasad Prasain and Mr Kumar Prasain who have encouraged me and assisted in several ways in my higher studies. I must thank my wife Mrs. Subhadra Devi and my son Pappu and daughter Pooza whose patience, support, encouragement, understanding and love helped me to bring this effort to fruition.

I would also like to place on record my profound sense of gratitude to Shri M.P. Mishra, proprietor, Akansha Publishing House, New Delhi, the publishers of this book who readily agreed to take up the assignment of publishing this book and extended the task within the shortest possible time.

Manipur University
Canchipur, Imphal

G.P. PRASAIN

CONTENTS

Foreword vii

Preface ix

List of Contributors xvii

KEYNOTE ADDRESS

1. Developing Entrepreneurship in North East Experiences and Strategies (With special reference to Small-Scale and IT Industries and Manipur) 3
   – *D.D. Mali*

ENTREPRENEURSHIP DEVELOPMENT IN MANIPUR

2. Industrial Policy and Small Scale Industries in Manipur 19
   – *E.Bijoykumar Singh*
3. The Prospects of Small-Scale Industries Development in Manipur 27
   – *B. D. Nayak and Shipra S. Nayak*
4. Entrepreneurial Motivation in Small Scale Industries in Manipur – An Analysis 41
   – *G.P. Prasain and E. Nixon Singh*
5. Managerial Problems in Small Scale Industries of Manipur: A critical Analysis of some selected units 55
   – *H. Ramananda Singh*
6. Working Capital Management of Small Scale Industries in Manipur: An Empirical Study 70
   – *Dr. N. Tejmani Singh*
7. Entrepreneurship Development in Manipur: Challenges and Opportunities 82
   – *Rajmani Singha*

8. Entrepreneurship Development in Small-Scale Industries in Manipur: The Challenges Ahead 93
– *Th. Priyokumar Singh*

9. Development of Entrepreneurship in Small Scale and IT Industries in Manipur 104
– *S. Herojit Singh*

10. Role of Promotional Agencies for Entrepreneurship Development in Manipur: A Case Study 121
– *Kh. Devananda Singh*

11. Hand-Woven Textiles & Home Furnishings: An Opportunity for Entrepreneurship Growth 129
– *Radhesyam Oinam and Memcha L.*

12. Problems and Prospects of Entrepreneurship Development in Small Scale Industries - A Case Study 139
– *Gautam Patikar and Ratan Kaurinta*

ENTREPRENEURSHIP DEVELOPMENT IN IT INDUSTRIES

13. Entrepreneurship Development and Information Technology 151
– *Purushottam Bhandari and H.C. Gautam*

14. Technopreneurship as the New Paradigm for E-business 161
– *Lai Prabhakar*

15. The E-Entrepreneur: Potential and Challenges 177
– *Kh. Tomba Singh*

16. Information needs of the Small Scale Industries: Prospects of E-Commerce in Manipur 190
– *L. Shanta Meitei and Dr. Th. Purnima Devi*

17. Entrepreneurship and Information Technology in Mizoram 205
– *R.K.P.G. Singha and K.C. Kabra*

18. IT Policy of Manipur: A Step for the Growth of SSI in IT Sector 217
– *S. Somokanta Singh*

19. Development of Entrepreneurship in Small Scale and IT Industries in Manipur 231
– *M. Minarani Devi*

WOMEN ENTEPRENEURSHIP

20. An Overview of Women Entrepreneurs in Manipur 245
– *Robita Sorokhaibam*

21. Women Entrepreneurs in Manipur: A Case Study of Khwairamband Women Market 256
– *G.P. Prasain and Kh. Dhiren Meetei*

22. Women Entrepreneurs and Self Help Groups 266
– *Kh. Somorendro Singh*

23. Problems of Women Entrepreneurs: A Case Study of Imphal and Kamrup Districts 280
– *Th. Prabha Devi*

ENTREPRENEURSHIP DEVELOPMENT IN NORTH-EASTERN REGION

24. Entrepreneurship Development in the North-Eastern Region of India: Experiences and Prospects 291
– *S.S. Khanka*

25. Sustainable Development of Tourism Entrepreneurship in the North-East India: An Appraisal of Tourism Entrepreneurship Incubator 313
– *Anjan Bhuyan*

26. ISO-9000 and TQM in SSI Units - Issues and Challenges 340
– *Ch. Ibohal Meitei*

27. Role of Entrepreneurship in Fruit and Vegetable Processing Sector: Perspectives of North-Eastern Region of India 354
– *R.M. Pant, P.K. Nema and Rituparna Datta*

28. Managerial Challenges of Small Scale Industries 370
– *S. Keshorjit Singh and Jibon Kumar L*

29. Co-operative Entrepreneurship in North-East States with Special Reference to Assam & Manipur 379
– *K.I. Meetei*

30. Prospects and Impediments on Industry in Manipur 391
– *L. Orenkumar*

Summary of Recommendations 400

Index 406

LIST OF CONTRIBUTORS

Bhandari, Purushottam, Jagiroad College, Assam.

Bhuyan, Anjan, Lecturer in Economics, Darrang College, Tezpur, Assam.

Datta, Rituparna, Department of Humanities and Social Sciences, North Eastern Regional Institute of Science and Technology, Itanagar, Arunachal Pradesh.

Devi, M. Minarani, Lecturer in Commerce, D.M. College of Commerce, Imphal.

Devi, Th. Prabha, Department of Commerce, Manipur University, Imphal.

Devi, Th. Purnima, Sr. Assistant Professor Department of Library & Information Science, Manipur University, Imphal.

Gautam, H.C., Professor of Commerce, Gauhati University, Guwahati.

Kabra, K.C., Lecturer in Commerce, North Eastern Hill University, Shillong.

Kaurinta, Ratan, Lecturer in Commerce, Nagaland University, Kohima.

Khanka, S.S., Dean, School of Management Science, Head, Department of Business Administration, Tezpur University, Assam.

Mali, D.D., Former Director, Indian Institute of Entrepreneurship, Guwahati.

Meetei, K. Ibomcha, Faculty Member, Institute of Cooperative Management, Imphal.

Meetei, Kh. Dhiren Faculty Member, Department of Commerce, Manipur University, Imphal.

Meetei, L. Shanta, Department of Library and Information Science, Manipur University, Imphal.

Meitei, Ch. Ibohal, Sr. Assistant Professor of Management, Manipur University, Imphal.

Memha L., Sr. Assistant Professor of Management, Manipur University, Imphal.

Nayak, B. D., Reader in Economics, North East Regional Institute of Science and Technology, Itanagar, Arunachal Pradesh.

Nayak, Shipra S., Dept. of Humanities and Social Science, North Eastern Regional Institute of Science and Technology, Itanagar, Arunachal Pradesh.

Nema, P.K., Department of Agricultural Engineering, North Eastern Regional Institute of Science and Technology, Itanagar, Arunachal Pradesh.

Oinam, Radhesyam, Research Scholar, MIMS, Manipur University, Imphal.

Orenkumar, L., Secretary, All Manipur Trained Entrepreneur Union, Imphal.

Pant, R. M., Reader in Economics, Department of Humanities and Social Sciences, North Eastern Regional Institute of Science and Technology, Itanagar, Arunachal Pradesh.

Partikar, Gautam, Lecturer in Commerce, Nagaland University, Kohima.

Prabhakar, Lai, System Analyst, MIMS, Manipur University, Imphal

Prasain, G.P., Head, Department of Commerce, Manipur University, Imphal.

Sharma, L. Jibon Kumar, Sr. Assistant Professor of Management, Manipur University, Imphal.

Singh, Th. Priyokumar, Lecturer in Economics, D.M. College of Commerce, Imphal.

Singh, E. Bijoykumar, Head, Department of Economics, Manipur University, Imphal.

Singh, E. Nixon, Lecturer in Commerce, D. M. College of Commerce, Imphal.

Singh, H. Ramananda, Reader in Management, Assam University, Silchar.

Singh, Kh. Devananda, Faculty Member, Institute of Co-operative Management, Imphal.

Singh, Kh. Somorendo, Faculty Member, Institute of Cooperative Management, Imphal.

Singh, Kh. Tomba, Lecturer in Commerce, Assam University, Silchar.

Singh, N. Tejmani, Sr. Assistant Professor of Commerce, Manipur University, Imphal.

Singh, S. Herojit, Faculty Member, Institute of Co-operative Management, Imphal.

Singh, S. Keshorjit, Faculty Member, MIMS, Manipur University, Imphal.

Singh, S. Somokanta, Faculty Member, MIMS, Manipur University, Imphal.

Singha, R.K.P.G., Lecturer in Commerce, Pachhunga University College Aizwal, Mizoram.

Singha, Rajmani, Sr. Assistant Professor of Commerce, Manipur University, Imphal.

Sorokhaibam, Robita, Sr. Assistant Professor of Commerce, Manipur University, Imphal.

KEYNOTE ADDRESS

1

DEVELOPING ENTREPRENEURSHIP IN NORTH EAST EXPERIENCES AND STRATEGIES

(With special reference to Small-Scale and IT Industries and Manipur)

D.D. MALI

Introduction

I consider it to be an honour and a privilege for me to have been invited to deliver the keynote address in the National Seminar on "Entrepreneurship Development in Manipur with reference to the small-scale and IT industries" organised by the Department of Commerce, Manipur University. Considering that the problems related to entrepreneurship development in other states of North East are also similar, I have taken the liberty to slightly modify the topic to talk about Developing Entrepreneurship in North East: Experiences and Strategies, with special reference to small-scale and IT industries and Manipur.

Entrepreneurs are individuals who recognise opportunities where others see chaos, confusion and contradiction[1]. There may be entrepreneurs in any field of activity, industry, agriculture, education, social service, health service etc. Again, they may emerge from families with any occupational background. They may be young and not so young; may be highly educated or not educated at all; may hail from rural or urban areas; may be male or female. They instigate social change and development. They are people who own, operate, manage and take the risk of business venture. They are engaged in entrepreneurship, the process of running a business of one's own.

It is observed that an individual enter into the field of entrepreneurship either by *choice*, or by force of circumstances (by *chance*), or by planned and systematic training (*created* entrepreneurs). However, in whatever way a person enters into entrepreneurial field, he/she is an entrepreneur. The society needs more such persons because of their role in industrial and economic development. They are highly sought after persons. The more the number of entrepreneurs, the higher is the level of industrial and economic development. They are the persons who take risk of business and lead the economy to the path of growth.

Efforts to Promote Entrepreneurship

In view of the importance of entrepreneurship in the economy, there have been systematic efforts to promote entrepreneurship both in developed and developing countries. In India, beginning with industrial campaigns during the 1960s entrepreneurship development is now a nation wide movement. Organisations and institutions have been set up at national, regional, state and even at the district level to promote entrepreneurship in the country. While Gujarat is credited as being the pioneer in starting planned and systematic efforts to entrepreneurship development, in the North East, Assam is the pioneer in this field. In 1973, the Government of Assam started a novel experiment to promote entrepreneurship among the educated unemployed youth of the state by setting up entrepreneurial motivation training centre (EMTC), a district level agency, to identify, select, and train prospective entrepreneurs and to provide them all support services to start and run their enterprises. The EMTC have now been merged with the district industries centres. However, in 2005 the Government of Assam has set up a state level "Institute for Development of Entrepreneurs in Assam" (IDEA) for promotion of self-employment in the state. In the North East, there are now several organisations directly engaged in promotion of entrepreneurship, such as Indian Institute of Entrepreneurship (IIE), North

Eastern Industrial Technical Consultancy Organisation (NEITCO), North Eastern Technical Consultants (NECON), National Small Industries Corporation (NSIC), and Small Industries Service Institutes (SISI), etc. Besides, there are many voluntary organisations engaged in entrepreneurship development activities.

Initially different organisations used to organise three different groups of training programmes for prospective and existing entrepreneurs, namely, new entrepreneurs creation programmes, programmes for existing entrepreneurs and awareness creation programmes. New entrepreneurs programmes are target-group oriented programmes (e.g. women, rural, general, science and technology entrepreneurs, etc.); product or process specific (e.g. jute product, food product, sports goods etc.), and also location specific, that is, they are organised in State capitals, district headquarters, and sub-divisional towns and even in remote areas. Programmes for existing entrepreneurs are organised on different aspects of management and development, such as financial management, marketing management, personnel management, production management etc. Awareness creation programmes are organised for creation of awareness of opportunities for self-employment and entrepreneurial activities in different areas such as service sector, agro-based activities etc. SIET Institute/NISIET/IIE organised programmes for personnel from support organisations, and for educated children of artisans, entrepreneurs and businessmen also.

In recent years, innovative programmes have been designed and experimented to promote new entrepreneurs, and for creating awareness of entrepreneurial and self-employment opportunities among the youth, e.g., entrepreneurial awareness camps for school, college and university students, faculty development programme on entrepreneurship for college and university teachers, and turnkey EDP for new entrepreneurs. Besides, new approaches have also been adopted to make the programmes more effective and successful. Earlier, the entrepreneurship development programmes (EDPs) were location specific. Now, in addition to location specific approach, area approach has been adopted by starting Rural Industries Programme (RIP), and District Rural Industries Programme (DRIP). SIDBI and NABARD have been supporting RIP and DRIP respectively. Besides, there is the Science and Technology Entrepreneurship Development (STED) project of Department of Science and Technology (DST), Government of India.

North-Eastern Council and Entrepreneurship Development

The North Eastern Council (NEC) recognised the crucial role of entrepreneurship in the economic and industrial development of the region. It got a study done on the entrepreneurial and managerial needs of the region through SIET Institute (now NISIET), Hyderabad, and based on the study; it took a number of steps for promoting entrepreneurship in the region.[2] In 1985, the NEC drew up an ambitious plan to train and develop 5000 prospective entrepreneurs during the sixth plan (1985-90). In its efforts Industrial Development Bank of India (IDBI) and its sister organisations, Industrial Finance Corporation of India (IFCI) and Industrial Credit and Investment Corporation of India (ICICI) also participated.

The initiative taken by the NEC in 1985 still continues. However, its emphasis is now on sector-specific programme. In its efforts there are now new partners. Small Industries Development Bank of India (SIDBI) started to co-sponsor Rural and Women EDPs with NEC. The Khadi and Village Industries Commission (KVIC) also started to participate in rural entrepreneurship programme. The KVIC (now renamed office of the Commissioner for Khadi and Village Industries-CKVI) has been organising programmes on its own. In addition, there are other agencies, which are supporting activities relating to promotion of entrepreneurship.

Impact of Entrepreneurship Development Efforts

Evaluation study (June 1990) on the effectiveness of EDPs in the North East revealed that overall rate of success of EDPs organised during April 1985 to March 1990 was 20.9 percent. This study covered 3609 trainees trained in EDPs organised during that period. Highest rate of success, 28.24 percent was reported from Manipur, followed by Mizoram, 26.32 per cent and Assam, 21.94 per cent.[3] Evaluation study (1998) of EDPs organised during April 1990 to March 1996 revealed that 25.2 per cent of the trainees could set up enterprises. This study covered 3713 participants. The success rate was highest in Manipur (37.7 %), followed by Assam (30.5 %), and Meghalaya 29.5 percent.[4] The rate of success in terms of number of enterprises set up has improved over the years.

Most of the units set up by trained entrepreneurs were micro enterprises only, though there were tiny enterprises also. There was practically no small enterprise. The average size of investment of units set up during April 1990 to March 1996 was Rs.0.88 lakh. The second all India census of small scale industrial units (1992) with 1987-88 as base year also revealed that the average size of investment in North East was Rs. 0.88 lakh as against Rs 0.95 lakh in the country. As per one study (2004), the average size of investment in SSI units was Rs 1.61 lakh. The average size of investment in Manipur was found to be Rs.0.37 lakh, as against Rs 0.32 lakh as revealed by the second SSI census.[5]

In Barpeta district of Assam, a study of 105 units promoted under a Rural Industries Programme (RIP) revealed higher average size of investment of Rs. 1.90 lakh, but still a micro enterprise.[6] Thus, the units promoted either under regular EDP or under area approach are micro enterprises only. Some day some of these enterprises will be tiny and small enterprises. Management of micro enterprise successfully will help in developing risk-taking capability of the entrepreneurs, and those who have the growth impetus will grow and prosper. Most of the entrepreneurs promoted in RIP district are willing to raise their level of investment and need support from banks and financial institutions.

The types of enterprises set up are mostly traditional. But there are now non-traditional products/ services that are also being taken up by new entrepreneurs. More and more entrepreneurs are coming up in service sector and also in agro-based activities. Many entrepreneurs have set up training institutes; particularly computer training, and many have set up franchise units to become business owners. There have been changes over the years in respect of entrepreneurial scenario in the region. More and more youth are now coming to take up entrepreneurial career by choice

A few trends are observed in the emergence of entrepreneurship in North East. More women entrepreneurs are entering into entrepreneurial field in recent years! The growing interest of women to take up entrepreneurial activities is because of a number of motivating factors, such as generating some additional income to contribute to the family income; to be economically independent to improve their status in family decision making process, for utilising their leisure time fruitfully by taking up entrepreneurial activity; to fulfil their creative urge; or because of force of circumstances. Many have taken up entrepreneurial activity because of economic compulsion. IIE study (2001) reveals that nearly 30 per cent women entrepreneurs set up their enterprise because of economic compulsion. Furthermore, there are now more women entrepreneurs emerging from SC/ST and OBC community.[7]

Another trend observed is that more and more retired persons (including those who take voluntary retirement) are taking up entrepreneurial activities. Due to increase in longevity and good health, the retired persons are coming forward to take up entrepreneurial ventures. Many of them have talent, ambition, experience, and retirement money to take up entrepreneurial activities. Many retired persons are taking up entrepreneurial activities for inducing their children to take up entrepreneurial career.

Again, group entrepreneurship has been emerging in the states of the North East. It is stated that there are more than 92000 Self Help Groups (SHGs) promoted in Assam alone during the last few years. Group entrepreneurship can help in overcoming the hurdles of finance in starting their entrepreneurial activities. The banks are willing to support SHGs, and also entrepreneurs in clusters. Hence, group approach and cluster approach may perhaps help in the growth of more entrepreneurs.

Opportunities in Village and Small-Scale Industries

Several entrepreneurial opportunities are emerging in village and small industries, wholesaling, retailing and service sectors, and even in agriculture and allied sectors. Old entrepreneurial activities are still undertaken, but new entrepreneurial opportunities are emerging.

In the village industries sector, two traditional industries, handloom and handicraft industries offer very good scope for entrepreneurial activities. In the North East, handloom is a class-less and caste-less activity. Handloom is still a women's activity, and that too, a leisure time activity. But the situation has been gradually changing for the better. People are taking up handloom as commercial activity. It is, however, necessary to identify the products that are in demand not only in the local market but also outside market including export market. Handloom development in clusters can be good entrepreneurial activities. Similarly, handicraft development can also be very good entrepreneurial activities. It is not only cane and bamboo handicrafts, but also other handicrafts that are traditional activities of the people of the North East. There are possibilities of conversion of some handloom products, particularly muga , eri and mulberry silk, into handicraft products for value addition, and also for getting wider market. For example, an innovator has developed a beauty umbrella using muga silk and an entrepreneur has purchased the right to manufacture the umbrella and market it worldwide. Both of them are from Guwahati.

For making the village industry products globally competitive, the office of the CKVI has introduced common brand name- *Sarvodaya* brand for village industry products and Khadi brand for Khadi products. Besides, they have introduced *deshi ahar* brand for natural and chemic free organic food products, the demand of which has been constantly increasing. Entrepreneurs in the village industry sector are emerging. This sector has better scope in the North East.

In the small-scale sector, varieties of entrepreneurial activities can be taken up. There are more than 9000 different items that are produced in the small-scale sector. In fact, sky is the limit to identify activities in the small-scale sector for entrepreneurship. Depending on the resource endowment, environment, demand and skill and craftsmanship of people, any activity can be undertaken. Every state government of the region has given priority to resource-based approach for the development of village and small-scale industries.

Opportunities in the service sector have been growing rapidly over the last few years. It is estimated that this sector now contributes about 52 per cent to the Gross Domestic Product of the country. There are abundant opportunities for businesses primarily engaged in providing a wide variety of services to individuals and business firms. The demand for many consumer services such as repair and servicing, tours and travels, lodging, restaurants, entertainment etc. has been increasing. Similarly, the demand for many business services such as consulting services, advertising services, and security services etc. have been increasing. As the economy continues to grow, the service sector will provide increased opportunities for new business. Besides, most of them will be small sized. The service sector enterprise will, thus, be a major target for would-be entrepreneurs. Again, many of the service enterprises have low barriers to entry and exit, that is, most of service enterprises require small investment, fewer formalities and also be closed quickly. This will also encourage new entrepreneurs to the service sector. The prospective entrepreneur is to identify the services needed by the customers and try to meet the need.

Opportunities are expanding in franchising. In India franchising has now emerged as a growth area. New entrepreneurs can consider this area for starting their enterprise.

There are new activities in health and fitness areas. People have now become more conscious about their health and fitness. They like to spend in good hospitals; nursing homes etc. instead of depending on government run hospitals. This has created opportunities for growth of nursing homes and hospitals. Doctors who treated patients earlier on the basis of symptoms no longer do so. Now treatment is mostly done on the basis of diagnosis made on the basis of clinical test. This has opened up opportunities for private clinical laboratories for different kinds of health check up.

There has been increasing interest among the girls and ladies to remain fit and beautiful. This has resulted entrepreneurs setting up beauty parlor, fitness centre to meet the growing demand of for beauty care services. Photography itself was not very common earlier. Now not photography alone but video photography is becoming popular. A marriage ceremony without video photography is practically unthinkable at least in cities. This has opened up opportunities for entrepreneurial activities in photography and video photography. Related to it is the development of training institutes for training youth to take up these activities. Repairing and servicing of mobile telephones has been emerging important entrepreneurial activities. Opportunities are many and varied for developing entrepreneurship.

Manipur is the fourth largest state of North-East in terms of area (22,327 sq km) and third most populous state (23.89 lakh). The state is known for its scenic beauty and rich cultural heritage. About nine-tenth of the state is hilly. The contribution of the secondary sector to the net State Domestic Product went up from 15.7 per cent during 1993-94 to 20.8 per cent during 2001-02. The per capita income of the State went up from Rs 5833 in 1993 to Rs 13213 in 2001-02. During 2002-03, the number of small-scale industrial units was 5974 as against 70579 in the region. The average size of investment was Rs 0.37 lakh as against Rs 1.61 lakh in the region. Average number of persons employed in SSI units in Manipur was 15.37 as against 5.41 persons in the region. As per the third all India census of small-scale industries with 2001-02 as base year, there was 4599 working units and 1226 closed units in the state. This can be compared with the number of working and closed units in North East, which were 25680 and 16394 respectively. Women entrepreneurs accounted for 15.12 per cent as against 17.46 per cent in the North East and 11.08 per cent in the country. More than 70 per cent of the SSI units were concentrated in Imphal East, Ukhrul and Bishnupur districts. From the data presented here it may be inferred that there is much scope to raise improve the condition of existing SSI units in Manipur in terms of level of investment and use of technology.

In Manipur, the Government has been focusing its attention to the development of small-scale and agro-based industries. Besides, it has been giving attention to the development of handloom and handicraft industries because of their potential for development. In addition, it has also been giving attention to the development of sericulture, which is a labour intensive agro-based industry. It has been implementing an externally aided project with the assistance from JBIC, Japan.

Opportunities in IT Sector

Today IT has become all pervasive. The changes in IT have effected all aspects of life- social, economic, cultural, political etc. Many are of opinion that the last 10 years have seen more changes in IT than the preceding 90 years of the 20th century. The barriers of natural boundaries have also changed. The world has now almost become a global village. Everybody now recognises the enormous potential of IT sector. It has changed our way of thinking and doing work. All the states of North East have recognised the potential of IT sector in their respective states.

The IT industry includes IT software, IT hardware, IT peripherals, IT networking, IT maintenance and. IT enabled services. IT enabled services include E-governance, call centres, medical transcription, online education, data processing, data digitisation, internet and E-commerce etc. IT maintenance, assembling and vending hardware, developing software, and IT peripherals, IT training Besides entrepreneurs have been setting up cyber café, call centres, medical transcription centre etc. This has resulted in setting up of IT training institutes, data processing activities and other information service related activities.

NEDFI pre-investment feasibility study of Software Technology Park for Manipur (2001) suggested a number of areas in IT sector having scope for promotion. These are: quality IT schools, Desk Top Publishing, back office operation, data entry job, medical transcription service, digital content development, software development for domestic market, customized software development, hardware and network maintenance service. For promotion of IT industries some basic infrastructure will be necessary.

Problems

In order to exploit the opportunities for entrepreneurship development in the village and small-scale and IT industries, it is necessary to understand the problems and take appropriate measures to overcome them. Environment plays an important role in entrepreneurship growth and development – environment in family, educational institutions, society and the support organisations at large. Environment in family helps or hinders the children in dreaming of an entrepreneurial career. In addition to environment in family, the environment in educational institutions in which they study, the social groups with whom they interact play a dominant role in shaping the mindset of the youth for a particular type of career, whether entrepreneurship or other. The social environment further influences this.

Besides, the availability of capital influences an individual's decision-making process to be an entrepreneur. Most often, finance becomes a major problem for first generation entrepreneurs. While the bankers say that they do not get worthwhile proposals, the entrepreneurs say that the banks are reluctant to lend to new entrepreneurs, particularly if the projects are new and innovative.

The problem of institutional finance takes various forms from delay in sanction and disbursement of loan to outright rejection of loan proposals. The delays occur because of procedural formalities, lack of persons capable of appraising loan proposals at bank branches, and to guide and counsel entrepreneurs, lack of clear and unambiguous communications from banks to entrepreneurs, delay in documentation formalities, lack of extension motivation of the personnel at banks/ financial institutions, etc. Most of these delays are, however, avoidable delays and can be avoided with little effort and proper mindset. If delays can be avoided or at least minimised most of the problems of bank finance can be solved.

Apart from family and social environment, an extension – oriented support system is extremely important for the growth of entrepreneurship. The organisational climate in the support system, including banks and financial institutions, can either help or hinder the growth of entrepreneurship. There is, however, a general feeling among entrepreneurs that organisational environment in the support system leaves much to be desired.

The existing industries can create a positive or negative environment depending on their performance. It is observed that the performance of existing industries, availability of raw materials and labour, infrastructure facilities such as dependable roads and railways, transport and communication, power, market etc. can have positive impact on entrepreneurial growth.

Positive environment can create a condition for growth of entrepreneurship. But environment alone is not sufficient to induce a person to take up entrepreneurial activity unless he wants to take a decision for entrepreneurial career. The entrepreneur as an individual is influenced by his motivational orientation, knowledge and skill about launching an enterprise and managing it successfully. However, knowledge and skill itself will not be adequate to influence an individual to become entrepreneur. In order to make knowledge and skill operative he must have sufficient motivation. The motivational orientation supported by his knowledge and skill will encourage him to choose an entrepreneurial career. Thus, there are several factors that help in the emergence of entrepreneurship in any society.

Strategies

In order to develop entrepreneurship, there must be a multi-pronged approach- develop knowledge, skill and motivation of the individuals to take up entrepreneurial career, create positive family and social environment, create required infrastructure facilities for entrepreneurship to grow, and entrepreneur-friendly environment in the support organisations, including banks and financial institutions. In the strategies everybody will have a role- the government, the support organisations, training organisations, and the entrepreneurs themselves.

The government has several roles to play for the growth of entrepreneurship: develop infrastructure facilities, provide policy support, adopt promotional measures and also help in creation of entrepreneur-friendly environment. Infrastructure, particularly power and transport are crucial for growth of entrepreneurship and industry. In the North East, except Meghalaya other states are deficient in power. Efforts are needed to improve power position and also roads and road transport.

In order to support and sustain the promotion and development of village and small industry and entrepreneurship there is a comprehensive organisational network. There are now central government, state government and even district level organisations to promote village and small industry and entrepreneurship. Besides, voluntary organisations (VO) have also emerged to play its role in the promotion of entrepreneurship. There are now organisations to train entrepreneurs, both for motivational development and skill development including technical training, help in technical upgradation of the existing enterprises, provide marketing support, infrastructure support and to provide finance including micro finance for the growth of entrepreneurs and entrepreneurship. However, organisational climate of the support organisations is much to be desired.

In the short-term, attention needs to be given new entrepreneurs creation and creation of awareness of entrepreneurial opportunities in the village and small-scale and IT industries. Awareness camps should also target college and university students who are the potential source of entrepreneurs for tomorrow. Some efforts in this direction have already been started. Besides, there should be orientation and sensitisation of the personnel of the support organisation at regular intervals to improve their knowledge and develop right kind of attitude to support entrepreneurs.

Major concern of the training agencies should be to develop motivation among the trainees, besides imparting knowledge and developing skill. Only highly motivated trainees take up entrepreneurial career. Hence, training agencies are to aim at improving the effectiveness of their training programmes through proper planning and implementation, and effective post-training follow-up, guidance and monitoring. Area approach to entrepreneurship development has been found to be more effective in promoting entrepreneurship. There should be both location approach and area approach to training of entrepreneurs, with greater emphasis on area approach. Area approach should be expanded both horizontally and vertically to cover more areas, and also to promote high value enterprises. Hence, they may put in more efforts in area approach to get better results.

In the long term, measures are needed to create environment for entrepreneurship. Organisations and institutions should go for networking with other organisations so that they can spread their activities to different areas. This will also facilitate growth of the organisations and institutions involved in entrepreneurship development. There will be need for collaborative activities to complement each other's strength. If efforts to promote entrepreneurship are to be geared up, sustaining activities in the entrepreneurship development cycle is to be accelerated. This would mean a constant monitoring of the units as a part of the development efforts so that entrepreneurs does not lose hope during the initial stage of setting up a unit and can overcome the problem. Mentoring can play an important role in developing entrepreneurship in the North East.

The need and importance of entrepreneurship education is gradually being realised. This has happened because of a number of developments. Most important of these developments are: firstly, in 1999, UGC advised the Universities to introduce entrepreneurship in the vocational streams; secondly, National Assessment and Accreditation Council (NAAC) started assessing the status of colleges. The first development induced the universities to introduce entrepreneurship in the vocational streams. The second development almost forced the colleges to think in the direction of doing something to guide and counsel students for self-employment and entrepreneurial career. I believe it should not be confined to vocational streams alone. The need is to develop an enterprising society for progress and prosperity. This will be possible only when entrepreneurship education form part of the education system.

In order to develop entrepreneurship in Manipur, there should be a comprehensive plan that will incorporate measures for stimulating, supporting and sustaining entrepreneurship. For stimulating entrepreneurship Manipur may consider setting up of an Institute of Entrepreneurship Development. In fact, once the state took some steps to set up such an Institute but no Institute could be set up. The Institute may work in close collaboration with banks and financial institutions for supporting trained entrepreneurs. Besides, there is need to identify type of industries having comparative advantage for development in the state for exploiting the potential of border trade. Emphasis is also needed to promote women entrepreneurship the scope of which is very high. There is also need to give emphasis on development of artisan-based activities where the state has very good potential.

A concerted and coordinated approach from all agencies will help in the development of entrepreneurship in the North East in general and Manipur in particular.

NOTES AND REFERENCES

1. Kuratko, Donald F. and Hodgetts Richard M. (1998), *Entrepreneurship – A Contemporary Approach.*
2. Pareek Udai and Nadkarni Monohar (1978), *Development of Entrepreneurship - A Conceptual Model*, Developing Entrepreneurship edited by TV Rao quoted from MMP Akhouri, *Entrepreneurial and Managerial Needs of North Eastern Region*, 1978.
3. NEC (June 1990), Evaluation Study of EDPs (mimeograph).
4. IIE (2000), *Promoting New Entrepreneurs.*
5. IIE (2004), *Study of Small Scale Industries in North East* (unpublished).
6. Speed (June 2004), RDC Report, (unpublished).
7. IIE (2001), *Study of Women Entrepreneurship in North East* (unpublished).

ENTREPRENEURSHIP DEVELOPMENT IN MANIPUR

2

INDUSTRIAL POLICY AND SMALL SCALE INDUSTRIES IN MANIPUR

E. BIJOYKUMAR SINGH

Introduction

The importance of small scale industry in India's development plans from the very beginning of planning is aptly summed up in the Industrial Policy Resolution of 1956 as follows:

> "The government of India would .... stress the role of cottage and village and small scale industries in the development of the national economy. In relation to some of the problems that need urgent solution, they offer some distinct advantages. They provide immediate large scale employment; they offer a method of ensuring a more equitable distribution of the national income and they facilitate an effective mobilization of resources of capital and skill which might otherwise remain unutilized.Some of the problems that unplanned urbanization tends to create will be avoided by the establishment of small centers of industrial production all over the country."

Small Industries sector consists of the following:

A. Traditional Industries

1. Khadi

   2. Village industry
   3. Handlooms
   4. Sericulture
   5. Handicrafts
   6. Coir

B. Modern Industries
   1. Small scale industries
   2. Powerlooms

C. Others

Over the past five decades SSI sector has acquired a place of eminence in the national economy. It accounts for nearly 40% of the gross value of output in the manufacturing sector and about 35% of the total export from the country. By March 2002 there were 3.4 million SSI units in the country employing 19.2 million persons, second only to agriculture. It produces about 8000 items. SSI creates new jobs, supplies a wide range of products, contributes to export, helps in more equitable distribution of national income and emerges as outsourcing destinations. The strengths of small scale industries are low capital investment, high employment generation, maximum utilization of capacity and flexibility in operation. It is also a part of the reorganization of the entire socio-economic structure on a decentralized basis.

Small scale industry relates not to the size of the industry as such but to the small size of the industrial unit whatever the criterion used for the measurement of size. SSI is officially defined in terms of investment ceiling in fixed assets such as plant and machinery whether held on ownership terms or on lease or hire purchase .Currently the limit is Rs 1 crore .It is Rs 5 crores in respect of 7 items of sports reserved for manufacturing in SSI. Total number of reserved items for SSI sector in October 2004 was 605. The reservation policy was initiated in 1967 with 47 items in the list. The process of dereservation is continuing.

The policy of protection and promotion of small industry since independence relates to information, consultancy, entrepreneurship development, training, modernization and technology support, industrial estates, raw material, marketing, finance, reservation, ancillary development etc.The case of preferential treatment to small industries by the state *vis-à-vis* large industry in a labour abundant, capital scarce country is on the consideration that it has capital saving and employment promoting characteristics.

The objectives of the article are as follows:

1. To highlight the SSI component in successive Industrial policy statements of Manipur.
2. To examine whether the macro data can throw any light on the efficacy of the policy

SSI Policy

Table 1 shows that though nominal plan expenditure in industry and mining in Manipur has been rising both in absolute terms and as percentage of total plan expenditure it does not emerge as a priority sector at any point of time. The provision for SSI also was meager in relation to its designated role in reviving the economy.

Table 1

Plan Expenditure in Industry and Mining in Manipur

Plan	Rs. in lakhs	% of total plan expenditure
1st FYP (1951-56)	0.68	0.66
2nd FYP (1956-61)	12.08	2.02
3rd FYP (1961-66)	35.28	2.75
1966-69	18.90	2.62
4th FYP (1969-74)	215.00	6.93
5th FYP (1974-78)	474.76	7.13
1978-80	322.55	5.27
6th FYP (1980-85)	1352.44	5.56
7th FYP (1985-90)	2759.61	5.47
8th FYP (1992-97)	5281.11	4.31
9th FYP (1997-2002)*	9540.64	5.75
10th FYP (2002-07)**	33294.00	11.87

Note: * Anticipated.
** Approved.

Source: *Statistical Handbook of Manipur* (various issues).

In the Tenth Five-year Plan the targeted annual compound growth rate of Manipur is 8.33%. During 1972-96 (at 1980-81 prices) manufacturing grew at the rate of 3.99% per annum and it was decelerating. During 1990-91 and 2000-01 the CAGR of gross domestic product of Manipur originating in industry in the broadest sense at 1993-94 prices was only 5.95. It shows how unrealistic our sectoral target is. Interestingly in 2000-1 among the north eastern states, industry consisting of mining,manufacturing, electricity, gas and water supply and construction had the highest share in real NSDP in Manipur. As per 55th round of NSS Manipur has the highest proportion of workers engaged in manufacturing among the north-eastern states though the rates are substantially lower than the all India figures.

The Industrial Policy of 1982 was the first attempt to look at industrialization of Manipur in a systematic manner. SSI units were to be encouraged. They enjoyed exemption from payment of stamp duty and registration charges for land and building, power at subsidized rates It was categorically mentioned that the effort of the state regarding SSI should not be for extensive and widespread coverage. The policy was to promote only those categories for which availability of raw materials was not a problem, we had skill and there was adequate internal market. Prior to the Industrial policy statement of 1991 the explicit focus of Industrial policy used to be in large and medium industries. In the 1991 Industrial Policy of Manipur the focus shifted to the development of the small scale sector. The following incentives were given to SSI units in the state:

1. *Allotment of land:* 25% of the cost of development will be subsidized by the state government for small scale sector.
2. *Allotment of sheds:* For new small scale industrial units built up factory sheds would be allotted to the entrepreneurs on monthly rent basis and the state government will reimburse 50% of the rent for a period of 5 years from the date of occupation of the shed.
3. Interest subsidy.
4. Power subsidy (to be notified from time to time).
5. Subsidy for technical knowhow (50%).
6. Price preference.

7. Reimbursement of stamp duty and registration fee (100%).
8. Subsidy for purchase of testing equipments (25%).

There is little change in the SSI policy in Industrial Policy of Manipur 1996.

Price preference to products of SSI is raised from 15% to 20% over the lowest technically and commercially viable rate offered by others.

For the small sector unit a cell in the Directorate of Commerce and Industries will be opened to monitor the sick units. A survey of existing small sacle units in the state will be carried out to categorise these units according to their potential for revival. Based on this survey a package of policy measures will be initiated to make these sick units viable.

It is hoped that the Industrial Policy of 2005 currently under discussion will provide a liberating environment for this sector

Database and Analysis

In India since the early 1950s the Industrial (Development and Regulation) Act, 1951 and the Factories Act, 1948 provided for the legal, regulatory and promotional activities for industrialization. A manufacturing firm has to register under IDR Act if it belonged to a schedule industry and also under the Factories Act if it employs 10 or more workers using power. It is 20 or more if it does not use power. Unregistered manufacturing income is the income originating from manufacturing establishments not governed by the factories Act i.e. manufacturing establishments employing less than 10 workers with power or less than 20 workers without power. One may roughly label unregistered manufacturing as the small industry sector. SSI is outside the purview of IDR Act but have to register with specialized promotional agencies meant for their development if they sought official assistance. Registration of small scale units with state directorate of industries or small industries development organisation is voluntary. Such a registration helps the unit to get different types of incentives and benefits offered by the central and state governments and the agencies sponsored by them. There is also an acute problem of sickness of SSI units due to selection of nonviable projects, inadequate availability of raw materials, power shortage, marketing problems, obsolete technology, inadequate working capital and inefficient management.

Annual Survey of Industries is a survey of production accounts of all factories registered under section 2m of the Factories Act 1948. Factories employing 10 or more workers using power (20 or more workers without using power) have to get registered under this Act. The survey consists of 2 parts – the census sector and the sample sector. A census was conducted of all factories employing 50 or more workers using power (100 or more workers without using power). For the remaining a 50% sample was taken every year. Since 1997-98 the census sector has been redefined to include factories with 200 or more workers; the rest are covered on a sample survey consisting of 1/3rd of the registered factories in each year.

Another source of data on SSI is the two All India Census of SSI units in 1972 and 1988.In the first census the limit of small and ancillary units were Rs 7.5 lakhs and Rs 10 lakhs. In 1988 the limits were Rs 35 lakhs and Rs 45 lakhs.

In the national accounts system the estimates of the contribution of SSI sector has been worked out using the estimates of value added per worker based on the state-wise results of the Second All-India Census on SSI Units with 1987-88 published by Development Commissioner, SSI and the corresponding work force. Estimates for manufacturing (unregistered) are compiled for the base year, i.e. 1993-94 and are extrapolated to later years using relevant indicators using workforce approach. The requisite data pertaining to the indicators for similar exercise in Manipur are unavailable.

In 1961 the number of factories registered with the Chief Inspector of Factories, Manipur was 66 which included 50 rice mills, 6 oil mills and 4 saw mills. In 2002 there were 2014 registered units in Manipur out of which 1618 were rice mills. The industries in order of importance are rice mill, saw mill, oil mill, flour mill, printing press etc. Considering the generally low level of investment in plant and machinery most industrial units, if not all, can be classified to be in the small sector. However it is difficult to reconcile this with the statement that the number of sick small scale industrial units in Manipur as on 31st March 1999 was 5237 (Indian Institute of Entrepreneurship, Guwahati).

Table 2 shows the growth in number of SSI units in Manipur during 1971-2001. It shows that Manipur's share has been declining. The paradoxically high share in 1981 and high growth in the preceding decade as well the fall in the following decade need deeper probing.

Table 3 also shows a high growth rate during the 70s though the base figures differ widely.

Table 2
Growth of Small Scale Industries in Manipur

Year	No. of units	% of North-east total
1971	8	0.8
1981	3422	34.8
1991	4059	15.1
2001	6000	13.57

Source: Basic Statistics of North eastern Region; Various issues.

Table 3
All-India SSI Census: Manipur

Year	No. of SSI units	Value of output in Rs. lakhs current price
1972	485	332
1988	2078	2988

Table 4 shows on the next page that the output of small sector as proxied by the income originating in the unregistered manufacturing sector has nearly doubled in 10 years .Its share has remained stagnant over the years. The share of manufacturing in NSDP rose marginally from 7.22% to 7.53% with the share of the unregistered component rising from 6.98% to 7.44 %. The compound annual growth rate of unregistered segment is 5.58% The declining phase during 1993-94 and 1995-96 may be due to revision of base period in real income statistics.

Conclusion

In the absence of a reliable database for the characteristics of SSI units it is hazardous to make any guess as to the effectiveness or otherwise of the SSI component of the successive Industrial policies of Manipur. However an inescapable inference is the inability of incentives/subsidies to take care of the debilitating impact of the law and order problem in terms of the stagnant share of unregistered manufacturing in the state income. The problem has been made more acute by the stiff competition from industrial products from industries based in the mainland and industries in China and other South East Asian countries. One can safely say that our industries have failed to cater to the fast changing taste of co0nsumers There is also the need to separate out the impact of measures adopted by the central government for SSI units.

Table 4
Income Originating in Unregistered Manufacturing Sector at 1993-94 Prices (1990-1 to 2000-01)

Year	Output in Rs. lakhs
1990-91	6713
1991-92	7618
1992-93	8414
1993-94	8219
1994-95	7924
1995-96	8239
1996-97	8834
1997-98	9239
1998-99	10632
1999-2000	12969
2000-01	11555

Source: Directorate of Economics & Statistics; Manipur Human Development Report.

NOTES AND REFERENCES

1. Government of India, *Basic Statistics of North East Region* (various issues), North-Eastern Council Secretariat.
2. Government of Manipur, *Statistical Handbook* (various issues), Directorate of Economics and Statistics.
3. Planning Commission (2003), *India's Five-year Plans – Complete Documents*, Academic Foundation.
4. Sandesara, J.C. (1993), "Modern Small Industry: Aspects of growth and Structural Chang", Reprinted in Uma Kapila (Ed.) (1999), *Indian Economy Since Independence*, Academic Foundation.
5. Sandesara, J.C. (1999), "Small Scale Industrialisation: The Indian Experience" in: Uma Kapila (ed) (1999), *Indian Economy Since Independence*, Academic Foundation.

3

THE PROSPECTS OF SMALL-SCALE INDUSTRIES DEVELOPMENT IN MANIPUR

B. D. NAYAK
SHIPRA S. NAYAK

Introduction

Development of viable and self-sustaining enterprises in rural areas have been identified for an intensive thrust with a view to address problems such as rural unemployment, urban migration, and under-utilization of rural resources and skills. Because, agriculture as the prime mover and green revolution as a panacea, has been unable to solve the problems of unemployment and poverty. Moreover, in recent past agriculture particularly in rural areas has become a relatively unrewarding exercise due to unfavourable price structures and low productivity, resulting in huge migration to urban areas. Also most of the rural households are small and marginal farmers and agricultural labourers. Due to seasonality of agriculture, employment is a major problem and millions of youths and women are joining the ranks of unemployed in rural areas. This is perhaps due to limited access to natural resources, skills, entrepreneurial training and also lack of support from institutions.

The organized sector has not been able to generate additional employment opportunities and the employment elasticities to output growth of all the sectors have gone down and agriculture sector is overburdened with unproductive employment. On the other hand, the large industries are catering to the needs of urban areas and even modern small-scale industries are also concentrated in urban and semi-urban centers. Thus, there is an increasing trend of migration to urban centers both for resources and skills.

Therefore, the only hope is to generate employment opportunities in the sustainable non-farm sector in the rural areas, as there is no dearth of resources amenable for value addition. Understandably, rural industrialization with respect to small scale units, household and cottage industries and other agribusiness units can provide an answer to the growing problems of poverty, unemployment and migration.

The importance of rural industries cannot be undermined since they play a vital role in the development of a developing economy like India in general and in North-Eastern Region (NER) of the country in particular. It is held that rural industrialization not only raises the per-capita income and standard of living of the people by providing employment opportunities but also enabling optimum utilization of local resources to serve the local needs.

Keeping in view the importance of rural industrialization particularly in NE Region of the country, small-scale industries have come to occupy a pivotal position in the economic dynamism of the region. This is so because of the fact that the NE Region has some vital bottlenecks like proper and adequate road and rail communication, transport facility, marketing networks, institutional credit facilities for the promotion of large-scale industries. On the other hand, unlike large industries, they are favoured with some advantages like easiness in starting, small capital involvement, higher employment potentiality, short-run planning, low gestation period, etc. Moreover, they aim at securing balanced regional development, equitable distribution of income and wealth and mobilizing small savings for productive channels. The comparative advantage of the small-scale sector over the medium and large-scale sectors in terms of capital, employment, and output is empirically evident from the statistics collected by the Annual Survey of Industries.

Development of an economy depends to a great extent on the expansion of employment potentialities. In the agrarian economies vast majority of the people live in rural areas and agriculture is not only their prime occupation but also their way of living. Underemployment and unemployment in rural sector have become a serious problem in the region because of their traditional farming systems. Hence to combat such a situation, development of small scale industries based on local resources and farm produce in rural and semi urban areas would help immensely in transforming the surplus labour force and agricultural products to the industrial force and semi-finished and final value added products. This, in effect, would improve the economic conditions of the villagers giving an impetus to the agricultural outputs; which in turn would lead to further increase in employment and income, and so on in the rural sector.

Thus, the role of small-scale industries for the removal of unemployment and poverty of an underdeveloped region/economy can hardly be exaggerated. Keeping this fact in mind, the development of SSIs has always received a popular acclaim in this regard. Moreover, there is a general consensus among the economists, policy makers and economic planners that the rural sector in general and agriculture sector in particular has got immense potential for employment generation and economic growth on a sustained basis. The fuller utilization of rural resources and other local potentials requires a comprehensive strategy for wide spectrum of occupations and economic activities in rural sector.

The diversification of rural economic activities in general and agricultural activities in specific is a process of broadening and strengthening of the income source of rural households. The recent experience in Asia, particularly in South East Asia, Middle East and North Africa indicates that policy-makers and planners are increasingly focusing on diversification of rural activities and agricultural diversification as well to promote agricultural growth and sustainable rural development (Petit and Barghouti, 1992).

Coming specifically to India, the states like Punjab and Haryana, which diversified crop sector in a big way, attained about 4.0 to 4.5 per cent trend rate of growth in net state domestic product of agriculture sector (NSDP Ag) in the past two decades. In contrast, the states like Bihar, Orissa, Assam, Tamil Nadu and Himachal Pradesh which experienced low degree of agricultural diversification showed poor growth in their NSDP (Agriculture).

It is observed that the crop-based farming system has not yielded desired level of output and optimum use of land resources in North-Eastern States in general and in Manipur in particular. Mountain agriculture not only in Manipur but also in the entire N.E. Region has been characterized by the internal variability with multiplicity of highly localized and complex micro-ecosystems. Therefore, the farming systems in the region has become invariably subsistence oriented and farming in North Eastern Region in general and in Manipur in specific is being carried on in fragmented and terraced fields, hilltops and hill slopes.

With the spread of modern and scientific farming system in post Green Revolution period Manipur agriculture has improved a lot yet it is still subsistence agriculture. Further, with the emergence of liberalization as well as globalization under 'New Economic Policy' the possibilities of commercialization of state agriculture having export-oriented bias has increased manifold. In this modern economic order, varied occupation and economic activities in rural sector and agribusiness provide a better opportunity for diversification of agriculture in view of its higher returns. Rural industries/SSIs help in enhancing farm income, generating employment, improving the economic condition of the farmers and entrepreneurs in one hand and it contributes considerably in enhancing exports and foreign exchange earnings of a nation on the other. Thus, rural industrialization with reference to small scale industries based on local resources, and the diversification of rural economic activities are not to be overemphasized in view of their vital role in employment generation and rural poverty alleviation.

Manipur, like other N E States, has an agricultural economy. Majority of its population are directly depending upon farm-related activities for their livelihood. The state can be divided into two segments of agricultural regions - (i) hilly and (ii) valley. Out of the total area of the state hill occupies 20,089 sq km and the area of valley is about 2238 sq km. Firm information regarding the land utilization of the whole state cannot be obtained except the valley because hill areas of Manipur are not cadastrally surveyed till now. In the hill areas, the villager does not collectively own lands. Settled cultivation is generally practised in the valley districts, while terrace cultivation is in practice in some pockets of the hill. Shifting cultivation, one of the oldest methods of agriculture, is also widely followed in most of the parts of the hilly districts. The irrigation system in Manipur is not fully developed and the prospect of agriculture, therefore depend largely on, timely occurrence of rain and also its equitable distribution over the cropping seasons. However, the percentage of irrigated area to its total crop area is the highest in the region (36%) while same is only about 15 per cent in the region and about 30 per cent at national level. Rice as the staple food of

Manipur, accounts about 90 per cent of food grains, and about 80 per cent of total cropped area and agriculture is mostly single cropping.

Majority of farming community have small and marginal land with about 45.26% in 1990-91 as per state's latest agricultural census. The operation size of the holding has slightly decreased from 1.26 hectare in 1985-86 to 1.23 hectare in 1990-91. The cultivation of horticultural crops is by and large practiced in non-commercial way in the homestead and orchard of farmers. It hardly helps in developing the proper market for horticultural crops. Agriculture, in the state, generally is a living proposition than a commercial proposition, though a little part of the production is for sale. Obviously due to infrastructure problem, agriculture is still gamble with nature and technology transformation is also slow. Even after 50 years of plan development the state could not become self-sufficient in food-grain production and productivity are also very low due to low cropping intensity, i.e. 125 per cent. Besides, there is little impact of green revolution, in the state and most importantly, the plan money for agricultural sector has been decreasing continuously. Farming in Manipur is either conventional or semi-subsistence. The prime objective of farming in the state is only to provide food security but not for commercial purpose. Thus, agriculture is the profession of the traditional and conservative farmers resulting low agricultural productivity in the state. The traditional agriculture, production of food grains for domestic consumption and non-diversification of agriculture are some of the basic causes of slow growth of agriculture in the state. However, the state has high potential and vast scope for developing its farming activities.

Industrial Growth in Manipur

The entire N E Region is characterized as industrially backward part of the country. It has not made much progress in industry sector. Besides Assam, other states in the region have made little progress with regard to the growth of large and medium industries. Though Manipur has only 12 such industries yet it has made significant progress in household industries and other small-scale enterprises by March 2000. The number of household industries is about 98 thousand while 80.5 thousand private small-scale enterprises are in the state by March 1998 out of which nearly 6.2 thousand are agriculture related enterprises and about 74.3 thousand are non-agri enterprises. As per the data shown in Table 1, Manipur has made considerable progress and it

Table 1
Vital Statistics of North Eastern States

Information	A.P.	ASM.	MAN.	MEG.	MIZ.	NAG.	TRI.	N.E.	INDIA
Total Population (000)	1097	26638	2388	2306	891	1989	1191	36500	10252.51
Total Male Population (000)	574	13788	1207	1168	460	1042	1636	19875	531277
Total Female Popul. (000)	517	12851	1181	1138	431	947	1555	18621	495738
% of urban popul in 2001	20.41	12.72	23.88	19.63	49.50	17.74	17.02	15.51	27.78
Density of popul. in 2001	13	340	107	103	40	120	304	151	312
Sex ratio in 2001	901	932	978	975	938	909	950	937	933
Literacy Rate (2001)	44.7	53.79	59.85	50.75	74.44	57.65	63.81	NA	55.18
Literacy Rate in 2001 (Male)	52.6	60.4	67.6	53	76.5	62	70.7	61.5	64
Literacy Rate in 2001 (F)	36	46.7	52	48	72	53	55.2	48.6	45.7
Total workers (000)	482	9557	1070	956	670	850	1151	14736	4025.12
Ratio of Male workers to total Male Population	51	50	49	47.8	57.4	47	50.8	50	52
Ratio of Female workers to total Female Population	37	21	40	35	47.6	38	21	25	25.6
Main workers (000)	414	7083	757	743	364	708	906	10975	3131.73
Ratio of Male Main workers									

to total Male Population	46	42	40	40	49	41	45.2	42.5	45.3
Ratio of Female Main workers to total F. Popul.	28	10	23	24	31.2	30	10.7	13.5	14.7
Marginal workers (000)	69	2474	313	214	106	142	252	3570	893.38
Ratio of Male Marg. W. to total Male Population	5	7.6	9.1	7.4	8.3	6.1	5.6	7.4	6.6
Ratio of Female Marg. W. to Total Female Popul.	8	11.1	17.2	11.2	15.8	8.2	10.4	11.3	11
Non workers (000)	614	17081	1318	1350	421	1139	2033	23956	6227.34
Cultivators (000)	282	3742	493	457	253	544	311	6082	127628
Agril.Lab. (000)	19	1290	121	173	27	34	278	1942	107448
Household Ind. (000)	4	329	98	18	7	18	34	508	16396
Other workers (000)	178	4197	358	308	182	254	535	6012	151040
No of Enterp. in 98 (000)	20.7	593.2	80.5	56.5	24.9	29.5	104.4	909.7	NA
Agri enterp. in 1998 (No)	201	194891	6173	2088	1744	508	2830	208435	NA
Non-Agri. Ent. in 98 (000	20.5	398.3	74.3	54.4	23.2	29	101.6	701.3	NA
No. of persons usually working in it 1998 (000)	80.5	2194.6	200.7	184.4	77.5	174.6	268.3	3180.6	NA
Large & Medium size Indust. March, 2000 (No)	17	129	12	10	1	7	2	178	NA

Source : Basic Statistics of NER, 2002.

occupys third rank in NE Region both in case of agri and non-agri enterprises. Similar is the picture in case of the number of persons working in these enterprises. More than 2 lakhs of persons were working in these units as on March, 1998.

Further, in conformity with the discussions made in foregoing paragraphs, the trend of development of SSIs as shown in Table 2 indicates that the number of these units has increased from about 4 thousand (1996) to over 6 thousand (2001) at the rate of over 10 per cent per year. On the other hand this state enjoys second position in the region by possessing about 15 per cent of the total SSIs in the region.

So far the growth of handloom sector in the region is concerned, Manipur is depicting a healthy picture. Manipur has made commendable progress in handloom units both for domestic and commercial purposes. In 1997-98, the number of handlooms for domestic use was 2.65 lakhs while the number of handlooms for commercial production was 2.84 lakhs. The number of commercial handloom units in the state was the highest and the units for household use in Manipur was the second highest i.e., next to Assam (Table 3). As far as the quantity of yarn consumed and cloths produced by handloom units are concerned, Manipur has achieved spectacular performance. Table 3 further reveals that out of total 13.91 lakh kilograms of yarn consumed and 6991.65 lakh metres of cloth produced in the region and Manipur alone has consumed 11.10 lakh kg yarns (80%) and 5828.75 lakh metres (83%) of cloth.

As per the data shown in Table 4, in Manipur 153 persons have been trained under EDP out of which about 55 per cent (84) trained persons applied for bank finance for setting up their enterprises during 1994 and 2001. Out of 84 applicants only 18 applicants (21.4%) received bank loan while 52 persons (about 62%) have set up their enterprises. It is further observed that the percentage of bank loan applicants out of total trained persons, the ratio of persons set up SSIs to total loan applicants and proportion of individuals set up SSI with bank finance to total loan applicants in Manipur are, however, not satisfactory as compared to other N E States.

But the growth of Khadi and Village industries in Manipur as well as in the whole North Eastern Region, as the data presented in Table 5, is satisfactory. The production, sale, earnings and employment are

Table 2

Trend of Development of SSI in Different States of NE Region (1996-2001)

State	1996	1997	1998	1999	2000	2001
Arunachal Pradesh	525(2.0)	1200(3.2)	2280(6.43)	3358(8.64)	4478(10.47)	4520(10.22)
Assam	12805(47.8)	18367(48.98)	20035(56.50)	21514(55.40)	23132(54.11)	23637(53.47)
Manipur	4059(15.1)	5034(13.42)	5188(14.36)	5578(14.36)	5829(13.63)	6000(13.57)
Meghalaya	1368(5.1)	177(5.27)	2079(5.86)	2229(5.74)	2514(5.88)	2621(5.92)
Mizoram	2478(9.2)	2880(7.68)	3466(9.77)	3677(9.46)	4028(9.42)	4333(9.80)
Nagaland	615(2.3)	731(1.94)	749(2.11)	779(2.00)	813(19.41)	982(2.22)
Tripura	4967(18.5)	7311(19.5)	1657(4.670)	1697(4.37)	1949(4.55)	2114(4.78)
N E Region	26817(100)	37500(100)	35454(100)	38832(100)	42743(100)	44207(100)

Source : Basic Statistics of NER, 2002.

quite impressive in Manipur during 1988-89 to 1997-98. The state is occupying second position in these fields in the region. The production of these industries has increased by around 14.5 per cent per annum from Rs.1290.6 lakh in 1988-89 to Rs.2978.6 lakh in 1997-98, while sales has increased by about 15 per cent annually from Rs.1357 lakh to Rs.3152 lakh during the same period and the earnings has gone up over 16 per cent per annum from Rs.4 crore (1988-89) to Rs.9.62 crore (1997-98). Moreover, the data presented in Table 5 also indicates that there is a vast scope for further growth of khadi and village industries in N E Region in general and in Manipur in specific.

Table 3
Handloom in NER – 1997-98

State	Nos. of Handlooms		Yarn consumed (in '000 kg)	Cloth produced (in '000 m)
	Domestic	Commercial		
Arunachal Pradesh	44937	653	3073	280
Assam	1251930	201803	17754	74876
Manipur	265302	283808	111012.2	582875
Meghalaya	11030	575	814	344
Mizoram	41041	5944	594	3689
Nagaland	1750	2170	232	1853
Tripura	95592	23480	5638	35250
NE Region	1711582	518433	139118	699166

Source: NEDFI Ltd., Guwahati.

Potentials for Small-Scale Industries

The literacy rate in Manipur is the third highest in the region with around 60 % which is next to Mizoram (77%) and Tripura (71%). As the data transpires in Table 1, the literacy rate of the state is much higher in comparison to the regional and national figures. Besides that the same for male and female in the state are 68 per cent and 52 per cent respectively. Again these figures are also quite impressive since 64 per cent male and 46 per cent female are literate in the country level. This implies that there are big chunks of educated youths both in male

Table 4

Small Enterprises set-up and those Financed by Banks among EDP Trained Persons in 50 Programmes Co-sponsored by NEC-IDBI and NEC-SIDBI (April 1994 – March 2001)

State	No. of Persons trained	Applicants for bank finance		Units Set-up		Units set up with bankfinance	
		No.	% of (3) to (2)	No.	% of(5) to (3)	No.	% of (7) to (3)
1	2	3	4	5	6	7	8
A. P.	172	91	52.9	82	90.1	41	45.6
Assam	410	193	47.1	147	76.2	53	27.5
Manipur	153	84	54.9	52	61.9	18	21.4
Meghalaya	193	113	58.5	51	45.1	17	15.1
Mizoram	100	65	65.0	24	37.0	14	21.5
Nagaland	143	82	57.3	44	53.6	20	24.4
Tripura	180	95	52.8	45	47.4	24	25.3
N E Region	1351	723	53.5	445	61.5	187	25.9

Source: Basic Statistics of NER, 2002.

Table 5

Khadi amd Village Industries in NE Region Key Data on Production, Sales, Employment and Earnings (Rs. in Lakhs)

State	Production		Sales		Employment (nos. in Lakhs)		Earnings	
	1988-89	1997-98	1988-89	1997-98	1988-89	1997-98	1988-89	1997-98
Arunachal Pradesh	0.13	86.24	0.13	87.83	**	0.01	0.08	35.74
Assam	1411.90	4066.55	1350.00	3468.73	1.10	1.11	454.17	1177.05
Manipur	1290.59	2978.57	1357.00	3151.84	0.32	0.42	400.08	962.13
Meghalaya	380.03	1411.87	450.00	1774.47	0.06	0.13	182.40	874.87
Mizoram	80.53	2085.46	77.00	1962.73	**	0.12	32.21	541.52
Nagaland	163.90	1946.13	180.00	2162.00	0.04	0.19	67.20	1064.21
Tripura	1324.20	1245.46	1390.00	1284.92	0.44	0.27	503.19	468.56
NE Region	4651.28	13820.28	4804.13	13856.5	1.96	2.25	1639.33	5129.97
All India	16872.20	451930.93	185618.00	506527.96	42.87	56.50	54699.00	154634.15

** Less than 500

Source: *Basic Statistics of NER, 2002.*

and female sections who are waiting for various self-employment business ventures or jobs in the state. Since the state is having considerably higher literacy rate and particularly among women, the scope of entrepreneurship development in the state is bright.

The ratio of workers to the total women population in the state is nearly 40% (next to Mizoram's 47.5 %) which is again a healthy sign for the state's economy. The data shown in Table 1 further reveal that the participation of women in bread earning in the state is commendable as compared to the levels at regional level and national level as well. The percentages of main workers and marginal workers among women are also significantly higher not only among NE States but also at country level. The statistics presented in said table reflect the work culture among women and their positive attitude towards self-dependence/economic independence in the state. This not only shows the healthy working environment for women but also boost the young women to start new business venture and take some risk to show their entrepreneurial skill/potential, prove their talents, and worth in the society.

In view of the higher literacy rate, ratios of total workers, main workers and marginal workers among women in Manipur, it can be unhesitately said that women in the state can be more effectively encouraged/motivated for entrepreneurship development and consequently facilitated for undertaking independent enterprises of their choice. Thus, the State Government should come foreword with regular Entrepreneurship Development Programmes to generate entrepreneurial awareness among educated youths, promote entrepreneurial culture and environment for the growth of Small Scale Industries in rural areas. This will no doubt help in diversifying the rural economic activities through crop diversification, occupational shift from agriculture to agri related business, rural business and commercial activities in rural areas.

Moreover, since Manipur is suitable for the development of horticulture the state has vast potential for the promotion of agribusiness. The major fruits grown in the state are pineapple, orange banana guava, pearches, and lemons, etc. In the recent years cultivation of horticultural crops as stated above are being developed on commercial scale in many places of the state both in hills and valleys. Therefore, the Department of Horticulture in the state can make some strategic measures in developing horticulture sector which would not only immensely help in diversifying agriculture, promoting agribusiness, undertaking several related activities in the rural areas but also generate huge employment resulting higher domestic income and standard of living in rural areas. Besides, it is known to all that the person i.e., the entrepreneur behind the success of enterprise is very important. Largely it is his effort, which gives the ultimate result i.e., launching and sustenance of an enterprise. It is emphasizes that the entrepreneurship training is the transformation of people from 'general' to specific i.e., 'person' to 'entrepreneur'. Whenever a general person undergoes with the training process of entrepreneurship development he comes out with new identity as an entrepreneur due to the effectiveness of training. Entrepreneur as an individual is influenced by his motivational orientation, knowledge and skill about launching an enterprise and managing it successfully. The motivational orientation supported by his knowledge and skill about launching an enterprise building will encourage him to choose an entrepreneurial career.

Conclusion

In view of the aforesaid discussion it is evident that though Manipur is industrially backward, yet the state Manipur and the entire North Eastern Region has got vast potential for industrial development based on local resources, local potential and skills in particular. Further, it is also observed that women of the North-Eastern Region are playing a significant role in the growth of small-scale and household industries. Hence, efforts should be made to divert the attention towards the development of women entrepreneurship and the provision of good and adequate support systems for the speedy growth of small-scale industries, household/cottage industries in Manipur and in the Region as well. This would no doubt boost the rural industrialization but also strengthen the economy of Manipur and of the entire North-Eastern Region.

4

ENTREPRENEURIAL MOTIVATION IN SMALL SCALE INDUSTRIES IN MANIPUR

An Analysis

G.P. PRASAIN
E. NIXON SINGH

Introduction

Entrepreneurship plays an important role in the economic development of a country. It instigates social and economic changes and development in terms of promotion of self-employment, in raising the level of income and standard of living of the people of the society. This is by and large, because of lack of Entrepreneurial motivation. Again, what makes a man is mostly his environment and his attitudes. The prevailing socio-economic, psychological and the cultural factors naturally influence a man and act as a source of inspiration to make a successful living in the society.

Environment and attitudes are not two different separable entities. The former influences the latter and *vice versa*. But the attitudes of people exert more influence on the environment. Sometimes, man becomes a prisoner of the environment of which he is the creator. Here again, the attitudes of man are not static. They are ever changing. Man constantly endeavours to conceive new ideas and better ideas and indulges in experimenting on them. This process guides to changed attitudes and the changed environments.

The level of economic development differs from one country to another country because the people of these countries are placed in different socio-economic setting with different attitudes. Wytinsky remarks that if it was possible to transplant overnight all the factories of Michigan, Ohio and Pennsylvania to India without changing the economic attitudes of the people, two decades later, the country would be about as poor as it is now. He felt that the main source of India's weakness lies in the human factor. What is lacking is not innate abilities or technical skills in her people but it is the lack of initiative or interest in improving their economic status.[1]

The paradise of the abundance of innate abilities and the lack of enterprising qualities in India is well exemplified by Ram K. Vepa. He cited the example of Bihar, Orissa, Assam and Madhya Pradesh which are endowed with rich natural resources and have, in the past produced amazing achievements both artistic and cultural. He cited the temples at Konark, Bhubaneshwar and Khajuraho which speak volumes about the skills of the master-craftsmen and the culture of the people of those areas in the past but which remained backward. Even today, these states remained backward despite massive investment in public sector projects there since the beginning of the era of planning in India.[2]

As such, of all the attitudes, innovation, risk taking and future planning is the most important from the point of view of industrial development. It is the entrepreneur who acts as a 'spark pug' to transform the economic scene and brings a sense of dynamism into it.[3] Entrepreneurs like any other careerists are not born but they are made. Career depends upon several factors other than the attitudes of the careerist himself. The attitudes of others like his family members, friends and relatives and the Government would exert influence on the career making. Entrepreneurship is no exception. Entrepreneurs are not only a product of their ambitions, but also those of the aspirations of their family members, friends and the nation.

Certain compulsions also, at times, push them to the entrepreneurial roles. The encouragement and help received from Government and non-governmental agencies are some of the important factors instrumental to the emergence of entrepreneurship.

Need of the Study

Unemployment is the most critical problem in India, more particularly among the educated youths. Manipur is also not an exception. It is a fact that Manipur is an industrially backward state. Economic reforms have failed to revive the down-trend in industrialisation. With the increase in unemployment, there arise many social evils. One of the important factors responsible for growing social tension in this state is the problem of unemployment. Thus, developing the spirit of entrepreneurship has become vital on the following grounds:

1. The government cannot provide jobs to all job seekers.
2. The private sector will be limited to only a few selected.
3. Jobs may be available out of home-towns but unwilling to move out.
4. The desired job is hard to find.
5. A job can support a family but an entrepreneurial effort can support more than a family.

Objectives of the Study

The specific objectives of the study are as follows:

i) To analyse the factors that have motivated and facilitated the transpire of entrepreneurship in the Imphal East and Imphal West Districts.

ii) To find out some suggestions for the growth and development of entrepreneurship in Manipur.

Research Design

As a matter of fact, the small scale industries of Imphal East District and Imphal West District has gained a lot of significance on account of several factors particularly due to its large number of population and non-existence of other organized sector in absorbing the labour force. According to the population enumeration of the census of India 2001, the population of the state of Manipur as on 1st March 2001 stood at 23,88,635 persons.[4] Imphal West District accounts for 18.40% of the total population of the state whereas that of Imphal East Districts accounts for 16.49%. In this connection, it may be mentioned that the problems of unemployment and population growth has given impetus for the growth of small scale industries. There are 5185 and 137 industrial units in Imphal West and Imphal East District respectively as on 31.03.2001. Hence, the s.ope of the present study has been confined to these two districts of Manipur. It comprises 106 samples of small scale industries which have been selected on random basis in such 56 samples from Imphal West Districts and the rest 50 from Imphal East District. The method of sampling adopted here is Stratified Random Sampling with proportional allocation in both stratum (two districts). The list of small scale industries is treated as sampling frame and the sample size is determined on the basis of a Pilot Survey (taking 10 small scale industries) say the mean ... S.D. of daily sales amount (in rupees) that is 2634.20 ... 2770.52 under the conditions that 95% degree of precision with 20% marginal error to the mean daily sales amount.

The formula used is

$$n = \frac{Zx^2 xs^2}{e^2}$$

Where, n = sample size,

e = marginal error/permissible error,

Zx = standard variate at "x" level,

s = standard deviation.

In the selection of the sample units for the purpose of the study, those with less than 5 years' existence and not working at present have been completely ignored. It had also been ensured to give representation to different types of industries.

Findings of the Study

A. Entrepreneurs' Ambitions

Ambitions motivate men. Ambition is an index of one's own resourcefulness. It activise men, broaden their vision and make the life more meaningful. Ambition is not something which is akin to greed or windfall. Greed results in disaster and windfall makes one a speculator. Like an individual, a nation or a region may have their own ambitions or aspirations which speak of their resourcefulness. "The people are poor because they prefer it that way". This is one of the causes of poverty attributed by Galbraith for the backwardness of many Asian and African nations. Galbraith further explained that because the people of those nations are lacking in ambition, they are lagging behind others in development."[5]

Ambition is the wrench of all motives. The intentions and initiative of a man are motivated by his ambitions. The importance of ambition in life can be justified by the common saying "aimless life is a goal less game." Hence, their aspirations and means to reach their goal is much more important than the man himself. However, ambitions differ from one person to another person depending upon the characteristics, priorities etc which they have set for themselves. Sometimes, personal ambitions may come in the way of achieving national aspirations. Well conceived notions, careful planning, calculated risk taking, timely decision-making and swift execution make the ambition meaningful and fruitful and hence the achievement of nations' economic growth and development.

As regards the entrepreneurs' ambitions under the present study, the entrepreneurs were asked to rank in the order of importance, any three of five given ambitions. The ambitions marked by them were ranked by weighted score by according three points to the ambition ranked first, two points to the ambition ranked second and one point to the ambition ranked third. On the basis of the percentage of total weighted score each ambition, overall ranking is made.[6] As can be observed from Table 1, the ambition of gaining independent living or self-employment was ranked first in Imphal West District (40.5%) as well as in Imphal East District (42.0%). In both the districts put together, 'to make money' received second rank (23.1%). 'To gain social prestige' was the third ranked ambition in Imphal East District while it was 'to make money' in the case of Imphal West District.

"To fulfil the desire of myself/my father/my wife" was the fourth ranked ambition in both the districts. The "other" ambition ranked fifth in both in districts while includes the desire to do something new or creative, self-employment to youths, etc. It is clear from the above analysis that the entrepreneurs in the two districts had mainly the ambition of gaining independent living or self-employment, making money, gaining social prestige and fulfilling the desires of himself and his family. It is also to be noted that basically there was only a slight, just an inter-changing, difference in the ambitions of entrepreneurs in Imphal West district and those in Imphal East District in respect of the top three ambitions.

Table 1
Entrepreneurs' Ambitions

Ambitions	Imphal West District					Rank	RankImpal East District				
	Entrepreneurs' Ranking			Weighted score	Rating (%)		Entrepreneurs' Ranking			Weighted score	Rating (%)
	One	Two	Three				One	Two	Three		
To make money	10	8	18	64	20.71	3	6	16	22	72	25.6
To gain independent living (self-employment)	30	16	3	125	40.45	1	30	13	2	118	41.99
To fulfil the desire of myself/ my father/my wife	6	10	12	50	16.18	4	2	12	10	40	14.23
To gain social prestige	914	10	65	21.04	2	11	6	3	48	17.08	
Others*	1	1	-	51.62	5	1	-	-	3	1.07	
No response	-	7	13	0	-	-	-	3	13	0	
Total	56	56	56	309	100.00	50	50	50	281	100.00	

* 'Others' ambitions includes the desire to do something new or creative, self-employment to youths, etc.

Reasons compelling Entrepreneurs to Enter Industry

Sometimes the compulsion rather than the ambition leads the man to success. At times, the initial aspirations and the opportunities may clash with each other. Then the destiny is shaped none other than by the compulsions encountered by the individual. Sometimes, one may be thrown out of his job all of a sudden or he may remain unemployed for long time after his education. There are also cases of people who start tiny industry as a diversification of economic interests and ultimately making lakhs of rupees and providing employment to others in hundreds. Such is the importance of the element of compulsion in everydays' life. Hence, it is thought appropriate to examine the reasons that might have compelled the entrepreneurs to pursue entrepreneurship.

Table 2 shows that the compulsion number one that have compelled the entrepreneurs in both the districts was the diversification of economic interests (31.3 %) 'Unemployment' was the number two compulsion of the Imphal West District that has driven 24.7 per cent of the entrepreneurs to the industry whereas 'dissatisfaction with the previous job held' was that the Imphal East District that has shaped the destiny of 25.7 per cent of the entrepreneurs to become industrialists 18.3 of the Imphal West District entrepreneurs ranked 'dissatisfaction with the previous job held' as number three compelling reasons while 22.0 per cent of the Imphal East District entrepreneurs mentioned 'unemployment' as the number three compelling reasons that ranked fourth in both the districts is making use of idle funds (12.6%). It may be interesting to note that 6 entrepreneurs, 2 from Imphal West District and 4 from Imphal East District, had no compelling reason to start industry. Moreover, 40 entrepreneurs, 22 from Imphal West District and 18 from Imphal East District had not mentioned any number two compelling reasons. Likewise, 35 entrepreneurs of the Imphal West District and 34 entrepreneurs of the Imphal East District didn't find any number three compelling reason to start industry.

It is not an easy task to differentiate between one's ambition and compulsion. What is an ambition for one entrepreneur may be a compulsion for another. It is the entrepreneurs' attitudes that ultimately make the difference.

Factors Facilitating Entrepreneurship

Ambitions or compulsions alone may not make an entrepreneur. Sometime, the encouragement he got from his family members or his

Table 2

Reasons Compelling Entrepreneurs to Enter Industry

Ambitions	Imphal West District					Rank	RankImpal East District				
	Entrepreneurs' Ranking			Weighted score	Rating (%)		Entrepreneurs' Ranking			Weighted score	Rating (%)
	One	Two	Three				One	Two	Three		
Unemployment	17	3	5	62	24.70	2	9	10	1	48	22.02
Dissatisfaction with the previous job held	9	9	1	46	18.33	3	13	8	1	56	25.69
To make use of idle funds	3	12	4	37	14.74	4	3	6	1	22	10.09
Diversification of economic interests	17	9	7	76	30.28	1	17	4	12	71	32.57
Others*	8	1	4	30	11.95	5	4	4	1	21	9.63
No compelling reasons	22	24	5	0	-	-	4	18	34	0	-
Total	56	56	56	251	100.00	50	50	50	218	100.00	

*

*Others includes maintenance of large families, revival of sick unit started by father etc.

friends and relatives, the experience he gained in employment, the skills he acquired or inherited etc., also facilitate the exercise of entrepreneurship. Many factors may come up in the way of starting an industry. For example, encouragement of the family elders is very much needed in the process of starting an unit. If they are reluctant, quite naturally, it is difficult to expect support from others including entrepreneur's wife. Moreover, first generation entrepreneurs generally faced strong opposition from their parents as occupation pursued by the family so far is different from what is going to be done by the entrepreneur. Therefore, an attempt has been made to examine whether there were any such facilitating factors.

Table 3 demonstrates the factors facilitating the emergence of entrepreneurship. Previous experience in manufacturing was rated highest (33.2 %) of all the facilitating factors in both the two districts. The next important factor facilitating entrepreneurship was the encouragement of family members/relatives/friends (26.5 %). Success stories of entrepreneurs were ranked as the third important factor (15.6 %). Closely followed, acquired or inherited professional and technical skills was rated as the fourth factor facilitating the entrepreneurship. This is the overall position in both the districts.

It is clear from the above analysis that there are at least two important factors facilitating entrepreneurship apart from a few others. They are previous experience in manufacturing and encouragement of family members/relatives/friends. These two were ranked first and second most important factors in both the Imphal West district and Imphal East District.

Expectations of Entrepreneurs

Expectations of the entrepreneurs, which stimulated their desire to jump into entrepreneurship and the degree of fulfilment of such expectations, is enquired in this section. It is quite natural that many of the entrepreneurs expect a lot from the state government and other non-government agencies. Whether these expectations get fulfilled or not, they initiate a useful function in stimulating the desire of the entrepreneur to start an industry.

In this study, a long list of possible expectations or aspirations are given to the entrepreneurs and asked to mark any expectation or

Table 3
Factors Facilitating Entrepreneurship

Facilities factors	Imphal West District					Rank	RankImpal East District				
	Entrepreneurs' Ranking			Weighted score	Rating (%)		Entrepreneurs' Ranking			Weighted score	Rating (%)
	One	Two	Three				One	Two	Three		
Success stories of entrepreneurs	11	6	2	47	15.41	3	10	7	-	44	15.77
Previous experience in manufacturing	27	6	-	93	30.49	1	31	4	-	101	36.20
Previous employment in industry	-	3	1	7	2.30	7	1	1	-	4	1.4
Property-inherited/acquired/ wife's	4	6	1	25	8.20	5	1	4	1	12	4.30
Encouragement of family members/relatives/friends	8	25	5	79	25.90	2	5	28	5	76	27.24
Acquired or inherited professional and technical skills	3	5	24	43	14.10	4	1	3	33	42	15.054
Others*	2	-	51	13.	6	1	6	-	-	-	
No. of entrepreneurs not responding	1	5	18	0	-	-	1	3	11	0	-
Total	56	56	56	305	100.00	50	50	50	279	100.00	

* 'Others' includes availability of raw material, nearness to markets, existence of similar units in the locality etc.

expectations that had stimulated their desire to enter industry. Table 4 shows the distribution of the expectations.

Table 4

Distribution of Expectations Stimulating the Entrepreneur's Desire to Start Industry

Expectations	District		Both
	Imphal West	Imphal East	
1. Allotment of plot/shed in industrial estate	1 (1.8)	- -	1 (0.9)
2. Financial corporations from State Govt./Financial corporations and other state agencies	40 (71.4)	33 (66.0)	73 (68.9)
3. Technical assistance from the Govt./non-government agencies	5 (8.9)	6 (6.0)	8 (7.6)
4. Government assistance in machinery and raw material.	1 (1.8)	-	1 (0.9)
5. Ancillary relation with large firms	3 (5.3)	1 (2.0)	4 (3.8)
6. Availability of skilled labour	5 (8.9)	2 (4.0)	7 (6.6)
7. Support of dependable partners/ shareholders	3 (3.6)	-	3 (2.8)
8. Others	2 (3.6)	-	2 (1.9)
9. No. of entrepreneurs not responding.	11 (19.6)	14 (28.0)2	5 (23.6)
Total	**56** **(100.0)**	**50** **(100.0)**	**106** **(100.0)**

Note : Figures in parentheses indicate percentages to total.

Even though a long list of expectations are given to the entrepreneurs, 19.6 per cent (11 out of 56 entrepreneurs) of the Imphal West district and 28 per cent (14 out of 50 entrepreneurs) of the Imphal West

District entrepreneurs admitted that they had no expectations as such. Many of the entrepreneurs (73 out of the total 106) expected financial assistance from State Government, Manipur Industrial Development Corporation (MANIDCO) and other state and national agencies. Expectation of getting technical assistance from the government/non-government agencies ranked second in Imphal East District (6.0%) as well as in Imphal West District (8.9%). Whereas in Imphal West District, expectation of availability of skilled and one in Imphal East District expected getting of anciliary relation with large firms. And 2 entrepreneurs of the Imphal West District had 'others' labour was ranked as equal as the expectation of getting technical assistance (8.9%). Only 3 entrepreneurs in Imphal West District expectations which includes financial assistance from moneylenders, government assistance in the sale of finished products, securing favours at political or official level etc.

This analysis draws the following conclusions: State agencies such as the MANIDCO, the nationalised banks and more particularly, the self-employment schemes initiated by the central Government are stimulating agents of entrepreneurship. Considerable assistance is also expected from the government agencies as regards technical aspects. What is expected from partners and shareholders, government assistance in machinery and raw-material are the least.

Entrepreneurs' Expectations and its Fulfilment

Here, the expectations of the entrepreneurs is sought to be self-assessed by the entrepreneurs themselves. Table 5 demonstrates the degree of fulfilment of the entrepreneurs' expectations.

Only 21.4 per cent of the Imphal West District (12 out of 56) and 26 per cent of the Imphal East District (13 out of 50) entrepreneurs fulfilled their expectations. The expectations of 29.3 per cent of the total entrepreneurs (31 out of 106) are partly fulfilled. Again, 13 entrepreneurs of the Imphal West District remained unfulfilled as regards their expectations. It is 12 in the case of Imphal East District. As pointed out earlier, 25 entrepreneurs had no prior expectations to enter into entrepreneurship. This explains the realistic attitude of the entrepreneurs in general. The expectancy gap is broader perhaps because many of them have the expectation of getting financial assistance from government or other sources.

Conclusion and Suggestions

It need not be repeated that a man is mostly influenced by his environment and his attitudes. Entrepreneurs covered by the study had mainly the ambition of gaining independent living or self-employment, making money, gaining social prestige and fulfilling the desires of himself and his family. But it is not easy to differentiate between one's ambition and compulsion. What is an ambition for one entrepreneur may be a compulsion for other. It is the entrepreneur's attitudes that ultimately make the different. Previous experience in manufacturing and encouragement of family members/relatives/friends are also at least two important factors facilitating entrepreneurship. State agencies like the MANIDCO, the nationalised banks and more particularly, the self-employment schemes initiated by the Central Government can also stimulate the desire of unemployed educated youths to jump into entrepreneurship.

Table 5
The Degree of Fulfilment of Entrepreneur's Expectations

Degree of Fulfilment	District		Both
–	Imphal West	Imphal East	
Fulfilled	12 (21.4)	13 (26.0)	25 (23.6)
Party fulfilled	20 (35.7)	11 (22.0)	31 (29.3)
Unfulfilled	13 (23.2)	12 (24.0)	25 (23.6)
No. of Entrepreneurs having no expectations	11 (19.6)	14 (28.0)	25 (23.6)
Total	**56** **(100.0)**	**50** **(100.0)**	**106** **(100.0)**

Note : Figures in parentheses indicate percentage to total.

NOTES AND REFERENCES

1. Batra, G.S. and Dangal, R.C. (2000), *Entrepreneurship and Small Scale Industries*, Deep & Deep Publications Pvt. Ltd. New Delhi
2. Cashin, P. and R. Sahay (1996), Regional Economic Growth and Convergence in India, Finance and Development, *IMF*, March issue.
3. Government of Manipur (2003), *Manipur Today*, Directorate of Information and Public Relations (DIPR).
4. Mali, D.D. and Bondopadhyay, D. (1993), *Small Industry Development in North East.*
5. Khanka, S.S. (1990), *Entrepreneurship in Small Scale Industries*, Himalayan Publishing House, New Delhi.

5

MANAGERIAL PROBLEMS IN SMALL SCALE INDUSTRIES OF MANIPUR

A Critical Analysis of Some Selected Units

H. RAMANANDA SINGH

Introduction

With the economic development, occupational structure of a country undergoes significant changes from agriculture and allied sector to indistry and service sectors (Table 1).

Table 1
Occupational Distribution of Working Population in USA, Japan, and India

Sector of economy	USA % of workforce		Japan % of workforce		India % of workforce	
	1870	1950	1877	1950	1951	1991
Agriculture & allied sector	50	12	83	48	72	66.7
Industrial sector	25	35	6	21	10.7	12.7
Service sector	25	53	11	31	17.2	20.6

Source: A.N. Agarwal *Indian Economy* 22nd edition, page 10-11.

India, with the growth of its economy, also experiences the gradual shift of its workforce from Agriculture to Industry and service sectors.

In Indian economy, SSI play a very important role. Considering the importance of SSI sector, its growth has been properly nurtured over the palnned period through policies of protection and reservation of items for the SSI sector.

The growth of SSI in India has been recording a stable growth rate over the year (Table 2).

Table 2
Growth of SSI in India

Year	Total No. of Units in Lakhs	% increase
1997-98	29.44	5.03
1998-99	30.80	4.60
1999-00	32.12	4.30
2000-01	33.11	3.08
2001-02	34.64	4.62

Source: IIE Guwahati.

The importance of SSI sector in the country is substantial. By 2000-03, with an estimated 5.572 million units, fixed investment of Rs 9045 crores, production of Rs 742020 crores and employment of 19.96 millions, SSI sector is playing a significant role in Indian economy. Export from the sector are estimated at Rs 71200 crores which is about 50% of exports from the industrial sector as a whole. SSI contribute 92% of employment (Mathew, 2004). And 80% of the total employment in the industrial sector of the country is contributed by SSI sector (Agarwal, 1983).

Though, there is stable growth rate of SSI in India, the sickness of SSI units is also high which is eroding away the benefits of the increased in the number of units registered (Table 3).

As for sickness is concerned, to unfold the cause of sickness, a study was conducted by the Reserve Bank of India which covered 378 units. The study revealed that 52% of the units had become sick due to management and managerial deficiencies (Table 4).

Table 3
Growth of Small Scale and the Percentage of Sick Units

Year	No. of SSI units in lakhs	% of sickness
1990-91	19.48	11.35
1991-92	20.82	11.74
1992-93	22.46	10.60
1993-94	23.81	10.77
1994-95	25.71	10.45
1995-96	27.24	9.63
1996-97	28.57	8.22
1997-98	30.14	7.25

Source: "*RBI Report on Currency and Finance*", Mumbai 1998-99.

Table 4
Broad Classification of Causes of Sickness and their Percentage

Group of causes	%
Management and managerial deficiencies	52
Faulty in initial planning and other techincal knowhow	14
Labour trouble	02
Market recession	23
Other (infrastructural factors and raw material shortage)	09
Total	100

Source: *Tiwari Committee report 1984*, p 24.

Further analysis of a study of industrial sickness in Small Scale Industrie conducted in Canada/USA revealed that management deficiencies in one form or the other is the single most important cause of failure of such industrial units. The proportion of units failing due to this reason in India was estimated at 66% with corresponding to 90% in case of Canada/USA (Table 5).

Table 5
Broad Classification of Causes of Sickness by a Study Conducted in Canada/USA

Group of causes	Units in %
Incomplete management	50
Lack of managerial experience	20
Imbalance managerial experience	15
Lack of experience in the area of business	05
Misc.	10
Total	100

Source: Mittal, B.M., "Industrail Rehabilitation of India", *Journal of Banking and Finance*, Jodhpur, Vol. 1 1987-88, p. 45.

The above discussion highlights the importance of management and managerial roles in the operation of units in SSI. In short, it is the nature of the unit's management which determines success or failure of the unit.

Small Scale Industrial Scenario of Manipur

Manipur with the geographical area of 22,327 sq. km is situated in the Noth-Eastern corner of India bordering Myanmar. As per Census 2001 the total population of Manipur is 23,88,634 persons. The economy of the state is basically agrarian in nature and is, therefore, dependent on the products coming from outside the state for most of the consumption items.

The industrial scenario of Manipur presents a dismal picture with very small size of industrial units operating in the state. Table 6 depicts the industrial scenario of Manipur.

By 1998-99, there were about 9247 units, with the total employment of 47157 persons, total investment of 33.84 crores. And in the year 2000-2001, the total number of units was 9374 which is 13.92 percentage of NE region and 0.28 percentage of all India. Though the state has recorded an inviable growth in the number of registered units, the performance is not satisfactory. The state's SSI sectors are mainly agro-based industries, electronics, and forest product-based industries.

The industrail activity was initiated in the state since the planning period and it gain momentum after accorded the status of full-fledged state. However there remain a gap between the initiative taken up and the requirement for the same for the development of the industrial sector of the state.

Table 6

No. of SSI Units, Employment, Average Investment, Production in Manipur

Year	No. of units	Employ-ment	Avg. employ-ment	Invest-ment in plant and machinery(crore)	Avg. invest-ment (in lakhs)	Produc-tion (in crore)
1987-88	3996	19900	4.98	12.30	0.31	67.26
1990-91	6788	33390	4.92	21.66	0.32	91.81
1991-92	7392	36910	5.00	23.59	0.32	101.45
1992-93	7696	38400	4.99	24.57	0.32	106.90
1993-94	8096	39680	4.90	25.70	0.32	116.70
1994-95	8341	42720	5.12	27.37	0.33	123.16
1995-96	8612	43949	5.10	30.19	0.35	127.65
1996-97	8916	45469	5.10	31.39	0.35	132.05
1997-98	8916	46390	5.20	32.05	0.36	134.89
1998-99	9247	47157	5.10	33.84	0.37	140.86

Source: Directorate of Commerce and Industries, Government of Manipur, Imphal 1999.

The slow growth of the sector (Table 7) coupled with the rampant closure of the SSI units has further aggravated the problems. The sickness in Manipur is about 30.36 percentage (SIDO report New Delhi 1999).

The growth in the registration of SSI units has considerably come down over the years. The performance of existing SSI units is discouraging the growth of SSI units. As per the IIE report, the slow growth of SSI in Manipur is attributed to the following reasons:

- the majority of the state are agrarian.
- people are not enterprising and preferred Government jobs.

- the infrastructure bottleneck of the state hampered growth of industries.
- the geographical isolation of the state is also regarded as a major retarding factor due to high cost of operation and production experienced by SSI units.
- the law and order problems that hold back the flow of investment.

Table 7
Status of SSI Growth in Manipur

Year	Percentage increase in registration
1993-94	6.00
1994-95	3.02
1996-97	3.55
1997-98	1.12
1998-99	1.43
1999-2000	1.67

Source: IIE, Report on "Status of Small Scale Industries in North-Eastern State of India".

Moreover, entrepreneurship as a profession or culture is yet to have its root in Manipur. A study revealed that 92% of the sick units belong to first generation entrepreneur who are educated youth belonging to lower middle and lower class strata (Table 8).

Table 8
Family Background of Sick Enterprises

Entrepreneurs	% of total sick units
First generation	92
Second generation	8
Total	100

Source: Kh. Tomba Singh, *Industrail sickness in Manipur- A case study of Small Scale Industries*, Thesis submitted to Commerce Deptt., Manipur University.

Keeping into consideration of the importance of SSI units in the economy of Manipur and various problems faced by SSI units leading to their closure, there is a need for looking into the main causes of the problems. This paper focuses on the managerial problems in Small Scale Industries in Manipur.

Managerial Problems in Some Selected Units of Manipur

The problem faced by the SSI units of Manipur can be divided into general and the problems in the functional areas of business.

(A) General Problems (Table 9)

The majority of the SSI units in Manipur faced general problems such as power supply problem, problems from society (e.g. discouragement, extortion), raw material and transportation problems.

Table 9
General Problems Faced by the SSI Units of Manipur
(Sample size = 40)

Types of problem	% of units facing problem	% of units not facing problem
From society	70.0	30.0
In getting licence	32.5	67.5
Transportation	62.5	37.5
Telecommunication	42.5	57.5
Power supply	82.5	17.5
Raw material	70.0	30.0

Source: Sample Survey.

(B) Problems in the Functional Areas of Business Enterprise

Finance and accounting, recruitment of employees and marketing are the main functional areas of business enterprise where SSI of Manipur are facing problems, while some have problems in production, handling of employees and technology (Table 10).

Table 10
Problems in the Functional Areas of Business Enterprise
(Sample size = 40)

Functional areas	%
Marketing	57.5
Production	12.5
Finance and accounting	67.5
Handling of employees	22.5
Recruitment of employees	60
Technology	37.5

Note: Some SSI units have more than one problem.
Source: Sample Survey.

A Peek into the Managerial Problems in Small Scale Industries of Manipur

Some of the causes leading to the managerial problems are discussed under different headings as given below:

(A) Inadequate State's Plan Allocation in the Industrial Sector

The pattern of plan allocation in the state plan over the planning period reflects that the industrial development did not received much priority in the state's plan which made the industrailization and development of the industrial infrastructure low in the state. The allocation pattern become clear from Table 11.

Table 11
Percentage of Allocation in the Industrial Sector in the State and Nation's Plan

	Plan period			
	VI (1979-85)	VII (1985-90)	VIII (1990-97)	IX (1997-2002)
State	6.00	5.6	4.0	5.21
National	15.4	12.58	- 10.92	10.55

Source: IIE Guwahati.

It is noticed that the state is not allocating enough fund for the purpose. This could be one of the reasons for slow growth of industries as private initiative is always lacking in the state.

(B) Inadequate Financial Support from Commercial Banks

It is seen that the SSI sector is facing the problem of finance and therfore, such units are set up with very little investment. The fact that entrepreneurs are new with less capital of their own makes the role of the commercial bank all the more important in the state. In spite of the state having satisfactory network of commercial banks, their role in terms of providing financial assistance to the SSI sector can not be termed satisfactory. The status as regard to the CD ratio of the commercial bank is given in Table 12.

Table 12
Comparative CD Ratio of the State, the North-Eastern Region and the Country

Year	Bank branches	Bank credit	Bank deposit	State CD ratio	CD ratio of NE	CD ratio of India
1994	85	9524	14576	72.13	39.5	56.6
1995	85	9865	17742	55.6	34.56	55.6
1996	85	12406	23093	53.72	34.51	61.90
1997	85	15195	26421	57.51	31.22	57.3
1998	85	16657	28343	58.76	29.86	55.5
1999	86	16923	40622	41.65	28.03	56.75
2000	81	17477	39070	37.45	28.06	57.1
2001	71	15723	44549	38.87	28.10	57.21

Source: IIE GUWAHATI.

CD ratio of the state is declining over the years which reflects the declining role of commercial banks. Even if the CD ratio is quite higher than that of other NE states, if the share of SSI is look into, it is not found to be significant. Even if the flow of fund to SSI is look into, in actual terms, it is not encouraging.

(C) Lack of Practical Knowledge of Business Enterprise

Majority of the proprietors/entrepreneurs concerning the SSI units claimed to have specialised knowledge of production and marketing. And also significant number of executives have the knowledge of technology, administration and finance (Table 13). In spite of their claim, SSI units have problems in marketing and finance etc. implying that they lack practical knowledge in the specialised areas which they claimed to posess the knowledge.

Table 13
Speacialised Knowledge Claimed to be Posessed by the Proprietor/Entrepreneur
(Sample size = 40)

Area of specialisation	%
Production	70
Marketing	85
Technology	47.5
Administration	40
Finance	47.5

Note: Some proprietors claimed to have more than one area of specialisation.
Source: Sample Survey.

(D) Lack of Qualification Relating to Commerce and Business

Proprietors/ entrepreneurs of the SSI units do not have the educational qualification relating to business management and commerce (Table 14). This is one of the main reasons for facing managerial problems by the SSI units of Manipur.

(E) Taking up Business Venture not by Choice

According to D.D Mali, former director of IIE, Guwahati, "people become entrepreneurs either by choice or by chance. But the person who becomes entrepreneur by choice has the inner spirit from within which will make him a successful entrepreneur."

Table 14
Educational Qualification of Proprietors/Entrepreneurs
(Sample Size = 40)

Educational qualification	%
Below X standard	15.0
X Standard	07.5
Graduate (Science and Arts)	45.0
Post Graduate (Science and Arts)	25.0
Degree (Technical)	07.5
Total	100

Source: Sample Survey.

Many a SSI units of Manipur were established by persons who at one point of time ware looking for Government jobs (Table 15) and also they established the enterprise with the main objective of self-employment and earning money. Only a minimal few have taken up the business venture to fulfill the dreams of becoming entrepreneurs/ businessmen (Table 16).

Table 15
Percentage of Proprietors/Entrepreneurs Applied for Government Jobs
(Sample Size = 40)

Response category	%
Applied for Government jobs	75
Not applied for Government jobs	25
Total	100

Source: Sample Survey.

(F) Non Participation of Training Programme

Various training programmes are conducted from time to time by various institutions such as IIE, NEDFi, SISI etc. For making the unit a successful and a viable unit, there is a need for continually upgradation of knowledge by the proprietors/entrepreneurs concerned with the business. It has been found that there is lack of participation by the persons who take up the entrepreneurial venture.

Table 16
Purpose of Establishing Enterprise
(Sample Size = 40)

Response category	%
To make money	22.50
To continue family busness	05.00
To secure self-employment	47.5
To gain social position	20.0
To fulfill the dream of entrepreneur	05.00
Total	100

Source: Sample Survey.

Table 17
Percentage of Proprietors/Entrepreneurs Attending Training Programme before Establishment of Enterprise
(Sample Size = 40)

Response category	%
Training attended	52.5
Not attended	47.5
Total	100

Source: Sample Survey.

(G) Wrong Choice of the Type of Product

Local availability of raw material is one of the factor leading to the success of small business. Establishment of enterprise for which the raw material is not locally available leads to various managerial problems. This factor was overlooked by a majority of SSI units of Manipur (Table 19).

Table 18
Percentage of Proprietors/Entrepreneurs Attending Training Programme after Establishment of Enterprise
(Sample Size = 40)

Response category	%
Training attended	55
Not attended	45
Total	100

Source: Sample Survey.

Table 19
Sources of Raw Material of SSIs
(Sample Size = 40)

Sources	%
Locally available	55
Bought from outside	45
Total	100

Source: Sample Survey.

(H) Lack of Awareness of Promotional Schemes of Various Financial Institutions

Various financial institutions are not only providing financial assistance but also the training programmes for the development of SSI units in North-Eastern states. Many a persons who are in the helm of affairs of running the units are not aware of this. So, majority of the persons invest their own money in the business vanture (Table 20).

(I) Lack of Using Sample Information for Studying the Viability of the Unit

A significant number of SSI units neither conducted survey nor used reliable information. Moreover they rely more on hunch and intuition. (Table 21).

Table 20
Mode of Financing the Units
(Sample Size = 40)

Mode of financing	%
Bank loan	7.5
Borrow from money lender	5
Own money	42.5
Bank loan as well as own money	22.5
Bank loan, borrow from other and own money	12.5
Union fund	5
Bank loan and state financial institutions	5
Total	100

Source: Sample Survey.

Table 21
Percentage of Proprietors/Entrepreneurs
Conducting Market Survey
(Sample size = 40)

Response category	%
Conducted survey	57.5
Not conducted survey	42.5
Total	100

Source: Sample Survey.

For the success of the firm, there is a need for regular survey regarding the change in test, preference of consumers, competitors strategy etc. so as to maintain competitive edge in the market.

Conclusion

Since SSI play a very important role in the economy of the state, Government should take enough measures to build the infrastructure facility for the same. A time has come for the society to recognise and appreciate entrepreneurship. And the persons who would like to take up the business ventures should be well aware of the various aspects of the business.

NOTES AND REFERENCES

1. IIE, *A Study on Status of Small Scale Industries of North-Eastern States of India.*
2. IIE, (1997), *A Study on the Impact of Industrial policy.*
3. A.N. Agarwal, *Indian Economy*, 22nd edition.
4. Mittal, B.M (1987-88), Industrial Rehabilitation in India, *Journal of Banking and Finance*, Jodhpur, Vol-1.
5. P.M. Mathew (2004), *Role Calls for Relook*, Survey of Indian Industries, The Hindu Publication.
6. Bedani S.N and Mitra P.K (1998), *Industrial Sickness Identification and Rehabilitation*, Vision Book, New Delhi.
7. Tomba Kh., Industrial Sickness in Manipur - A Case Study of Small Scale Industries, Thesis submitted to Department of Commerce, Manipur University.

6

WORKING CAPITAL MANAGEMENT OF SMALL SCALE INDUSTRIES IN MANIPUR

An Empirical Study

N. TEJMANI SINGH

Introduction

With the increase of economic development associated with the pace of industrial growth and its activities, the need for the development of Small-Scale Industries in India has been the objective of the Government, since independence. Over the years, Small Scale Industries have gained increasing significance in the economic development of our country. They have achieved a high degree of sophistication and made significant progress in quality upgradation and standardisation.

Beginning with simple consumer goods like soap, detergents, leather goods, etc., the Small Scale Sector has made strides and now entered into sophisticated fields of production including electronics and electro-medical devices, I.Ts. etc. The importance of Small Scale Industries (SSIs) was specifically spelt-out in the Industrial Policy Resolution dated the 6th April, 1948. And Section 4 of the New Industrial Policy of Manipur, 2002.

These industries are particularly suited to the better utilization of local resources and for the achievement of local self-sufficiency in respect of certain types of essential consumer goods.

The distinguishing characteristics of the SSIs lies in its potential for creation of gainful employment and specially self-employment opportunities, which is engaged in the processing, preserving, manufacturing or servicing activities including of all those modern manufacturing and repairing units with an investment in plant and machinery of not exceeding Rs.1 crore in respect of Small Scale Industries and Ancillary, according to extraordinary issue of the Gazette Notification No.798 in New Delhi, on December 24, 1999.

The Small Scale Sector is the second major contributor to the industrial economy of our country. Thus, the significance of Small Scale Industries as one of the keys to rural development hardly needs to be emphasized, where motivation of development is present among the rural population, the Small Scale Industries acts as a stimulant, where motivation is lacking, it acts as a lubricant.

The term "Working Capital" is particularly appropriate expression for denoting the wealth of an enterprise which is continuously revolving through the stages most desired by the customers (inventories) and the firm (Cash). The intervening stage (receivable) identifies the current relationship between the firm and its customers. Almost every activity of business or everything that happens in the business, is related to working capital decision.

Rationale

The problem of managing working capital has got a separate entity as against different decision-making issues concerning current assets individually. The skills for working capital management are somewhat unique, though the goals are the same as in managing current assets individually, viz. to make an efficient use of funds for minimizing the risk of loss to attain profit objectives. Hence, working capital management is concerned with the problems that arise in attempting to manage the current assets, the current liabilities and the inter-relationship that exist between them.

Entrepreneur needs cash to buy raw materials and put the raw materials into production process. The goods so produced are either sold for cash or on credit. After a disposal of the turnover, cash is again needed for buying and manufacturing purposes. Under the manufacturing process raw materials are to be purchased and wages are to be paid. Thus, it enlightens the necessity of working capital and therefore, sufficient working capital is necessary to sustain sales activity.

The management of working capital has assumed added significance in respect of SSIs in India in general and Manipur in particular, as the most of firms/units/industries have weak financial base and limited access to financial institutions to supplement their scarce resources.

No significant and comprehensive study as well as enquiry into the functioning of all the various aspects of SSIs and its policies of working capital management in Manipur, has been done before as well as experienced over the entire plan period. Hence, the present study on the "Working Capital Management of Small Scale Industries in Manipur is an attempt to fill up the gap.

The Small Scale Industries have been accorded a vital role by the Government of India for achieving socio-economic objectives. The proper calculation and maintaining of the working capital provides the business, the right amount of cash to maintain, regular flow of its operation and enhances the credit of the concern.

Objective and Approach of the Present Studies

In order to bring out the clear analysis is of the working and functioning of Small Scale Industries in Manipur, the specific objectives of the present study is:

(i) to analyse and examine the management of inventories, management of cash and management of account receivables; and some findings and conclusions.

The management of working capital is one of the important aspects of overall financial management. Since, Manipur remains mainly as a State of Small Scale production, it is necessary to analyse the issues concerning working capital to the possible extent.

The present study which covers the various dimensions and aspects of working capital management in SSIs in Manipur examines how far the objectives of the SSIs are fulfilled, accelerated or weakened of financial assistance and assessing the regional gap. And this empirical study highlight the working capital management of selected 144 SSIs/Units in Manipur and the components of working capital have been intensively examined with the help of different accounting and statistical techniques such as ratios, averages and percentages, etc.

Methodology Adopted

To analyse and evaluate the objective of the present study primary data from the sample units were collected by the Researcher through personal interviews, on the basis of a pre-tested structured Questionnaire in all the 9 districts, namely Imphal East, Imphal West, Ukhrul, Senapati, Churachandpur, Tamenglong, Chandel, Thoubal and Bishnupur. Here, Imphal East and Imphal West districts are combined together as 'Imphal' district. Keeping in view of this 144 units were collected from the District Industries Centres (DICs) Manipur, registered under Small Industries Development Organisation (SIDO) and secondary data for the present study were collected through various records from the publications and bulletins of District Industries Centres (DICs), Department of Industries, Government of Manipur, Manipur Industrial Development Corporation (MANIDCO), Industrial Development Bank of India (IDBI), National Small Industrial Corporation (NSIC), Small Industries Servicing Institutes (SISI), Planning Department, Government of Manipur, Economics and Statistics Department, Government of Manipur, Information and Public Relations, Government of Manipur and also from different Financial Institutions functioning in the State.

The study has come out with findings and suggestions, which may be of practical advantage to various Small Scale Industrial units in Manipur, in managing their working capital effectively and efficiently to sustain the liquidity as well as profitability position of the selected sample units.

Since the main components of working capital management are management of Cash, management of Account receivable and management of Inventories, the analysis of these parameters in the selected sample units in Manipur are present in the following paragraphs.

Selection of the Sample Units

The Researcher has selected 144 units (Small Scale Industries) for sample survey from each and every districts of Manipur through the concerned General Manager of the District Industry Centre, which were working smoothly or properly in Manipur. And the selected sample units are categorised in the following manner (depicted in Table 1).

Working capital analysis has acquired significance primarily because the investment in current assets bears a direct relation with sales growth

Table 1
Selected Sample Untis (No. of Units for each Districts)

Sl. No	Industry Group	IMP	UKL	SPT	CCP	TML	CDL	TBL	BPR	Total	Total in P.C.
1.	2.	3.	4.	5.	6.	7.	8.	9.	10.	11.	12.
1.	Engineering and Metal Based Industries	15	02	03	06	03	03	05	09	46	31.95
2.	Printing and Publishing	02	01	00	03	01	00	01	02	10	6.95
3.	Agro Based Industries	01	01	00	01	02	05	02	02	14	9.72
4.	Ready Made and Garment	02	02	05	02	07	04	01	03	26	18.06
5.	Forest Based Industries	05	04	07	03	03	08	09	06	45	31.25
6.	Miscellaneous (including Brick fields, Hotel Keeping Bee keeping Unit)	01	00	01	00	00	00	01	00	03	2.08
		26	10	16	15	16	20	19	22	144	

Source: Compiled personally from questionnaire.

Note: IMP = Imphal (East+West)UKL=Ukhrul SPT = Senapati
CCP = Churachandpur, TML=Tamenglong; CDL = Chandel
TBL = Thoubal BPR=Bishnupur.

Table 2
Distribution of Sample Units by Total Investment

Sl. No.	Investment Group(in rs.)	IMP	UKL	SPT	CCP	TML	CDL	TBL	BPR	Total	Total in P.C.
1.	2.	3.	4.	5.	6.	7.	8.	9.	10	11.	12.
1.	Below 10	0	0	0	0	1	1	0	1	3	2.08
2.	10-20	0	1	4	1	9	3	2	4	24	16.67
3.	20-30	1	2	6	1	4	3	4	1	22	15.28
4.	30-40	2	3	2	2	0	4	1	1	15	10.41
5.	40-50	2	3	1	1	0	1	1	3	12	8.33
6.	50-60	1	1	1	2	0	3	3	4	15	10.41
7.	60-70	1	0	1	2	1	1	0	0	6	4.17
8.	70-80	0	0	1	2	1	1	0	0	5	3.47
9.	80-90	2	0	0	1	0	1	1	1	6	4.17
10.	90-100	3	0	0	3	0	1	3	0	10	6.95
11.	100 & above	14	0	0	0	0	1	4	7	26	18.06
Total:		**26**	**10**	**16**	**15**	**16**	**20**	**19**	**22**	**144**	

Rupees in thousand range.
Source: Compiled personally from questionnaire.

Table 3

Various Institutions Providing Loans to the Simple Unit

Sl. No.	Districts	MANIDCO	MRB	UBI	SBI	PNB	NSIC	URBAN BANK	DIC	AFS	Total	No Response
1.	Imphal	09	01	03	02	01	02	00	00	01	19	07
2.	Ukhrul	00	00	01	01	00	00	00	03	00	05	05
3.	Senapati	00	00	01	00	00	00	01	03	00	05	11
4.	C.C.Pur	00	00	02	00	00	02	00	01	00	05	10
5.	Tamenglong	00	00	00	01	00	00	00	04	00	05	11
6.	Chandel	00	00	04	00	00	00	00	07	00	11	09
7.	Thoubal	04	00	02	00	00	01	00	02	00	09	10
8.	Bishenpur	03	00	02	00	00	00	00	06	00	11	11
	Total	16	01	15	04	01	05	01	25	01	70	74
Total in p.c.		22.85	1.43	21.43	5.72	1.43	7.14	1.43	37.14	1.43	48.61	51.39

Source: Field Survey.

Note: MRB = Manipur Rural Bank; UBI = United Bank of India; SBI = State Bank of India; PNB = Punjab National Bank; NSIC = National Small Industries Corporation; DIC = District Industries Centre; APC = Assam Financial Corporation.

rate. Out of 144 units selected, there were 26 units in the investment groups of above Rs.100 thousand, which was the highest category of this range of investment group with the highest number of units. The lowest number of units was found in the total investment range of below Rs.10 thousand to the extent of only 3 units (Depicted in Table-2).

Under the present study, only 70 units could secure loans from the Financial Institutions like MANIDCO, UBI, SBI, PNB, AFC, etc. and the remaining 74 unit were not the aware of loan facilities which is shown in Table 3.

The purpose for keeping cash balance by the sample units Table .4 as revealed by the study that only 34 units hold cash balance to meet their current obligations followed by 22 units and 16 units hold the cash balances to meet their contingencies as well as for other purposes. Only 10 units were keeping their cash in order to available of the advantages accruing through price changes/fluctuations.

Table 4
Purpose for Keeping Cash Balance

Sl. No.	District	To meet current obliga-tion	To meet contin-genciesin	To take advantage percent-ages	Any other purpose	No Response	Total
1.	Imphal	07	04	04	03	08	26
2.	Ukhrul	03	02	01	01	03	10
3.	Senapati	05	05	02	03	01	16
4.	C.C.Pur	04	02	00	00	09	15
5.	Tamenglong	04	02	00	02	08	16
6.	Chandel	06	03	00	01	10	20
7.	Thoubal	03	02	00	05	9	19
8.	Bishenpur	02	02	03	01	14	22
Total		34	22	10	16	62	144
Total in p.c.		**23.60**	**15.28**	**6.95**	**11.11**	**43.06**	**100.00**

Source: Field Survey.

The statistical evidence on the procedures adopted by the selected units for their collection of debts accounts revealed that compromise and persuation as well as writing remainders appears to be the main strategy of the sample units, which shows 43 units and 42 units in respect of compromise and persuation as well as writing remainders (depicted in Table 5).

Table 5
Collection of Credit Information Followed by Sample Units

Sl. No. District	Writing Reminder	Compromise & Persuation	Collection Agent	Legal Action	No Response	Total
1. Imphal	08	04	05	01	08	26
2. Ukhrul	04	02	01	00	03	10
3. Senapati	05	05	00	00	06	16
4. C.C.Pur	03	07	01	00	04	15
5. Tamenglong	02	08	01	00	05	16
6. Chandel	06	04	00	02	08	20
7. Thoubal	06	07	02	01	03	19
8. Bishenpur	08	06	02	02	04	22
Total	42	43	12	06	41	144
Total in p.c.	**29.17**	**29.86**	**8.33**	**4.17**	**28.47**	**100.00**

Source: Field survey.

Nearly 15% of the various units maintained the maximum level of inventory only to take advantage of opportunity cost. 56 units and 23 units prepared the inventory report monthly and quarterly respectively, which is shown in Table 6.

Findings

The present study is related to the efficient management of working capital in SSI's in Manipur (144 Units have been selected for the study). Working capital analysis has acquired significance primarily because the investment in current assets bear a direct relation with Sales growth rate. Failure to prepare comprehensive financial plan is one of the main causes for the sickness of some industries. In the survey it was found that even banks/financial institutions have financed the SSI's indiscriminately to achieve their targets either in pressure or with over enthusiasm, without an adequate and critical evaluation of the Project/ Unit. Most of the times feasibility report is not prepared by many units. Even if it is prepared, it will be depicting a rosy picture to satisfy the requirements of lending institution(s).

Table 6
Frequency of Inventory Report in the Sample Units

Sl. No.	District	Monthly	Quarterly	Half-Yearly	Yearly	No Response	Total
1.	Imphal	11	05	00	04	06	26
2.	Ukhrul	03	01	00	01	05	10
3.	Senapati	07	03	02	00	04	16
4.	C.C.Pur	06	02	03	02	02	15
5.	Tamenglong	04	00	00	05	07	16
6.	Chandel	08	04	01	01	06	20
7.	Thoubal	07	03	00	03	06	19
8.	Bishenpur	10	05	02	01	04	22
Total		56	23	08	17	40	144
Total in p.c.		38.89	15.97	5.55	11.81	27.78	100.00

Source: Field survey.

Therefore, while sanctioning loan for a unit, the qualities in the entrepreneurs like risk-taking, organising ability, competence, integrity, honesty creativity and so on must be X-rayed. Further, the entrepreneurs should actively participate in short term programmes organised by the SISI, AMEA, NECON etc. in the area of Finance, Marketing, Production Planning for up-to-date knowledge.

The list of debtors prepared by the Units did not indicate the length of the period for which the different accounts had remained unpaid after the due dates, according to the length of period (age) they remained uncleared. Hence, every entrepreneur should follow a clear-cut collection procedures to speed up the collection dues from the customers/debtors.

The availability of raw materials at the concessional rate through the Govt. agencies found most irregular and uncertain and many of the units seldom prepared the inventory reports as they do not have the sound knowledge of inventory management. Therefore, they should chalk out proper forecasting of the requirements of various types of raw materials and storage and spares on continuous basis to run the production operation smoothly and efficiently. And in order to improve their competitive base and resources, joint marketing programme should be undertaken with properly standardized and identified by trademarks.

Conclusion

Entrepreneur needs cash to buy raw materials and put the raw materials into production process. The goods so produced are either sold for cash or on credit. After a disposal of the turnover, cash is again needed for buying and manufacturing purposes. Under the manufacturing process raw materials are to be purchased and wages are to be paid. Thus, it enlightens the necessity of working Capital and therefore, sufficient working capital is necessary to sustain sales activity and growth of the entrepreneurs.

The Management of Working Capital has assumed added significance in respect of Small Scale Industries in India, in general and Manipur in particular, as the most of these firms/units/industries have a weak financial institutions to supplement.

NOTES

1. Wytinsky, India: *The Awakening Giant*, P. 187
2. Ram K. Vepa, *Entrepreneurship for Development of Bcckward Areas, National Productivity council*, New Delhi, 1973, pp. 14-15.
3. *Ibid.*, p.16.
4. Census of India, 2001: *Provisional Population Totals*, Directorate of Census Operators, Manipur.
5. John Kenneth Galbraith, *Economic Development*, Havard University Press, Cambridge, 1969, p. 15.
6. Data relating to reasons compelling entrepreneurs to enter industry, *factors facilitating entrepreneurship, entrepreneurs choice of type of industries* etc. is also elicited and evaluated similarly in the ensuing sections of this chapter.

REFERENCES

1. Agarwal, N.K. (1983), *Management of Working Capital*, New Delhi, Sterling Publishers Pvt. Ltd.
2. Goel, B.S. (1978), *Production Operation Management,* Pragati Prakashan, Meerut.
3. Goyal, O.P. (1979), *Financial Institutions and Economic Growth of India*, Light and Life Publishers, New Delhi.
4. Saeed, M. (1962), *Financing Small Scale and Cottage Industries in U.P.*, Thesis submitted for the award of Ph.D. Thesis to the University of Allahabad.
5. Joseph, Simon, (1996), New SSI Policy and Economic Restructing, *Yojana*, Dec. 31, 35(23).
6. Subash, J. Rele, (1980), Small Scale Sector, Modernisation, *Crucial for Progress*, *Eastern Economist*, 75(21).
7. Sugam, C. Jain and Mathur, N.D. (1991), *Working Capital Management-Analysis and Cases,* Research Development Association, Jaipur.

7

ENTREPRENEURSHIP DEVELOPMENT IN MANIPUR

Challenges and Opportunities

RAJMANI SINGHA

Manipur is economically and industrially backward state in the North-Eastern corner of India bordering with Myanmar on the east, Nagaland on the north, Assam on the west and Mizoram on the south. About 9/10th of the total area of the state is covered by hills and remaining 1/10th is covered by valley. On the other hand 9/10th of the total population are settled in the valley.

Industrialisation and entrepreneurship are inseparable factors and the crucial role of the entrepreneurs needs to be highlighted in any study relating to industrial and economic development. The individual as an entrepreneur is a critical factor in economic development and an integral part of socio-economic transformation. Because it can generate large scale employment with relatively low capital investment; promote more balance regional development; equitable distribution of income; make use of untapped capital, natural and human resources; and finally it also urge to take risk in the face of uncertainties and intuition.

Despite massive development efforts taken by both central and state governments through various schemes and programmes, the pace of economic and industrial development of the state is very poor. As a result the number of educated unemployed youth of the state has crossed 4.60,143 as in January 2005 of which 1,18,121 were female unemployed youth. The rate of unemployed youth against the total population was 19.26 per cent which is much higher than the national average of 2.81 per cent. Of which Kerala has 21 per cent highest unemployment rate in the country in 1999-2000.

This growing unemployment problem can be solved only when the educated youth of the state are trained and involved in entrepreneurship oriented vocations. Because entrepreneurship is a purposeful activity through which it help in initiating, promoting and maintaining various range of economic activities for the production and distribution of wealth.

Thus, entrepreneurship development usually implies development of small scale industries and it has a significant role in the economic development indirectly and directly solving the alarming growth of unemployed educated youth of the backward state like Manipur in particular and North-Eastern Region in general.

Recognising the importance of entrepreneurship development for industrial development and economic development of the state in one side and lack of entrepreneurship development of the state on the other side, the Central Government, North- Eastern Council and State government through various agencies such as IDBI, SIDBI, SISI, IIE, ICM, NEDFi, Directorate of Commerce and Industries and NGOs have been organising various entrepreneurship development programmes over the past few decades. Such programmes have facilitates direct and indirect training and education to the potential entrepreneurs specially in the area of managerial, technical, marketing, financial and accounting to established their own small and medium enterprises. But unfortunately the pace and progress of entrepreneurship development in Manipur is not encouraging one.

Entrepreneurship Development: A Retrospect

Entrepreneurship development of the region and state over the past few decades can be examined from the following paragraph:

During 7th Five-Year Plan NISIET, NEITCO, NECON and EDII together have organised 152 different training programmes all over the region and trained 3609 prospective entrepreneurs selected from seven states. Base on it an evaluation study conducted by the North Eastern Council in June 1990 revealed that the overall success rate who have established their own enterprise of the region after training was 20.88 per cent. Further, state-wise successive rate of entrepreneurs for Manipur per cent. Further, state-wise successive rate of entrepreneurs for Manipur was 28.24 per cent followed by Mizoram 26.32 per cent and Assam 21.94 per cent respectively.

Another similar study was conducted by IIE Guwahati (1998) to know the effectiveness of the EDPs co-sponsored by NEC and organised by NISIET, NEITCO, NECON, NSIC and IIE. This study also trained 3713 participants during April 1990 to March 1996. Out of which 935 participants had started their own enterprises. Thus, the success rate of the region has increased to 25.2 per cent, which was 20.88 per cent up to 1990. In this study too Manipur occupies the highest success rate with 37.7 per cent followed by Assam 30.5 per cent and Meghalaya 29.5 per cent respectively (Mali 2004).

Table 1 shows the number of entrepreneurs trained and units set up in different North-Eastern states sponsored by NEC, IDBI, SIDBI and financed by commercials banks.

Table 1
No. of Entrepreneurs Trained and Units set up in North-East India (April 1994 to March 2002)

State	NEC-IDBI-SIDBI Sponsored and Commercial Banks Financed			
	Participants	SSI Units	Success rate in %	Rank
Arunachal Pradesh	495	123	12.85	1
Assam	927	200	21.57	3
Manipur	475	70	14.74	7
Meghalaya	446	68	15.25	6
Mizoram	219	38	17.35	5
Nagaland	286	64	22.38	2
Tripura	395	69	17.47	4
NE Total	**3243**	**632**	**19.49**	

Sources: Basic Statistics of North Eastern Council, 2002, P-211 and CMIE, Bombay.

It gives a totally different picture against the previous results. The success rate of the region has declined to 19.49 per cent, which was 25.2 per cent during 1998. Further, the success rate for Manipur has also declined to the lowest rank against first in previous two evaluation studies. It is also noticed from the table that the performance of Arunachal Pradesh has increased significantly and it accounts the highest successive rate among the seven states representing establishment of 123 enterprises out of 495 participants trained.

If we analyse the successful rate of trained entrepreneurs in the region in general and particularly in Manipur over the past few decades shows a quite encouraging as well as discouraging scenario. The fluctuation in the successive rate of entrepreneurs in the region and state may be because of the different in infrastructure available, methodology of training imparted, attitude, behaviour, willingness and also the selection process of the participants. However, change in successive rate of participants (so-called entrepreneurs) may be varied from time to time. But the main question arises in author's mind is their follow up rate of success. Initially after receiving training and education of entrepreneurship development, most of the participants may start their enterprises (so-called success rate) but after 5/10 years of duration their morale and enthusiasm has declined due to lack of financial and other infrastructural support. Resulted, most of units have become sick and finally closed down their shutter which is considered as one of the main reason behind the slow progress of industrialisation in Manipur.

Keeping in this view, the present artical is focus on two main themes, one CHALLENGES face in the process of entrepreneurship development and two OPPORTUNITIES emerging through entrepreneurship development in Manipur (See Diagram). Identifying various challenges and converting various opportunities into realities will have the way for entrepreneurship development, industrial development and economic development of Manipur.

CHALLENGES

Unlike past, the present entrepreneurship development in Manipur as well as in the region and country have to overcome many hurdles. Many challenges have emerged along with the process of liberalisation and globalisation. Some of the important challenges are:

WTO and Small Scale Industries

These days are the days of intense competition. There is WTO regime to oversee free trading, services and investment. India being a

DIAGRAM

OPPORTUNITIES AND CHALLENGES ON ENTREPRENEURSHIP DEVELOPMENT

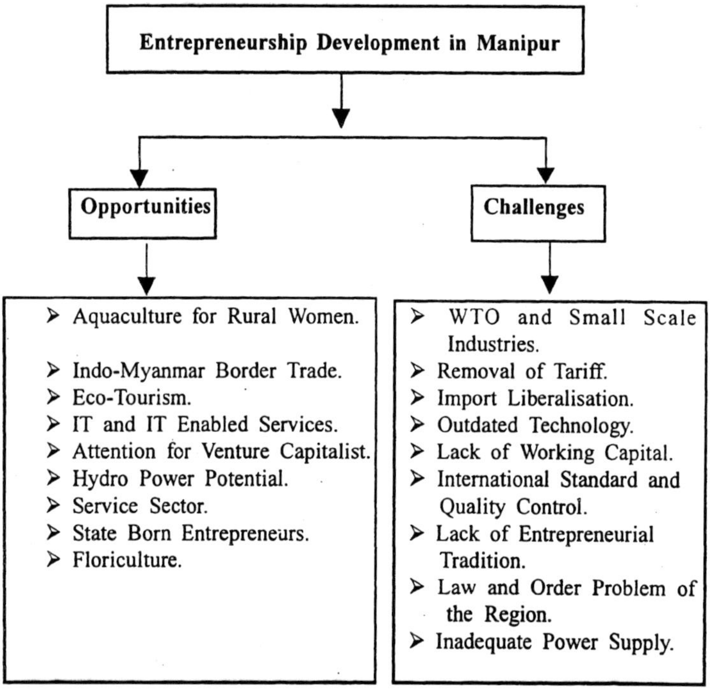

member of WTO cannot avoid the free entrance of MNCs in the state, region as well as in the country. With this entrance, a new cut throat competitive era has been emerged with the industrial, services and investment sector. The giant Asian and European MNCs will wipe out the small and inferior manufacturer from the domestic as well as export market. Which causes a great challenges to the upcoming new enterprises as well as new prospective entrepreneurs of the state/region.

Removal of Tariff

The small scale industrial sector has now been facing a number of challenges arising out of the commitments made by India for removal of tariff and non-tariff barriers in this globalised trade. India has to keep its commitment to bring down the tariff rates to ASEAN level or 12 per cent. In fact, its trade reforms in recent years have already brought down the average custom duty across the commodities from 71 per cent in 1993-94 to 35 per cent in 1999-2000. The custom duty has further been reduced in recent budget. Lowering the tariff will facilitate the price advantages of MNCs imported goods than the goods produced within the country and region.

Import Liberalisation

The quantitative restrictions (QR) on import has been removing in phase manner over the past few decades. In 1997 India had 2714 items on restricted list for import. Since then many of the items have been brought under Open General License (OGL) list. Till March 2000, there were 1429 items in the restricted list. During 1st April 2000 another 714 items has removed quantitative restrictions on import by the government and furtheremoved the restrictions of remaining 715 items from 1st April 2001. Removal of quantitative restrictions will freely allow the entrance of MNCs in the country and facing direct competition without any protection from the government.

Outdated Technology

Another challenges face by the entrepreneurs in Manipur is the use of obsolescence and outdated technology. Most of the units are unable to replace their units with modernize and sophisticated technology because of paucity of fund and other technical difficulties. Until and unless they changed with modernise technology the units have been lagging behind from their competitors qualitatively as well as price of the products. For, example most of the regional manufactured product or state manufactured product were unable to compete with national brand, likewise most of our domestic products are unable to face competition with imported third world countries products.

Lack of Working Capital

One of the most important challenges face by the entrepreneurs in Manipur are possesses of inadequate working capital. The poor credit repayment ratio of the borrower, lengthy process of getting loans and financial aid, fewer financial instruments and sources of funds are some of the challenges face by the SSI units in the state. The problem associated with inadequate working capital helps an units towards sickness.

International Standard and Quality Control

In this advance technological era , quality of product play the pivotal role for success or failure of an unit. ISI marks issued by the BIS and ISO series for international standards are some of the measuring standard and quality for a products. To get such standard by a small units operating in Manipur is a great challenging task. As a result many products have high demand but fail to meet the demand because of poor standard and quality.

Lack of Entrepreneurial Tradition

The North-Eastern Region especially the hilly region do not possess any entrepreneurial tradition. The young potential entrepreneurs have never seen their elders take up any major entrepreneurial activity, as a result of which they themselves are a little apprehensive and perhaps unsure of themselves to undertake any major entrepreneurial risk, despite the existence of numerous facilities that are currently prevalent in the region and state.

Law and Order Problem of the Region

North-Eastern Region is in the realm of insurgency prone and any activities undertaken for the development of region and state had been hindered by the law and order situation of the place. Frequent bandh, strike, economic blockade call by the various organizations to protest against non fulfilment of their demand. In the process of entrepreneurship development of the state and region, our prospective entrepreneurs were facing many obstacles directly and indirectly.

Inadequate Power Supply

Power shortage is another big challenges to our small scale industries in general and particularly in the process of new entrepreneurship development. Frequent load shedding, low voltage of power, high power tariff has hindered the normal function of small scale industries in Manipur.

OPPORTUNITIES

Given the opportunities that emerge in the current liberal trade scenario, it is important to understand the following area for entrepreneurship development:

Aquaculture for Rural Women

Aquaculture is a new area for entrepreneurship development in Manipur specially rural women. A fisher-women can earn Rs 1,000 to Rs. 1,500 per unit per month by selling fruits of Eurile Ferox (Thangjing) Memosa Plants (Ekai Thabi) Arum Plants (Singjupan) and Trapa (Heikak). The selling of fish from fish rearing pond can earn Rs 50,000 to Rs 60,000 per unit per season. (within six month).

Indo-Myanmar Border Trade

Promotion of Indo-Myanmar border trade for solving of unemployment educated youth of Manipur is another opportunities areas. Strong potential for future trade in both foreign and domestic market is emerging with this globalisation and privatisation era. Potential investors should tap the vast contiguous market of Myanmar, China, Malasia, Thailand, Singapore, Philippines, Indonesia and other East and South East Asian countries. The phenomenal bio-diversity – be it the forest wealth, agro base, fruits and vegetables, herbs, aromatic plants, exotic flowers, other flora and fauna could be the prospective area for entrepreneurship development.

Eco-Tourism

Countries such as Kenya, Costa Rica, Canada and United States of America have successfully tap their natural beauty in the form of nature based tourism (Ecotourism). They are managed by the local community in that area which helps in the upliftment of the standard of living of rural people and of the development of the nation as a whole (Binu 2004). Manipur is having an ample scope for the development of eco-tourism which is less capital involvement with more labour intensive. In the same pattern and way, our potential entrepreneur should find out the suitable site/area where Eco-tourism can be developed. This will help in development of an area and people without affecting ecological and natural beauty.

IT and IT Enabled Services

IT, IT-enabled services and Business Process Outsourcing (BPO) play a significant role in solving the unemployment problems. They not only provide employment opportunities to the unemployed educated but also improve the communication network. The latest study reveal that the IT and IT-enabled service sector would be able to earn nearly US $50 billion of export by the year 2008. The proposed IT park at Mantripukhri will provide job opportunities for the potential entrepreneurs specially IT degree-holders.

Attention for Venture Capitalist

Venture capitalist firm such as IDBI, ICICI should come forward and must invest in the areas for entrepreneurship development where state has ample scope for development such as Agro-food processing Industries, Energy, Herbal, Medicinal plants, Eco-tourism, Handloom and Handicrafts.

Hydro Power Potential

The state has large potential for Hydro power resources. The state has hydro power potential of 2241 MW of which only 105 MW Hydro power has generated so far. (as per the report of the many studies – conducted by Central Electricity Authority in October 2001). Once this resources are tapped fully, the power problem of the state can be solved and would facilitate the growth and development of SSI and IT based industries of the state.

Service Sector

Nowadays more entrepreneurs are emerging in services sector too. Entrepreneurial activities in service sector such as computer training, internet services vendor, digital photography, film making, non-banking financial services, management consultancy services, and entertainment service etc. The educated unemployed youth of the state can think of this sector for exploiting their skills, knowledge and experiences in different field.

State Born Entrepreneurs

The state government, NGOs, social workers and educational institutions should invite state born entrepreneurs who are working outside the state and abroad in different capacity as entrepreneurs, managers, professionals in different field to motivate and change the interest of the young generation unemployed youth of the state to make enable to create as job giver rather than job seekers.

Floriculture

Floriculture is another emerging areas for our young prospective entrepreneurs. India has shown a sign of playing a significant role in world flower market. Apart from increasing the domestic demand in last five years export has also increased significantly. In the similar way the state has also increased the business of potted flower, cut flower trade with neighbouring states of Nagaland and Assam. Further, the rare species Orchid, Shiroy Lily which are available in the state can be sources of good foreign exchange, if proper care is taken. Some of the essential oils from different flowers such as Jasmine, Rose and Tuberoses used in the manufacture of these cosmetics are prices as high as Rs 8,000 to Rs 12,000 per kg.

Conclusion

From the above study, it is conclude that entrepreneurship is the life blood of any economy. It is now recognised both in the developed and in developing societies as an essential resources in the development process. The backwardness of the North-Eastern Region and state may be attributed largely to the inadequacy of the supply of entrepreneurs in the state. If this deficiency were removed, the state would compete favourably with the rest of the country. The prospective entrepreneurs of the state should be dominated by a need for achievement and be driven by a high degree of motivation, in the absence of which even the highest degree of the opportunities may remain unexploited. To resolved this problems, entrepreneurs, state government, North Eastern Council, and central government's initiation, strong will and firm commitment is need of the hour.

NOTES AND REFERENCES

1. Shamshad Ahmad, (2005), NGOs and the Development of Rural Entrepreneurship, *Kurukshetra*, Vol 53, No 5 March, pp 27-29.
2. Behera M.C. (2004), *Globalisation and Development Dilemma Reflections from North East India*, Mittal Publications, New Delhi –59, pp 273-282.
3. Kanwat Manish (2004), Introduction of Floriculture Industry in India. *Kurukshetra*, Vol. 52 No. 8, June, pp 30-32, 36.
4. R. Binu *et al* (2004), Ecotourism and Rural Development, *Kurukshetra*, Vol 52 No.8 June, pp 33-36.

5. Khanka, S.S. (2003), Ethical Entrepreneurship – Challenges and Rewards, *Yojana,* Vol. 47 No. 7 July, pp 19–22.
6. Mushra Pulak *et al*, (2003), Developing Entrepreneurship in India. *Yojana*, Vol. 47 No. 12 Dec., pp 15-18.
7. Vaidya V. Bankimchandra (2003), Entrepreneurship Development, Transforming Rural Scenario, *Kurukshetra*, Vol. 52 No. 2, December, pp 37-40.
8. Vaidehi . S. *et al*, (2003), WTO and Small Scale Industries, *Khurukshetra*, Vol 52 no. 2, pp 30–36.
9. Mali, Dr. DD., (2001), A Case for Entrepreneurship Education, *Journal of the NEC* Shillong Vol. 21 No. 1. Jan–March, pp 14-17.
10. Mali, D.D. (Dr) (2000), The WTO the challenges before the SME sector, *Journal of the NEC*, Shillong, Vol 20 No 2 (April-June), pp 31-34.
11. Kharpujari, R.P (2000), Entrepreneurship: The Gateway to progress and self reliance, *Journal of North Eastern Council*, Shillong, Vol 20 No 3, (July- Sept), pp 14-16.
12. Ray B.Datta *et al* (1998), Sociological Constraints to Industrial Development in North-East India, Concept Publishing Co., New Delhi, pp 252-267.
13. Khanka, S.S. (1998) Making the Entrepreneurial Society. *Yojana* Vol. 42 No. 2 Feb., pp 9–11
14. Gopal Swaroop (1995), *Advances to Small Industries and Small Borrowers: A practical guide*, Sultan Chand & Co., New Delhi, pp 346-367.
15. Barua Sanjib, Foundation of BCIM Trade Agreement, WWW.Google.
16. Manipur: Gateway to the South East Asia, DIPR, Government of Manipur.

8

ENTREPRENEURSHIP DEVELOPMENT IN SMALL SCALE INDUSTRIES IN MANIPUR: The Challenges Ahead

TH. PRIYOKUMAR SINGH

Introduction

Entrepreneurship has always been a key factor in making any economic activity successful. That is why, the developing countries laid much stress on the growth of entrepreneurship, particularly in the small-scale sector. Likewise, small enterprises may serve as seedbeds of entrepreneurship in Manipur.

An entrepreneur who is an organiser of an economic venture should have qualities such as firm determination, high degree of patience, sincerity in approach, capacity for hard work and respect for dignity of labour. Essentially, an entrepreneur bears uncertainty or risk to become one who is responsible for the existence of new enterprises. These enterprises unfold many new opportunities which would contribute to economic growth.

In the midst of industrially backward economy and huge unemployment problem (the number of persons on the live register in Employment Exchanges was 3.97 lakhs as on 31-12-2002), prevailed in the state, the entrepreneurship development particularly in the small-scale sector is highly imperative. The small-scale industries spread out employment avenues throughout the state. The Industrial Policy, 1996 of the state have failed to achieve a remarkable growth in the industrial sector, mainly due to ineffective implementation of various incentives/ subsidies included in the policy. Also a New Industrial Policy of the state has been drawn in 2002 but yet to abridge the gap between forward and backward linkages on the limited impact experienced with the previous industrial polices of 1982, 1989, 1990 and 1996. Besides, the emerging scenario of globalization, with the more exposer of the state in the world market, entrepreneurs of this tiny state are being threatened increasingly day by day in their survival, since they are having lack of competitive strength in the international arena. The state becomes a captive market for the products produced in other parts particularly in the mainland of the country and for those goods coming from via Myanmar.

The study followed random sampling method in the selection of some entrepreneurs of SSIs, each of them deals in the production of different commodities by adopting different machines and technologies. Information are collected from these entrepreneurs through personal interviews. Opinions and suggestions are also collected from the expertise of Small Industries Service Institutes (SISI), Imphal, the people of All Manipur Entrepreneurs Association (AMEA). In the process of analysis, secondary data are mainly used.

Objectives

This paper is developed with three main objectives:

(I) To examine the scope of entrepreneurship developement in the small-scale industries in Manipur;

(II) To identify the problems faced by the entrepreneurs at present in the state;

(III) To analyse the challenges ahead of the state in creating successful entrepreneurs in the sector concerned.

Emerging Industrial Scenario in the State

Industrialisation in the state, particularly in the public sector, is worrisome that out of the 10 (ten) PUs existed earlier, 5 (five) have been wond-up and 2 (two) are on their way to wind-up in due course of time, mainly due to paucity of fund for maintenance. Only three undertakings i.e. Manipur Handlooms and Handicrafts Development Corporation Ltd. (MHHDCL), Manipur Industrial Development Corporation Ltd. (MANIDCO), and Manipur Electronics Development Corporation Ltd. (MANITRON) are in exist but in a shaky footing (ESM:2002-03, pp.102-103).

Small-Scale Industries (SSIs)

SSI is an industry whose investment in fixed assets such as plants and machineries does not exceed Rs.1 crore. The investment limit for tiny units is Rs.25.00 lakh. By the end of March 2003, the number of registered permanent small-scale industries both SIDO (Small Industries Development Organsiation) and NON-SIDO stood at 9,852 with an investment of Rs.37.73 crores in plants and machineries and providing employment to 51,122 persons where annual production was estimated to be Rs. 168,84 crores (ESM: 2002-03, p.103). Data relating to growth, employment, investment and production of SSIs in Manipur over the years are shown in Table 1 at pages 96-97.

Scope of Entrepreneurship Development in SSIs in Manipur

To examine the scope, it is indeed needed to bring a clear picture of the various opportunities available in this regard in the state under various heads.

(A) At the National Level

Among the various opportunities/ incentives recommended by the study group of development of small enterprises and later on implemented by the government, the followings can be viewed as important:

i) Marketing Development Assistance (MDA) being operated by Ministry of Comemrce.

ii) A credit linked capital subsidy scheme for adoption of new/ improved technology.

iii) Technology Development and Modernisation Fund Scheme (TDMF) being operated by Small Industries Development Bank of India (SIDBI).

iv) A scheme for setting up Testing Centres/Laboratories by Industries Association.

v) Subsidy for obtaining ISO-9000 quality certification.

(B) New Industrial Pakage for the North-East

The Government of India has approved a new industrial policy and other concessions for the North-Eastern Region. Important among the various policy packages includes:

i) Development of Industrial Growth Centres with central assistance has increased from Rs.10 crores to Rs.15 crores.

ii) Growth Centre/ Integrated Infrastrucure Development Centre/ Industrial Estates would be a Tax Free Zone from Income Tax and Excise for a period of 10 years from the date of commencement of production with provision to be made for exemption of local sales tax and municipal tax on the part of State Governemnts.

iii) 15% Capital Investment subsidy is provided to industrial units located in growth centres subject to a ceiling of Rs. 30 lakhs.

iv) Grant of 8% interest subsidy on working capital loans for 10 years from commencement of production.

v) Exploration and development of market for export to neighbouring countries particularly Myanmar, Bhutan and Bangladesh.

vi) Relaxation of PMRY norms namely, maximum age limit raised to 40 years. Family income limit raised to Rs.40,000 per annum, subsidy ceiling raised to Rs.15,000.

(C) District Industries Centre (DIC)

The centre provides all the resources with its facilities required by the entrepreneurs including identification of suitable schemes, preparation of feasibility reports, arrangements for supply of machinery and equipments, provision of raw-materials and facilities for marketing and extension services. Prime Minister's Rozgar Yojana (PMRY), a special scheme, has been drawn-up to be operated through the DIC since 1993 for providing self-employment opportunities to educated unemployed youths and the scheme is being instrumental in the growth of industries in the state.

(D) Small Industries Service Institute (SISI), Imphal

The institute is engaged in promotion and development of small-scale industries in the state of Manipur. The entrepreneurs are guided

Table 1
Growth, Employment, Insvestment and Production of SSIs in Manipur

Year	No. of units	No. of employment	Average No. of employment per unit	Investment (Rs. in crore)	Average investment per unit (Rs. in '000)	Production (Rs. in crore)	Average per unit production (Rs. in lakh)
1	2	3	4	5	6	7	8
1987-88	3,996	19,900	5.0	12.30	30.78	67.26	1.68
1988-89	5,417	27,000	5.0	16.31	30.11	80.26	1.48
1989-90	6,319	31,500	5.0	19.20	30.38	89.11	1.41
1990-91	6,788	33,390	5.0	20.70	30.49	94.81	1.40
1991-92	7,392	36,910	4.9	22.63	30.61	101.45	1.37
1992-93	7,696	38,400	5.0	23.61	30.68	106.90	1.39
1993-94	8,096	39,680	4.9	24.74	30.56	116.70	1.44
1994-95	8,341	42,613	5.1	26.41	31.66	123.16	1.48
1995-96	8,612	43,842	5.1	28.23	32.78	127.05	1.48
1996-97	8,910	45,460	5.1	29.51	33.12	133.90	1.50
1997-98	9,088	46,464	5.1	30.72	33.80	139.39	1.53
1998-99	9,240	47,388	5.1	31.53	34.12	143.33	1.55

(Contd.)

Table 1 (Contd.)

Year	No. of units	No. of employment	Average No. of employment per unit	Investment (Rs. in crore)	Average investment per unit (Rs. in '000)	Production (Rs. in crore)	Average per unit production (Rs. in lakh)
1	2	3	4	5	6	7	8
1999-2000	9,415	48,514	5.2	33.19	35.25	150.69	1.60
2000-01	9,635	49,792	5.2	35.08	36.41	157.70	1.64
2001-02	9,744	50,374	5.2	36.10	37.05	162.34	1.67
2002-03	9,852	51,122	5.2	37.73	38.30	168.84	1.71

Source: *Economic Survey Manipur: 2002-03*, p.104.

suitably to enable them to start their own ventures. Entrepreneurship Development Programmes (EDPs) have been organized from 3 to 4 times in a financial year in the state in the past and more of such programmes are likely to be organised in the year 2004-05. Generally such programmes are each of 1 month duration and target educated unemployed youths, rural artisans etc. Year-wise entrepreneurs trained under various EDPs sponsored by the institute and the number of units set-up are detailed in Table 2. Main assistance provided to the entrepreneurs by the institute is in the following areas:

i) Identification/ Selection of products of manufacture;

ii) Selection of suitable Plant and Machinery;

iii) Selection of appropriate technology, manufacturing process and technique;

iv) Quality control and standardisation;

v) Economic information related to the product;

vi) Assistance in marketing related areas.

Table 2

Year-wise Entrepreneurs Trained under various Entrepreneurship Development Programmes Sponsored by SISI, Imphal and No. of Units set-up

Year	No. of EDPs	No. of Entrepreneurs Trained	No. of units	Percentage of col. 4 to col. 3
1	2	3	4	5
1999-2000	03	92	31	33.69
2000-2001	03	133	38	28.57
2001-2002	04	121	48	39.66
2002-2003	04	114	52	45.61

Source: Industrial Management Training (IMT) Section: Small Industries Service Institute, (SISI), Takyelpat, Imphal.

Besides the above backgrounds, there are large numbers of educated unemployed youths in the state seeking for employment avenues. There is a concencious opinion among the economists, social workers, politicians and other educationists that the state has the scope of establishing agro-based, forest-based, food-based and herbal industries. The geographical location of the state is linking to the South East Asia through Myanmar and therefore, the state is favourable in expanding the market size of its products through trade. Opinions are also given by the expertises of SISI, Imphal, people of AMEA and DICs that the Manipuris have inborn creative and innovative instincts which are basic qualities that an entrepreneur need.

Keeping all the matters discussed above in mind, now, it is in a position to say that there is an ample scope in the entrepreneurship development in the state. But the reality will depend on how effectively we seize the opportunities to do so.

Problems of the Entrepreneurs at Present in the State

i) **Socio-environment problem** – Prevailing social unrest in the state, numerous bandhs and blockades called by various organizations on the National Highway hampers the efforts of the entrepreneurs in procuring enough raw materials from outside the state. The problem is accumulated due to lack of railway services in the state. Consequently shortage of raw material arises which ultimately leads to the non functioning of some SSI units which uses imported raw materials.

ii) **Electric-Power Shortage** – It is a real headache to the entrepreneurs and it oftenly interupt the smooth functioning of industries.

iii) **Marketing problem** – Different forms of marketing problems are faced by SSIs of the state. Some industries are yet to obtain ISI-mark for their product from the Bureau of Indian Standard and it become a big burden to the entrepreneurs to compete with the products having such symbol in the market. Sometimes, due to no export market of some products of homogeneous type produced by various SSIs, they face too much competition among them in the local market.

iv) **Procedural bottlenecks** – In getting various governmental documetns, such as ISI-symbol, FPO (Food Product Order), AGMARK etc., entrepreneurs of the state faced a long governmental procedure as the authorised offices are located outside the state. Besides entrepreneurs faced various legal hurdles in the estalishment of new enterprises.

v) **Capital Constraints** – It is a common problem of most of the entrepreneurs in the state. A more liberal release of fund by various agencies including commercial banks is pertinent to improve the situation.

vi) **Technological Adaptation** – Incapability of adapting new techniques of production makes the entrepreneurs of the state unable to increase production level of their products with up-to-date quality and feature.

vii) **Lack of Infrastructures** – Due to lack of infrastructures like cold-storage, warehouse, some SSIs whose production based on seasonal raw materials like fruits, agro-products etc., could not function for many months in a year, as raw-materials are exhausted within a short period. So, the entrepreneurs used extra money in the reorganisation of its service when the raw-materials are at their disposal.

To overcome the various problems discussed above, most of the entrepreneurs like to attract the attention of the government towards them with a sincere attitude. In this regard, they long for a totally new industrial policy in the state in which main component consists of marketing assistance, power subsidies, capital assistance etc. They feel that present industrial policy of the state is only a paper-work and not properly implemented. In short, they like to implement the policy very effectively in the best possible way. Besides, they like more interference of the various commercial banks in this particular sector with better provision of capital assistance.

Challenges Ahead of the State

The state has to face various challenges in order to uplift SSI-sector and to create an environment for successful entrepreneurship. Some important challenges are discussed hereunder:

i) Government must be able to bring into picture the untapped potentials and unutilised opportunities that await exploitation in the state. Hereupon, a policy having concrete strategies for the growth of SSI is needed to be framed in the state with the actual implementation.

ii) More interference of the government is sought in the marketing policy of the products produced by home entrepreneurs so that their prducts' market can be expanded.

iii) Search for a more effective strategy is needed in order to utilise the material, human, technolgical and social resources that we possess, in the most rapid, efficient and organised manner.

iv) Training and technology upgradation are two important tools for increasing productivity. Therefore, such provision must be there in a continuous process in the state and it should be the key policy concern.

v) Suitable strategy is to be taken up with strong determination to overcome the problems of raw-material shortages.

vi) For the growth of entrepreneurs, industrial-friendly environment is to be created in the state in which there is socially peace and politically stable.

In fact, the extent of the challenges that the state has to face is to catch-up with the capability levels in the particular sector in the rest of the country.

Table 3
State-wise Entrepreneurs Trained and Units Set-up for NEC-IDBI and NEC-SIDBI Co-sponsored Programmes (April 1994 – March 1999)

Sl. No.	State	No. of Entrepreneurs Trained	No.of Units Set-up	Percentage of (4) to (3)
1	2	3	4	5
01	Arunachal Pradesh	172	71	41.3
02	Assam	410	136	33.2
03	Manipur	125	40	32.0
04	Meghalaya	178	42	23.6
05	Mizoram	100	18	18.0
06	Nagaland	143	39	27.3
07	Tripura	128	34	26.6
Total:		**1256**	**380**	**30.3**

Soruce: Basic Statistics of North Eatern Region 2000, p.143.

Conclusion

An industrial-friendly environment is yet to be developed fully in the state. But keeping in mind, the various opportunities arises in the state, one can say that there is an ample scope of entrepreneurship development in the SSIs. However, the reality will depend on how effectively we seize the various opportunities. It is also encouraging to realize that the percentage of number of units (i.e. 40) set-up in the state against the number of entrepreneurs (i.e. 125) trained under the NEC-IDBI and NEC-SIDBI co-sponsored programmes during (April 1994 – March 1999) is 32 as it is above the North-East average which is 30.3. (see Table: p. 101). Now, the challenges that lies ahead of the state is to find out the effective strategy for utilising the materials, human, technological and social resources that we possess in the most rapid, efficient and organised manner. A totally new industrial policy is sought by the entrepreneurs for actual implementation in the most effective way in which main component consists of capital assistance, marketing assistance, power subsidies etc. More and above, it is also needed to bring into view the untapped potentials and unutilised opportunities that await exploitation in the state.

NOTES AND REFERENCES

1. Government of India (2002), *Basic Statistics of North Eatern Region, 2000*, North-Eastern Council, Ministry of Home Affiars, Shillong.
2. Government of India (2nd), *SISI at your Service Small Industries Service Institute*, Ministry of SSI, Imphal-1.
3. Government of Manipur (2004): *Economic Survey Manipur 2002-03*, Directorate of Economics & Statistics, Imphal.
4. Gupta, S.P. (2002), *India Vision 2020*, Planning Commission, Govt. of India, New Delhi.
5. Gupta, S.P. (2002), Report of the Special Group on Targeting Ten Milion Employment Opportunities per year over the Tenth Plan Period, Planning Commission, Govt. of India, New Delhi.
6. Kulshreshta, Kalyani (1999), *Successful Entrepreneurship*, Kanishka Publishers & Distributors, New Delhi.
7. Patrick, Martin (1999), *Self-employment and Successful Entrepreneurship*, Kanishka Publishers & Distributors, New Delhi.

9

DEVELOPMENT OF ENTREPRENEURSHIP IN SMALL SCALE AND IT INDUSTRIES IN MANIPUR

S. HEROJIT SINGH

Before discussing the present scenario of Entrepreneurship Development in Manipur, this paper attempts to highlight about Entrepreneurship. Defining the concept of entrepreneur, it comprises different intrinsic qualities, which the individual has to acquire in order to be a successful Entrepreneur. He brings an overall change in the societal environment. Through his innovative and leadership quality meaningful interaction can be made with leverage to personal, economic and human resources.

In short, an entrepreneur takes leverage responsibility involving a very high risk factor to serve for the betterment of the Society. By and large, the activity of an entrepreneur encompasses all fields/sectors for the welfare of the Society. So, the application of the entrepreneurial intrinsic qualities in action is termed as Entrepreneurship (i.e. to run an enterprise/unit).

So, entrepreneurship can be viewed as a creative and innovative response to the changing environment and ability to recognize, initiate and exploit an economic opportunity.

Introduction

In the context of Manipur, few groups of people consist of academician, intellectual, literate and those who are connected with the related departments are aware of the concept of entrepreneurship and its importance. But majorities of people both in urban and rural area have less awareness about it. The simple concept of Entrepreneurship, which is perceived by the masses, is that, a person who is operating any kind of business to earn for his livelihood, regardless of innovative and scientific management.

As time changes, people have become a little aware of entrepreneurship through awareness programmes conducted by different organizations, training institutes etc. Much remains to be done. A telling example is misconception of the Prime Minister Rozgar Yojana (PMRY) – this scheme is taken merely as loan getting programme, not as EDP. As a result, this programme cannot ensure real impact in terms of mind set change and creation of entrepreneurship ability. Accessibility of loan alone does not serve the basic purpose of entrepreneurship development. In short, cultivation of basic ideas is the mother of producing human capabilities in long term. Essentially, for enabling idea germination, need-based entrepreneurial development training's are called for.

Looking to the raising requirements, various institutions have attempted to undertake entrepreneurial development training programmes. These programmes incorporate managerial skill development, technical skill development and fitting in the given business environment. On the other hand, various financing and promoting agencies have made possible attempts to develop enterprises through entrepreneurship development approach.

Objectives

The main objectives of this academic exercise are:

1. To study the development of Entrepreneurship in SSI and IT industry in Manipur.
2. To discuss the activities undertaken by various supporting Institutes/financial institutions to develop SSI units.
3. To recommend the possible suggestion for future development.

Methods and Database

This article is prepared based on the field exposure, data collected from various institutes/funding Agencies, sponsored programme and published data. Thus this exercise is based on both Primary and Secondary data.

For finding the primary data, interview technique was adopted for collection of information from officials of department of Commerce and Industries, NEDFI, AMEA, CKVI, MKVIB, NSIC, RIP official (SIDBI sponsored programme) and faculty of I.C.M., Lamphelpat.

Background

During the plan period various possible efforts have been made for the development of small-scale industries (SSIs) in India. From time to time various policy resolutions were made.

In the strategic development of SSIs, it is worthwhile to mention the initiatives taken up for setting up of District Industries Centres (DICs) in India in 1974-75. As a part of DIC approach 8 (eight) DICs were set up in the initial year. The SEEUY was a major programme for DICs. Later this programme has been merged to the PMRY in 1994-95.

In recent years commercial banks and financial institution started taking up specific steps for the development of SSIs in Manipur. Mention may be made of the initiative taken by SBI.

The first 3 months Entrepreneurship Development Programme was started under the sponsorship of **STATE BANK OF INDIA, IMPHAL** (1982). At these EDP–25 participants attended the training programme. These EDP creates the pioneers, who are listed among the successful categories and others are still pursuing their respective activities.

Then in 1983-84, NISIET, Hyderabad conducted a 3 months Entrepreneurship Development Programme at Johnston School, Imphal (Now, Johnston Higher Secondary School). Ex. Minister Shri Paonam Achou Singh inaugurated the EDP. The programme coordinator was Shri Dr. Sharma, NISIET. 25 young and bright Entrepreneurs of Manipur attended the EDP. As part of the EDP schedule, went to Okhla Industrial Estate, New Delhi as field visit. Perhaps, this training was considered to be the 2nd batch of Entrepreneurship Development Programme held at Manipur.

The Beginners

The entrepreneurs who had attended the EDP sponsored by SBI had gathered themselves and formed a State level association called **ALL MANIPUR ENTREPRENEURS ASSOCIATION (AMEA)** in the year 1983, head office at Takyel Industrial Estate, Imphal West. AMEA played a vital role in the beginning stage providing consultancy, marketing support, training, organized State level industrial exhibition, seminars, workshops, conference etc. Such programme are organized in its own or collaboration with other agencies like Directorate of Commerce and Industry, Manipur NSIC, SISI, MANIDCO, CKVI etc. from time to time, to support and encourage entrepreneurs.

At present, AMEAs activity is decreasing as compared to those periods. The public had a great expectation that formation of such an association would provide an ample service to the young and needy future entrepreneurs.

The Manipur Industrial Development Cooperation (MANIDCO) was one of the leading organizations to finance composite loan (initially up to Rs 1 lakh) to the Entrepreneurs. SINGLE WINDOW SCHEME (up to Rs 5 lakhs) was introduced after two years.

Role of Financial and Promotional Institutions

The imperatives of the leading agencies may be discuss as follows:

Rural Employment Generation Programme (REGP)

Commissioner, Khadi and Village Industries (CKVI) launched a salient feature of the Gramodyog Rojgar Yojana in Manipur, under the Ministry of Agro and Rural Industries, Govt. of India. Under the purview of CKVI and MKVIB promotes a good number of SSI units through REGP. In the context of Manipur, food processing industry is included in SSI category.

The National Small Industries Corporation Ltd. (NSIC a government of India Enterprise) was established in the year 1955 by the Government of India, with a view to promote, aid and foster the growth of Small Industries in the country.

NSIC through its Regional Office at Guwahati and branch office at Imphal (Uripok Achom Leikai) formulated different strategies to help the small industries to stand at their own feet. NSIC extend technical as well as financial support to SSI units. But, the contribution from NSIC toward the growth and development of SSI seems to be scaling down.

The North Eastern Development Finance Corporation Ltd. (NEDFI) is one of the public financial institute. By and large, NEDFI encompasses diverse sectors such as health care, jute, tea, info-tech, agri-business, horticulture, cement, handloom and handicraft etc.

In Manipur, NEDFI also contributed their share in developing smali scale industry. The most effective tools of financing is through MICRO-FINANCE to NGO's. Under these NGO's, there are good number of SHGs, who received financial assistance to run their small unit. Most of these SHG's activities are covered under SSI and considered as group Entrepreneurship. Many of them are non-registered body.

The Small Industries Development Bank of India (SIDBI) was set up in April 1990 by an Act of Indian Parliament to function as the principal financial institute for promotion, financing and development of Industrial concern in the small-scale sector and to coordinate institute engaged in similar activities. SIDBI became operational on 2 April, 1990 and has since completed 12 years of service to the small-scale sector.

SIDBI operation encompasses based on 3 principal namely, (i) Indirect Assistance (ii) Direct Assistance and (iii) Development and support services. Refinance support is extended to the SSI units through Prime lending institution such as Commercial Banks and State Finance Cooperation.

In Manipur, SIDBI's MICRO-FINANCE scheme was availed by an NGO, "Youth Volunteers Union", Thoubal. Apart from other developmental task took great effort in Rural Industrialization through RURAL INDUSTRIES PROGRAMME (RIP). RIP is a comprehensive enterprise support service programme for the benefit of Entrepreneurs and aims at promoting viable rural enterprises leading to employment generation in rural areas. RIP encompasses manufacturing and service industry only, which are under the purview of Small Scale Industry.

Rural Industries programme was launched in Manipur in the year 2002, implementing agency being Indian Institute of Entrepreneurship (IIE), Guwahati. This project is for 3 years, targeting two districts of Manipur, Imphal East and Imphal West.

The National Bank of Agricultural and Rural Development (NABARD) gave main emphasis on agricultural and allied sector. But, the attention encompasses Non-farm sector also. Through various credit agencies, NABARD provide refinance assistance (build-up Credit linkage) to promote and developed SHGs and other non-farm sector (include SSI units). NABARD also organized various entrepreneurship development programmes in collaboration with various training institutes like EDII, Ahmedabad, I.C.M., Lamphelpat, AMEA etc.

Small Industries Service Institute (SISI), under the Ministry of Small Scale Industries, Government of India, open a field office of SIDO in 1971. The institute engaged in promotion and development of SSI in the State of Manipur. They provide consultancy service and technical guidance to the entrepreneurs. SISI conducted a good number of Entrepreneurship Development Programme in diverse field. These training programmes are organised with an objective to identify persons with entrepreneurial quality motivate them, trained impart with basic inputs to start their own ventures. Indeed, SISI trained many people but there is a limitation on the part of the trainer i.e., handholding support system is not a part of their activities.

Under the banner of STATE BANK OF INDIA, Imphal sponsored one week Entrepreneurship Development Programme and conducted at the INSTITUTE OF COOPERATIVE MANAGEMENT, Lamphelpat from June 21–26, 2005. These special EDP is perhaps first of its kind because it targeted only women Entrepreneurs. 28 Entrepreneurs participated, out of which 26 of them avail financial assistance from SBI after the training programme. Among them, 20 Entrepreneurs are covered under Small Scale Industries.

The present status of entrepreneur in Information Technology (IT) sector is countable in hands. SOFTWARE TECHNOLOGY PARK OF INDIA (STPI), Mantripukhri, Manipur was started functioning from September 2004, which gave a wide scope in IT sector in our state. Among the objective laid down, STPI targeted to provide incubating center facilitating, infrastructure office space, general amenities for the small and medium entrepreneurs (SMEs).

A group called MANIPUR DATA SYSTEM (MDS) established on 25th February 2001, which perform the task of Medical Transcription (Information technology service) grasps these opportunities and continue their service at the building of STPI, Imphal.

Presently, MDS employed 45 employees to run their service unit (included under SSSBE). They had a vision to employed 120 employees by March 2006. As per data collected from STPI, two more parties are on the pipeline to launch their operational activities in IT sector.

Development Pattern

Development pattern of SSI may be discussed in terms of units, employment and production. The number of SSI units was 678 in 1990-91, it increased to 8096 in 1993-94. Further increased to 8916 in 1996-97 and to 47999 in 2001-02 (3rd All India Census of SSIs 2001 -02). During the period of 11 years a substantial growth in SSIs was recorded–by nearly six-fold increase.

If the SSI units are classified in three categories – manufacturing, repair and maintenance and services, manufacturing dominated with 65.74 percent of all categories, followed services (20.12 %) and repair and maintenance (14.14 %)–as shown in Table 1. The percentage share of manufacturing is one of top ranking states, which shows much ahead of all India average (39.69 %). Almost similar feature of India is marked for repair and maintenance. Less contribution is recorded for services. It is encouraging to note that 1,36,811 persons could be employed in SSIs in 2001-02 by contributing 0.55 percent of the total employment generation SSIs in India. Contribution margin may be less in all India level, but looking to the population size it is quite encouraging. Compared with NE states except Assam, Manipur takes a lead. Employment generation in selected states of India is shown in Table 2.

Considering only SSIs under SIDO, 149 units were set up in 1999 –2000 with avenue of employment of 1005 persons. In 2003-04 set up of SSI was to the tune of 105 units which employed 582 persons (Table 4). During the period from 1999-2000 to 2003-2004 less effort of employment generation is observed. The index value of employment declined from 97 in 2000-01 to 57.9 in 2003-04. The invest index and production index indicate growth momentum. The index value of invest was 1000 in 2001-01, it rose to 1018.5 in 2003-04. On the other, index value of production has shown increased from 100 in 1999-2000 to 561.9 2003-04. Tables 6 and 7 set out gross output and employment generation for selected industries set up in various districts of Manipur.

Presenting a scenario of SSIs units promoted by various financial/promotional institute, Rural employment generation programme

Table 1

Percentage Distribution of Units in the Total SSI Sector by Nature of Activity

Sl. No.	Name of State/UT	Manufacturing		Repair & Maintenance		Services		Total
		Rural	Urban	Rural	Urban	Rural	Urban	
1.	Uttar Pradesh	30.73	11.47	10.90	8.16	22.11	16.63	100
2.	Haryana	12.46	17.11	10.16	14.88	17.79	27.42	100
3.	Delhi	1.26	31.16	0.78	16.60	1.45	48.74	100
4.	West Bengal	35.69	21.44	8.65	7.36	11.29	15.56	100
5.	Orissa	55.86	5.54	5.76	3.34	20.28	9.22	100
6.	Madya Pradesh	26.50	9.92	9.51	6.76	26.00	21.32	100
7.	Gujarat	13.53	18.67	10.93	11.16	18.56	27.15	100
8.	Tamil Nadu	6.83	15.82	4.52	7.79	23.53	41.52	100
9.	Sikkim	32.07	31.79	0.00	2.99	1.09	32.07	100
10.	Arunachal Pradesh	12.38	22.20	2.24	29.47	3.67	30.03	100
11.	Nagaland	62.77	11.75	9.88	1.22	9.44	4.95	100
12.	Manipur	52.44	13.30	6.90	7.24	12.48	7.64	100

(*Contd.*)

Table 1 *(Contd.)*

Sl. No.	Name of State/UT	Manufacturing		Repair & Maintenance		Services		Total
		Rural	Urban	Rural	Urban	Rural	Urban	
13.	Mizoram	17.04	32.53	0.03	2.69	31.64	16.08	100
14.	Tripura	10.06	15.14	5.83	12.00	22.56	34.40	100
15.	Meghalaya	47.32	12.61	0.79	16.59	2.55	20.14	100
16.	Assam	32.70	8.99	18.89	8.14	22.30	8.98	100
17.	All India	25.31	14.38	8.37	7.99	21.53	22.42	100

Source : 3rd All India Census of Small Scale Industries 2001 - 2002

Table 2
Employment Generated in SSI Sector in India

Sl. No.	Name of State/UT	Total Employment	Percentage
1.	Uttar Pradesh	4002374	16.05
2.	Haryana	553399	2.22
3.	Delhi	626909	2.51
4.	West Bengal	2169105	8.70
5.	Orissa	923176	3.70
6.	Madya Pradesh	1344584	5.39
7.	Gujarat	1266676	5.08
8.	Tamil Nadu	2018137	8.09
9.	Sikkim	1322	0.01
10.	Arunachal Pradesh	3687	0.01
11.	Nagaland	56795	0.23
12.	Manipur	136811	0.55
13.	Mizoram	24850	0.10
14.	Tripura	56962	0.23
15.	Meghalaya	65586	0.26
16.	Assam	429003	1.72
17.	All India	24932763	100

Source : 3rd All-India Census of Small Scale Industries 2001–2002.

(REGP) recorded the highest. In 2002-03, 50 units assisted by Manipur Khadi Village industries Board, (MKVIB) as compare to 29 units of Commission Khadi Village industries (CKVI). (As per Chart-1, target is 100 units per year). But in 2003-04 MKVIB is nil, CKVI promoted 56 units, indicating a sharp increase. There is marginal increased of units from 2003-04 to 2004-05 of 60 units under CKVI whereas MKVIC promoted 37 units in 2004-05 from 0 level in 2003-04. Under Rural Industries Programme (RIP), SIDBI sponsored programme of 3 years duration, 80 units are promoted as against the target of 100 from 2002-03 to 2004-05. North-eastern Development Finance Corporation Ltd.

Table 3

Percentage Distribution of Gross Output in SSI Sector in india

Sl. No.	Name of State/UT	Percentage Gross Output
1.	Uttar Pradesh	9.72
2.	Haryana	7.08
3.	Delhi	5.41
4.	West Bengal	6.26
5.	Orissa	1.86
6.	Madya Pradesh	3.44
7.	Gujarat	4.70
8.	Tamil Nadu	6.47
9.	Sikkim	0.01
10.	Arunachal Pradesh	0.02
11.	Nagaland	0.13
12.	Manipur	0.17
13.	Mizoram	0.05
14.	Tripura	0.11
15.	Meghalaya	0.12
16.	Assam	1.17
17.	All India	100

Source : 3rd All India Census of Small Scale Industries 2001 – 2002

(NEDFI) promoted SSIs unit in an average during the period from 2002-03 to 2004-05. Among the financial institutions, National Small Industries Corporation Ltd. (NSIC) stood at the lowest rank.

Analyzing the present scenario of achievement of units as per Chart-1, REGP promoted the maximum no. of units yet they are far behind to achieve the set target of 100 units per year. Sometimes question can be arise whether it should go on counting no. of units produce or maximum utilization of allocated budget?

Table 4
Production and Employment of Manufacturing Industries in Manipur (SIDO)

(Rupees in lakh)

Year	No. of Units	Total Investment (Rs.)	Total Employment	Total Production (Rs.)
1	2	3	4	5
1999-2000	149	16.00	1005	68.34
2000-2001	191	160.00	975	504.00
2001-2002	89	87.00	468	390.00
2002-2003	105	142.00	638	545.00
2003-2004	105	162.97	582	384.07

Source: Data/Information are collected from Directorate of Commerce & Industries, Government of Manipur, of those SIDO units covering all districts of Manipur.

Note : SIDO didn't include those SSIs which come under the purview of CKVI, Silk board, Handicraft Board, and textile commissioner etc.

Table 5
Indices of Development Parameters of SSIs under Sido

Year	Investment Index	Imployment Index	Production Index
1999 - 2000	100	100	100
2000 - 2001	1000	97	737.4
2001 - 2002	543.8	46.5	570.6
2002 - 2003	887.5	63.4	797.4
2003 - 2004	1018.5	57.9	561.9

* Compiled based data on furnished in Table 4.

Table 6
Registered SSI Sector having 100 or more Units Producing the Same Product/Service

Sl. No.	Product Name	District name	No. of units	Fixed asset (Rs)	Gross output (Rs)	Employ-ment
1.	Furniture & Fixture (Wooden)	Imphal West	168	9291148	38484529	641
2.	Rice Raw Excl Basmati	Imphal West	121	9467272	17813726	402
3.	Cardigan; Sweeter etc. Woollen	Ukhrul	101	4176000	7239643	401

Source : 3rd All India census of SSI, Ministry of Small Scale Industries, Government of India (2001-2002).

Here, discussion is based on no. of units promoted. An advantage of REGP is the scheme include margin money portion 30% of the project cost. Margin money scheme (MMS) attracted more beneficiaries but this scheme is meant for the first timer. Those who already established couldn't apply this scheme.

On the other hand, bankers are reluctant to finance new unit because of past trend of non-repayment of loan. So, the banker recommended beneficiaries whom they had a good linkage, but unfortunately the units are existing one. While making adjustment to achieved bankers target, maximization part seem to be neglected.

The most difficult part in promoting SSIs, units under Rural Industries programme (RIP) is Credit-linkage with banker/funding agencies. Though various training institution provide Entrepreneurship Development programme, a good credit linkage with funding agencies is very important. The matrix combination of training institute, funding agencies and potential entrepreneur is a much.

Conclusion

In Manipur, Small-Scale Industrial sectors face many problems for both registered and unregistered units. Problems are of similar nature

Table 7

Unregistered SSI Sector having 500 or more Units Producing Same Product/Service

Sl. No.	Product Name	District Name	Units	Fixed asset (Rs)	Gross output (Rs)	Employ-ment
1.	Rice Milling	Senapati	2672	356587399	109647287	6678
2.	Almirah/Cabinet/Cupboard, (Wooden)	Imphal West	2163	92820349	346307449	6095
3.	Chicken, (Live)	Imphal West	1,255	70294946	124658107	2556
4.	Rice Milling	Imphal West	1202	63909727	158762598	3564
5.	Benches (Wooden)	Senapati	1130	113006667	21923293	2260
6.	Wooden sleepers and poles	Senapati	1130	97185734	10961647	1130
7.	Furniture & fixture Wooden	Churachandpur	1028	10273334	70372333	2568
8.	Other woollen knitted wears	Imphal West	911	33658840	87700930	2690
9.	Rice Raw Excl. Basmati	Churachandpur	908	56224700	105920100	2676
10.	Embroidery work (By Mech. Pro.)	Imphal West	578	23115000	27449062	1156
11.	Agriculture Implement	Churachandpur	514	9524022	25369540	1519
12.	Sculpture	Churachandpur	514	4623000	34415667	1541

CHART - 1

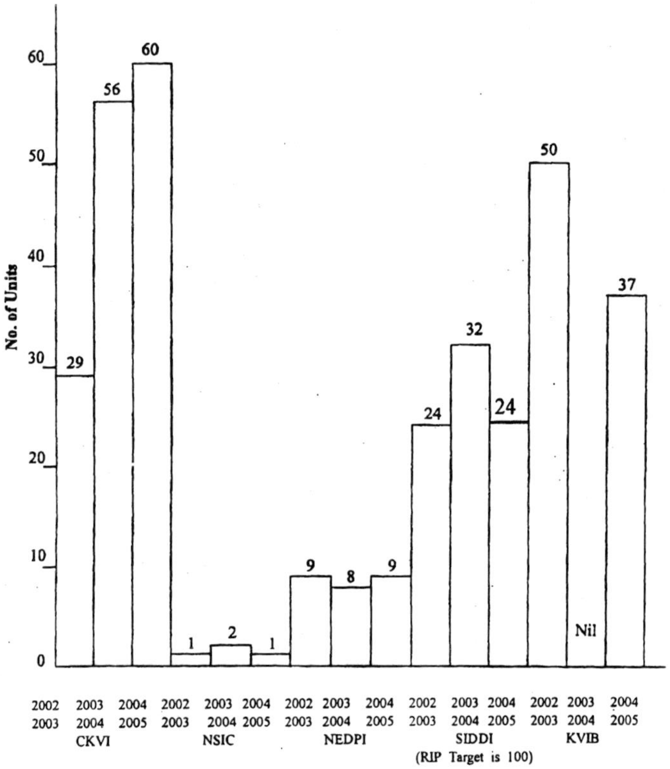

NOTE: Bar chart shows the no of Units assisted by Various financial / promotional Institute in the last three years.

viz., lack of financial assistance (especially working capital), less demand, scare or non-availability of raw material, power shortage, labour problem, marketing, new technology and management problem etc.

Recommendation

To minimize the difficulties / problems face by Small scale Industrial sector, the following measure are necessary to bring growth & development namely,

1. Entrepreneurship Development Programme (EDP) should emphasis more on specific target oriented programme for a longer period.
2. Time-consuming process of financial Institute/commercial banks needs to be reviewed to encourage the young and potential entrepreneur.
3. Identified EDP trained potential entrepreneurs should be provided handholding support system by the promotional institute.
4. Human Resource Management is an important core area. The knowledge of HRM will help in alleviating the standard of working environment. Short-term course (as special package) should be made mandatory.
5. Infrastructure improvement will enhance performance of the SSI's sector, which depends on basic amenities of power, water, communication, road, transport system etc. Takyel industrial estate is a good example of lack of such basic amenities.
6. The Government needs to focus from the grass-root level, its policy to minimize the non-availability of raw material.
7. Technical Institute should provide their support system at various level and plan according to its requirements.
8. An effective production and marketing network can alleviate economy and growth for the small-scale Industrial units.

NOTES AND REFERENCES

1. Desai, Vasant, *Dynamics of Entrepreneutcial Development and Management Himalaya Publishing House*, Mumbai, 2004, Reprint Editor.
2. 3rd All India Census of Small Scale Industries, 2001-2002, Development Commissioner (SSI), *Ministry of Small Sale Industries*, Government of India, Nirman Bhavan, New Delhi-110011
3. State Fours Paper, 2004-2005, Manipur, *National Book for Agriculture and Rural Development*, Manipur Regional Office, Imphal.
4. Promotional and Development, *Small Industries*, Development Bank of India (SIDBI), Published by SIDBI, Lucknow.
5. AMEA at a Glance, Economic towards 2001. A.D, All Manipur, *Entrepreneurs Association*, Takyel Industrial Estate, Imphal.

6. Rural Industries Programme (RIP), *SIDBI Sponsored Programme*. Quarterly Report of March, 2005.
7. Data/Information for Economics upto 2003-2004, *Directorate of Commerce and Industries*, Government of Manipur.
8. SISI New Letter, *Quarterly Publication from Small Industries Service Institute*, Ministry of SSI, Government of India, Imphal, Vol-2, October 2003, Issue 6.
9. Taking Indian Software Towards, *Global Leadership*, Software Technology Parks of India, Imphal, Manipur.
10. Personal Interview Conducted, Singh, P. Voken, *President AMGA*, Official of DIC, CKVIC, MKVIB, NSIC, NEDFI, I.C.M. and Official of STPI.

10

ROLE OF PROMOTIONAL AGENCIES FOR ENTREPRENEURSHIP DEVELOPMENT IN MANIPUR:

A Case Study

KH. DEVANANDA SINGH

The term "Entrepreneur" is rooted in the French word "entrepredre" which means, "to undertake". Many scholars define an "Entrepreneur" in different words but with same central ideas. In broad sense, anybody who is engaged in any economic activity is an entrepreneur. Being an economic man, an entrepreneur aims to optimise his profits through innovative means. He/she should have a will to act, is ready, to assume risks and organise human resources for production of products and services. This generates and multiplies economic and social activities that induce change in the society. Indeed, an entrepreneur is a change agent. An entrepreneur has a great responsibility to the society and accountable not to his ownself to ensure a continued existence of his enterprise, but also to the different segments of the society and the community as a whole.

The development of our country depends on the advancement of each and every entrepreneur's activity. The Indian economy needs to generate a large number of entrepreneurs to arrest the rising generate a large number of entrepreneurs to arrest the rising unemployment problem in the country. Being a change agent, an entrepreneur has to change. It may be the development of new innovative ideas, knowledge of technical know-how, sources of finance etc. In Manipur, there are many promotional agencies to impart knowledge to our entrepreneurs. District Industries Centres (DICs), Manipur Industrial Development Corporation (MANIDCO), National Bank for Agriculture and Rural Development (NABARD), Small Industries Service Institute (SISI), Institute of Cooperative Management (ICM) etc. can be cited.

Some of the active promotional agencies are discussed below:

National Bank for Agriculture and Rural Development (NABARD)

In December 1981, the NABARD Act was passed by the Parliament. It has been established by merging the Agricultural Credit Department, Rural Planning and Credit Cell of Reserve Bank of India (RBI). NABARD commenced its business from 12th of July 1982 as per notification of Government of India under NABARD Act. The National Bank came into existence in the year 1987 as Sub-office and upgraded as Regional Office from August 1998 onwards in the State of Manipur.

For the past two decades, NABARD is marching towards Rural Entrepreneurship Development Programme (REDP). This programme comprises three phases. These are pre-training phase, actual training and Follow up/post-training phase. Pre-training phase includes identification of potential activity, location and final selection of candidates through systematic and sound selection process. Preparation of project profile, management of men, materials and money, technical know how, market feasibility etc. are falling under actual training phase. The above mentioned activities are examined and evaluated under Post training phase.

NABARD provides promotional assistance to capable agencies with good track record and professional competence to successfully implement REDPs. The agency should satisfy the following criteria:

1. It should be a legal entity and should have been working in rural areas, at least, for three years.
2. Its officials should not be the office bearers of any political party/or elected members of any legislative body.

3. It should have necessary professional and organisational competence to plan, execute and monitor REDPs.
4. It should be highly committed to the philosophy of REDP.
5. It should have exclusive trained and qualified trainer-cum-motivator as a permanent employee.
6. It should have the required minimum training infrastructure to conduct the programme effectively.
7. It should have good rapport with banks, local administration/ people and possess grass-root level linkage.
8. It should have the willingness and potential to become self-sustained in conduct of REDPs in due course.
9. It should be prepared to facilitate economic diversification in rural areas.
10. It should be prepared to ensure escort services and proper monitoring and
11. It should be prepared to conduct REDPs in the approved manner to achieve good success rate.

In 2004-05 NABARD, Imphal released loan assistance of Rs. 10 lakh to Rural Development Organisation (RDO). Lamshang for on lending to REDP trained youths. Further, the bank has provided Rs 4.94 lakh for conducting REDPs, to the same organisation. Rs 0.42 lakh for conducting REDPs for craftsmen and Rs 0.75 lakh were sanctioned for conducting one REDP to Craft Society of Manipur and ICM, Imphal respectively.

The bank also sanctioned Rs 1.71 lakh for conducting 3 EDPs on agro-processing industries to Association of Food Scientist Technologies (AFST) Imphal.

Small Industries Service Institute (SISI)

SISI Imphal, Ministry of Small Scale Industries, Government of India was set up in the year 1971. This is one of the 30 such Institutes all over the country. The Institute is engaged in promotion and development of entrepreneurs in Small Scale Industries in the State.

The main functions of SISI for enterpreneurship development are:

i) To provide technical information about the supply and the availability of raw materials, machines and equipment, technical know-how and also about the process of production.

ii) To provide technical training to the workers employed in various enterprises as well as the entrepreneurs in order to improve standards of quality and labour.

iii) To play a significant role in the efforts regarding export promotion.

iv) To guide the entrepreneurs in the quality upgradation, modernisation and improvement of productivity, and

v) To act as a developer of the market.

Again, the services provided by the Institute include techno-economic and managerial services, basic inputs in the form of information and technical guidance required setting up new units and running successfully by improving quality and productivity. The entrepreneurs are guided suitably to enable them to start their own venture. As a part of development of entrepreneurs, SISI Imphal conducts Entrepreneurship Development Programme (EDP), Management Development Programme (MDP) and Motivation Campaign in different districts of Manipur. The same programmes are also conducting internally in the premises of the Institute.

In order to guide and assist the prospective entrepreneurs to set up new units or expand the existing activities, the Institute prepares project profiles on technically feasible and economically viable new products and updates the existing project profiles.

The number of Entrepreneurship Development Programmes (EDPs) completed by SISI, Imphal during the last 4 years are shown in Table 1

Table I
No. of EDPs completed by SISI, Imphal

Year	No. of EDPs	No. of Participants
2001-02	4	121
2002-03	Not available	Not available
2003-04	5	145
2004-05	6	250

Source: SISI, Imphal.

Institute of Cooperative Management (ICM), Imphal

ICM, Imphal was established in the year 1988. The Institute is one of the 19(nineteen) such Institutes in India under the aegis of the National Council of Cooperative Training (NCCT), New Delhi and also under the umbrella of National Cooperative Union of India (NCUI), New Delhi which is fully funded by the Ministry of Agriculture, Department of Cooperation, Government of India.

The focal objective of this institute is to develop human resources through catering need-based training to the manpower of State Governments of Manipur, Nagaland and Mizoram, cooperative organisations, Non-Governmental Organisations (NGOs) and Entrepreneurs. As a part of entrepreneurship development in the State, the Institute offers various short term courses on credit and banking, marketing, processing, consumer, handloom handicrafts, dairy, fisheries, general management, account and audit, agriculture and allied activities, project planning and management etc. to our entrepreneurs. Since its inception in 1988, the Institute has successfully completed to train 21,844 trainees in different courses up to Jan, 2005.

Training achievement chart 1988-89 to 2004-05 (up to January 2005)

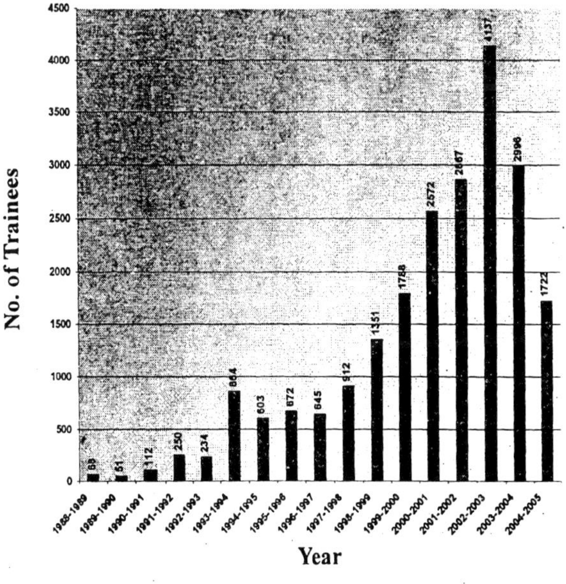

Table 2
Training Achievement under Various Programmes (1988-2005)

Year	Training achievement at a glance								
	HDCM	Sectorial Mgt. Course	PGDCA	PGDBM	STC	LDP	Seminar/ Workshop	No. of Prog.	Total Trained
1988-1989	32	-	-	-	36	-	-	3	68
1989-1990	43	-	-	-	8	-	-	2	51
1990-1991	-	-	-	-	112	-	-	6	112
1991-1992	31	26	-	-	116	-	77	10	250
1992-1993	31	29	-	-	149	25	-	10	234
1993-1994	35	50	-	-	398	34	347	29	864
1994-1995	30	43	-	-	488	-	42	27	603
1995-1996	32	50	-	-	590	-	-	30	672
1996-1997	26	27	-	-	592	-	-	29	645
1997-1998	27	25	-	-	661	199	-	40	912
1998-1999	42	23	-	-	1020	266	-	57	1351
1999-2000	27	19	-	-	941	801	-	67	1788

2000-2001	38	-	-	-	1609	575	350	85	2572
2001-2002	45	-	-	-	1894	928	-	94	2867
2002-2003	30	-	-	-	-3149	795	163	124	4137
2003-2004	31	-	-	-	1808	500	657	81	2996
2004-2005 (upto Jan. 2005)	37	-	30	30	1625	-	-	62	1722
Total	500	292	30	30	##	##	1636	756	###

Note: HDCM: Higher Diploma in Cooperative Management

STC: Short Term Course

LDP: Leadership Development Programme

EDP: (included under STC)Entrepreneurship Development Programme

PGDCA: Post Graduate Diploma in Computer Application

PGDBM: Post Graduate Diploma in Business Management

Source: ICM, Imphal

The success of any enterprise depends upon the survival of the product in the fast changing market scenario. Therefore, quick decision-making and problem solving approach are to be developed among our entrepreneurs, which will help to solve managerial problems. Due to various constraint imposed by traditional society, our entrepreneurs lack confidence in their own abilities. The promotional Institutions can accelerate motivational programmes to increase the confidence level of entrepreneurs. To prevent the entrepreneurs from being "week" management inputs like business planning, administration, marketing, finance, labour laws, taxations etc. are to be imparted frequently.

To conclude, such promotional agencies in Manipur are taking great role for development of entrepreneurs. They cater training needs, value based professional management, and action research, problem research and policy based research to enterprises. They also take up socio-economic development enterprises, in the context of sustainable development and render management and project consultancy services to them. As it continues, the development of our state will grow.

NOTES AND REFERENCES

1. Awasthi Sebastian, (1996.), *Evaluation of Entrepreneurship Development Programmes*, Sage Publications, New Delhi,
2. Kaulgud Aruna, (2003), *Entrepreneurship Management*, Vikas Publishing House Pvt. Ltd, New Delhi.
3. Singh, Jasmer, (1996), *Entrepreneuship Development*, Deep & Deep Publications, New Delhi,.
4. *ICM, Imphal*, Guard File.
5. NABARD, Imphal (2004-05), State Focus Paper.
6. SISI, Imphal, *Newsletter*, Various issues.

11

HAND-WOVEN TEXTILES AND HOME FURNISHINGS

An Opportunity for Entrepreneurship Growth

RADHESYAM OINAM
MEMCHA L.

McKinsey and Co. has reported that export of made ups *(value added home furnishings)* are likely to provide 60% of the growth opportunity after the elimination of quotas in 2004. In the year 2002-03, the total cotton textiles exports stood at Rs. 16,827 crores and the share of made ups/value added home furnishings was 35%.[1] During the same period, India's handloom exports stood at Rs. 2,634 crores; out of these, made ups constituted 68% and fabrics constituted 32% with madeups having a growth of 14.4%.[2]

Against the above global background, the handloom sector of Manipur can be described as an industry, which has remained, hitherto fragmented, disorganized, mismanaged, bereft of market linkages and a testimony to the stagnant economy of the state. With information technology sweeping the state, surface transport getting geared up for the Trans Asia Network and with the 'Look East Policy' of the Central Government, the winds of change is slowly beginning to blow. Manipur will remain no more a landlocked cul-de-sac. Thus, the time is ripe to exploit and explore this segment of the economy with a new dimension.

As Peter Drucker quoted, "an entrepreneur has to redirect resources from areas of low or diminishing results to areas of high or increasing results. He has to slough off yesterday and to render obsolete what already exists and is already known. He has to create tomorrow"[3]. The state of Manipur with scarce resources and enormous logistic constraints is truly in need of a new and a coordinated approach by the Entrepreneurs of the new millennium. The concepts of "efficiency" which is doing things right or the right means of resource usage and "effectiveness" which is doing the right thing or right goal attainment have to be the primary tools for achieving any worthwhile usage of the available resources.

A SWOT Analysis of the Handloom Industry of Manipur

Strength

- **Abundant Resources**: As per the 1995-96 handloom census conducted by the Ministry of Textiles (MOT), Manipur had 2.77 lakh looms against a national total of 34.86 lakh or a 8% of the country's total. And against a total of 65.5 lakh persons engaged in handloom weaving and allied activities, 3.40 lakhs were from Manipur which is 5.2% of the national total.[4]
- **Existing Markets and High patronage**: There is a high patronage of Manipur handloom products not only in the local markets but also in the national domestic markets. Deliverance of the right products is the key to convert the patronage into brand equity.
- **Low Entry Barriers:** To quote Michael E. Porter, "nearly all fragmented industries have low overall entry barriers. Otherwise, they could not be populated by so many small firms".[5] This aspect can be perceived as an advantage by the aspiring young entrepreneurs.

Weakness:

- **Low Productivity**: The MOT estimates of production of handloom fabrics in the year 2000-2001 for the state of Manipur was 265.16 million sq. mtrs against the national total of 7,475 million sq. meters; a meager 3.5% of the national total.[6]

- **Backward Technology**: All the looms are the traditional fly shuttle looms, throw shuttle looms or the loin looms. Traditional and conventional methods of warping, sizing, finishing are still in use.
- **Women Predominance**: In Manipur, weaving is the prerogative of the women, thus limiting the labour market. The household chores also acts as an hindrance in achieving "just in time production". Another drawback is in production of fabrics which require extreme physical endurance.
- **Unorganized**: The looms, handloom units are all scattered and fragmented, with about 92% of the looms in the domestic segment.
- **Outsourcing Dilemma**: Most of the registered handloom units are in the co-operative sector which are mostly commercially non- viable. Due to the non existence of successful and large business oriented units, outsourcing becomes a big dilemma thus thwarting the viability of sustaining and fulfilling large purchase orders.
- **Non-Existence of Common Facility Services**: Absence of pre weaving and post weaving facility centers such as the modern dye houses, quality testing centers, processing units or finishing centers render it impossible for any worthwhile competitive production.
- **Non Availability of Good Quality Yarn**: Due to various reasons, the quality of the yarn available in the local markets has been declining and the variants available have been static and stagnant. Neither the yarn traders nor the weavers have shown any enthusiasm to experiment with new variants of yarn.

Opportunity

- **Vast Home Textiles Market**: There is an enormous opportunity for the handloom industry of Manipur to enter the vast household textiles markets with new innovative products. The key lies in innovative fusion and transformation of the beautiful and eleganct local motifs and designs into creative home products. The source of inspirational designs is unending whether it be from the checks of the *khudei* or the *Ngotekherh,* the colors and motif of the *Radapai* and *Chiinasa,* the colorful stripes of the *Puans,* the colors and motifs of the *Ngumphai* or the *Moirang Phee.* . . [7]

- **Untapped Markets:** Improved quality and variants of home textiles will lead to higher consumption even by the local markets. The national markets, especially the National level exhibitions are all ready points of sale for improved and innovative hand woven products.
- **Value Added Products**: Silk, especially Eri variety, and Pineapple Yarn[8] could provide value additions. The expertise and the inputs of *kauna* reed could be fused with hand-woven fabrics to create household decorative items.
- **Functional Utility Products**: Conversion of the traditional textiles and fabrics into wide array of universally functional utility items holds the key for unending experimentation and endless penetration into various market segments.
- **Transport Subsidy:** Under the Industrial Policy of Manipur, 1996, there is provision for Transport subsidy for transportation of raw materials and finished products. [9]
- **Freight Reimbursement**: Ministry of Textiles, Government of India, has made provision for transport subsidy for yarn purchased through the National Handloom Development Corporation (NHDC) at the rate of 3% of the non silk/jute yarn value; 1.5% of silk yarn value and 8.5% of jute/jute blended yarn.[10]
- **Weavers' Service Centre (WSC)**: The WSC at Takyel, Imphal is one of the 24 WSC's in the country which imparts training and up gradation of skills to weavers. The Imphal WSC covers the three states of Manipur, Nagaland and Mizoram.

Threat

- **The Handlooms Reservations Act may be discontinued**: The Handlooms (Reservations of Articles for Production) Act, 1985 provides for reservation of eleven items for exclusive production by the handloom sector which includes the Sarees, Moirang phee, phaneks, shawls etc. But, in the post MFA (Multi Filere Agreement), the handloom reservation remains at stake.

- **Increased Competition from the Power loom and Mill Sector**: There will be increased price competition from the mills and power loom sector, with these two sectors taking up modernization plans to attain global competitiveness. With the abolition of the Handlooms Reservation Act, replication of various handloom products by the mills cannot be ruled out.
- **Increasing No. of Idle Looms and Handloom Units:** Today, shrinking local markets, diminishing compensation to the weavers, stagnant product line, outdated modes of production, non-application of commercial principles, declining quality of yarn and dyes have brought the handloom sector to the brink of disaster, rendering this mode of employment unfruitful. The number of idle looms has been on the rise with people seeking alternative opportunity.

The Role of the Entrepreneurs

Recently, a significant body of literature has emerged on the interface between marketing and entrepreneurship (MEI). G. E. Hills has summarized these commonalities as, "Good marketing is inherently entrepreneurial, ... and good entrepreneurship is inherently marketing oriented. "[11]

Thus, the first and foremost requirement by the entrepreneurs is to start with the markets and work backwards. All these years, the handloom products of Manipur have been homogenous, low value, large volumes and targeted at the mass traditional markets. In the bargain, the handloom produce has been perceived more as a "commodity" than a "product".

Apart from the innovations in small quantity, majority of items produced caters to the local functional usage only. To expand and to reach out to other markets, the handloom products have to fulfil the needs of the consumers of different markets by product diversification and modification. Converting the local designs, weaves, motifs, colors into universally functional utility fabrics and products is the answer for any commercial foray in the vast textile market, including the local textile markets as well.

As there is tremendous potential in the home textiles segments the local colors, weaving expertise, designs-motifs of this region could be converted into the following universally functional utility products by blending the right yarn, designs, sizes, colour and texture:

a. Hand –Woven fabrics:

- Saree and salwar kameez variants by using and blending different varieties of yarn.
- Shirtings, Lungies and any other fabrics

b. Home Furnishings and Made-up items

- Bedlinen – bedsheets, bedcovers, pillow cases, duvets and other quilt coverings.
- Tablelinen table cloth, table covers, napkins, place mats etc.
- Furnishing fabrics – for draperies and upholsteries
- Rugs, durries – can be converted from *lashing phee*
- Wall hangings, lamp shades – blending silk/ kauna/ pineapple yarn etc.
- Toilet / kitchen linen
- Towels

The following strategic parameters could be used by the entrepreneurs to achieve entrepreneurial growth:

I. The Marketing Parameters

a. The identification of the right markets – the local and domestics markets offer huge potential for market expansion and extension. The non-traditional handloom markets have to be also explored.

b. Suitable Products and Pricing have to be identified taking into account the possible backward linkages.

c. Appropriate packaging and promotional inputs have to be arranged to enhance product image.

d. The supply chain logistics for purchases of inputs, distribution and inventory management have to be arranged.

II. The Production Parameters

a. ***Improved Technology***

To increase the production and reduce wage: Looms Flyshuttle sley and in broad width, Semi-automatic looms, take up motion attachments, double and multiple box sleys, let off motion, roller shuttles;

To improve designing capacity: Dobbies and Jacquards.

Winding: improved cycle wheel charkha with or without chain, winding machines working on hand, pedal or electric power with provisions of multi spindles.

Warping machines: Horizontal warping machines with or without automatic measuring machines

Other machines such as Doubling machines, Twisting machines, Sizing machines could be used to economise production.

b. ***Raw Materials and Equipments***: More varieties of yarn, improved yarn quality, better reeds, improved fly shuttle sleys and shuttles

c. ***Organizational Structures***: a shift from the co-operative oriented handloom units towards individual commercial units with application of sound business practices.

d. ***Human Resources***: the service and consultancy of qualified designers, alumni of the Indian Institute of Handloom Technology (IIHT), and textile engineers.

e. ***Financial Facilities***: Tie ups with commercial banks should be explored, as a deviation from the regular practice of over dependence on governmental schemes.

f. ***Weavers' Remuneration and Compensation***: an innovative compensation and remuneration system so that the weavers take up weaving as a full time profession.

Conclusion

With numerous logistics and service provider bottlenecks, the immediate approach to be adopted by the entrepreneurs is the "Consortium Approach". This approach will give them the leverage to achieve economies of concentration and attain economies of scale through bulk purchases of raw materials, design development facilities, common processing facility centers, common participation in national and international exhibitions, full load booking of outward trucks etc. And, above all, the 'just in time' delivery schedules for export orders could be achieved by intra outsourcing of the consortium participants.

Nevertheless, policy makers also have to identify the special needs and problems to make the sector more competitive. Flexibility in the funding pattern and financial assistances, may not be the only criteria. A separate handloom directorate as in the case of Assam may be the immediate requirement (Assam-Handloom and Textiles Dept.). Immediate revamping and restructuring of the North Eastern Handicrafts and Handlooms Development Corporation (NHHDC) as planned by Department of Development of North East Region (DONER) may provide the much needed forward market linkages. Simultaneously, provision of special and proactive role to the Weavers' Service Center at Imphal will provide the much needed technological support to the aspiring entrepreneurs.

Lastly, with the complete integration of the textile sector into the World Trade Organisation (WTO) from the 1st January, 2005, the Multi Fibre Agreement (MFA) completely phased out, the survival of the handloom sector will soon depend on the competitiveness both from within and outside the country. The key to the global markets is to concentrate on designs and weaves which cannot be imitated by the mills. Weaving need not be just the prerogative of the woman any more. It is the coordinated efforts of the entrepreneurs which can link the handloom products with the commercial textile markets and give this sector a new dimension.

"The coordinated approach and efforts of the entrepreneurs can make 'that difference' to make it happen"

NOTES

1. *Report of the Cotton Textiles Export Promotion Council* (TEXPROCIL): The Economic times, 10th Nov, 2003.
2. *Handloom Export Monthly Newsletter*, Oct., 2003, The Handloom Export Promotion Council, Chennai.
3. Peter Drucker, Management: *Tasks, Responsibilities, Practices* (Mumbai: Allied Publishers Pvt. Ltd.) p 45.
4. Census Report on Handloom, 1996-97, Directorate of Commerec and Industries, Government of Manipur.

5. Michael E. Porter, *Competitive Strategy: Techniques for Aanalyzing Industries and Competitors*, (The Free Press, New York) p 196.
6. Draft report of the sub-group of Handlooms for Xth Five Year Plan, Ministry of Textiles, GOI, p 82.
7. Bahadur, Mutua, *Tribal Hand woven Fabrics of Manipur*, 2000.
8. *Handoom Export Monthly Newsletter*, December, 2004 (HEPC, Chennai) p 25.
9. *Industrial Policy of Manipur*, 1996, Directorate of Commerec and Industries, Government of Manipur, p 9.
10. Plan schemes of the office of the Development Commissioner for Handlooms, Ministry of Textiles, Government of India p 76.
11. Andreu Blesa and Maria Ripolles 'The Role of Market Orientation in the Relationship between Entrepreneurial Proactiveness and Performance', *The Journal of Entrepreneurship*, 12 (2003), Sage Publications New Delhi.

REFERENCES

1. A Brief Note on Panipat Textile Industry, Weavers Service Centre, Panipat.
2. Andreu Blesa and Maria Ripolles, (2003), The Role of Market Orientation in the Relationship between Entrepreneurial Proactiveness and Performance, *The Journal of Entrepreneurship*, 12, Sage Publications.
3. Bahadur, Mutua, (1997), *Traditional Textiles of Manipur*.
4. Bahadur, Mutua, (2000), *Tribal Hand Woven Fabrics of Manipur*.
5. Bannerjee, Amalesh and Kar, Biman, (1999), *Economic Planning and Development of North-Eastern States*, Kanishka Publishers, New Delhi.
6. *Census Report on Handloom*, (1996-97), Directorate of Commerce and Industries, Government of Manipur.
7. *Cluster Update* (issue 1, Sept 2003) a quarterly newsletter on cluster development initiatives of Textiles Committee, Textiles Committee, Ministry of Textiles, Government of India.
8. *Compendium of Textile Statistics*, (2003), Office of the Textile Commissioner, Ministry of Textiles, Government of India.
9. Darlie O. Koshy, (1997), *Garments Exports: Winning Strategies*, Prentice Hall of India Pvt. Ltd., New Delhi.
10. *Draft Report of the Sub-group on Handlooms for Tenth Five Year Plan*, Office of the Development Commissioner, Handlooms, Ministry of Textiles, Government of India.
11. Drucker, Peter, (1973), *Management: Tasks, Responsibilities, Practices*, Harper and Row, New York.

12. Ganguly, J.B., (1983), *Marketing in North East India.*
13. *Handloom Export Monthly Newsletter*, (December, 2004), HEPC, Government of India.
14. *Handloom Export Monthly Newsletter*, (Oct., 2003), The Handloom Export Promotion Council, Government of India.
15. *Indian Hand Woven Textiles*, (1996), The Handloom Export Promotion Council of India, Development Commissioner for Handlooms, Government of India.
16. *Industrial Policies of the North Eastern States*, (2002), NEDFI.
17. *Industrial Policy of Manipur*, (1996), Directorate of Commerce and Industries, Government of Manipur.
18. Integrated Handloom Training Project (IHTP), Office of the Development Commissioner of Handlooms, Ministry of Textiles, Government of India.
19. Kotler, Philip and Armstrong, Gary, (1996), *Principles of Marketing*, Prentice Hall of India Ltd., New Delhi.
20. Kotler, Philip, (2001), *Marketing Management*, The Millennium Edition, Prentice Hall of India Private Limited, New Delhi.
21. *National Textile Policy*, (2000), Ministry of Textiles, Government of India.
22. Plan schemes of the office of the Development Commissioner for Handlooms, Ministry of Textiles, Government of India.
23. Porter, Michael, E., (1980), *Competitive Strategy: Techniques for Analyzing Industries and Competitors*, Free Press, New York.
24. *Report of the Cotton Textiles Export Promotion Council, Texprocil*, (10th November, 2003), *The Economic Times.*
25. Rangarajan, S. HEPC *Product Manual*, (1994), The Handloom Export Promotion council of India, Development Commissioner for Handlooms, Government of India.
26. Scheme for North East Handloom and Handicrafts (SNEHH), North Eastern Development Finance Corporation Limited (NEDFI).
27. Service Charter, Weavers' Service Centre, Development, Commissioner, Handlooms.
28. Minsistry of Textiles, Government of India.
29. *Textiles in North -Eastern Region NER* (2000), Programmes for Development, Ministry of Textiles, Govternment of India).
30. *The Handlooms* (Reservation of Articles for Production Act, 1985, Ministry of Textiles, Government of India.
31. Verghese, B.G., (1996), *India's North East Resurgent.*

12

PROBLEMS AND PROSPECTS OF ENTREPRNEURSHIP DEVELOPMENT IN SMALL SCALE INDUSTRIES – A Case Study

GAUTAM PATIKAR
RATAN KAURINTA

Every country irrespective of its economic system wants to increase its productivity so as to provide maximum welfare to its citizens. Towards this end numerous organisations are engaged in the production of goods and services. Here, special mention may be made of business enterprises that hold the key of rapid economic development. Of late, there has been a growing realisation about potential contribution of small enterprises. Healthy small business sector is rightly considered to be the backbone of every economy. This is the reason why entrepreneurial training is encouraged through out the world and thereby promotes local entrepreneurship and accelerates the pace of small enterprise development. "Research studies conducted in U.S.A. (Birch, 1987) suggest positive link between economic development and entrepreneurship".[1] Although such type of systematic research are rarely available in our country. But such absence does not suggest that such a positive relationship does not exist. Developing countries like India, China, Pakistan, Sri Lanka, Malaysia and many other South Asian

China, Pakistan, Sri Lanka, Malaysia and many other South Asian countries have always considered small business sector as an important sector of economy. Through this paper an attempt has been made to study the various problems associated with entrepreneurship development and pin-point future prospects in the field of small-scale industries with special reference to the state of Manipur.

Much of the discussion on entrepreneurship and its contribution would be of insignificant importance unless we clearly define development process as such and its linkages with entrepreneur. It is therefore necessary to clarify the meaning of development process and how entrepreneur comes in picture before discussing problems and prospects of entrepreneurship development.

Meaning of Development

Economic development has been a focal point right from the days of Adam Smith, Ricardo and other noted economists. Adam Smith did not assign any significance to entrepreneurial role in his monumental work 'An enquiry into the Nature and Causes of the Wealth of Nations' published in 1776. According to Ricardo, profit leads to saving of wealth, which ultimately goes to capital formation and leads to economic development.

The thinking of the economists during 1950s and early 1960s focused mainly on the concept of 'stages of economic growth' in which the process of development was viewed as a series of successive stages through which all countries must pass. It was primarily an economic theory of development in which the right quantity and mixture of saving, investment, and foreign aid were all that was necessary to enable developing nations to proceed along an economic growth path that historically had been followed by the more developed countries. Development thus became more synonymous with rapid, aggregate economic growth. It is however, the producer who as a rule initiates economic change, and he if necessary; they are as it were educates consumers, taught to want new things or things, which differ in some respect or other from those, which they have been in the habit of using. The producer combines material and forces so as to meet the wants of consumers. In fact, development is dragged along by such changes in the surrounding world.

According to J.B.Say, the entrepreneur's function is to combine the productive factors, to bring them together. Carrying out of new combination of productive factors is called 'enterprise' which in fact is fundamental phenomenon of economic development. The individual whose function is to carry them out is what we call 'entrepreneur'.

The entire change and development of the civilization to a large extent is the result of trade, commerce and industrialisation. In this development the human resource in general and entrepreneur in particular plays a pivotal role. There is a growing realization that both quantity and quality of entrepreneurs are of utmost significance for achieving the goal of economic development. Active and enthusiastic entrepreneurs can fully exploit the potentialities of a country's available resources like labour, technology and capital.

Entrepreneurship - Meaning and Concept

Entrepreneurship in recent times has become a serious area of study. It is considered to be a panacea for creating wealth, generating employment and providing new and better goods and services. Despite the spirit of entrepreneurship among the young it has also become vital because the government cannot provide jobs for all kinds of unemployed youth and the corporate sector will provide limited jobs only to the best and that too without any job security and often it is difficult to find an ideal job.

Entrepreneurship is a buzzword both in India and abroad, yet it is scarcely understood as a concept or construct. The word entrepreneur is applied to 'a *paanwala*' as well as to such entrepreneurs as Mukesh and *Anil Ambani* of *Reliance* fame or *Krishnabhai Patel* of *Nirma fame*. The theory at its present stage of development cannot pass a judgement whether a 'paanwala' on the street is an entrepreneur or not and what he has in common with Mukesh Ambani.

Entrepreneurship has very little to do with money. It is instead an attitude, a way of thinking. It goes beyond simply starting a company. In other words not all people who start their own organizations can necessarily be categorised as entrepreneurs. Entrepreneurs challenge assumptions, recognize opportunities in periods of change, reveal patterns where others see chaos and mobilize limited resource to achieve an objective.

Entrepreneurship Development

Entrepreneurship is simply finding new opportunities, commitment to innovation and challenging traditional boundaries of thought and this is what entrepreneurship is all about. With change like globalization, deregulation, open competition and technological changes taking place, our society is becoming an entrepreneurial society. In an entrepreneurial society, individuals face a tremendous challenge, a challenge they need to exploit as an opportunity, the need for continuous learning and relearning and thereby inculcate qualities of entrepreneurship in an individual. In this process development of entrepreneurship takes place in a society.

Entrepreneurship development is closely connected with human resource development. Development is nothing but acquisition of capabilities - capabilities that are needed to do the economic activities for the welfare of the living human in the world.

As a matter of fact, most of the industrial development in India has been concentrated round a few metropolitan cities and big towns. Therefore, development of entrepreneurship in backward regions has been adopted as a basic strategy of economic planning in India.

Although, up to sixties no systematic plan and policy were undertaken for entrepreneurship development. "Later a purposeful policy has been taken in our country in this respect as a strategy for removal of unemployment problem and to promote industrialisation through indigenous enterprises".[2]

In the northeastern region, plantation industry emerged in the eighteenth century, but it was started mostly through British entrepreneurs. Indigenous entrepreneur was a rare phenomenon at that time. However, numerous skilled craftsmen were engaged in various cottage industries. Indigenous planters emerged at the later part say towards the end of the nineteenth century. Assam is the first state to take initiative to develop entrepreneurship in a planned way.

Since the state of Manipur being a part of the backward region of the country, small industries occupy a significant place in its overall economic development. Henceforth a study on entrepreneurship development in small-scale industries becomes essential. Therefore, an attempt to highlight the problems and prospects of entrepreneurship development in small scale industries should include the present development trend in the growth of small scale industries and the various problems faced by the entrepreneurs in carrying forward the development in this sector.

Industrial Overview of Manipur

The land of Manipur is a land of contrasts. On the one hand it has vast natural resources for the development of different types of industries especially in medium and small-scale sectors; on the other hand the standard of living of the people of Manipur is somewhat lower than many of the states in the country.

Manipur continues to be one of the industrially backward states despite its vast minerals, forests and agricultural resources. The state has a net domestic product of Rs.2,208 crores at current prices during 2000-2001. While per capita state domestic product at current prices is Rs.12,228 crores during the same year. Over the years several industries have come up in the state under various schemes for industrial development. However, industrialisation has apparently not yet made its full impact on the state's economy. The state lags far behind the industrially developed states like Maharashtra, Gujarat, and West Bengal etc. although the number of large and medium scale industries as on 31st March 2000 was 12 and the numbers of SSI units were 5,829 units.

Table 1
Trend of Development of SSI

Year	Manipur		Nagaland	
	No. of Units	% of increase	No. of Units	% of increase
1996	4059	-	615	-
1997	5034	24.02	731	18.86
1998	5188	03.05	749	02.46
1999	5578	07.51	779	04.00
2000	5829	04.49	813	04.36
2001	6000	02.93	982	20.78

Source: Basic Statistics of NER, 2002.

Table 1 shows the trend of development of SSI in Manipur as compared to its neighbouring state of Nagaland for the period of six years from 1996 to 2001. It is observed that there has been a continuous increase in the number of SSI units in Manipur. It was only 4,059 units in 1996 and went up to 6000 units in 2001. The percentage of increase was highest with 24.02 per cent in the 1997 and the lowest increase was 02.93 per cent in 2001. While comparing the trend of growth of SSI units in Manipur with Nagaland it is revealed that there has been a corresponding increase in the number of units during the period under study. The total number of SSI units in Nagaland was 982 units in 2001 as against 615 units in 1996. The percentage increase of SSI units in both the states has been haphazard while the difference lies in the total number of units.

Obstacles and Problems

Manipur being one of the backward states of the country the entrepreneurial activities could not make any significant headway resulting in low pace of economic and industrial development. The main sector of the economy in this state is agriculture, which engages about 75 per cent of the total population. But this sector is not fully developed to offer facilities to secondary and tertiary sectors. About 95 per cent agriculturists are marginal farmers with the help of family members and only 5 per cent carry on who work agricultural activities with the help of hired workers. As a result of low level of agricultural activities in the state the identification and development of entrepreneurship is difficult one.

There is no encouraging entrepreneurship culture amongst the local people except in cottage and village industries. About 80 per cent of the people live in villages with their own agricultural land. Substantial portion of this population do not like to take any risky ventures other than agriculture. But this attitude is gradually changing in recent years.

Similarly, the absence of industrial culture in the state has been one of the important factors for low level of entrepreneurship development. The fruit of modern technological development is yet to reach to the remotest parts of the state. The level of industrial growth particularly of large and medium scale obviously hampered the pace of entrepreneurship development.

Natural barriers like climatic condition, topography, rainfall etc. are the main hurdles for the development of economic activities in the state. These natural barriers accompanied by insurgency problems vitiated the whole atmosphere and as a result people are reluctant to take up the risky ventures.

Entrepreneurship training provided by various institutions has not been very effective in the state. As a matter of fact, 322 entrepreneurs were trained during the period from 1st April 1994 to March 2002 but only 52 units were set up. The percentage of units set up to number of entrepreneurs trained stood at only 16.1 per cent which is less than the overall percentage of 23.5 for North-East India as depicted in Table 2. Although the number of entrepreneurs trained in Nagaland were only 143 but the units set-up were 44 representing 30.8 per cent which is the highest in the region and Manipur recorded the lowest rate of units set-up to number of entrepreneurs trained during the period.

Table 2

State-wise Entrepreneurs Trained and Units Set-Up for NEC-IDBI & NEC-SIDBI Co-Sponsored Programmes (April 1994- March 2002)

Sl. No.	State	No. of entrepreneurs trained	No. of units set-Up	Percentage of col. 3 to 4
1	2	3	4	5
1.	Arunachal Pradesh	323	84	25.4
2.	Assam	517	147	28.4
3.	Manipur	322	52	16.1
4.	Meghalaya	253	51	20.2
5.	Mizoram	119	24	20.2
6.	Nagaland	143	44	30.8
7.	Tripura	215	45	20.9
	Total	**1892**	**445**	**23.5**

Source: Basic Statistics of NER, 2002.

In Manipur, women entrepreneurs are very active and expert in their native skills and craftsmanship. However, for lack of suitable EDPs, women entrepreneurs failed to progress significantly.

Besides, there are some general problems as well, which are similar in all the states of Northeastern region. Among them we can easily mention about the tedious formalities of banks while issuing loan to small scale industry, lack of infrastructural development, lack of analytical EDP, lack of appreciation for industry unit with native skill, absence of information regarding feasibility, lack of consultancy organisation to induce entrepreneurs etc.

On the other hand, an institution cannot prosper and progress unless it has the capacity to manage change. This change can take place in the following three ways:

- Change in attitude
- Change in technology
- Change in system

The states in the northeastern region face a very serious challenge in regard to these three types of change. Taking up the question of change in attitude, one finds that there is a great resistance to change in northeast. The attitudes that have been built upon over a very long period of time have taken an extremely strong grip over the peoples mind and somehow there is a latent fear that changes in attitudes may result in an alteration of the power equilibrium and social structures in this area and therefore there is a resistance to change.

The serious dilution of the educational system in the area is to a great extend responsible for this. A number of schools and colleges have been opened with no attention to the quality of education. Most of the educational institutions have not kept pace with the changes and the syllabi have not been made uptodate in accordance with the need of the hour. The society leadership has not shown any particular anxiety to bring about change and on the contrary the anxiety to preserve group identities and cultural heritage often reinforces the resistance to change.

As regards change in technology, there is somehow a fear that technological changes will result in unemployment. This fear combined with the incapability of the educational system to produce manpower capable of understanding the latest developments in technology and contributing to the adoption of technology for the regions requirements is indeed a difficult situation to handle.

On the question of change in systems, the situation is not any brighter. Technological changes by themselves do not and cannot bring about substantial and continuous improvements in productivity if they are not accompanied by suitable modifications in organizational structures and procedures. Systems analysts play an important role here. However, in the northeast, no effort has been made in this direction so far.

Future Prospects

Despite the various obstacles and problems the future prospect of entrepreneurship development is very bright in the state of Manipur. It is also evident from the trend of development of SSI, which signifies the gradual growth in the number of industrial entrepreneurs besides agriculture, which accounts for substantial contribution to entrepreneurship development. To enhance this process of entrepreneurship development we must give due consideration to four essential ingredients, namely (1) resources – human and material, (2) organisations, (3) infrastructure, and (4) the entrepreneurs.

Since the state is abundant with material and human resources, it provides a sound base for development of both potential and active entrepreneurs. The requirement is only to develop the organizational and infrastructural facilities, which will undoubtedly brighten the prospect of entrepreneurship development. Awareness and interest of the entrepreneurs must be created through proper publicity in order to get a successful result from EDPs. The local or native entrepreneurs of this state mostly come from the artisan and the farming family. According to a study undertaken by NISIET, Guwahati, 75 per cent of the local entrepreneurs comes from these two categories.

Conclusion

Thus, to conclude, it can be said that it is the work culture and strong conviction on the part of the individual to be an entrepreneur in the true sense of the term. There are many instances that without any training and incentives a large number of entrepreneurs are doing very good services to them and thereby create an enviable industrial growth. For better result all efforts must proceed in a systematic way. An integrated and multi dimensional approach is required for the growth of entrepreneurship in backward areas such as Manipur and for identifying opportunities that have growth prospects based on local resources. It is necessary to provide the technology, finance and other assistance, which small-scale entrepreneurs need very acutely. The planners and policy makers should be fully familiar with the problems and priorities of entrepreneurship development in this part of the country. It is therefore suggested that a road map requires to be planned for the promotion of local entrepreneurship with specific targets and all concerned authorities take due responsibility, be it in the area of training, finance, marketing, technology, infrastructure etc. with strict monitoring so that there is a vibrancy and visibility in the performance of the SSI sector.

NOTES AND REFERENCES

1. Saini, Jasmeer Singh , *Entrepreneurship Development: Programmes and Policies*, p 3.
2 Baruah, H.K., *Entrepreneurship Development in the NER and its impact on indusrialisation of the region.*

ENTREPRENEURSHIP DEVELOPMENT IN IT INDUSTRIES

13

ENTREPRENEURSHIP DEVELOPMENT AND INFORMATION TECHNOLOGY

PURUSHOTTAM BHANDARI
H.C. GAUTAM

Introduction

Entrepreneurship is one of the main indicators of economic development in the context of privatisation, liberalisation and globalisation of Indian economy. Development is a function of entrepreneurs. Without entrepreneur, there is no development of enterprises. The Dictionary meaning of the word "Entrepreneur" according to *Oxford Encyclopaedic Dictionary* is "Organizer, manager, of (esp. musical), entertainments; manager one who undertakes an enterprise, esp. contractor acting an intermediary between capital and labour. The term 'entrepreneur' became popular in economics in the 18th century. Ricard Cantillon (1680-1734) an Irish International banker (a French Economist) defined the term 'entrepreneur' as "an agent who buys factors of production at certain prices in order to combine them into a product with a view to selling it at uncertain prices in future." Jean Baptiste Say (1767-1832), a classical economist, was a pioneer for the introduction of the concept of an entrepreneur into economic theory, and also the division of the fundamental factors of production into three - Land, Labour and Capital. J.B. Say defined the term 'entrepreneur' as "one who combines the land of one, the labour of another and the capital of yet another to produce a product." Joseph Alois Schumpter (1883-1950) stated that an entrepreneur is one "who institutes new combinations of factors of productions i.e., innovation." In common parlance, entrepreneurs have to perform three objectives (i) what to produce, (ii) how much to produce and (iii) what technique of production should be adopted to maximize output and profit margin. In modern economic development strategy, an entrepreneur has to perform six functions, as (i) an organizer, (ii) an innovator, (iii) a risk taker, (iv) a creator of new system, (v) an uncertainty bearer and (vi) a change agent.

Entrepreneurship is a creative human act. It creates new thing or adds value to the existing one. It involves mobilisation of resources from one level of productive use to a higher level of use. Entrepreneurship involves a willingness to take responsibility and ability to put mind to a task and see it through from inception to completion. Another ingredient of entrepreneurship is sensing opportunities, while others see chaos, contradiction, and confusion. Essence of entrepreneurship is going against time with maturity and serving as a change agent. Entrepreneurship is an outcome of the development process, which also encompasses the emergence of economic and social innovations.

The first and perhaps most important requirement for success as an entrepreneur is a passion for the work at hand with a sense of optimism, with a sense of purpose, with a sense of challenge.

Now a days, it is not that entrepreneurial success is all about entrepreneurial abilities of an individual. In reality entrepreneurial success is a highly collaborative process. A good entrepreneur has to bring out creative ideas and the entrepreneurial spirit from all his people. All entrepreneurs are faced with adversity at some point of time. But he is expected to convert every adversity into opportunity.for the work at hand with a sense of optimism, with a sense of purpose, with a sense of challenge.

Why Entrepreneurship Development Programme is Essential?

The importance of EDP is generally felt on account of the following. These are as follows:

(i) It opens up avenues for the generation of self-employment.

(ii) It encourages development of small-scale units and household enterprises.

(iii) It facilitates effective mobilisation and utilisation of resources, human and physical, which otherwise remain idle and unutilised.

(iv) It has an impact on raising the level of livelihood by eradicating poverty.

(v) It ensures more equitable distribution of National Income of the country.

(vi) It facilitates the maximum utilisation of indigenous resources raising productivity of traditional sector.

(vii) Besides reducing unemployment problem of the country, it is helpful in rehabilitation of those labourers, skilled and unskilled, who are thrown out of jobs after the economic reforms in the country.

(viii) Entrepreneurship development precedes industrial development. It will benefit the community in the long run.

(ix) Entrepreneurship development has the ability to innovate and introduce advance technology.

(x) It creates a competitive skill, which paves the way to the global market.

(xi) It stimulates faster development and Optimum utilization of financial institutions.

(xii) It creates potential entrepreneurs in various sectors of the economy.

(xiii) Entrepreneurship development helps to generate innovative climate in industrial sector.

IT as an Aid to Entrepreneurs

Entrepreneurs generally face various types of problems. Many of these problems can be solved with the assistance of Information Technology. Some of such problems are listed below:

(i) Search for a viable project.

(ii) Product identification and analysis.

(iii) Acquiring professional competence.

(ii) Preparing the blue-print of the project

(iii) Search for a financier.

(iv) Fund Management.

(v) Choose a proper technology for production, warehousing, and distributional (marketing) functions.

(vi) Technology transfer, Counselling and Legal formalities.

(vii) Selection of manpower.

(viii) Creating information network.

(ix) Motivating the people for better efficiency.

(x) Managing the stress that may confront the process. Knowledge of managing risks and uncertainty.

(xi) Creating an environment for adoption of modern technology.

(xii) Preparing the people to accept the change.

(xiii) Establishing Global Linkages.

All entrepreneurs are faced with one or more of these adversities at some point of time. But he is expected to convert every adversity into opportunity. In the solution of the above problems information technology can be of great help.

Emerging Areas for EDP- IT Coverage

To speak the truth, there is no limit for area coverage under EDP. It is especially true for a developing country like India in general and North-Eastern Region (NER) in particular. The development of the region, which is predominantly rural and hilly but full of natural resources, is intimately associated with the issues of rural development and proper utilisation of these resources without detriment to the sustainability. The entrepreneurs, present and prospective, have to shoulder this responsibility. Information Technology enriches these entrepreneurs in tuning their line of action in the process of performing the activities they select to carry on in this regard.

A few areas where EDP-IT has a role to play are mentioned below:

1. Education, though is a social responsibility of the Government, it is a fact that the people must supplement the action initiated by the government. So, education is a sector, which is waiting for an entrepreneur to exploit the possibilities; especially in

the country like India where in addition to the rural areas the small towns also are found lacking the right kind of infrastructure for education.

2. In the area of health, the entrepreneurs may look into establishing hospital chains. It is already recognised that this part of the country is rich in medicinal plants. Production of Herbal Medicines and raw materials for this could be well taken by the entrepreneurs. There are many villages in this region, which are completely dependant on the traditional herbal medicines. The entrepreneurs may ponder over this area to commercialise the system.

3. The emerging areas in agriculture sector in which entrepreneurs may venture are horticulture, food processing including fruit-based units, floriculture, cattle feed, dairy, pisci-culture including ornamental fish. The people in this region are more or less acquainted with all these activities. By giving modern approach to the conventional production system for making the product more market friendly, entrepreneurs may start Small Business opening an opportunity for more employment. This is possible with an addition to their existing stock of knowledge through IT. It is often reported that during the peak season, the price of cabbage and tomato in some parts of Assam come down to Re.0.50 to Re1.00 per kg, a price, which even, does not cover the variable cost of cultivation. The entrepreneurs may look into the prospect of converting these and other vegetables into processed food (e.g. banana and potato chips).

4. In the service sector, Tourism is an area with a very high growth potential in NE region. The specific areas in this industry are hotel business, Tour and Travel agencies with conducted tour facilities, Tour-guide, etc.

5. Border trade with neighbouring countries is another emerging area for the entrepreneurs .The agreement for augmenting trade relations with the Association of South East Asian Nations (ASEAN) is already there. The entrepreneurs may exploit this opportunity by to explore the possibility of starting new enterprises in export business.

6. Small and household business create majority of new jobs in the economy. In the context of North-East it may be said that

household industries are traditionally run by the people in handloom, handicraft and light food items from rice like *Chira, Moori, Khandah, Akhoiguri* etc. Women Association like Self-Employed Women Association (SEWA) may help the women of this region to develop an entrepreneurship mentality at the grass root level.

7. There are thousands of self-help group working in the villages and trying to boost their economic condition but without the knowledge of EDP-IT Assistance. NGOs, Government agencies and individuals who are in IT line may extend their helping hands to upgrade the skill and technology.

There is possibility of exploring new projects in the areas mentioned above. As for support organisations entrepreneurs required data and information on raw materials, skill formation, production technology, market intricacies, emerging opportunities and resources to take decisions on production, diversification and capacity utilisation. Information Technology has an important role to play in these areas. The development in IT and use of Internet has made Information Availability easy.

IT Applications in Entrepreneurial Development

The applications of Information Technology in Entrepreneurial Development may be in the following specific field: (i) Project Preparation, (ii) Institutional Arrangements, (iii) Education and Training, (iv) Support Mechanism, (v) Financing, (vi) Innovation Function, (vii) Infrastructure (viii) Market Network, (ix) Advertisement, (x) Risk Management, (xi) Quality Management, and (xii) Environmental considerations.

i. Project Preparation

* Cost estimation
* Viability of project
* Site selection
* Mode of Financing
* Market prospective

ii. Institutional Arrangements

* Entrepreneurial Motivation Training Centres (EMTCs, 1973),

* The National Institute of Small Industry Extension Training (NISIET),
* The North Eastern Industrial and Training Consultancy Organization (NEITCO),
* Indian Institute of Entrepreneurship (IIE, Guwahati),
* District Industrial Centres (DIC),
* Entrepreneurship Development Institute of India (EDII),
* The North Eastern Council (NEC),
* Industrial Development Bank of India (IDBI),
* Industrial Financial Corporation of India (IFCI),
* Industrial Credit and Investment Corporation of India (ICICI),
* Small Industries Development Bank of India. (SIDBI),
* State Small IndustriesNorth-Eastern Industrial Consultant Ltd. (NECON)
* North-East Women Entreprenuers Association (NEWEA).
* National Small Industries Corporation (NSIC).

iii. Education and Training

* General and technical education
* Confidence in business running
* Management skills
* Identification of potential entrepreneurs
* Motivational training
* Help and guidance in selecting products
* Knowledge of cost-benefit analysis
* Outlook and attitude

iv. Support Mechanism

* Registration of unit
* Providing land, shed, power, water etc.
* Getting licences
* Granting subsidyOffering consultancy

V. Financing

* Entrepreneur's own share
* Micro-credit through SHGs
* KVIC
* Development Banks
* Commerical Banks
* RRBs
* Non-banks
* Private Banks

vi. Innovation Function

* Introduction of new products
* Use of new method of production
* Opening of a new market
* New source of raw materials
* New form of organizations

vii. Infrastructure

* Settingup Industrial parks
* Export-promotion zones
* Setting up industrial growth Centres
* Transport subsidy
* Power subsidy
* Central Govt. Packages
* Comprehensive Insurance Scheme
* Research and Development

viii. Market Network

* Information on market demand
* Technology transfer
* Trade Marks and Patent Laws
* Global Linkages

* Future outlook. Risk Management
* Insurable and non-Insurable risks
* Wisely selected risks
* Unforeseen risks like change in demand, price, supply etc.
* Uncertanity of future
* Hazards of business falls
* Change in economic policy.

ix. Advertisement

* Salesmanship
* Sales promotion measures
* Home delivery scheme
* Media
* Development of websites. Quality Management
* Creation of quality awareness
* Quality Assurance scheme
* Creation of quality councils
* ISO standards
* Quality testing
* Maintenance of global standards

xii. Environmental considerations

* Cleaner technology
* Pollution control projects
* Environmental Laws
* Setting up Common Effluent Treatment Plants

Conclusion

Entrepreneur may not be a technical person, but he must be able to determine the level of technology required for the enterprise at every step of the progress. The future will see Entrepreneurship, as the key driver of economic development. Technological obsolescence will become order of the day. He must take initiatives to determine technical innovations. It is true that the IT driven economy will limit number of jobs and will demand sophisticated skills. The retirement age will decrease with the business institutions demanding younger people who are not resistant to change. But at the same time it must be kept in mind that these technical innovations shall not, in any way, contradict the National Economic Objectives. Hence the technical innovations shall be commensurate with the National Economic Objectives. Here lies the role of a successful Entrepreneur to trade-off between the Enterprise Goal and National Objectives.

NOTES AND REFERENCES

1. Prasain, G.P. [(ed.), 2003], *Entreprenuership Development*, Sunmarg. Publishers and Distributors, New Delhi.
2. Rani. C., *Entrepreneurial Development Cycle*, Faculty Member, National Institute of Small Industries Extension Training, Hyderabad.
3. Mali, D.D. (2000), *Entrepreneurship Development in North-East,* Indian Institute of Entrepreneurship, Guwahati.
4. Mali, D.D. and Dutta Gautam, (2000), *Promoting New Entrepreneurs,* Indian Institute of Entrepreneurship, Guwahati.

14

TECHNOPRENEURSHIP AS THE NEW PARADIGM FOR E-BUSINESS

LAI PRABHAKAR

Introduction

We have seen tremendous changes in the field of information technology. Different organizations are using information technology in different field of their business. This gives a chance to establish IT industries big or small. Today we have seen the new revolution based on Information Communication Technology (ICT). The computer has evolved from being a number crunching calculator in the 1950s to a data processor in the 1960s; a tool for information management in the 1980s, for communication in the 1990s and now to better manage knowledge in the new millennium. Coupled with the pervasive nature of the Internet and multimedia, a new digital economy has emerged which is set to change the nature of human civilization. In this new economy, the players and rules of business are to change dramatically. From traditional 'brick and mortar' businesses, the digital economy gave rise to new electronic businesses or e-businesses which are global in nature and extensively web-based. We define e-business as the process of using Web technology to help business streamline processes, improve productivity and increase efficiencies. E-business will enable companies to easily communicate with partners, vendors and customers, connect back-end data systems and transact commerce in a secure manner.

Linking Today's Business with Tomorrow's Technology

It's happening right before our eyes: a vast and rapid reconfiguration of business on an unprecedented scale. Conventional wisdom says that e-commerce is an economic solvent. It dissolves old business models, changes the cost structure, and rearranges links among buyers, sellers, and everyone in between. The impact of e-commerce is happening in three different phases.

In the first phase (1994-1997), e-commerce was about presence: making sure that everybody had a Website, meeting the demand that every company, large or small, get out there and have at least something on the Internet. People weren't quite sure why they were doing it, but they knew that they had to have an online presence.

The second phase (1997-2000) of e-commerce was about transaction – buying and selling over digital media.

Today, e-commerce is entering the third phase (2000-?), with a focus on how the Internet can impact profitability. And profitability is not about increasing gross revenues but rather increasing gross margins. We call this phase e-business. It includes all the applications and process enabling a company to service a business transaction. Thus, e-business is not just about e-commerce transactions or about buying and selling over the Web; it's the overall strategy of redefining old business models, with the aid of technology, to maximize customer value and profits. To paraphrase *Business Week*, "Forget B2B or B2C, E-business is about P2P- Path to Profitability."

There are certainly many benefits to venture into e-business. An e-business can provide high personalization, high quality customer service and better supply chain management compared to a traditional 'brick and mortar' business. Above all, high efficiency productivity at reduced costs and very low overheads meant big profits for any company willing to venture into the new electronic business. They are also low entry barriers to start an electronic business. An idea, a computer and connection to the Internet is all that is thought to be needed to start selling on the Net. With such an alluring attraction, no wonder many 'dot com' companies were formed worldwide to cater for various types of e-commerce and e-business.

What is Technopreneurship?

According to Gates, "While 2001 has been a challenging year, in fact the toughest in several decades for both the world at large and the technology industry, the next decade holds huge potential". Gates said he is excited about the 2001-2010 time period, which he said will be known as the 'Digital Decade' and where digital innovations will become an integral part of everyday life. It's the vision of a world where the number of people using e-mail to communicate will quadruple from today and where e-commerce will finally take off in the way visionaries and analysts have talked about for years.

"The productivity gains that technology will drive during this Digital Decade will be double those of the 1990s," he said. "An economic revival will be driven by technological advances. The wave of hardware and software innovation currently being seen will provide the impetus for renewed investment in information technology across every business and economic sector."

Interestingly, in his book "Business @ The Speed of Thought," Gates (1999) earlier outlined 12 steps he said companies should take if they want to reinvent the way they work and succeed in the coming digital decade. Gates' 12 steps were:

i. Insist that communication flow through e-mail.

ii. Study sales data online to share insights easily.

iii. Shift knowledgeable workers into high-level thinking.

iv. Use digital tools to create virtual teams.

v. Convert every paper process to a digital process.

vi. Use digital tools to eliminate single-task jobs.

vii. Create a digital feedback loop.

viii. Use digital systems to route customer complaints immediately.

ix. Use digital communication to redefine the boundaries.

x. Transform every business process into just-in-time delivery.

xi. Use digital delivery to eliminate the middle man.

xii. Use digital tools to help customers solve problems for themselves.

The 12 steps are certainly steps for a successful e-business operation. If Bill Gates prediction of a Digital Decade is true, how can e-business succeed after experiencing such a bad experience? What is its critical success?

The focus of e-business is changing to one of empowerment, not technology for its own sake. E-business is also not simply defined as e-commerce transactions. It's about using technology to redefine business. The big winners of the future are going to be those companies that provide industries with enabling technology. To succeed, an infrastructure flexible enough to absorb new technologies, maximize efficiency across organization, and support business model changes will be needed. Thus we can define Technopreneurship as being an entrepreneur by using existing technologies and pertain it to newer application or invent a new product.

Who is a Technopreneur?

Organizations need individuals who take it upon themselves to make IT a meaningful and profitable aspect of organizational functioning. These individuals need to be present in all parts of an organization. Such individuals tend to empower themselves in terms of thinking about new ways of working, incorporating technology into workplaces, and managing and dealing with people. These individuals working within organizational confines are often referred to an ***Intrapreneurs***. When these self-appointed stewards take it upon themselves to make IT work in an organization, they become ***Infopreneurs*** who generate new ideas regarding IT usage. They attempt to push through creative ideas in spite of any criticism and are not afraid to go along alone in demonstrating localized IT-related success. It is in that sense that they become techno-entrepreneurial. Hence the term technopreneur is coined. Thus, ***Technopreneur*** can be defined as ***"Someone who uses technology to do something new or invents new devices and then makes a business from selling these inventions."***

Why Technopreneurship?

High-tech and entrepreneurial skills are driving our economy back to prosperity. Technopreneursip-merging technology prowess and entrepreneurial skills - is the real source of power in today's knowledge-based economy. A technopreneur distinguishes logic from tradition, tradition from prejudice, prejudice from common sense and common sense from nonsense while integrating a variety of ideas from diverse groups and disciplines.

Technopreneurship is not a product but a process of synthesis in engineering the future of a person, an organization, a nation and the world. Strategic directions or decision-making processes are becoming more demanding and complex. This requires universities, and in site professional development programs and training to produce strategic thinkers who will have skills to succeed in a rapidly changing global environment.

Traditional University programme, however, lack the teaching methods to turn today's students into creative, innovative, visionary global leaders who understand the importance of technopreneurship. Recent technological advances and global competitiveness have changed and broadened the nature of liberal arts to embrace humans and machines. The answer is not creating new liberal arts or soft-skills courses, but integrating them into the general technical curriculum. These changes take time. Also, what about present and past universities' graduates? The solution is to increase in site training and development at all levels of a corporation.

These programme should focus on what workers and professionals should be able to do. These include functioning on multidisciplinary teams, communicating effectively, acquiring updated knowledge of technological developments, and understanding the basic technical concepts and there new applications and improvements.

Creativity is breaking the conventional mental blocks and playing with imagination and possibilities, leading to new and meaningful connections and outcomes while interacting with ideas, people and the environment. Technopreneurship is the only source of long-run sustainable competitive advantage. In an era of man-made brainpower industries, individual, corporate, and national economic success will all require both new and more extensive skills sets than have been required in the past. By themselves skills don't guarantee success. They have to be put together in successful organizations. But without skills and technopreneurship there are no successful organizations.

According to a study conducted by a team led by Dr. Andrew Whinston, the Hugh Roy Cullen Centennial Chair Professor in Information Systems at the Graduate School of Business in the University of Texas, Information Technology capital (computer hardware, software and networking equipment) contributed significantly to financial performance measures for the digital dot coms. However, the IT contribution for physical dot coms was uniformly insignificant across all financial measures. The result involving physical dot coms attributed to the fact that beyond the digital customer interface, such companies were not fundamentally different from traditional business operations.

There is also a distinction between two types of dot com companies - digital and physical. Digital dot coms are Internet based companies such as Yahoo, Ebay and America Online, whose products and services are digital in nature and are delivered directly over the Internet. By contrast, the physical dot coms sell physical products such as books, flowers and gifts that are shipped to consumers.

Technopreneur Development

We are living in challenging and exciting times. The world economy and the way businesses are run are being transformed by the triple driving forces of technological innovation, globalisation and liberalisation. Under the onslaught of these forces, old paradigms are being examined and new paradigms are being thrown up almost by the day. In a more competitive world economy, businesses have to concentrate their resources not just on value adding but increasingly on value-creating. These changes are unsettling not only for businesses but also for Government, Trade Unions, employers, workers and society in general. The following areas should be emphasised in the technopreneur development.

Culture development

- Research opportunities for undergraduate students.
- Exposure to the technology updates and trends.
- Student participation in selected university operation (library, computer labs, etc).
- Wide range of innovative and special activities that promote student running small business.
- Encouraging multi-disciplinary (inter-faculty) networking· Strong industry linkage in student projects, assignment, industrial placement and final year projects.

Conducive Environment

- Fast internet access.
- Wide selection of information resources on technology trend, market, financial market, venture capital.
- company operation and project management.
  Abundant part-time project opportunities.
- Easy broadcast of info, news and contacts through many notice boards and online channels.
- Availability of small development areas and web hosting facilities.
- Practical technology development facilities (software tools, testing equipment).
- Business plan competition, entrepreneurship competition.

Technopreneur Training

- Project management training.
- Startup company support in terms of consultancy and advices.
- Software development and hardware development training.
- Basic technopreneur skills training.

Technopreneur Support

- Facilitation of seed money, development resources and entrepreneur support.
- Small university venture funds.
- Contacts to patent filing companies, investment companies, venture capitalist.
- Setting up of online technopreneur resource web site.

How to Set-Up a Techno Enterprise - Decision to be a Technopreneur

The overriding reason for anyone to think of establishing a SSI unit can be summarised in one word - opportunity. An opportunity to be your own boss, to provide a product or service, to implement your ideas which can generate sufficient surplus is reason to think of starting up a SSI unit.

Starting a small business takes a lot of courage. To be successful - to stay in business - you need a combination of hard work, skill and perseverance.

Generally, people who start their own businesses can be grouped into two broad categories. The first group consists of people who know exactly what they want to do and are merely looking for the opportunity or resources to do it. These people may have already developed many of the skills necessary to succeed in their chosen field and are also likely to be familiar with industry customs and practices, which can help during the startup phase of a new business.

The second group consists of people who want to start their own business, but don't have any real definite ideas about what they'd like to do. They may have developed skills in the course of their employment or education, but may not be interested in opening a business in the same field of endeavour.

How a person will proceed depends on, mainly, to which group they belong to. To evaluate the aptitude for small business ownership, technopreneur needs to:

Understanding the Responsibilities of Ownership

Before starting a business technopreneur should know what's involved in owning a business and what are the roles s(he)'ll have to play if they start on their own one? Most important fact to keep in mind is - Owning a small business is not just another job but a lot more than that. You are totally and completely responsible for its growth, development and its future. It's a completely different lifestyle. Technopreneurs have to ask themselves whether they are ready for a complete commitment to the success of their business.

Ability to Set Your Goals

What do you want from your business? If you want to "succeed," how will you know if you get there? What should be the next goal once you reach the initial goal? Knowing what you want from your business permeates all of the other decisions you'll have to make in starting a new business. It will affect which business you choose, how you evaluate your chances for success, and how you determine if you have the right skills.

Estimate the Impact On Your Everyday Life

Your life will change completely once you start your own business. Try to comprehend the degree to which your life is going to change when you become a business owner? Many of the more "secure" aspects of employee life do not exist/will vanish once you open up your own business. You might have to be perform more than one function, work at all irregular hours, juggle between business and household demands. You will need to repriortise your schedule, work and personal life.

Evaluate Your Skills

Evaluate your own skills and make judgments about whether you're ready to own your own business. There are many technopreneurial quizzes available on the net and with Entrepreneurship Development Institute which test your technopreneurial capabilities.

Assessing Your Strengths

Successful small business owners know their own strengths and weaknesses. They build their businesses around their strengths and compensate for their weaknesses. If you're to succeed, you'll have to be able to identify what you do well and what you don't do so well.

While evaluating yourself, be honest otherwise you'll only hurt yourself if you're not. Also, don't panic if you discover that you have weaknesses. Every one including small business owner has them. The key to success is not so much in having every skill as it is in finding ways to compensate for those weaknesses.

By evaluating yourself, you are making a list of what you like to do and what you don't like to do. Generally, you like to do things you are good at and you don't like doing things you're not good at. It's a simple approach, but it should help you start to focus.

Technopreneurial Characteristics

Though the list is not exhaustive it does tell you about the major characteristic of a technopreneur.

Good health

Technopreneurs keep themselves physically resilient and in good health. They need to work for extended periods of time, and while they are in the process of building their business, good health is a must.

Self-Control

Most technopreneurs believe they can do the job better than anyone else and will strive for maximum responsibility and accountability. A technopreneur needs to maintain his/her calm even in face of adversity. Technopreneur realises loosing temper won't help the situation.

Goal setting

Technopreneurs enjoy creating business strategies and thrive on the process of achieving their goals. Once they achieve a goal, they quickly replace it with a greater goal. They strive to exert whatever influence they can over future events. They have a compelling need to do their own thing in their own way. They need the freedom to choose and to act according to their own perception of what actions will result in success.

Self-Confidence

Technopreneurs are self-confident and tackle problems immediately with confidence and are persistent in their pursuit of their objectives. Most are at their best in the face of adversity, since they thrive on their own self-confidence. Before anyone else you have to believe in yourself and your product or services. It will show when you will meet your future customer, and suppliers.

Sense of Urgency

Technopreneurs have a never-ending sense of urgency to develop their ideas. Inactivity makes them impatient, tense, and uneasy. They thrive on activity and are tireless in the pursuit of their goals.

Comprehensive Awareness

Successful Technopreneurs should have ability to comprehend complex situations that may include planning, making strategic decisions, and working on multiple business ideas simultaneously. They are farsighted and aware of important details, and they will continuously review all possibilities to achieve their business objectives. At the same time, they devote their energy to completing the tasks immediately before them.

Realism

Technopreneurs are realistic, they accept things as they are and deal with them accordingly. They will change their direction when they see that change will improve their prospects for achieving their goals. They will verify any information they receive before they use it in making a decision.

Conceptual Ability

Technopreneur should possess the ability to identify relationships quickly in the midst of complex situations. They identify problems and begin working on their solution. They are not troubled by ambiguity and uncertainty because they are used to solving problems. Technopreneurs are natural leaders and are usually the first to identify a problem to be overcome. They quickly identify an alternative problem-solving approach.

Status Requirements

Technopreneurs like the business they have built to be praised. When they need help, they will not hesitate to admit it especially in areas that are outside of their expertise. During tough business periods, Technopreneurs will concentrate their resources and energies on essential business operations. They want to be where the action is and will not stay in the office for extended periods of time.

Interpersonal Relationships

Technopreneurs are more concerned with people's accomplishments than with their feelings. They generally avoid becoming personally involved and will not hesitate to sever relationships that could hinder the progress of their business.

Technopreneurs are impatient and drive themselves and everyone around them. They don't have the tolerance or empathy necessary for team building unless it's their team, and they will delegate very few key decisions.

Technopreneurs need good interpersonal skills to be able to adjust and survive as their organization grows and becomes more structured.

Emotional Stability

Technopreneurs should have a considerable amount of self-control and should be able to handle business pressures. They should learn to relax in stress situations and are challenged rather than discouraged by setbacks or failures. Technopreneurs are uncomfortable when things are going well. They'll frequently find some new activity on which to vent their pent-up energy. They are not content to leave well enough alone.

Technopreneurs tend to handle people problems with action plans without empathy. Their moderate interpersonal skills are often inadequate to provide for stable relationships. However, the divorce rate among technopreneurs is about average.

You might possess three or more of the characteristic listed above, you don't necessarily need them all use your strengths to compensate for your weaknesses.

Once you've decided that you have the right stuff to be a technopreneur, check out the following prime considerations for determining if your business idea has a chance to succeed before you pump your life savings into a small business.

Does the idea fire up your motivation and is it adequate enough to keep you going for next 1-2 years?

Is it a viable business proposition in your area?

Does it match the needs of your clientele, local or otherwise?

Check it out with basic market research

Test it out at market place

Consult with the experts

Look out for competition in the field

Is it a sunrise industry?

Your business opportunity

Project conceptualisation

Once the ideas are screened and a viable business opportunity emerges the project has to be conceptualised in all its dimensions. The 4 P's of Project Conception are:

Product (Shape, Size and Nature)

Process (Technology to produce the product)

Place (Location of Plant)

Partner (Technological or Financial Collaborator)

Having a business plan will help you in defining these 4 P's and chalking out the strategy for future of your business. It will help you establish goals, targets and identify the strengths and weaknesses.

How to Set-Up a Techno Enterprise - Preparation of Business Plan

A Business Plan is a document where you plan your Business to have an organized and effective response to a situation which may arise in future. Business plan is not just for a start up company but also for those which are growing. It can be used it to establish realistic goals or targets to achieve and to determine the current position. A workable business plan:

Determine where the company needs to go

Forewarn of possible roadblocks along the way

Formulate responses to contingencies

Keep the business on track to reach its planned goals

Start a business plan with describing your business and product or services. Tell about the market you are targeting and the stage of development your company is in. If you get stuck up on a particular part of the plan-leave it for time being-and come back later and finish it. You can't make a perfect first draft - so just get some thoughts down to start the process and you can always come back and change it or polish it up later. While making a business plan keep following points in mind.

Keep Target Audience In Your Mind

While writing your business plan keep in mind the intended audience and why you are writing the plan. For example, if you are trying to get debt financing emphasis should not be on the huge profit potential - but on the certainty that the debt can be repaid. If you are writing a plan to help you run the business better you may start with general background information on the company and the industry, and focus on the areas of your plan that are currently most important to you.

Strategy - Core of Your Business Plan

Basically the first part of the business plan should be geared towards helping develop and support solid business strategy. The plan should explain the market, the industry, target customers and competitors. Write about customer needs and the benefits of current products and services. Evaluate the strengths and weaknesses of each competing firm and draw out the opportunities for your product or service in the marketplace. All of these steps largely aim to help you in creating a strategy for your business. The second half of the business plan should explain how to execute your selected business strategy. Your products and services, your marketing and operations should all closely tie in with your strategy. Have a strategy that will set the course for your business rather than having a smart-sounding strategy for your plan.

Think Competitively Throughout Your Business Plan

In present competitive market, you would probably be facing some serious competition sooner or later no matter how unique your business idea is. You need to think competitively throughout your business plan. As a technopreneur, you need to identify where you will do things in similar manner as your competitors, where you will do things differently, what will be your real strengths and real weaknesses, where will you create your niche. Focus your plan on being different than your competititors and compete with existing players less directly. Find a particular market niche to focus on. Think over the points, can you find a unique strategy? Can you position your products differently? Can you use different sales or marketing vehicles? Your business plan should be able to answer these questions.

Be Realistic With Your Business Plan

Lots of business plans sound good on paper, but don't work in the real world marketplace. It's difficult to attract people to a new product or service, just because it's better. People or companies have established buying patterns and are currently doing business with someone else. To do business with you, it takes more than attracting them to your business. You've got to steal your customers from someone else's business and create your own base of loyal customers. It is possible that your competitors may launch new products or services or cut their prices to counter your entry in the current market. For a new start up company it's easy to overestimate sales projections as it's easy to underestimate costs. There are always going to be some unseen expenditure, hefty amount of cost overruns, expensive problems, and items that you simply overlooked. So forecast conservatively and try to have an extra cushion of cash tucked in reserve.

Tips on Creating Plans

People

In seeking fund from banks, venture capitalists or other outside investors, you will increase your chances of success if you get someone committed to your management teams who at least have a recognizable name.

Alternately, you can include as exhibits to your plan any positive media clippings you can find, such as items from trade publications, about members of your management team. If you don't have any clippings, try contacting relevant publications to get media coverage-perhaps about your start-up business proposal.

Keep Your Business Plan Factual and Succinct

Try to keep the plan factual; don't use hyperbole or generalizations to describe the potential of your business plan. Use more factual information you present to reach their own conclusions. Keep it succinct. Don't put too much detail when creating plans. If a business plan is too long, it might be skimmed and focus on what is really important might be lost.

Involve Everyone

Involve use expert opinion or key employees to create business plan. Then work with them until you are satisfied. Have key people get together to get the plan in synchronized fashion and to get any disagreements out in the open. The more input people have in creating the plan, the more responsibility they will feel toward it.

Conclusion

We believe there is a significant difference between an entrepreneur and a technopreneur, with the latter having an advantage on the mastery of the technology element besides possessing good business acumen. But mastering the technology alone is not enough, the intellectual, emotional and spiritual intelligences of the person must also be strong and this require special programs to forge the technopreneurship spirit.

Technopreneur development programmes and training are required to produce strategic thinkers who will have skills to succeed in a rapidly changing environment. Universities should take an important role in this regard. Students are to be taught to enrich their creativity, innovative ideas.

To be a successful technopreneur one should have a well define business plan with the aim that existing technology can be utilized to innovate new product. Once after defining the 4 P's of project conception, it will be helpful to establish goals, targets and identify the strengths and weakness of your SSI. Creativity and innovation are important factors for the successful technopreneur. Without skills and technopreneurship there are no successful organizations.

NOTES AND REFERENCES

1. Bajaj K, Nag Debjani, (2000), *E-Commerce – The cutting edge of business*, Tata McGraw-Hill Publishing Company Limited.
2. Boddy D, McCalman J. and Buchanan A.D. *The New Management Challenge – Information Systems for improved performance*, Croom Helm.
3. C.S. Rayudu (2004), *E-Commerce E-Business*, Himalaya Publishing House.
4. Dewan Bushan, (2001), *E-Commerce*, S. Chand and Company Ltd.
5. Dot-Coms, (June 19, 2000), Can They Climb back, *Business Week*, p.101
6. Gates, W. H. (1999), *Business @ The Speed of Though*, Warner Books, Inc., New York.
7. Goel Ritendra, Kakkar. D.N. *Computer Applications in Management*, New Age International Publishers
8. Joseph P.T. (2002), *E-Commerce: A Managerial Perspective*, PHI
9. Kalakota Ravi, Robinson Marcia (2004),. *E-business 2.0 Roadmap for Success*, Pearson Education.
10. Kanungo Shivraj, (1999), *Making Information Technology Work*, Sage Publications.
11. Parameswaran R., (2002), *Computer Applications in Business*, S. Chand and Company Ltd.
12. http://www.amigospais-guaracabuya.org/oagmc160.php. Manuel Cereijo (July 2002). Technopreneurship
13. http://www.mmu.edu.my/~cctd/CCTD/services_techno_dev.htm
14. http://www.nzcs.org/site_default/x-files/4916.doc
15. http://www.techno-preneur.net/new-timeis/howto/decision.htm
16. http://www.techno-preneur.net/new-timeis/howto/business_plan.htm.

15

THE E-ENTREPRENEUR

Potential and Challenges

KH. TOMBA SINGH

Introduction

Recent changes in the world economy have made the pursuit of entrepreneurial opportunity increasingly important to wealth creation. Globalization has begun to dismantle the barriers that traditionally segregated local business opportunities and local firms from their international counterparts. Local markets are becoming integral parts of broader, global markets. As globalization proceeds a pace, entrepreneurs and small business will play a more prominent role on the global business arena.

Information Technology has brought revolutionary changes in energy walk of life. It has accelerated the pale of globalization. Use of internet and computers for different purposes is increasing rapidly. Internet has facilitated an efficient, speedy and transparent process for disseminating information to the public and other agencies working in different fields. The rapid strides made by the telecom sector in India continue to amaze us. It gives me great joy to see a young boy in Manipur strike a spontaneous conversation with someone in Kerala. To see fishermen bargain for the best price on their catch while they are still on water, or a farmer in Punjab accessing commodity rates in various mandis at the push of a button, is equally in spinning. India has very quickly transformed from an era of snail mail, scarcity in phones and occasional long distance phone calls to an era of having the sixth-largest telecom network in the world. At the core of all this and many more similar milestones is the E-entrepreneurship revolution.

The advent of electronic commerce and the internet has changed forever the nature of starting a business for those who incorporate technology into their operations and products within the frame work of the resource-based theory. The resource-based theory is the most appropriate to understand new venture creation because it best describes how entrepreneurs themselves build their business from the resources and capabilities they currently posses or can realistically acquire. Successful entrepreneurship is not simple an analytical exercise. Industry and competitor analysis – the application of the theory of industrial organization economics – alone is in-sufficient. The resource-based theory argues that the choice of which industry to enter and what business to be in is not enough to ensure success. The theory says that the nature and quality of the resources, capabilities and strategies the entrepreneur possesses and can acquire can lead to long-term success. These resources are rare, valuable, and hard to copy and have no good substitutes to obtain a sustainable competitive advantage. Choosing the appropriate resources is ultimately a motive of entrepreneurial vision and intuition. Bill Botton and John Thompson define an entrepreneur as a ***"person who habitually creates and innovates to build something of reorganized value around perceived opportunities"***. Among the key behavioural characteristics of an entrepreneur, the most crucial are the talent to perceive an opportunity and his creativity to innovate and build something of value.

The two basic roles of an entrepreneur are:

1. Entrepreneur as an opportunity spotter.
2. Entrepreneur as a project champion.

This suggests that it is not enough for an entrepreneur to perceive an opportunity. He should also be able to nurture it into a creative venture that is developed in to a viable project. We can perceive it as a process that begins with an idea and ends as a profitable project.

Potential of E–Entrepreneur Around the World

Over the last few centuries, human beings have experienced two major revolutions – industrial and electronic. As we enter the 21st century, we are seeing the beginning of a new revolution, namely the net work revolution. It enter connects different parts of the world, enabling the seamless flow of information. The internet is the engine of this revolution and electronic commerce is its fuel.

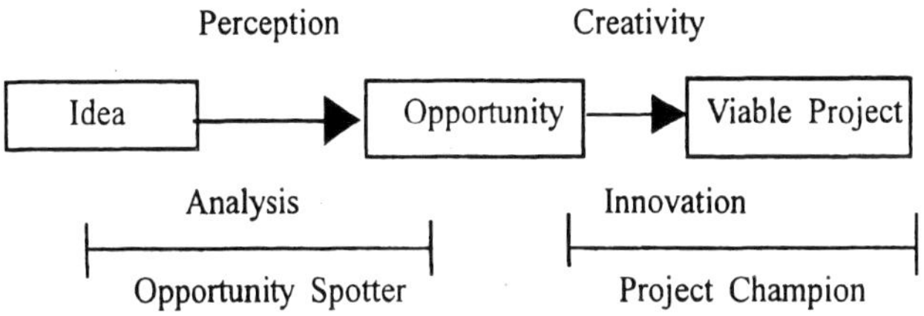

Tables 1 and 2 show the computer infrastructure worldwide. Table 1 reveals that the United States still leads the world in the number of computers in use. Growth rates indicate that the Asia Pacific region and the European Union countries may pass the United States by 2005.

Table 2 show where the greater growth per capita in computers has been and will be. These statistics show that the E-entrepreneur is operating internationally. It is clear that the growth of the e-economy and Internet opportunities will be global and the E-entrepreneurs who possesses some specialized advantage (such as language or contracts) in a particular high growth country will have distinct advantages.

Table 1
Computer in Use Worldwide

Region	1993	2000	2006 estt:
Asia Pacific	25	116	257
European Union	44	135	250
United States	77	159	230
Latin America	3	18	44

Source: *Computer Industry Almanac*, The Wall Street Journal, *World Business*, Sept. 25, 2000.

As shown in Table 3 worldwide internet users increased by 60% from 2002 to 2004. In 2002, one-third of all internet users in the world wide in North America, however, by 2004, North American users was amount for only a quarter of the world's active internet users. In 2004, more internet users are living in Asia pacific countries than in North America. Latin America has just 6% of the world's active internet users in 2004, will experience the greatest percentage increase in growth.

Between 2002 and 2004, the number of Latin American internet users increased by a substantial 84%. Finally, in 2004, Europe which was projected to be home to the largest number of internet users in the world.

Table 2
Growth Rate in Computer

Country	Growth Rate %(1993 – 2000)
China	1052
India	604
Russia	580
Brazil	565
Indonesia	552

Source: *Computer Industry Almanac*, The Wall Street Journal, *World Business*, Sept. 25, 2000.

Table 3
Worldwide Internet Users (in millions)

Country	2000	2001	2002	2003	2004
North America	97.6	114.4	130.8	147.7	160
Europe	70.1	107.8	152.7	206.5	254.9
Asia/Pacific Rim	48.7	63.8	85.4	118.8	173.0
Latin America	9.9	15.3	22.1	31.0	40.8
Africa & Middle East	3.5	5.3	7.2	9.0	10.9
Worldwide Total	229.8	306.6	398.2	513.0	640.2

Source: Adapted from e-Marketer (2004).

Table 4 shows that, the top 10 countries in 2002, in terms of absolute number of users, account for nearly 382 million internet users (72% of all users). Some of the smaller countries, such as Iceland and Sweden, enjoy 50% to 60% internet penetration in their population.

E-Entrepreneurs should research the country's computer, information, internet, and social infrastructures in more detail before selecting specific country targets. The E-Entrepreneur will be everywhere – everywhere there are personal computers, cell phones, or PDAs. language capability and fluency in the local delivery language will be skills that the E-Entrepreneur will need to possess or acquire.

Table 4
Top 10 Countries in Number of Percentage of Internet User

Rank	Country	No. of internet users (millions)	Country	% of population internet users
1	Unites States	149	Iceland	60.1
2.	China	56.6	United States	53.6
3.	Japan	51.3	Hong Kong	54.2
4.	Germany	32.0	Sweden	49.4
5.	United Kingdom	29.0	Norway	48.9
6.	South Korea	16.7	United Kingdom	48.7
7.	Canada	14.2	Switzerland	46.6
8.	France	11.00	Canada	44.9
9.	Italy	11.00	The Neatherlands	42.5
10.	France	11.00	Finland	41.3

Source: www cyberatcas. Internet. Com. (2002).

There are now almost 25 million households in India with part time or a full time home based worker. Working at home certainly has its conveniences and advantages. We do not have to waste hours fighting traffic in order to get work. We can dress casually most of the time. We may set your own schedule, working from 4 P.M. to midnight if that's what's best for us. If the matter is nice we can work on a laptop or make phone calls from our choice lounge on the back deck. A world without borders and boundaries – a world restricted only by our imagination – this is the world of technology.

Liberalization has provided the much-needed boost to the Indian economy. The opening up of the telecom sector in the early 1990s has created a paradigm shift in the way people communicate. The mobile phone population has zoomed ahead of television, stereos and the personal computer. There are over 1.5 billion mobile phone users in the world today, more than three times the number of PCs. India today has the sixth largest telecom network in the world up from 14th in 1995 and the second largest among the emerging economies. It is also the world's 12th biggest telecom network is expected to become the second largest after China in the next five years.

The opening of the cellular market has unleashed a powerful dynamism in market place. Cellular mobile telephone subscribers in India increased from 77,000 in 1995 to 7.3 million by June 2002 to 44.5 million in October 2004 Table 5. This still relatively low compared with the average penetration of about 25% achieved by low income countries and upwards of 50% unit by upper middle income and high income countries. The mobile explosion is helping improve telecom penetration, bring economic benefits of enhanced accessibility, while at the same time generating employment and fostering a facilities like e-health and e-education, video and teleconferencing, e-commerce, telemedicine, distance learning, new job opportunities, skill development.

Table 5
Cell Phone Users (in thousands)

Country	1990	1999
China	18	43240
Egypt	4	465
Finland	226	3445
France	283	21434
Germany	273	23470
India	0	1195
Ireland	25	1400
Israel	15	2800
Japan	868	56849
Sweden	461	5125
United Kingdom	1144	23944
United States	5283	86047

Source: Marc J. Dollinger; *Entrepreneurship–Strategies and Resources*, Pearson Education, Delhi, 2004.

Today, about 60 million mails are sent on the internet everyday. Applications such as distance education and telemedicine are being implemented. Classrooms across the country are connected through the electronic-photonic system. Velya Vahini connects 6000 high schools in seven districts. It provides real time audio and video interactivity.

Lectures can be conducted in 5000 schools simultaneously. Similarly, the linking of hundreds of hospitals is taking the benefit of specialist doctors from cities to small towns. All these developments are transforming the nature and process of business, commerce governance and education in India. An efficient and rapid flow of information is a catalyst for economic and social development. Vision 2020 conceives of India evolving into an information society and knowledge economy e-entrepreneurship will be the spring board.

Table 6
e-Commerce Savings

	Traditional System	Internet	Savings (%)
Airline tickets	$ 8.00	$ 1.00	87%
Banking	$ 1.08	$ 0.13	89%
Bill Payment	$ 2.22 to $ 3.32	$ 0.65 to $ 1.10	71% to 67%
Life Insurance	$ 400 to $ 700	$ 200 to $ 350	50%
Software	$ 15	$ 0.20 to $.0.50	87% to 99%

Basically, the internet has the following potential:

1. It lowers the cost of communication between people and companies and within net works.
2. It lowers the cost of transactions between people and companies and within networks.
3. It lowers the cost of searching for information.
4. It lowers the cost of monitoring transactions and search processes.

The internet is predicted to have the most impact or information – intensive industries such as:

a. Financial Services
b. Entertainment
c. Health Care

d. Education

e. Government

The internet is predicted to have less impact on industries that create, transform or transport some physical entity, including:

a. Retailing

b. Manufacturing

c. Travel

d. Power

These brief analysis suggests that as internet access and use accelerates around the world, so, too, will e-entrepreneurship opportunities, yet where will the greatest challenge be? We believe they will be in countries with emerging economics – countries such as Russia, India, Nepal and China which prompt different and sometimes difficult decisions for e-entrepreneurs.

What is an Entrepreneur?

An entrepreneur is one who creates a new business in the face of risk and uncertainty for the purpose of achieving profit and growth by identifying opportunities and assembling the necessary resources to capitalize on those opportunities. Basically, an entrepreneur is an innovator, job and wealth generator. In addition to the above he is a:

- Change Agent
- Problem Solver
- Pace Setter
- Excellence Seeker
- Marketing Executive
- Concept Promoter

Entrepreneurs are the corner stone of the Indian private enterprise system. They play a leading role in creating and developing new products and services, which results in news business opportunities. Furthermore, entrepreneurs bring together the funds needed to the business, organize and direct it toward goal accomplishment, and often play the leading role in managing the business operation to provide economic goods and services to consumers.

Characteristics of the Typical Entrepreneur

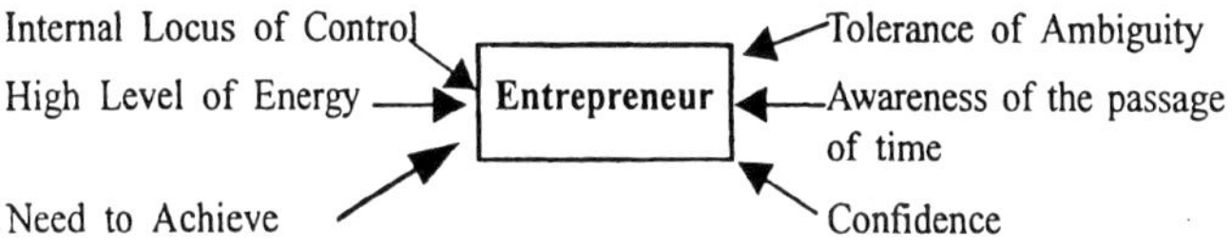

Characteristics of an Entrepreneur

To be a successful entrepreneur, a person has to acquire and develop certain qualities, which can be inculcated by training and motivation. These characteristics often attributed to the entrepreneurs are:

1. Confidence
2. Perseverance, determination
3. Energy, diligence
4. Resourcefulness
5. Ability to take calculated risks
6. Dynamism, leadership
7. Optimism
8. Need to achieve
9. Versatibility, knowledge of product, market, machinery, technology.
10. Creativity
11. Ability to influence others.
12. Ability to get along well with people.
13. Initiative.
14. Flexibility
15. Intelligent.
16. Orientation to cheer goals
17. Positive response to challenges
18. Independence
19. Responsiveness to suggestions and criticism.
20. Time – competence, efficiency.
21. Ability to make decisions quickly.

22. Responsibility.
23. Foresight
24. Accuracy, thoroughness
25. Cooperativeness
26. Profit orientation
27. Ability to learn from mistakes
28. Sense of power.
29. Pleasant personality
30. Eqotism.
31. Courage
32. Imagination
33. Perceptiveness
34. Tolerance for ambiguity
35. Aggressiveness
36. Capacity for enjoyment.
37. Efficacy.
38. Commitment
39. Ability to trust workers
40. Sensitivity to others
41. Honesty, integrity
42. Maturity, balance.

Entrepreneurship has been considered for long as a process primarily aimed at creating ones own business venture, and contributing to economic development and employment generation.

Entrepreneurship is the result of a disciplined, systematic process of applying creativity and innovation to needs and opportunities in the market place. It involves applying focused strategies to new ideas and new insight to create a product or a service that satisfies customer's needs or solves their problems. It is much more than random, disjointed tinkering with a new gadget. Millions of people come up with creative ideas for new or different products and services, most of them, however, never do anything with them. Entrepreneurs are those who marry their creative ideas with the purposeful action and structure of a business. Thus, successful entrepreneurship is a constant process that relies on creativity, innovation, and application in the market place.

Creativity	Innovation	Entrepreneurship
Thinking new things	Doing new things	Creating value in market place.

Who are the E-Entrepreneurs?

Though Electronic Entrepreneur or E-Entrepreneurs in short, is new accepted as one of the most important developments in conducting E-Entrepreneurship business, there is as yet no universally accepted definition. The E-Entrepreneurs are young and ambitious, older and corporate based, international and risk taking dreaming for E-commerce. E-Entrepreneurship is in its infancy but still it is the most popular way for a business to expand its customer base and increase productivity. Every business is found with a site on the web and online shopping has become popular in recent years. With an earth link total commerce package, we can sell our products world wide through our web-based store.

Many E-Entrepreneurs are just like normal entrepreneurs. A recent survey of school placement offices shows that E-commerce start-up are a serious consideration for business school graduates at some of the United States' most prestigious business school. Although consulting and banking are still more popular, start-ups have their attractions to many newly minted B-School graduates.

E-Entrepreneurs involved following features:

- Online point-of-sale and transaction processing
- Web retailing and wholesaling
- Electronic Data Interchange (EDI)
- Electronic Fund Transfer
- Electronic Banking
- Interactive Marketing and
- Supplying Chain Management

E-Entrepreneurs collaborate some systems they are:

- Electronic Mail
- Voice Mail
- Discussion Forums
- Data Conferencing
- Video Conferencing
- Electronic Meeting Systems.

Most of the E-Entrepreneurs are high degree of risk bearer. They are dedicated to their businesses and to the life of E-Entrepreneurship. E-Entrepreneurship is a worldwide phenomenon. Japanese E-Entrepreneur, Sonny Koike even after the internet bubble had burst, Sonny's business continued to flourish. The e-biz, 25 is an annual listing of the top E-Entrepreneurs published by business week's e-biz magazine. Listed these most powerful people by their achievement and contribution to their industry, and aspiring E-Entrepreneurs would be well served to know their names, study their business, and monitor future developments. Clearly, technological resources are valuable in the start-up and running of the e-commerce business. Many of these firms' basis for existing rests on their technological abilities. E-Entrepreneurs who promise technological adeptness and cutting-edge technology products, and cannot deliver, are simply doomed.

The challenges for E-Entrepreneur in India:

- Language barrier.
- Internet connectivity is very slow and access costs are still very high.
- High legal and regulatory barriers.
- Poor telecom and communications infrastructure for reliable connectivity.
- High illiteracy rate.
- PCs and other devices to access the net for individuals are less than 1%.
- Telephone line penetration is limited to less than 3% of the population.

Conclusion

The E-Entrepreneur needs scanning and analyse to spot opportunity. Some opportunity will depend on local knowledge of language, custom and network of contracts. The other opportunity may be constrained by industry and economic forces that remain unchangeable for the E-Entrepreneur. However, entrepreneurs who are well prepared culturally have an advantage. Those that enter industries where the primary focus is formation, not some physical product, may expect the best results. It has opened new vistas to the entrepreneur in India and the real success depend upon the effort and attitude of business units as well as consumer to make use of opportunity by availing the protection and security measures provided in the IT act.

NOTES AND REFERENCES

1. The Economist, (2000), *E-Commerce – Shopping Around the Web*, London, February and March.
2. Dollinger, Marc J, (2004), *Entrepreneurship – Strategies and Resources*, Pearson Education, New Delhi.
3. Strauss, Judy, (2003), E-*Marketing, Pearson Education*, New Delhi,
4. David H. Holt, (2003), *Entrepreneurship – New Venture Creation*, Prentice-Hall, New Delhi.
5. Murthy, C.S.U., (2003), *E-Commerce-Concept – Models, Strategies*, Himalaya Publishing House, New Delhi.

16

INFORMATION NEEDS OF THE SMALL SCALE INDUSTRIES: Prospects of E-Commerce in Manipur

LAIRENLAKPAM SHANTA MEITEI
THOIDINGJAM PURNIMA DEVI

Introduction

The industrial revolution of the last era gave some countries the status of a developed economy, the information of the current era is transforming the whole of society into a single borderless entity. As we step into the new millennium's new century and recount what Information Technology (IT) in the field of information revolution has contributed, all of us those who know about it can visualise its wonderful or tremendous challenges and opportunities. In this stage our success in the new millennium, therefore, would lie not only in capitalizing on the available opportunity, but more important on the context to which we can convert the challenges into opportunities to ensure a win-win situation. Today we draw upon the Internet to communicate with thousands of people in a few seconds. There is also Intermedia (merger of internet with multimedia), net Fusion (merger of network with object), and web DB (merger of web computing with Database) etc. Business today is conducted through Electronic Commerce (e-commerce) or e- business; Government operations through e- governance; education and learning are through e-education.

Information has become an essential ingredient for the progress of civilization and society for all the times. Lack of information transfer and its effective means of communication are now widely recognised as being limiting factors in socio-economic development of the people. Basically, small scale industries constitute an integral part of our national economy, and play an important role in the economic development of our country. The small scale establishments are acting as ancillaries in the course of development planning and are playing an important role in establishing the country's economy. Identification of information needs and the sources of obtained information regarding production, marketing, emerging new technology and technical know-how etc are important if one has to plan for the development of such industries. Keeping the above facts in view, a survey was conducted during my research work on the Community Information Needs by the rural people. A part of this study, specially the information needs of the small scale industry in the rural areas of valley districts of Manipur as a case study has been taken up.

Objectives of the study

- To study the information needs of the people who are engaged in small scale industries;
- To examine the use of information channels and information sources of the persons who are engaged in small scale industries;
- To examine if the people have knowledge of IT, computer literacy, and information literacy and if not the problem faced thereby;
- To study and identify the possible areas of application of e-commerce to the service centers of small scale industries; and
- To indicate the prospects of e-commerce in Manipur.

Methodology

For the present study a questionnaire was designed for the rural community of the villages of valley districts of Manipur and distributed during 2003-04, interviewed the representatives of the villages including heads of the villages, specially the Adhyaksha, Pradhan, Up-pradhan of panchayat and villagers particularly those who are engaged in small scale industries of the rural areas. It covered 116 persons through simple random sampling method, of the 116 questionnaires distributed 104 were received. The data thus obtained were analysed to draw the conclusions.

Observation

For speedy growth of small scale industries, the Government has already brought about simplifications in the SSI registration procedures. By the end of March, 2003, the numbers of registered permanent small scale industries both SIDO (Small Industries Development Organization) and NON SIDO stood at 9,852 with an investment of Rs. 37.73 crores in plants and machineries and providing employment to 51,122 persons where annual production was estimated to be Rs. 168.84 crores. A total of 108 manufacturing units are found registered in Manipur during 2002-2003. Among the districts, Imphal West district has the highest number of registered industrial (SIDO & NON SIDO) units with 31 (28.70%), followed by Bishnupur with 24 (22.23%) units. The lowest was recorded in Senapati and Tamenglong districts having only 2 (1.85%) each. The district wise SIDO and NON SIDO break-up of industrial units, employment, investment and production during 2002-2003 at four valley district of Manipur are presented in Table 1.

Distribution of Respondents by Age and Sex

Table 2 indicates that, of the 104 respondents, there were 75 (72.11%) males and 29 (27.89%) females. The distribution of respondents by age and sex (Table 2) showed that maximum of males belonged to the age group of 21-25 years (26 i.e. 25.00%), followed by the age group of 26-35 years (22 i.e. 21.15%) whereas maximum females belonged to below 20 years (12 i.e. 11.54%), followed by the age group 21-25 years (8 i.e. 7.69%).

Distribution of Respondents by Educational Attainments

The educational level of the respondents was categorized into: (i) under matric, (ii) matric level, (iii) secondary level, (iv) graduate, and (v) post graduate level. The distribution of respondents according to their educational attainment is provided in Table 3, which showed that maximum number of males (28 i.e. 26.92%) were educated upto secondary level while maximum number of females (13 i.e. 12.50%) studied upto matric level. Twenty five (24.04%) males studied up to

Table 1

District-Wise Distribution of SIDO and NON-SIDO Industrial Units (Employment, Investment, and Production at Four Valley Districts of Manipur)

Sl. No.	District	No. of Units			No. of Employment			Investment (Rs. in crores)			Production (Rs in crores)		
		SIDO	Non-SIDO	Total	SIDO	Non-SIDO	Total	SIDO	Non-SIDO	Total	SIDO	Non-SIDO	Total
1	Imphal West	26	5	31	173	49	222	0.47	0.10	0.57	2.79	0.36	3.15
2	Imphal East	12	5	17	120	22	142	0.53	0.07	0.60	1.32	0.10	1.42
3.	Bishnu-pur	21	3	24	174	18	192	0.14	0.01	0.15	0.80	0.03	0.83
4.	Thoubal	11	2	13	56	23	79	0.07	0.01	0.08	0.18	0.52	0.70
	Total:	70	15	85	523	112	635	1.21	0.19	1.40	5.09	1.01	6.10

Source: Commerce & Industries Department, Government of Manipur, Imphal, 2003.

matric level whereas nine (8.65%) females under matric level and remaining other figures were indicated in the following Table .3.

Table 2

Distribution of Respondents by Age and Sex

Age group	Males		Females	
	No.	%	No.	%
Below 20	7	6.73	12	11.54
21-25	26	25.00	8	7.69
26-35	22	21.15	5	4.81
36-55	18	17.31	4	3.85
56 Above	2	1.92	-	-
Total:	75	72.11	29	27.89

Source: Questionnaire.

Table 3

Distribution of Respondents by Educational Attainments

Status	Males		Females	
	No.	%	No.	%
Under matric level	12	11.54	9	8.65
Matric level	25	24.04	13	12.50
Secondary level	28	26.92	5	4.81
Graduate level	7	6.73	2	1.92
Post graduate level	3	2.89	-	-
Total:	75	72.12	29	27.88

Source: Questionnaire.

Information Needs of the SSIs Units

Table 4 shows that, 73.08% of respondents need information on raw materials which is maximum amount of percentage of response, followed by 70.19% of respondents need information on market facilities and its current prices of the products, new arrival of the products, expected demand for their products and services. 65.38% of respondents need information credits system, loans, subsidies of the raw materials and need financial assistance from different financial institutions.. 54.81% of respondents required information on maintenance and repair of the tools/ products and many of them need information regarding the design, technique, quality and quantity of the products. 50.00% of respondents required information on skills of the manpower, experience, improvement, replacement of defective tools and handling the tools. And 47.12% respondents need information on import and exports facilities including agencies, taxes, transactions, transportation and communication information.

Table 4
Information Needs of the SSIs

Sl. No.	Information Needs	No. of respondents	% of respondents
1.	Information on Raw materials (availability of raw materials, readily available in the fields or markets etc.)	76	73.08
2.	Information on Maintenance/production (design, technique, quality, quantity etc.)	57	54.81
3.	Information on Markets (new market area, current prices, demand, services etc.)	73	70.19
4.	Information on Manpower/Machine/tools (skills, experience, improvement, handling, replacement of defective tools etc.)	52	50.00
5.	Information on Credit System/Loan/Subsidy	68	65.38
6.	Information on Imports and Export (agencies name, transportation, taxes, transaction, Communication etc.).	49	47.12

Note: Percentage is more than 100 because of multiple choices.
Source: Questionnaire.

Use of Information Channels/Sources by the Respondents

In order to find out the main information providers regarding the availability of raw material, improvement of defective tools, maintenance/ repair of tools, about new market areas/ prices/ demands, credit/ subsides/ taxes/ transaction, each respondent was asked to mention the sources of information to solve such problems or to get fuller understanding of them. They were also asked to mention those sources which they had either consulted earlier or proposed to consult them in the future. The sources of information were categorized into 9 broad head which is provided in Table 5, which showed that, important information providers regarding availability/non-availability of raw material were self/ personal experience (72.12%), followed by fellow professionals (68.27%), mass media including print and electronic media (63.46%), family members (50.00%).

Improvement and replacement of defective tools, the most important information source was the shopkeeper (69.23%), followed by fellow professionals (66.35%), friends, neighbours, relatives (36.54%).

On maintenance and repair of tools, the most important sources of information was self/personal experience (75.00%), followed by fellow professionals (74..04%) while on new markets it was the friends, neighbours, relatives (72.12%), followed by mass media (52.89%), and on credit system/ taxes it was mass media (53.85%), followed by fellow-professionals (49.04%).

Opinion about the use of IT, E-Commerce

The respondents were requested to indicate their awareness about the use of IT, and E-Commerce, whether the peoples were aware about the new emerging technique and technologies or not, which is (shown) in the following table no.6. 72 (69.23%) of respondents were not aware about the IT, knowledge of computer literacy and access to internet. 86 (82.69%) of respondents were willing to receive IT based E-commerce services and 70 (67.31%) of respondents did not understand the idea and knowledge of E-Commerce or e-business services.

Application of E-Commerce and Prospects in Manipur

Overview

The most talked about phenomenon on the Internet today is e-commerce. Everyone wants a piece of this pie. They will sell books,

Table 5
Use of Information Channels/Sources by the Respondents

Sl. No.	Channels/Sources	Availability/ of raw materials		Improvement/ replacement of defective tools		Maintenance/ repair of tools		New market areas/ prices/demands/ services		Credit system/ Subsidies/ taxes	
		No.	%	No.	%	No.	%	No.	%	No.	%
1.	Self/personal experience	75	72.12	33	31.73	78	75.00	42	40.38	36	34.62
2.	Friends, neighbours, relatives	48	46.15	38	36.54	38	36.54	75	72.12	30	28.85
3.	Family members	52	50.00	27	25.96	36	34.62	47	45.19	31	29.81
4.	Fellow professionals	71	68.27	69	66.35	77	74.04	43	41.35	51	49.04
5.	Market/Shopkeeper	50	48.08	72	69.23	46	44.23	53	50.96	47	45.19
6.	Block/panchayat office	22	21.15	7	6.73	3	2.88	5	4.81	6	5.77
7.	Library & Information Centres	5	4.81	2	1.92	2	1.92	3	2.89	2	1.92
8.	CICs/DICs	6	5.77	3	2.89	2	1.92	4	3.85	3	2.89
9.	Mass media	66	63.46	30	28.85	27	25.96	55	52.89	56	53.85

Note: Percentage is more than 100 because of multiple choices.
Source: Questionnaire.

music, software, toys, flowers, food, cloth, cosmetics everything you want. It is all on-line. So the word Electronic Commerce and Internet are used widely. E-Commerce involves much more than simply selling large volumes of mass market products over the web. It also deals with butting and selling of goods and services on the Net. This involves both business-to-business (B2B) and business to customer (B2C) transaction. E-business embraces e-commerce, including Internet based communication and web enabled business process. E-commerce save a lot of time, energy and manpower. It is also a boon for businessmen who are in interaction with business online. We can define E-commerce as "It is a business on the Net".

Table 6
Use of IT, E-Commerce by the People

Sl. No	IT based E-Commerce Services	No. of respondents with percentage		Total Percentage
		Yes	No	
1.	Awareness about IT, knowledge of computer handling, & Internet access	32 (30.77%)	72 (69.23%)	100
2.	Knowledge of E-Commerce or E-Business	34 (32.69%)	70 (67.31%)	100
3.	Willingness to receive IT based E-Commerce Services	86 (82.69%)	18 (17.31%)	100

Source: Questionnaire.

During the last decade, e-technology or e-activities (e-learning, e-communities, e-commerce, e-management, e-marketing, e-governance, tele-working etc) has developed (at a fast rate) in the new millennium and it is considered as one of the essentials of human life. Electronic equipment like 'computer, e-typewriter, e-watches, wireless telephone and so on has developed with unimaginable speed, India has taken very powerful steps towards e-world which was heralded by the new millenium. While global market continue to be lucrative the domestic market is also growing by leaps and bounds. India is strongly positioned to benefit from the wave of electronic industrial and social restructuring.

Manipur is one of the states in the North-Eastern Region of India. According to the 2001 Census, the population of Manipur is 23,88634. Out of the total population of Manipur 76.12% are living in the villages while only 23.88% live in urban areas with more than 50% of them illiterate and 30% of the population falling below the poverty line. In a State like Manipur with agro-based rural economy, small scale industries play a vital role in the economic development of the state. More particularly its role in rural development is significant because of the importance of agriculture in the rural economy. Small Scale Industry (SSI) help to improve the state income and lead to an equitable distribution of the same among different sectors and regions in the economy and it can play a very important role in industrial development and solving unemployment problems in the state of Manipur.

Therefore, it is necessary to implement the SSI units in Manipur with the emerging Information and Communication Technology (ICT) facilities along with the electronic financial transaction, online payment for services or products delivered to the customer, marketing online while delivery or payment of the service or product is made offline, and online promotion encourages people to visit your institution and pay an admission fees or a voluntary contribution.

Application

Considering the importance of information to our academic purposes and our day to day work, there is great need to start efficient information dissemination services in libraries, by identifying information needs to the users. Taking into consideration the library as a service oriented industry or enterprise, the application of e-commerce in library services and operations would serve well. E-commerce can be applied in Academic, Public and Special libraries. Generally academic library means the library which is attached to academic institutions. Any library can start transaction once the delivery mechanism, collection methodology and back office are in place. Further, to step into e-commerce in the library environment, the infrastructure i.e. Internet is to be established which means overall organization structure should be designed to facilitate a networking mode of functioning.

Road map to consider when developing an e-commerce strategy:

- Determine the library's primary goals in relation to e-commerce.
- Study how others have met this goal.

- Assess the technical capabilities and need to train digital workers.
- What are the monetary realities and what is the budget for setting up an e-commerce strategy.
- Examine legal issues-intellectual property, taxation, privacy, advertising etc.

The functions and services of e-commerce can also be applied in State and District Information Centres situated in different locations of Manipur State. This will be done with the coordination efforts and sharing of information and networks facilities among the Government agencies like NICNET and their State Informatics Centre/Districts Informatics Centres along with the State/ Districts Information Centres for the benefit of the users specially those who are working in the SSIs units.

The Community Information Centres (CICs) is also one of such centre which will provide various facilities regarding the IT, internet access, advertisement and sales of rural products particularly agricultural and small scale industries products on internet. The CICs and other information centres will provide the tele-trading for selling agricultural and its allied products including small scale industries products on Internet.

Moreover, the Government agencies should take more responsibility In organizing and establishing a well IT based E-commerce service centres by providing the appropriate tools and support in the rural areas of Manipur State.

Prospects

Technologies especially computer and telecommunication have greatly revolutionized in the field of business activities and giving rise to a new aspect called E-Commerce or E-Business. The explosive growth in network connectivity and rapid advances in computing power to the functions and activities of business environment has dramatically changed over the last decades.

But, due to lack of infrastructural and manpower facilities there is lack of IT awareness among the peoples, the construction and establishment of well IT based E-Commerce Industries in the state of Manipur is still lagging behind. Besides these, Manipur has been facing many problems due to transportation and communication facilities being very poor. There is shortage of power supply. Flow of institutional finance is negligible in Manipur. Recovery rate of loan sanctioned by the banks and financial institutions is very poor. There is no proper industrial policy of the Government which is suitable for the growth of SSIs. Due to law and order problems, investment environment gets endangered and looks unattractive and there is no Foreign Direct Investment as well as lack of resource inventory and competitive production technology has greatly influenced the creation and management of a well Entrepreneurship Development and IT Industries in the state of Manipur.

However, in the small scale sector in Manipur, there is prospect for IT based E-commerce industries like mechanical, electronic, glass and ceramic, auto-parts components and ancillaries, transport equipment, paper products, plastic products, lime products, rubber products, citronella oil, stationary items oka ink, electrical units, dairy products, bakery units, leather and tanneries etc. The indigenous secondary sector chiefly consist of handicraft, reed, cane and bamboo wearing, pottery, embroidery, agricultural implements and aluminium utensils. There is a need to strengthen and modernize cluster of traditional industries to make them vibrant market and quality savvy, finished goods with high consumer demand made from locally available raw materials should be encouraged and should give the concept of IT based E-commerce awareness programmes to the people, particularly in the rural areas of the of Manipur.

Implied Suggestions

The view and comments offer by the people of the villagers and persons those who were working in SSIs units of the state of Manipur have enabled the investigators to offer some feasible suggestions. They are the followings:

1. The present study has seriously considered the lack of proper information service centres at the village level; rural people particularly, those who are working/engaged in SSIs units are not getting/aware of the information of their needs. Majority of the people lack of knowledge in the use of new ICT facilities specially e-commerce services. This will lead to the slow development of the rural mass. Hence, it urges the state

government to implement the proper industrial policy which is suitable for the growth of SSIs.

2. The network would progressively have to be extended to all the villages or at least the larger villages for the promotion and motivation of the people to use and access information which they require. The type of Multipurpose Community Telecentres developed by the International Telecommunication Union (ITU) in rural areas of the Rajkot District of Gujarat can be used as an example
3. Extensive IT awareness programmes would have to be extended at the village level through panchayat and community education programmes.
4. It is suggested that the different educational institutions and government agencies of the state can provide all the technical skills necessary for the content creation and management of the IT industries in the state of Manipur.
5. It is suggested that the information centres, community information centres, libraries etc. should have content preparation programmes including continuous updation based on new technologies. Content preparation requires the knowledge of the subject, knowledge of the concerned rural areas so as to make the content area specific, knowledge of the local dialects and the terminologies used so as to communicate better and the basic knowledge of creation of multimedia packages. The network would progressively have to be extended to all the villages.
6. State Institutes of Rural Development (SIRD) and Directorate of Industries & Commerce (DIC) should be strengthened, and National Institute of Rural Development (NIRD) is an apex and all the rural development libraries at the base should form a pyramidal structure of grid system. Further, all the educational institutions, research centres, public libraries, information centres and community information centres should also integrate their coordination and cooperation with the village libraries at the local level. This will build the infrastructure in the rural areas and state as whole.
7. Government should pen down a State Policy of Small Scale Industries and State Information Literacy Policy, to make

knowledge based society and where information should reach to all the section of the society.

It is known fact that without a computer networking system we cannot walk into the 21st century.

Conclusion

By adopting the above road map the investigator strongly felt that institutions and government agencies of the state can play a major role in bridging the information gap for the rural population of the state in this era of IT, using computer and internet, they can transmit local relevant knowledge and information in all areas such as agriculture, small scale industries, live stock management, water management, waste management, health, career guidance etc. to different population segments in rural areas. While conducting the survey, it is strongly felt that, entrepreneurs in rural/remote areas need market information, such as current prices and expected demand for their products availability of raw materials in the market and services, e.g. agricultural products, small scale industries products, fish products, handicrafts, natural resources, tourism, and transport and to reach of with information about these products. Easy access to government information, such as records of property ownership and transaction, and information about taxes and subsidies, would help business to develop in rural areas. Good data communication facilities would enable city based IT industries enterprises to establish virtual offices for tele-workers in rural areas. Community-owned networks, using computer mediated conferences and bulletin boards, provide powerful tools for generating and sustaining local business and social initiative. All of this will contribute to reversing the current trend of urbanization, IT based E-commerce services and to reducing pollution.

NOTES AND REFERENCES

1. Balliarsingh R.K. and Mahapatra, M., (1988), Reading Interests Among Adult Literates in a Semi Urban Community of Orissa, *Annals of Library Science and Documentation*. Vol.35,
2. *Census of India*, 2001.
3. *Economic Survey Manipur*, (2002-2003), Directorate of Economics and Statistics. Government of Manipur.
4. Multipurpose Community Telecentres–The Rajkot Project (1998), *Today and Tomorrow*, Vol. 17, 3, 22-23.

5. Musib, S.K., (1991), Information Needs of the Cottage Industries: A Survey Report. *CLIS Observer*. 8(2):14-17.
6. Prasain, G.P., (2004), *Small Scale Industries in Manipur: Problems and Prospects. Dimensions of Rural Development in North-East India*, Akansha Publishing House, 128-137.
7. Sangam, S.L., and Keshava (2001), Application of E-Commerce in Libraries. *Indian Journal of Information, Library and Society*. 14(1-2):1-8.
8. Veeranjaneyulu, K., and Sudharani, D.V., (2000), Information Sources and Services for Rural Development. *Indian Journal of Information, Library and Society*. 13(3-4):123-126.
9. http:// www.rirdc.org.

17

ENTREPRENEURSHIP AND INFORMATION TECHNOLOGY IN MIZORAM

R.K.P.G. SINGHA
K.C. KABRA

Introduction

Economic development through expansion of Industrial base is the most vital issue these days and an entrepreneur is an essential key inputs for qualitative industrial development of a country. Entrepreneurship being associated with natures human resource is different from other material resources of the key inputs plays a premium mobile role in promoting industrial development of an economy. In a way, differences in the levels of economic development across the countries and among the regions within a country may be attributed to the differences in levels of their entrepreneurship attainment. Again, "entrepreneur precedes entrepreneurship". Entrepreneur is the person who tries very hard to find out new opportunities, new techniques, new lines of production, new products and co-ordinates all other peripheral activities. An entrepreneur is the leader who takes all initiatives to start a risky venture. It can be said that entrepreneurs constitute an important and most valuable human resource of a nation.

In India, entrepreneurship development has been considered as a strategy for achieving the twin goal of solving the present burning problem of unemployment particularly among the educated youths and also for rapid industrialisation. It may be said that entrepreneurship and economy go side by side and bears the relationship of cause and effect. One can sum up it as "an economy is the effect for which entrepreneurship is the cause". In the present day, the economic progress of any country, or state or district can be achieved only through a systematic Industrial Development. This is an unchallengeable fact in today's context. Following this, to promote and foster industrial and economic development particularly in remote, backward, and undeveloped areas, the entrepreneurship development has become a subject of great concern and is in serious discussion these days.

The present educational system in India and particularly the North-East lacks to a great extent in inculcating entrepreneurship among the youths. The North-Eastern Region (NER) with its vast resource base has virtually remained industrially and economically backward. . Further, the level of industrial advancement within the region varies from state to state just because of complete absence of entrepreneurship in general. Year after year the region has to import large number of mass consumption goods from rest of the country.

It was Assam which initiated entrepreneurship development at first in November 1973 by setting Entrepreneurial Motivation Training Centres (EMTCs) at district level which rose to 9 in number as against 6 in the beginning. EMTCs merged with DIC, Assam, in 1999 followed by other N-E states. Later, during the last three decades, Small Industries Service Institute (SISI), North-Eastern Industrial and Technical Consultancy Organisation (NEITCO), North-Eastern Consultants Ltd. (NECON), National Small Industries Corporation (NSIC) and Indian Institute of Entrepreneurship (IIE) were established and made responsible for spread of entrepreneurship in the region. So far, nothing significant could be achieved in this regard, and the situation remains more or less stagnant.

In the present article, an attempt has been made to assess the performance and progress achieved so far in respect of entrepreneurship development in Mizoram. Besides, an effort also made to discuss the problems, prospects, government's support, institutional initiatives and necessary infrastructural support to uplift the entrepreneurship development in the state. The data/results presented in this article are drawn from various sources such as North-Eastern Consultant Limited

(NECON), Small Industries Service Institute (SISI), Directorate of Industries (DI) located at Aizawl in Mizoram.

Entrepreneurship Development

Coming to Mizoram, the status as regards to entrepreneurship development is not different than any other N-E states rather it is yet to occupy a place on the industrial map of India as it is still identified as "no industry area" at national level. Among the industries of Mizoram, barring one or two medium scale industries, only small scale, tiny village, cottage, handloom and handicrafts industries are dominating with very little capital investment. Till today, not even single large scale industry exists in Mizoram.

The reason for such a grim situation prevailing over the whole state may be attributed to historical reasons and to some extent political and social causes, lack of entrepreneurship as well as future vision and acuteness of job scarcity; it did not make any headway in the field of Industrial development in the land-locked state of Mizoram as it is clear from the high ratio of government jobs in proportion to total population of the state. The authors believe that the people are inclined to white color jobs. However, the employment situation in Mizoram becoming acute day by day causing changes in scenario. Agriculture being not in position to bear increased population load combined with no industrial development so far and saturation in government jobs as prevailed earlier making the employment scenario grimmer. Something is to be done immediately before the situation takes 'U' turn. To us, the only solution to the problem is making rapid growth in entrepreneurs. It is a challenge lying ahead of policy makers responsible for economic development and institutions imparting higher and technical education in particular and society itself in general as there is a need to change the mind set of coming generation. Their horizons are to be opened up by bringing change in their thought.

In view of the above situation, under the Department of Industries, Government of Mizoram, various training programmes are being conducted for promotion of industrial environment in the state. These include:

1. One-year artisan course in handloom weaving at Weaving Training Centre at Aizawl, Lunglei and Saiha.
2. Six month training in knitting and tailoring at craft centres

at Aizawl, Lunglei, Saiha, Champhai and in Cane and Bamboo craft at Hnathial, Haulawng and Diltlang.

3. One-year certificate course in blacksmithy, wireman, carpentary, tinsmithy, auto-mechanic, turner and welding and foundry.
4. One-year PC hardware maintenance course and one year diploma in computer

Science at Golden Republic IT Centre, Aizawl and DOEACC "O" level course, COEACC "A" level Course and Repair and Maintenance of Consumer Electronics Course at Academic of Computer and Electronics Centre at Lunglei.

In addition to the above, awareness campaigns, entrepreneurship development programmes are also conducted at intervals in collaboration with agencies like NECON, SISI, IIE etc. and some entrepreneurs are also sponsored for in-plant training outside state.

Table 1 discloses the year-wise training programmes conducted on weaving at various training centres in Mizoram including the number of participants from 1990-91 to 2001-02. It depicts that the number of participants were more or less same at respective centres during the period of the study. Further, it shows that these programmes were not conducted on large scale yet the results may be considered encouraging. It also discloses the year-wise number of programmes and participants in the training programme on knitting and tailoring at various crafts centres in Mizoram from 1990-91 to 2001-02 as conducted by the Department of Industries, Government of Mizoram. As is envisaged, the number of participants in all the three craft centres has recorded a marginal increase over the period of the study. The participants have shown interest in the training programme, which may be considered encouraging. However, the year-wise total number of participants on training programmes of cane and bamboo crafts are reducing from 1990-91 to 2000-01. The cases of Haulawng and Hnahthial are noteworthy in this regard, which is not a good sign from industrial prospectives Table 1.

Coming to the ED programmes conducted by SISI which was opened in 1973 as a part of Small Industries Development Organisation (SIDO), an apex body under the Ministry of Small Scale Industry, Government of India, which show a mixed trend as far as the participants' ED is concerned (Table 2). The Branch SISI works in close cooperation with State Government, Zoram Industrial Development Corporation Ltd.

Table 1

Various Training Programmes Conducted by Directorate of Industries, Mizoram

	Weaving craft training[1] programme No. of participants			Knitting and tailoring[2] training programme No. of participants			Cane and bamboo crafts[2] training programme No. of participants		
	Aizawl	Lungli	Saiha	Aizawl	Lunglei	Champhai	Diltang	Haulawng	Hnathial
1990-91	18	14	05	37	29	40	30	20	20
1991-92	14	17	07	39	28	39	30	20	10
1992-93	19	15	11	42	37	36	30	20	-
1993-94	22	13	06	39	36	40	31	20	-
1994-95	22	15	06	36	38	40	23	20	20
1995-96	14	18	05	39	31	39	24	09	06
1996-97	30	17	06	34	32	39	30	05	18
1997-98	19	18	06	51	42	47	-	13	18
1998-99	12	14	01	49	41	48	-	10	-
1999-00	14	09	06	59	43	50	27	-	08
2000-01	12	10	08	52	46	47	25	01	06
2001-02	-	-	-	47	45	52	-	-	-

Note: [1]1 year programme. [2]6 Months programme.

Source : Directorate of Industries, Government of Mizoram, Aizawl.

(ZIDCO), District Industries Centre (DIC) and other agencies concerned with promotion, development and modernisation of small scale industries in Mizoram. It conducts various training programmes such as:

- Entrepreneurship Development Programme (EDP).
- Managerial Development Programme (MDP).
- Export Packaging Training Programme (EPTP).
- Skill Development Programme (SDP).

Table 2 discloses the various EDPs conducted so far by Branch SISI, Aizawl to educate unemployed youths of the state for self-employment.

Table 2
EDPs Conducted by Branch Small Industries Service Institute, Aizawl

Year	Name of programme	Duration	No. of participants
1997-98	Motivation Campaign	1 day	62
	EDP	1 month	26
	EDP	1 month	30
1998-99	EDP	1 month	
1999-00	EDP	1 month	38
	EDP	1 month	32
2000-01	EDP	1 month	51
	Motivation Campaign	1 day	Mass Participation
2001-02	EDP	1 month	21
2002-03	EDP	1 month	34
	EDP	1 month	
	Motivation Campaign	1 day	88
2003-05	EDP	1month	18
	Motivation Campaign	1day	Mass Participation

Legend: EDP = Entrepreneurship Development Programme.
Source: Branch Small Industries Service Institute, Aizawl.

The table reveals that the branch SISI has been conducting various EDPs at various places in Mizoram for the common good of new generation entrepreneurs. The number of participants has shown a fluctuating trend rather than rising is a cause of concern.

On the similar lines the North-Eastern Consultants Ltd. (NECON) is also committed to the entrepreneurship development programmes and present a series of programmes for different target groups, e.g. educated unemployed youths, engineering graduates and diploma holders, science graduates, women, ex-servicemen and PMRY beneficiaries.

With a view to provide industrial consultancy, assistance and professional services to tiny/rural/cottage/small and medium scale enterprises a Branch of NECON was established on 21st November, 1989 at Aizawl. It also helps voluntary organisations for establishment of socio-economic development activities suitable in their locality.

Table 3 exhibits the EDPs conducted by NECON. The table reveals that NECON has conducted various programmes for various target groups covering a wide area in the state which may be considered very encouraging.

Besides, it undertakes Appraisal of Projects and Techno Economic Viability, prepares State Industrial Profile, provides Economic Information Service, and has also undertaken Industrial Potential Survey to identify feasible SSIs. These are as follows:

Scope of Entrepreneurship Development

The scope of EDP in Mizoram can be enormous. In fact, EDP can substantially boost the economy and manpower in the state. As per the survey made by NECON, Aizawl, the state harbours various industries such as consumer based, local resource based, capital good,, ceramic and engineering based industries covering a diverse variety of products Table 4.

Enterprenuership Potentials in Information Technology

Development of information technology ensures accelerated employment. Mizoram its very high literacy has significant potential in this field. High literacy intricate capabilities work force is as reflected in their traditional fine handloom products of the state, pleasant and agreeable climate of the Mizoram are all conducive for the development of electronics. The only need is to train them properly by giving exposure to modern computers, computer programming and designing. Zoram Electronic Corporation Ltd. (ZENICS) and DEOACC may take lead

Table 3
ED Programme Conducted by NECON, Aizawl

Place	1991-92	1992-93	1993-94	1994-95	1995-96	1996-97	1997-98	1998-99	1999-00	2000-01	2001-02
Aizawl	75	-	-	25	25	25 (w)	25	25	45	5(w)	41,25(w)
Champhai	25	-	-	25	-	25	-	-	-	-	25
Hnathial	-	25	-	-	-	-	-	-	-	—	-
Kolasib	25	-	-	25	-	-	25	-	-	28	-
Lunglei	50	-	-	-	-	-	-	25(w)	25	25(w)	-
Lungsen	-	-	25	-	-	-	-	-	-	-	-
Mamit	-	-	-	-	-	-	-	-	-	-	25
Ratu	-	-	-	-	-	-	-	28	-	-	-
Serchhip	-	-	30	-	-	-	-	-	-	-	25
Saiha	25	-	-	-	-	-	-	-	-	-	-
Tlabung	-	30	-	-	-	-	-	-	-	-	-
Thingsei	-	30	-	-	-	-	-	-	-	-	-
Thenzawl	-	30	-	-	-	-	-	-	-	-	-
Thingsulthlia	-	-	-	-	-	-	-	-	-	-	27(w)
Vairabi	-	-	30	-	-	-	-	-	-	-	-

Note: w: Women
Source: Compiled from various Reports of NECON, Aizawl Branch.

Table 4
Different Industries of Significance and their Products

Industries type	Product component
Consumer based	Plastic injected moulded components, Polythene carry bags, poly-packs etc., Hawai chappals from rubber, Detergent powder, Washing soaps, Vim powder, vessel cleaning chemicals, Paper bags, envelopes, Exercise notebooks, Bags for school children, Paper pins, Stapler pins, Office gum and pastes, Office file covers, File pads, tags etc., Ready mixed paints, varnish, thinner, Wood polish, fence polish etc.
Local Resource based	Wooden furniture, wooden handicrafts, Wooden doors and windows, Wooden rulers, graduated scale, Handmade pencils, Cane furniture, bamboo crafts, and baskets, Wooden packing box, packing materials etc., Tent poles, bamboo ladders, Agarbatty sticks, dhoop, Artistic photo frames, trays etc.
Capital good based	A full-fledged ferrous foundry unit to produce castings, and to the repairments of other SSI's A machine tool industry to manufacture machine tool accessories and small machines like drilling machine, hand saw machine, grinder etc.
Ceramic based	Light roofing sheet, Cement, mosaic-flooring tiles, Chemical porcelain wares, Tile, Glass mirror, polishing unit, Salt, glazed pipes, Printing ink, ball pen ink, Manufacture of phenyl, deodorant, Re-cycling and reclamation of used lube oil, Leaf cups and plates, Hospital equipment and absorbent, cotton, bandage etc.
Engineering based	CI sluice valves, wheel valves, pipe fittings, Manufacture of PVC pipes, Special purpose fasteners, Manufacture of slotted angles, Mild steel electrodes, Trailers, trolleys etc. GLS lamps and miniature lamps, Milk chilling plant etc.

role in providing software development facility ensuring full exploitation of the qualified engineering manpower that is currently available in the state and through import of software expertise so as to convert the same into meaningful tangible asset .In view of initiating a program for computerization and office automation in different sectors by Government of Myanmar, there exists a scope for software exports. Young Mizos who are trained and have acquired the requisite expertise in the field of computers and allied services can take advantage of the opportunities lying ahead. They will be best suited in Myanmar owing to their proximity.

Problems of Enterprenuership Development

The problems relating to EDP in Mizoram can be basically of two types: (a) of general nature and (b) of specific nature. The general problems include: lack of comprehensive programme, absence of post-entrepreneurship follow-up, absence of suitable organisational climate among promotional agencies, lack of infrastructure particularly transport and communication, lack of information regarding industrial potentiality, general awareness of people, lagging of collaborative efforts by a number of organisations, callousness on the part of bankers to finance small business while the specific problems are: lack of programmes for women entrepreneurs, lack of emphasis on the establishment of industrial complexes and ancillarisation, lack of openness to outside investments, restrictions on free flow of trade, restrictions on movement of goods, commodities as well as agricultural product, frequent social and political disturbances, etc.

Besides, there has been lack of awareness among educated youths on discounting entrepreneurial opportunities. The socio-psychological attitude towards industrialisation has also been hindering entrepreneurial development. Entrepreneurs need a package of services at different stages like stimulatory, support and sustaining which are applied in an environment conducive to entrepreneurial growth. A good entrepreneurial growth on the other hand is possible only when the various components of entrepreneurial environment such as political, economic, social, technological, cultural etc are in synchronous manner Table 5.

It is also very crucial on the part of Government, institutions, voluntary organization, political parties and mass people to create such an environment which is congenial for development of entrepreneurship in the state as well to boost the economy as a whole.

Table 5

Model on Entrepreneurial Environment, Factors Affecting ED

Political	Economic	Social	Technological	Cultural
1. Political atmosphere.	1. Economic Policies.	1. Consumers and Risk.	1. Competition	1. Aspirations.
2. Quality of leadership.	2. Labour. 3. Trade. 4. Industries. 5. Subsidies.	2. Labour. 3. Opinions. 4. Motives.	2. Efficiency. 3. Productivity. 4. Profitability.	2. Values.

Conclusion

Despite the fact that many EDP have been conducted by numerous agencies/organization since the past 3-4 decades, the result is very groomy. As of the participation of the local people is concerned, there is absolutely no problem, however, when it comes to effective implementation, the follow up is very minimal, may be at the best 25-30%. The reasons for this poor feed back of EDP are mainly due to special hindrances coupled with no-supportive integrated approaches from different corners. The weak process of entrepreneurial environment further becomes another hurdle in successful EDP and IT in Mizoram. Therefore, the concerned machinery should take steps to develop a growing business and trade environment with the help of the new generation entrepreneurs in Mizoram. In nutshell, a long-term sustainable industrial development through the optimum utilisation of available natural and human resources and through building up of physical infrastructure of the state should be taken up in a planned manner by giving proper training to the new age entrepreneurs for the overall development of the state.

NOTES AND REFERENCES

1. Khanka, S.S., (2004), *Entrepreneunial Development*, S. Chand and Co. Ltd., New Delhi p.17
2. Mali, D.D., (2002), Entrepreneunrship and Social Cultural Ethos and Values in the North-East Region, *Kangleipak Business Review*, 2(1): 26 (Department of Commerce, Manipur University, Imphal).

3. Singha, R.K.P.G. and Gupta, A.D. (2003), Industrial Development in Mizoram - Towards Sustainable Development, In: *Modernization of the Mizo Society*, Prasad, R.N., and Agrawal (Eds.), Mittal Publications, New Delhi, p. 92.
4. Gupta, A.D. and Singha, R.K.P.G. (1996), New Economic Policy, Human Resource Development and Entrepreneurship – A Case Study of NE India, *Kangleipak Business Review*, 1: 65 (Department of Commerce, Manipur University, Imphal).
5. Kabra, K.C. and Singha, R.K.P.G. (2003), Border Trade of Mizoram, Paper Presented at the National Seminar of *Challenges of Development in North-East India* held on 21-23rd Oct. organised by the ICSSR, Regional Centre, Shillong, p. 24.
6. Various *Reports of NECON*, Aizwal Branch.
7. Various *Reports of Branch* SISI, Aizwal.

18

IT POLICY OF MANIPUR:
A Step for the Growth of SSI in IT Sector

S. SOMOKANTA SINGH

Introduction

There is growing realization about potential contribution of small enterprises both in developed and developing countries. A healthy business sector is rightly considered to be the backbone of any developed economy. Today people are anticipating that small business and entrepreneurship will lead the way to new economic development. On the other hand, underdeveloped economies usually suffer from paucity of funds, lack of skilled labour and non-existence of minimum social and economic overheads. In the absence of industrial background and a well developed institutional support, entrepreneurs in such economy try to copy innovations introduced by innovative entrepreneurs. Developing economies need greater number of people possessing entrepreneurial qualities and capable of taking decisions under conditions of uncertainties.

A few large scale industries started by entrepreneurs from outside the state in economically backward areas may help as modules of pioneering efforts, but ultimately the real strength of industrialization in Manipur depends upon the involvement of local entrepreneurship in such activities. Medium and large scale industries can only be started with huge investment which is either available with well-established industrial houses or need to be drawn from the public exchequer. An important advantage of establishing small scale enterprises in Manipur is that they can be started with meager financial resources and little or no previous experience or entrepreneurial background.

Information Technology is one of the fastest growing industries in India and one of the largest foreign exchange earners. IT services industry does not require transportation through trains and roads. It is viable for a State like Manipur as geographical inaccessibility is not a limiting factor and depends upon the quality of manpower and communication link. Also Manipur posseses a temperate climate with dust-free and eco-friendly environment.

Opportunity for IT Entrepreneurs

Recognizing the vast potential of IT industry in the state, the Government of Manipur accords high priority to the electronics and IT sectors as a major thrust areas of development. A special package of incentives is provided to facilitate competitive growth of the sector. Manipur has vibrant manpower potential ideally suited for electronics and IT based industries in view of unpolluted and eco-friendly environment conditions and ever growing qualitative work force. In order to bring significant progress in the socio-economic development of Manipur, the state Government has evolved a dynamic and co-ordinated IT policy.

The objectives of the IT policy are as follows:

1. To set up the Institutional Framework to implement and monitor the IT Policy.
2. To use E-Governance to upgrade the standard and quality of administration, and to provide citizen oriented, efficient and cost-effective government.
3. To promote investments and growth in IT industry, and encourage private sector initiative in IT related infrastructure and services, so as to increase the contribution of IT in the economic growth of the state.
4. To provide adequate infrastructure in the State so that the IT sector can flourish.
5. To encourage percolation of IT literacy and education in the State.

6. To generate IT related employment opportunities for the educated youth.
7. To use the power of IT to enhance earning capacity of the citizens for a better quality of life.

IT Areas where Private Participation is Encouraged

In order to promote investments and growth in IT industry, and increase the contribution of IT in the economic growth of the state, the Manipur government encourages private sector initiatives in the following areas:

1. Setting up of an IT park to facilitate IT Entrepreneurs.
2. Setting up of IT enabled Service Centres such as Call Centres, Medical Transcript Centres, etc.
3. Development of backbone network "Manipur State Wide Area Network (MANNET)" for voice, data and video transmissions and dissemination. The network will be utilized for inter-department connectivity, multi-users and multi-service facilities, video conferencing, file transfer facility, e-mail, on-line application processing, query and response etc.
4. Issue of multi-function smart cards to citizens that enable citizens to interact with services, make payments and serve as ration cards, driving license and identity card, etc.
5. Implementation of IT literacy programme in schools and colleges to be taken up jointly by the Education and IT Department.
6. Encouragement of all educational institutions to have Internet connectivity and to set up Internet cafes/clubs for students.
7. To create infrastructure throughout the State for promotion of distance learning through IT, through the use of electronic classrooms of Universities, other educational institutions, vocational training and technical education centres.
8. Setting up of computer laboratories in School.
9. Setting up of training centres for the unemployed.
10. Setting up of Advance Institute of Information Technology and Specialised Schools of Information Technology as Centres

of Excellence in IT to provide high end education in IT and upgradation of skills for the IT industry.

11. Setting up of Information Kiosks using touch screens without using keyboard or mouse all over the State.
12. Internet over Cable and other new technologies for Internet penetration.

Present IT Infrastructure in Manipur

The state has remained economically and industrially backward primarily due to its remote location and geographic disadvantage. Information Technology can overcome geographic disadvantages provided reliable and necessary telecommunication infrastructures along with power supply are in place. The following are the present infrastructure and Internet scenario in Manipur:

- Independent Satellite link with Delhi and Shillong.
- Microwave link with Kohima and beyond.
- 40 digital exchanges.
- Internet C-II Networking at Imphal with 810 connections to all district headquarters.
- Imphal has a 'C' type Node which is connected to 'B' type Node at Shillong and further A1 node at Kolkata which is directly connected to a Gateway.
- Bandwidth presently available is 2 Mbps streams. Upgradation is in process.
- Number of subscribers through BSNL is 630.
- Number of subscribers through Big Byte NE Line is 600.
- No more subscribers are accepted through BSNL since the capacity is already saturated.

IT Manpower in Manipur

The state has a large pool of IT trained manpower within and outside. Manipur University, CEDTI, and Government College of Engineering are presently conducting Degree/Diploma and Certificate IT Courses. There are also a number of private institutions in the State providing IT education, like Symphony, APTECH, NIIT, Dhani

Computers, Technocraft, IIIT, GROM, ARENA, LCC, etc. Computer education has also been introduced in the School, College curriculums.

The following is the indicative figures of IT manpower in Manipur:

Manipur University	:	240 MCA, 320 PGDCA, 400 Certificate Course in Computer Applications.
CEDTI (DOEACC Centre)	:	62 '0' level, 9 'A' level, 742 Hardware/ Software Certificate Course.
Private Institutions	:	8800 Certificates.

The above figures highlight the fact that, with a little effort, Manipur with all its strong manpower can achieve excellence in the field of IT industry.

Small Scale Industries in IT Sectors Having Scope in Manipur

Sl. No.	Product having scope	Total Proposed investment (Rs. in Lakhs)	Employment Generation
UNDER ELECTRONICAL BASED INDUSTRIES			
1)	Cyber cafe/Internet browsing centre	4.50	3
2)	Computer training institute	6.00	5
3)	Web Page designer	3.00	2
4)	PC repairing	4.00	3
5)	Computer repairing/Maintenance	1.75	2
UNDER SERVICE BASED INDUSTRIES			
1)	Cyber Cafe	1.20	2
2)	Computer Training Institute	4.50	3
3)	Medical Transcription	15.00	10
4)	Animation/Multimedia TV studio	5.50	3
5)	Data Processing Centre	2.00	2

Categories of Industries included in the scope/definition of Information Technology Industry

A) Computing devices including:

Desktop

Personal Computer

Servers

Workstations

Nodes

Terminals

Network PC

Lap-top Computers

Note Book Computers

Palm top Computers/PDA

B) Network Controller Cards/Memories including:

Network Interface Card (NIC)

Adaptor-Ethernet/PCI/EISA/ Combo/PCMICA

SIMMs- Memory

DIMMs - Memory

Central Processing Unit (CPU)

Controller-SCSI/Array

Processors-Processor/Processor Power Module/Upgrade

C) Storage Units including:

Hard Disk Drivers/Hard Drives

RAID Devices and their Controllers

Floppy Disk Drives

CD ROM Drives

Tape Drives-DLT Drives/DAT

Optical Disk Drives

Other Digital Storage Devices

D) Others

Keyboard

Monitor

Mouse

Multimedia Kits

E) Printers and Output Devices including:

Dot Matrix Printers

Laser Printers

Inkjet Printers

LED Printers

Line Printers

Plotters

Pass-book Printers

F) Networking Products including:

Hubs

Routers

Switches

Concentrators

Trans-receiver

G) Software including:

Application Software

Operating System

Middleware/Firmware

IT Enabled Services

H) Power Supplies to Computer Systems including:

Switch Mode Power Supplies

Un-interrupted Power Supplies

I) Networking/Cabling and related accessories (related to IT Industry)

Fibre Cable

Copper Cable

Cables

Connectors, Terminal Blocks

Jack Panels, Patch Cord

Mounting Cord/wiring Blocks

Surface Mount Boxes

J) Consumables including:

CD ROM/Computer Disk

Floppy Disk

Tapes DAT/DET

Ribbons

Toners

Inkjet Cartridges

Inks for Output devices

K) Electronic Components:

Printed Circuit Board/populated PCB

Printed Circuit Board/PCB

Transistors

Integrated Circuits/ICs

Diodes/Thyristor/LED

Resistors

Capacitors

Switches/(On/Off, Push button, Rocker, etc)

Magnetic heads, Print heads

Connectors

Microphones/Speakers

FUSES

L) Telecommunication Equipment including

Telephones

Videophones

Facsimile machines/Fax cards

Tele-printers/Telex machine

PABX/EPABX/RAX/MAX-Telephone

Exchange

Multiplexers/Muxes

Modems

Telephone answering machines

Telecommunication Switching Apparatus

Antenna and Mast

Wireless datacom equipment

Receiving equipments like pagers,

Mobile/Cellular Phone etc.

VSATs

Video Conferencing Equipments.

*Including Set Top Boxes for both Video and digital signalling.

Package of Incentives

The State Government has introduced a comprehensive new industrial policy which includes infrastructure support and both project and production related benefits that are meant for all industrial activities including those of small scale industries. The salient features of the policy are:

1. Allotment of Land

i) The developed land will be allotted on hire purchase basis with suitable terms of installments subsidizing of the cost of land development @ 25% for SSI units, 30% for EOUs and units owned by weaker sections and 15% for large and medium units.

ii) Rules for allotment of land including recovery of cost of land development shall be framed and modified by the State Government.

2. Allotment of Sheds to SSI Units

The State Government will provide available sheds to SSI units in infrastructural centres at monthly rental basis. Subsidy on the monthly rent will be eligible @ 50% for entrepreneurs of all categories and 55% in case of EOUs and units set up by weaker sections. This subsidy will be applicable for 5 years only from the date of occupations, of the shed.

3. Manpower Development

Subsidy @ Rs. 10,000 per trainee or 50% of the actual cost of training, whichever is less subject to a maximum of ceiling of Rs. 30,000 per year shall be provided to industrial units which depute their workers for technical training in Government recognized/reputed training institutions or established industrial concerns.

4. State Capital Investment Subsidy

The State Government will provide Subsidy to the industries establish in thrust areas 30% on total capital investment on plant and machinery and miscellaneous fixed assets subject to ceiling of Rs. 15.00 lakhs per unit. For EOUs, the rate of subsidy shall be 35% subject to a maximum of Rs. 20.00 lakhs per unit.

5. State Transport Subsidy

Subsidy @ 10% of the actual freight and air transport charges subject to a maximum of Rs. 1.50 lakhs per unit shall be provided to industrial units for transportation of raw materials from Calcutta/ Patna/ Silliguri to the industrial location in Manipur and for transportation of finished product to Kolkata/ Patna or for both, for EOUs the maximum limits will be Rs. 2.00 Lakhs.

6. Interest Subsidy

SSI units will be provided an interest subsidy of 5% per annum on working capital and term loan taken from banks and financial institutions. This subsidy will be available for the first five years from the date of commercial production or from the date of release of loan in case of revival of sick units. In case of weaker sections and EOUs, the subsidy will be 7% per annum.

7. Power Subsidy

a) Power subsidy will be provided to SSI units for the first 5 years from the date of commercial production of the unit at the rates fixed by the Government from time to time.

b) 50% of the cost incurred on linking of power from the main line to the factory shed will be subsidized subject to a ceiling of Rs. 50,000 per unit for such units which are not provided land in developed industrial areas. In case of Weaker Sections and EOUs the subsidy will be 55% subject to a maximum of Rs. 55,000 per unit.

c) 40% subsidy will be admissible for purchase of Diesel Generating sets of 10 H.P. or more subject to ceiling of Rs. 90,000. In case of Weaker Sections and EOUs, the subsidy shall be 50% subject to a maximum of Rs. 1.00 lakhs.

8. Subsidy for Technical Know-How

A subsidy of 50% will be admissible to meet the cost of technical know-how obtained by SSI unit from organisations approved in advance by Government of Manipur. The subsidy will be released only on commencement of commercial production. The subsidy will be 60% in case of Weaker Sections and EOUs.

9. Exclusive Purchase Programme

The State Government will commit to the policy of purchasing the products of SSI units in the State for Official requirement whenever their products are manufactured locally subject to fulfillment of the quality, standards and specification.

10. Reimbursement of Stamp Duty and Registration

SSI units will be reimbursed in full for the amount paid towards Stamp Duty and Registration Fee for securing loans and other incentives from financial institutions including mortgage of fixed assets.

Special Incentives of IT Industries

In addition, all IT industries employing a minimum of 25 persons would be entitled to:

a) 50% concession on floor space rentals for a maximum of 5 years [including clause (b) below wherever applicable].

b) All IT industries set up by local entrepreneurs would be given 50% concession on floor space rentals for a period of 2 years from the date of setting up of the unit. Provided that the 50%

concession on the floor space rentals will be subject to a ceiling, to be notified by the State Government.

Present IT Commercial Activities in Manipur

- Beside a number of private IT educational institutes, Computers have been used for Desk Top Publishing (DTP) since the last 10 years and is a well established industry.
- Two Medical Transcripts Training institutes have been set up.
- Two Internet Service Providers VSNL and NE Lines Big Byte are currently in operation in Imphal.

Future Scopes

1. Repairing and Maintenance

Personal Computers have occupied an important role in a modern office. Increased IT awareness, dropping of PC prices, increasing buying power and spread of computer literacy have made PCs increasingly popular. Presently, training and hardware repair facilities are inadequate in view of the potential users and this is the right time for entrepreneurs to make use of the available opportunities.

2. Software development centres

Information Technology Industries is very versatile since there is no area of manufacturing or services where we cannot apply information technology and get better results in terms of saving in time, cost, energy as well as better service. Accordingly the use of software is constantly on the rise. Some years back software constituted 20 per cent out of the total electronics business and 80 per cent was hardware. However now the figure stand at 40 and 60 per cent respectively. Software professional in Manipur can join hands for establishing Software Development Centre of excellence in the North-Eastern Region for software export to South Asian regions.

3. Information Kiosks

The Government will encourage entrepreneurs to set up Information Kiosks all over the State. The kiosks shall provide access to a wide range of citizen-oriented information and E-governance related information. They need not have Internet connection and could simply have data stored for access by the citizens. The government will assist the entrepreneurs in getting space in government/public locations. In addition STD/ISD booth owners will be encouraged to convert them to Cyber cafes/Cyber communication centres.

4. Animation/Multimedia Studio

Recent boom in the production of digital films in Manipur paves the way for film editing and other related activities. Entrepreneurs can set up animation/multimedia studio for providing services to the promotion of local film industry. Persons with proper knowledge of multimedia software can start their ventures in this field.

5. IT-enabled Services

IT enabled services like Medical Transcription, Call Centres, Data Conversion, Data Processing, and Back-Office operations will provide opportunities to entrepreneurs.

Conclusion

The contribution of the IT service industries to the development of economy of the State is almost nil. Non availability of proper data may be one of the factors for difficulty in finding the relationship between the two. India is projected to become an IT superpower by 2008. With a little effort, Manipur with all its various advantages, mainly the strong manpower can piggy-ride the country's success in this field. So, persons with suitable training and support can set up their ventures with minimum inputs in terms of investment both in rural and urban area of the state. While much has been spoken over the past decades about a new momentum being imparted to India's "Look East" policies, these only serve our national interest only if technopreneurs try to foster it to the promotion of economic progress and welfare of the North-East. Only then the State Governments vision of transforming Manipur into Information Technology driven economy and society can be fulfilled.

NOTES AND REFERENCES

1. International Note (1 Jan 1991), "Will Business be the Answer for Developing Countries", *Journal of Small Business Management*, Vol 29.
2. Alexander P.C, (26th and 27th May, 1975), Key-Note Address, Summary of Proceedings of the *National Seminar on Entrepreneurship Development in Small Scale Industries*, Development Commissioner, Small Scale Industries, New Delhi.

3. Dua, T.R. (June 1997), *Private Sector Participation: An Engine for Growth,* Telematics India, pp. 20-21.
4. Vittal, N. (June 1996), Information Technology: Futuristic Scenario, *Technorama*, 40(1): 18-26.
5. Saini, J.S, Dhameja, S.K, *Entrepreneurship and Small Business*, Rawat Publications, New Delhi.
6. Kuppuswamy, C.S., (2001), India's Policy: Looking Eastward-An Update, *South Asia Analysis Group,* Note No. 123.
7. Government of Manipur, (2003), *Information Technology Policy of Manipur.*
8. Department of Commerce and Industries, (2002), *New Industrial Policy of Manipur*, Government of Manipur.
9. Government of Manipur, *Manipur, Gateway to the South East Asia.*
10. http://www.nedfi.com/tedf/status_and_prospect_of_it.html, Status and prospects of IT sector in NE States.
11. http://www.themanipurpage.tripod.com/economy/ecoappr.html, Economy of Manipur by Somorendro Oinam, NedFi.
12. http://www.investinmanipur.nic.in/it.html, Invest in Manipur.
13. http://www.nerdatabank.nic.in/manipur/html/, IT Industry and Infrastructure.
14. http://www.inomy.com, Globalization and Information Society Development Perspective.
15. http://www.techno-preneur.net/timeis/STRUCTURE/finalstructure/incentives/maipur.html, Incentives for entrepreneurs in Manipur.
16. http://www.indiacityguides.com/manipur.html, GDP, GDS GDCFCSO, NSSO.
17. http://chalo-india.tripod.com/cybercafelc, Cyber cafe in India.
18. http://www.sisimanipur.nic.in/services.htm. The role of Small Industries Development Bank of India (SIDBI) in SSI.
19. Government of India, Ministry of SSI (2003-04), *Report on State Industrial Potentiality Survey of Manipur.*

19

DEVELOPMENT OF ENTREPRENEURSHIP IN SMALL SCALE AND IT INDUSTRIES IN MANIPUR

M. MINARANI DEVI

Entrepreneurship is the capacity of doing things in the face of uncertainty which should come to brilliant success in the long-run. Development is a radical change towards the optimum exploitation of the available resources. A small scale (SS) industry is an Industrial Undertaking in which the investment in Fixed assets in plant and machinery, whether held on ownership terms or on lease or on hire purchase, does not exceed rupees three crores[1].

In section 4 of the New Industrial Policy of Manipur[2], 2002 of Department of Commerce and Industries, Government of Manipur, it has been identified "Electronics and Information Technology (IT) industries" as Thrust Areas. This New Industrial Policy regards "information" as one of the important industrial inputs. The organizational behaviour, production efficiency, technological response and quality improvement are considerably changed by the market signals. Poor information breeds poor planning, poor planning produces poor performance. The "information package" needs to be delivered at the doorstep of the enterprise. The Information Technology Centres will be essential part of the New Policy. This IT sectors does not required to obtain clearance from State Pollution Control Board as other sectors do at the very setting up of new units.

For IT industries (hardware and software) all the other incentives stated in the new policy, would be applicable as a thrust sector industry. In addition, IT industries would be given the following incentive support:-

All IT industries employing a minimum of 25 persons would be entitled to:

(a) 50% concession on floor space rentals for a maximum of 5 years [including clause (b) below wherever applicable]

(b) All IT industries set up by local entrepreneurs would be given 50% concession on floor space rentals for a period of 2 years from the date of setting up of the unit. Provided that the 50% concession on the floor space rentals will be subject to a ceiling, to be notified by the State Government.

This paper discussed some of these aspects with special emphasis given towards the use of computers and development of entrepreneurship in small scale and IT industries in Manipur.

Introduction

Any person born on this earth whether blind, lamb, deaf or physically handicapped who can undertake any work physically or mentally is an Entrepreneur. Entrepreneurship[3] is the quality of an entrepreneur to enable him or her to discharge any sort of activities in the present day world. Here, it may be mentioned the divine gift of humanity, "Man has Talent"; "Talent = Aptitude + Capacity + Ability". Aptitude is the habitual tendency of work done within a scheduled time. Measured capacity is ability. Ability of a man when trained, practiced and researched enhances capacity. Therefore, the significance of entrepreneurship is to mobilize human and material resources. In other words, man is of (i) skilled (ii) semi-skilled and (iii) unskilled. The first and second are workable and value oriented when put into work. The third is not so. This skill imposition is with the entrepreneurship development. A man is resourceful when imbibed in the qualities of being an entrepreneur. Resource is of two kinds - *one* is human resource i.e. skill importation as stated above and the *second* is material resource which is of two kinds - (i) scarce and (ii) unscarced materials. Normally, scarce materials are precious and as such, establishment of SS and IT industries with scarce materials as raw material seems not suitable in Manipur where there is no such mines and easy procurement. Rather unscarced materials heap up in Manipur can easily be converted into capital products. These unscarced materials which may be said as money are scattering here and there e.g. bio-gas plant, gobber gas plant, fuel frequenting, hard boards for partition of walls, ceiling from husk leave, straws, water treatment plant etc. may be made as SS and IT industrial products. This is purely a socio-environmental protection and also a step towards the capital formation. Skill is the richest cultural heritage of our nation. Again now-a-days, everything could be commercialized and nothing of the unscarced material could not be commercialized.

Entrepreneurship is risk taking, decision making, wealth creating, welfare promoting and above all, an indispensable leadership of any organization, because, entrepreneurship is by nature, proprietory. Entrepreneurship itself is the initiation and creation of new ideas. In short, it is a software system. Entrepreneurship is an irrepressible urge for creation of value and wealth by taking risk as distinguished from uncertainties and maximizing opportunities at every stage. It is the art of effective integration and creative utilization of the available resources. It is therefore to nourish production and productivity programmes in a profitable, dynamic and desirable manner.

Entrepreneurship is the capacity to perceive environment to identify opportunities, to mobilize resources to execute projects of SS and IT industries in order to augment wealth and also to promote social responsibility. Entrepreneurship is solely a developing linkage in the society and in our changing socio-economic pace of Manipur; Entrepreneurship is the human quality that generates the intensity of development.

Entrepreneurship is the nurse and if not mother for growth of economy, it is the solace in the perception of environmental opportunities and more specifically, in the competence of management skill.

Methodology

The training programmes of entrepreneurship had been launched in the past decades by various organizations both private and public as sponsored by SIDBI (Small Industries Development Bank of India) Imphal, Ministry of Human Resource Development, Government of India and NEC (North Eastern Council), Shillong etc. The launching organizations for Manipur specially are IIE (Indian Institute of Entrepreneurship) Guwahati, NISIET Guwahati, NISIET Hyderabad[4], the Entrepreneurship Institute of India, Ahmedabad, NRDC (National Research Development Corporation of India), New Delhi. The target groups are the officials and candidates from general category more emphatically from educated unemployed youths (man and women).

Among the existing organizations in Manipur, AMEA (All Manipur Entrepreneurs Association), Takyel, AMTEU (All Manipur Trained Entrepreneurs Union), Rupmahal Tank, Imphal and more supporting organizations, namely, NECON (North Eastern Consultancy Organization), Lamphel had undertaken innumerable ED Programmes with a view to catering to employment avenues and also advancing financial assistances from banks in varied fields of industries, Service and business as sponsored by financing agencies, like, SBI, SIDBI and NABARD, Imphal. The programme includes project formulation, business management, financial management, recruiting the right type of person, problem diagnosis, marketing management, inventory control, setting up of SS and IT industries and its modality etc. Total quality management (ISO-9000) by IIE in collaboration with UK had also been launched at Guwahati where Manipuri participants could avail.

Literature Survey

Looking into the details of SSI, it reveals that SSI[5] classifies as:

i. Small Scale Industrial Undertaking

ii. Ancillary Industrial Undertaking

iii. Tiny Enterprise

iv. Women Entrepreneur

v. Small Scale Service and Business (Industry related) Enterprises (SSSBEs).

For instance, Small Scale Industrial Undertakings have the following requirements.

- The following requirements are to be complied with by an industrial undertaking to be graded as Small Scale Industrial undertaking w.e.f. 21.12.1999
- An industrial undertaking in which the investment in fixed assets in plant and machinery whether held on ownership terms on lease or on hire purchase does not exceed Rs 10 million.

(Subject to the condition that the unit is not owned, controlled or subsidiary of any other industrial undertaking)

Department of Information Technology, Punjab[6], India defines information technology and IT industries as follows:

Information Technology (IT)

"IT Software" means any representation of instructions, data , sound or image, including source code and object code, recorded in a machine readable form, and capable of being manipulated or providing interactivity to a user, by means of an automatic data processing machine falling under heading, ` I.T. Products`, but does not include 'non I.T. Product', 'IT Service' is defined as any service which results from the use of any IT Software over a system of IT products for realizing value addition. The IT Industry shall cover development, production and services related to IT products. The term 'IT-Software' shall be substituted in place of 'Computer Software' in all notifications.

Information Technology Industry

IT includes IT and Telecommunications; IT Industries includes IT Hardware and Software Industries; IT Software Industries include IT Software, IT services and IT enabled services. IT Infrastructure means the physical Infrastructure build by a firm or a builder and sold to an IT Industry for its own use or the Infrastructure build by an IT Industry for its own use.

The New Industrial Policy of Manipur 2002 mentions about entrepreneurship development in SS and IT industries as follows. The New Industrial Policy seeks to update, upgrade and enrich the entrepreneurial skill of the "Winners" and "upcomings" with a twin - programme of new orientation and "on the job-training".

The follow-up is considered absolutely necessary for sustaining the rising entrepreneurial spirits and professional acumen. As such the New Industrial Policy intends to emphasize the follow-up (physical support package) more than training programme. "Trade Mission" should be a necessary component of the entrepreneurial development.

In section 4 of the New Industrial Policy of Manipur, 2002 of Department of Commerce and Industries, Government of Manipur, it has been identified "Electronics and Information Technology (IT) industries" as Thrust Areas. This New Industrial Policy regards "information" as one of the important industrial inputs. The organizational behaviour, production efficiency, technological response and quality improvement are considerably changed by the market signals. Poor information breeds poor planning, poor planning produces poor performance. The "information package" needs to be delivered at the doorstep of the enterprise. The Information Technology Centres will be essential part of the New Policy. This IT Sectors does not required to obtain clearance from State Pollution Control Board as other sectors do at the very setting up of new units.

For IT industries (hardware and software) all the other incentives stated in the new policy, would be applicable as a thrust sector industry. In addition, IT industries would be given the following incentive support:-

All IT industries set up by local entrepreneurs would be given 50% concession on floor space rentals for a period of 2 years from the date of setting up of the unit. Provided that the 50% concession on the floor space rentals will be subject to a ceiling, to be notified by the State Government.

Finally, N. Mohendro Singh[7] in a paper "Development Experience In Manipur (1891-1969) and "The Lost Article of Self-Reliance" has discussed up-gradation and modernization of traditional skill as [In this connection a reference may be made to the observation made by the Economic Report submitted by the National Council of Applied Economic Research, New Delhi (1961).

1. "The importance of development of Manipur flows from a variety of reasons among which its strategic importance is the most important" (page 81).
2. "The development policy should be directed towards development local enterprise and local skill" (page 78).
3. Thus while the major objective should be to develop local initiatives immediately, the government will have to pale an active, determined and direct role in the field of small industries" (page 79)].

He further commented "The token outlay of Rs. 0.60 lakhs in the First Five-Year Plan was increased to Rs. 13.06 lakhs and Rs. 49.39 lakhs in the Second Five-Year Plan and Third Five Year Plan respectively. During the Third Plan the sericulture received a share of Rs. 4.29 lakhs only as plan allocation. No state policy of industrial development was announced. No skill inventory was prepared. However the number of small factories registered a modest increase from 27 in 1957 to 66 in 1961 and 130 in 1967. The tempo remained visibly low. The factories were too small to create any perceptible impact and basically meant for local needs." It is also worth mentioning that IT industries, though the government launches many attractive incentive policies and STPI, Imphal has been emerged, as compared to other states it is not so developed. We have to see and applying section 4 of this paper as well as computerized inventory control (e.g. in a grocery shop many items of consumable goods like salt, rice, mustard oil etc. numbering about 100/200 items are being sold daily and the whole sale proceeds are kept in the cash box which is quite clumsy and indistinguishable without proper inventory control and gains/profit are not understandable for each item) may help in developing entrepreneurship in SS and IT industries in Manipur. In this connection, it is worth mentioning that Draft Information Technology Policy 2001 of Manipur which will provide the followings for IT Industry and IT Infrastructure.

1. State Wide Area Network
2. Software Technology Parks of India
3. Internet over Cable
4. Promotion of IT Industry
5. Electronic Commerce
6. Preferential allotment of land
7. Change of land use
8. IT industries in residential localities
9. IT Enabled Services
10. Seminars, Workshops and Exhibitions
11. Village Telecom infrastructure for Internet
12. Floor Area Regulation (FAR)
13. Clearances and Support
14. Registration and Stamp Duty
15. Sales Tax Concession
16. Applicable rate of Sales Tax
17. IT as priority sector for lending

18. ROW Clearance
19. Permission for three shift operation
20. Exemption from Pollution Control
21. Self-certification/ exemption from various Acts
22. Awards of excellence

Now-a-days, SS and IT industries are being globalised so as to disperse balance economy and manpower.

A brief note on System Analysis and Design[8] (which will promote entrepreneurship development using computers)

The followings are the steps in systems analysis and design:

1. System Analysis
   - Recognition of Problem or Defining the Need (For example, to computerized a hospital, we have to answer one out of two when we ask ourselves why we need computerization to understand the needs. That is, we should understand that whether they need computerization in substitution of their old manual system for effective and efficient productivity or they have already computerized but they need further improvement.)
   - Feasibility Study
   - Investigation and Analysis
2. System Design Concepts
   - Design Objectives
   - Elements of Design
   - Elementary Concepts on Data Processing
3. Design of Systems Components
   - Designing Outputs
   - Designing Logical Files
   - Designing Inputs
4. System Documentation
   - Organization of Documents
   - Outline on Document Contents

5. System Design Methodologies
   - System Development Life Cycle Method
   - Structured Design Development Method
   - Systems Prototype Method

Further, due to the introduction of "spreadsheet" in the history of software, business decision making is perfected and "what-if analysis" can be performed. Hence, with a little knowledge of system analysis and design and use of spreadsheet software, an entrepreneur may enhanced the productivity in SS and IT industries - thanks to IT.

Resumption

To resume the topic it is to mention that entrepreneurs are to be resourceful with the imposition of techniques for setting up SS and IT industries in Manipur and thereafter production and productivity programmes are to be tackled. The Statistical Report of District Level details of Registered Units of SSI in Manipur from 1997 to 2001 are shown in Table1. These are to be followed by skillful management practice with proper linkage systems and adoption of centrifugal type of industries (Fig. 1), service and business sectors establishment in the nook and corner of Manipur state rather than the centripetal type only concentrated at town of Imphal so that there may have been equitable and balance economy to a great extent.

Table 1 District Level Details of Registered Units of SSI in Manipur from 1997 to 2001

Name of District	Code	No. of Regd Units
Imphal West	01	2905
Ukhrul	02	670
Senapati	03	242
Churachandpur	04	425
Tamenglong	05	277
Chandel	06	199
Thoubal	07	437
Bishnupur	08	507
Imphal East	09	117

Today, the world is becoming smaller and smaller not in size but in communication system (e.g. internet). Any information from the remotest area of the Globe can easily be obtained by the Information

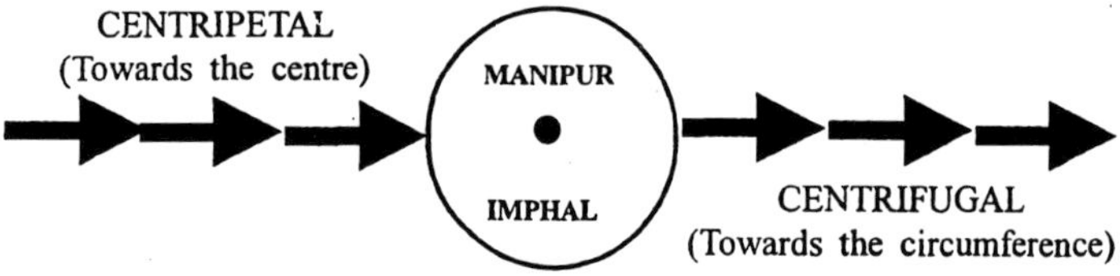

Fig. 1: Diagram Showing Centrifugal Type of Industries.

Technology became an indispensable part which will help create in developing Industries, Service and Business Ventures. As to cite an example, in a grocery shop many items of goods are being sold daily. But the sale proceeds of each and every item is never recorded but the total sale proceeds of all the items in the shop for the particular day. Hence, Information Technology can reveal the loss and gain of each item so that profit motive may readily be increased. Therefore unsystematic management leads to damp the huge amount of working capital without profit. IT plays a vital role in this modern fast changing economic scenario. As such, establishment of SS and IT, industries by developing Entrepreneurship may in the long run, make Manipur state a rich and self sufficient Manipur state along with the optimum utilization of unscarce raw-materials into capital goods . Because, the unscarce raw-materials in the form of money scattering here and there in all areas of Manipur could easily be collected by the use of modern technology which is of low energy consumption and also nourishment of surrounding environment and ecology of Manipur.

Conclusion

Broadly[10], successful projects: (a) embrace the notion that durable competitiveness of small producers in a competitive economic environment requires that they develop internal capabilities to effectively assimilate, use and adapt product and process technologies; (b) are demand-driven; (c) target the assistance to groups of producers with common interests and problems, and help them to organize themselves in collective bodies that can evolve into self-help institutions; and (d) include appropriate incentive structures based on market principles.

To conclude the theme, it may be mentioned that our lives are solely dependent on industrial products for various necessities - shelter, nutritious food, health, work condition to be available communication (internet/IT) etc. These are present day needs of human being and any failure of the needs in quality may result inconveniences of economics and social breakdown, menace and even loss of life. Consequently, entrepreneurship is to channelize the available manpower to the appropriate vocations. Secondly, it also aims at increasing number of employabilities through training. Thirdly, entrepreneurship envisages providing vocational guidance and career information system at every appropriate stages.

Last but not the least in the process of developing Entrepreneurship, the maximum of "Treat every man as genuine unless he or she proves otherwise" and "good for all and all for good" will bring proper linkage, because, it is an instrument of management practice in persuading people to work for economic and social satisfaction. In another word, it is to induce an effective motivation of individuals to achieve the goal of life. Because, it means a matter of understanding how the human mind works at the time of emotion. "Understanding comes only when I, you and he she meets at the same place, at the same time and for the save purpose".

NOTES AND REFERENCES

1. Gazette of India, dated 11-12-1997.
2. www.nic.net.in *New Industrial Policy of Manipur 2002*, Department of Commerce and Industries, Government of Manipur.
3. *Brochure of NISIET* Guwahati, 1981.
4. *Brochure of NISIET* Hyderabad.
5. http://www.exim.indiamart.com/ssi-corner
6. Information Technology Incentives Special Package of Incentives (Notification No. 15/4/99-51B/2174 dated: March 15, 2000) Department of Information Technology, Govt. of Punjab, India
7. www.themanipurpage.tripod.com/economy/mani_economics.html
8. DCO-1 (Office Environment and Data Processing) Block-4 (Introduction to Data Processing), IGNOU, 1991.
9. Directorate of Commerce and Industries (2002), Nucleus Cell, Government of Manipur
10. Romijn, Henny (2001), Technology Support for Small-scale Industry in Developing Countries: A Review of Concepts and Project Practices, *Oxford Development Studies*, 29(1).

WOMEN ENTREPRENEURSHIP

20

AN OVERVIEW OF WOMEN ENTREPRENEURS IN MANIPUR

ROBITA SOROKHAIBAM

Introduction

Pandit Jawaharlal Nehru rightly said, "When women moves forward the family moves, the village moves and the nation moves". Women have been regarded as the nuclei of a nation and the builder and moulder of its destiny. The position and status of women in any society is an index of its civilization. Employment gives economic status to women. Economic status paves the way of social status. With the impact of globalisation, women are now seeking gainful employment in several fields in increasing numbers. With the spread of education and awareness, women entrepreneurs are spreading their wings to higher levels. However, it cannot be said that women entrepreneurs are spreading their wings to higher levels. However, it canot be said that the women entrepreneurship has completely taken off the ground and it is felt that the movement is still in a transition period. Emergence of women entrepreneurs in the economy is an indicator of women's economic independence and their improved social status. The role of women entrepreneurs helps industrial development, promotes economic development and helps to solve the problems of unemployment and poverty.

Women Entrepreneurship - A Need of the Day

Women constitute nearly half of the population in India, they have had a very limited access to the developmental programmes. Women's work participation rate in the country as a whole has been significantly lower than men. Their lower literacy rate, which was 39.49% according to 1991 Census, is the cause and effect of their subordinate position in the society. Majority of the women perform domestic and household duties, which are never paid. Infact, women play a dominant role in agriculture where it account for 65% of total employment in which women's share is 82% whereas in the advanced countries of the world, there is a phenomenal increase in the number of self-employed women after the world war. In the US, women own 25% of all business, Canada 1/3rd, France 1/5th, UK it has increased three times as the number of self- employed men. Hence, they have been making a significant impact in all segment of the economy. Likewise, Socio-economic problems in India in general and Manipur in particular lie in Gandhiji's idea of "Production by masses instead of mass production. This can be made possible through self-employment drive based on women entrepreneurship development to a great extend.

Women Entrepreneurship in Northeast India

Northeast India is the home of eight sisters of Assam, Meghalaya, Manipur, Nagaland, Arunachal Pradesh, Tripura and Sikkim. In the northeastern part of the country, several financial institutions, banks and organization have come to the rescue of small entrepreneurs. Here, the entrepreneurial class is usually the small business owners and specially the tiny and cottage unit owners. The region is however lacking in infrastructure and suffering from law and order problem. Nevertheless, ambitious young women entrepreneurs are on the rise.

The role of modern women is much more than what it was before. Empowering women through entrepreneurship is essential for achieving the goals of sustainable development. Present day women started taking full participation in decision-making processes in all walks of life. Women increasingly took an important role in this globalised economic order. With the advancement in the field of education, employment of the people both educated and uneducated is a big challenge in the developed as well as the developing world today. This situation may create serious socio-economic problems. an effective developmental process of entrepreneurship, tapping the talent in the unorganised sector, can clearly address these problems.

The Government of India defines a women entrepreneur as "An enterprise owned and controlled by a woman and having a minimum financial interest of 51% of the capital and giving at least 51% of employment to women". Moreover, the president of India Dr. APJ Abdul kalam in his recent independence day speech outlined a three-pronged strategy to devise employment-oriented education system i.e. education system should highlight the importance of entrepreneurship and prepare the stdents right from the college education level to get oriented towards setting up of the enterprise. Secondly, the banking system should provide venture capital right from every Village level to the prospective entrepreneurship for udertaking new ventures, and lastly, the overall development of all.

Economic development is not only a quantitative phenomenon but has qualitative dimensions too. Economic development of any country or any state is related to its naturally available resources like climatic condition, soil, vegetation and many other natural phenomenons. Most of the social scientists agreed that human resource is the centre of economic activity and it takes a vital role in any developmental process. For economic development, there is the need for proper arrangement of human and material resources. This arrangement is known as entrepreneurship. Now it is widely accepted that the availability of entrepreneurship is the most important determinant in the process of industrialization.

Economic development is the result of purposeful human activity. Socio-economic development of any region is closely linked with the necessity of optimizing the use of existing resources, labour and economic infrastructure. For doing these works effectively there is the need for a good entrepreneur and for proper utilization of these resources (natural as well as other resources) small enterprises are very important. A large-scale industry is not feasible in this part of the state. In small-scale industries there is less capital investment as compared to medium or large-scale industries. And it facilitates the optimum utilization of locally available resources. This industrial sector occupies an important position in planned development of Indian economy and has grown to be the most vital sector of our nation.

Women Entrepreneurs in Manipur

The industrial backwardness of the state needs concerted effort from the Government departments, Banks and financial institutions and other support organization to put a thrust on the development of small-scale industries as a vehicle of employment generation. Above all, the women are hard working and produced different designs of the product through experimentation and innovative technique. The New Industrial Policy of Government of India has specially highlighted the need for special entrepreneurship programme for women entrepreneurs in the nature of product-process oriented courses to enable them to start small scale industries with a view to uplift their status in the economic and social fields. Due to the aforesaid fillip, the state laid emphasis on creating a strong industrial base and employment opportunity through provision of various growth-inducing factors based on locally available resources.

Non-governmental and other voluntary organization also takes initiative for women entrepreneurs and become the link between entrepreneurs and credit agencies. Professional associations of women entrepreneurs may identify certain women entrepreneurs and make them available for consultation and advice as and when needed. For industrially backward district and other backward areas, the association have also taken a number of promotional measures such as conducting techno-economic survey, establishment of technical consultancy organzation (TCO), encouragement of Entrepreneurship Development Programme (EDP), etc.

Women Entrepreneurs Working in Different Sectors

Women entrepreneurs in the Northeast contributed in a large scale in the economic development of the region. The women folks run most of the small enterprises. These small enterprises can be started with a small investment. The large and the medium scale industries need a huge amount of capital in which only few fortunate can afford to do, majority of the enterprises in the region are small enterprises, which is dominated by the womenfolk. For the large-scale industries, it had a long gestation period, and generally, takes more time to generate employment but the small industries had advantage regarding this matter over the large-scale industries. The women entrepreneurs of the region are very artistic, they designed different types of product especially in the traditional industrial sector like handloom and handicraft. Their product had customers in most of the major international markets. They are not only bringing economic gain but also fame for their respective state with the laurel they brought from national and international promoters of women entrepreneurs. Most of the women entrepreneurs are engaged mainly in traditional activties like weaving, handloom, handicraft, knitting and embroidery, fruit processing industries etc. However, in recent years it has been observed that women entrepreneurs are venturing into non-traditional activities like beaty parlour, xeroxing, inccese stick making, candle making, restarant etc.

Table 1
Women Entrepreneurs in Different Sectors

Different sector	No. of W.E.	Percentage
Handloom	11	22
Handicraft	17	34
Fruit processing	3	6
Embroidery	5	10
Knitting	3	6
Other Sector	12	24
Total	50	100

Source: Field Survey.

Handloom related enterprise is dominated by women folk. So, out of fifty women entrepreneurs selected in prospective sampling in Manipur about 22% of them turn out to be handloom related entrepreneurs Table1. They produced different range of products ranging from phanek (it is an important type of cloth for women), Khudei (Lungee), bed cover, pillow cover, table clothes and many other different types of chadar. Some of the handloom products has been demanding in national and international markets. Besides, the handloom sector, handicraft is also one of the important industrial sectors in the State. The State is known for their handicraft products like pottery, mattress items (cushion, sofa-seats, morahs, handbags, shoes, flower pots, etc.), potloi dress making, etc. there are many national awardee in this sector. Thus, it is discovered that from among the total fifty women entrepreneurs selected in Manipur, 34% (maximum number according to the survey report) of them turn out to be engaged in handicraft related sectors. This is because of that their products are very demanded in the national and international markets. According to the survey report only 6% of the women entrepreneurs in Manipur were engaged in fruit processing industry. From the very early days in Manipur, women are engaged in embroidery work. This is reflected in its cultural and traditional dresses. This needlework shows the status and class of the people in the society. For example, royal family member such as King and Queen wore different designs of embroidered clothes. In Manipur, 10% of them were engaged in this sector and some of them are national awardee. Knitting industry is not so well developed in this State compared to some States like Rajasthan, Gujarat, Kashmir, etc. Thus, there are only about 6% of women entrepreneurs in Manipur. Besides, the above discussed different industries, there are various sector like beauty parlour, restaurant, eroxing, incense stick making, poultry farming, candle making, sericulture, etc. where women entrepreneurs have intension at diversifying their business into many other areas from the traditional enterprises. One of the reasons may be because of the need of the customer and their satisfaction. Thus, it is observed that 22% of women entrepreneurs in Manipur were engaged in the new sectors.

Growth of Women Entrepreneurship

In Manipur, women are taking prominent role in developing the economy of the State. With this view; a special chapter in the economic planning has covered the integration of women in economic development. It is observed from the testing using the statistical tool i.e. measurement of central tendency in different sector where women entrepreneurs are engaged in Manipur, that the monthly income of the enterprise is highest in fruit processing sector, followed by handicraft sector, embroidery and handloom sector.

The highest income calculated in the Fruit Processing Sector is Rs. 15,833. The women entrepreneur engaged in fruit processing is few, their income is found to be the highest. Therfore, women entrepreneurs working is this sector should be given special package of incentives to enable them expand and improve their enterprises.

The monthly income of the enterprise in embroidery sector is found to be Rs. 11,500/- and it is the second highest income generator among the different sectors discussed in this present study. In order to maintain the income level of the embroidery sector, the handloom sector needs to be strengthened.

The handicraft sector, which is the highest numerically, among the different sector, ranked third position when compared with the monthly income generated from other sectors. Despite the numeral advantage handloom sector is forth position. The reason for this is most of the people are not willing to pay huge amount in handloom products except in occasional cases.

Common Problems Faced by Women Entrepreneurs in Manipur

Beside the above factors, women entrepreneurs are facing many problems. The problems may vary and different from enterprise to enterprise, place to place and from time to time. Some of these problems may be common, but other are more specific and related with the live of activity of the enterprise. Some may be due to the internal environmental factors, while some of the problems are because of the external environmental factor. These problems directly or indirectly affect the enterprise. This is shown in the following Table 2.

Table 2
Common Problems Faced By Women Entrepreneurs in Manipur

Sl. No	Different Problems	No. of W.E.	Out of 50 %
1.	Social Taboos	26	52
2.	Searching of raw material	30	60
3.	Transportation	25	50
4.	Telecommunication	20	40
5.	Power	14	28
6.	Problems looking for employer	8	16
7.	Technological problem	20	40
8.	Marketing	26	52
9.	Production	15	30
10.	Finance	34	68

Source : Field Survey.

It is one thing to declare women socially equal to men but quite another to accept the traditionally maintained differences between their nature characters behaviour, social and psychological mindsets. Women suffered social problem because of the prevalent inequality, discrimination due to the social altitude of males and the existing customs and tradition male chauvinistic attitude still affects the female movement, women still suffered from male reservation about women role, ability and capacity and are meted accordingly. This social attitude especially that of male acts as a big hindrance especially for women entering into business. In the State of Manipur out of 50 Women Entrepreneur, 52% of them faced this problem. If this problems decreases turn economic participation will automatically increase. So, general public need to understand this problem faced by the women entrepreneur.

Another important problem is scarcity of raw materials. In Manipur out of 50 Women Entrepreneur, 30 of them i.e. 60 % faced this problem. Sometimes price of the raw materials fluctuate in the markets, and at times the price of the material rises higher than price of the final product. This affects the entrepreneurial works. In large industrial units they buy material in bulk quantity and the Government also offered incentive for them. But in small units these types of incentives are not available, Non-available of quality raw material also hampers in the process of production. So, we need special attention from Government and non-Governmental organisation for removing this problem, then their economic strength will be increased.

Inadequate infrastructural facility is also one of the reasons for underdevelopment. After fifty years of Indian independence the Northeastern region is still neglected in the field of transportation. The survey observed that 50% of the women entrepreneur faced this problem in the State of Manipur. This is one of the reason for the under-development of the industrial sector in the region.

In Manipur out of the total 50 women entrepreneur surveyed, 52% of them had suffered from marketing problem, marketing problem is also related with quality control, transportation and communication system etc. without proper transportation and communication system there cannot be much headway in development of the enterprise and it will be very difficult to market the various products. There are few opportunities where one can sell their products in the State or national level trade fair, which is being regularly held in different parts of the region. For proper marketing of the products, the State needs proper arrangement of marketing through Government and Non Governmental agencies.

Finance is one of the important organ of an enterprise. And it is a powerful developmental tool, which greases the productive process of the industries in various ways. Without adequate financial resources there is no proper development in the work. According to this survey,

68% of the women entrepreneurs in the state of Manipur have finance related problem and this is one of biggest problem faced by them in almost all the sector. Due to the lack of finance many of them are facing a stiff competition from other firms and their counterpart from outside the State. Their lack of competitiveness leads to loss of many markets for their product, if they have sufficient Capital for investment then they can earned more money and boost the economy of the State. Economic condition of the state is very poor as compared to other part of India.

Education is an important instrument for increasing and improving the chances of employability in many sectors. Inspite of many inadequacies, education has made a definite impact upon enterpreneurial development. It opens up an area of which women can compete with men and prove their independent indentity. It ultimately leads them to adventures. Education has been reported as a crucial factor for developing modern entrepreneurship. So, education is known to be the best means of developing a precious resource which income pass different dimensions of entrepreneurship. Thus, formal education will benefit entrepreneurs by marking available more skills necessary for entrepreneurial endeavour. However, in the State of Manipur the survey had found out that only a minimal number of women entrepreneurs are well educated. So, most of them are not getting the opportunity for advancement in many areas like financial facilities, export and import promotional activities and technical know how etc.

Suggestions

1. Access to information. Special efforts have to be made by the Government for this purpose.
2. Access to Credit. Bank and Financial institution needs to come forward to extend loans without insisting on collateral securities and margin money provided it is a feasible one.
3. EDP's should be tailored to suit varying requirements. Various vocational educations needs be given.
4. The Government should extend all the services/benefits at the disposal of their marketing department and other network of distribution to the women entrepreneurs.
5. Minimizing of social taboos by creating mutual understanding, A Societal-Approach is essential.

6. National organizations such as NRDC, NISC, NABARD, SIDBI etc needs to establish centers for training, counseling and production for women entrepreneurs.
7. Removal of "Fear Complex" and "Inferior Complex".
8. Wide publicity through different medias, conferences, seminar and other related activities must be conducted to educate and the need for more women entrepreneur.
9. Design, plan and implement various programmes for the benefit of women student in all the educational institution to attract young women to take up entrepreneurial activities.
10. Improvement in the health condition of women is very important.

Conclusion

Manipur, one of the North Eastern region is blessed with abundant natural resources if there are properly exploited, it can tremendously boost its economy. But the pace of economic development is very slow and the region is still industrially backward. There are various natural and economic factors for its industrial backwardness. Today, there is a greater awakening among women. Given an opportunity, they will deliver the results. In education, they have not only excelled but also become top makers. The need of the hour is to provide an opportunity in a conducive atmosphere free from gender differences. The need for awareness motivation to be an active member of the society is a great challenge today. It is, therefore, encouragement of the growing intensity of motivation amongst educated young women for coming in the entrepreneurial stream and extend support with scientifically designed package of the technical and financial assistance. Towards this end, an integrated approach is necessary for making the movement of women entrepreneurship a success.

NOTES AND REFERENCES

1. Balu, U. (1991), *Entrepreneurial Development*, Sri Venkatesevara Publications, Madras.
2. Basotia, G.R. and Sharma, K.K. (1999), *Handbook of Entrepreneurship Development*, Mangal Deep Publications, New Delhi.
3. Mali, D.D. (2002), *Entrepreneurship Development in North East*, Experience and Strategy, I.I.E.

4. Rani, Lalitha (1996), *Women Entrepreneurs*, A.P.H. Publishing Corporation, Delhi.

5. Rapporters Report, (1998), Women Entrepreneurs in India, *Indian Journal of Commerce*.

6. Srinivasan, N.P. (1994), Entrepreneurial Development and Development Banking, Department of Commerce, University of Madras, Madras.

7. Singh, Kamala (1998), *Women Entrepreneurs*, Ashish Publishing House, New Delhi.

8. Desai, Vasant (2003) *Dynamics of Entrepreneurial Development and Management*, Himalaya Publishing House, New Delhi.

9. IIE, (2000) *Promoting New Entrepreneurs*.

10. Census of India, Manipur (2001), Directorate of Census Operation, Manipur.

11. *Statistical Abstract of Manipur* (2004), Directorate of Economics and Statistics, Government of Manipur, Imphal.

12. *Draft Annual Plan (2004-05)*, Planning Department, Manipur.

21

WOMEN ENTREPRENEURS IN MANIPUR: A Case Study of Khwairamband Women Market

G.P.PRASAIN
KH. DHIREN MEETEI

Introduction

In Manipur, Khwairamb and Women Market occupies an important place in the history of Manipur. Manipuri women took major share in the socio-economic life of the state. Women are not confined within the four walls of their domestic life. They freely moved from place to place for the purpose of business. S.K. Bhuyan quote that " Manipur women have been enjoying a freedom which their sisters in India have failed to attain even up to the present day. Their activities are not confined to the four walls of their domestic life. They go out freely for purpose of petty traders mainly in the scale of the products of their own hands." Women take a great role in the financial matters of the family.

According to R. Brown "Many women walk miles in the morning and buy things from distant villagers and sell it again into capital in the evening. In the evening the women were hurrying along with their wares on their heads and little baby slung on their backs. In the bazar the women sat in long row raised on card without any cover in the rainy seasons". Women also engaged in promoting handlooms and handicrafts industries.

Historical Background of Khwairamband Women Market

King Khagemba established Khwairamband Bazar in the sixteenth century. The Khwairamband Bazar is an important market place of the state of Manipur. The southern part of the Bazar is known as Paona Brajabashi Market, the northern part as Thangal Market and the eastern part are called Bir Tikendrajit Market.

The roads passes from the women market to the southern side is Paona Road, the northern part as Thangal Road and the eastern part as Bir Tikendrajit Road. From the historical point of view, Khwairamband Bazar is the only market centre for women.

The establishment and development of new market in Manipur were completely in the hands of the king of Manipur. The socio-economic life of the people of Manipur was fully regulated by the laws framed by the administrative office of the king. These laws were announced in the market place. In the market place, the king conducted various types of activities. In 1806 king Chourjit accompanied by the Queen used to visit markets to enhance smooth, peaceful and effective functioning of the state. The people in the market areas also performed the sports activities and festivals during the king Gambhirsingh (Chinglen Nongdrenkhomba) 1833.

The market place was the main centre for administering justice in Manipur. From the historical records, it was shown that for any unhealthy happenings, the culprits were brought in the market place and various typed of punishments were given by the king himself to ensure justice. The king in this market settled the conflicts and the quarrels among the common people and nobilities. Between men and women illegal relationship were given punishment in the market. During the war period, floods and natural calamities, the king used to announce the closure of the market.

There are many factors for the development of women market in Manipur in the early part. They are:

All the adult male members of the family had to render the military service in the palace.

All the adult male members of the family accompanied the king during the warfare against the neighbouring kings.

Constant warfare between Manipur and Burma reduced the number of male members in Manipur.

Due to above factors, women had to come forward and earn money from the business in order to maintain the family members which ultimately helped women to develop their skill in business.

Modernisation and Women Entrepreneurs

Since 1949, women of Manipur have developed their skill in handlooms and handicrafts, knitting and embroidery, developing fashionable dress etc. as a result of the process of modernisation and urbanisation. Today, some women in groups started the saving transaction of money in the form of Chit funds/Marups. Women of all sections, educated, uneducated, household wives, workingwomen, etc. have taken keen interest in marups as either organisers or members. By doing so, women get a lot of financial benefit.

Women traders doing business in the women market of Manipur act as the backbone for economic development in Manipur. The contribution of women in the economic development can be traced to the early part of the history of Manipur. Mr. Mc.Culloch, the Political Agent in Manipur quote that "There is a market daily attended only by women. Every women carries a basket containing something not immediately required for the consumption of her households and she barters it for something immediately wanted or she sell it and purchased what she wants with the proceeds."

Manipur is an agricultural state. Women takes an active part in the field of agriculture and in course of time, they developed their skills, knowledge and management as small traders taking various forms and in different situations. The economic activities of the women were confined in the state due to lack of communication and traditional method of cultivations. In course of time due to better communication system and transport system, Manipuri women are becoming more experts in their trade and business.

Different Types of Khwairamband Women Bazar

The most important and popular market in Manipur is called Khwairamband Bazar. The Women Market of Khwairamband bazar can be divided into the following heads: -

Purana Bazar

Purana Bazar was established in 1915 during the period of British rule in Manipur. It is the largest type of women market in Khwairamband

Bazar. The main items available in this market are food items, women jewelleries, handicrafts items, flowers, vegetables, fruits, fishes, coins, etc. This market is popularly known as Ima Keithel i.e. Mothers Market. Muslim women also sell eggs in this market.

The following table (Table 1) shows the main items, shed No. and seat capacity in Purana Bazar.

Table1
Main Items of Purana Bazar

Sl. No.	Main Items	Shed No.(s)	Seat Capacity
1.	Tilak Material (Chandon)	1	83
2.	Jewellery	2	86
3.	Vegetables, Spices	3, 4, 8, 9, 12, 16, 18, 25	529
4.	Betel leaf and nuts, rice, fruits, Eggs	5, 6, 7, 13	339
5.	Dry Fishes, Fresh Fishes	14, 17, 19, 26, 27	365
6	Women frock dress	10, 11, 20, 21, 22	90
7.	Pot	15	66
8.	Dry pea and chana gram	23, 24, 28	82
	Total		1899

Source: Imphal Municipal Council and Personal Survey.

New Market and Lingthoingambi Market

The New Market and Lingthoingambi Market consist of 18 sheds i.e. 14 sheds in the New Market and 4 sheds in the Lingthoingambi Market. The main items available in the New Market are of locally produced clothes for men, women and children to be used on various occasions. Table 2 shows the various items, shed No and seat capacity in the New Market.

Lingthoingambi Market is the name of another women market, which was given by the Members of Municipal Board on 25th May 1990. Table 3 shows the main items, shed No. and seat capacity in the Lingthoingambi Market.

Table 2
Main Items of New Market

Sl. No.	Main Items	Shed No.	Seat Capacity
1.	Silk clothes	1	42
2.	Miscellaneous spined clothes/ clothes for daily uses	2, 9, 10, 3	(42+102+100+40) = 284
3.	Frock for children and women	4, 5, 8, 13	(42+68+66+132) =308
4.	A costly thin shawls for women	6	72
5.	Local cotton towel, fishing net, local loin	7, 14, 11	(64+113+118)= 295
6.	Ready garments	12	90
	Total		1091

Source: Imphal Municipal Council and Personal Survey.

Table 3
Main Items of Lingthoingambi Market

Sl. No.	Main Items	Shed No.	Seat capacity
1.	Local made towel, bed covers, Loin clothes etc.	1, 2	(32+32) = 64
2.	Woollen clothes, tribal clothes etc.	3, 4	(48+48) = 96
	Total		160

Source: Imphal Municipal Council and Personal Survey.

Laxmi Bazar

This market deals in mainly clothes, utensils and local lamps. The total number of sheds in this market is 14. Shed 1 deal with local cotton towels, shed 2 sells miscellaneous spined clothes, sheds 3, 4, 5 sell pieces of clothes used for ritual purposes. Sheds Nos. 6 and 7 sell utensils for ritual purposed, shed 8 deals with local lamp (podons). Readymade quilt cover available in shed Nos. 9 and 10. Handloom products, bed cover etc. sells in shed No. 11. Dresses of cotton clothes for womenfolk (pungou phanek) sell in shed Nos. 12 and 13. Shed 14 is reserved for selling mosquito nets of local varieties and designs. The details of these are shown in Table 4.

Table 4
Main Items of Laxmi Bazar

Sl. No.	Main Items	Shed No.	Seat Capacity
1	Local Cotton Towel (Gamsha)	1	32
2	Miscellaneous Spined Clothes	2	48
3	Pieces of Clothes used for Ritual Purposes	3, 4, 5	47+42+47=136
4	Utensils for Ritual Purposes	6, 7	48+48=96
5	Local Lamp (Pondon)	8	48
6	Readymade quilt cover	9, 10	48+47=95
7	Handloom Products, bed cover	11	48
8	White Cotton Clothes for Women	12, 13,	47+48=95
9	Mosquito Net	14	48
	Total		646

Source: Imphal Municipal Council and Personal Survey.

Chakrikom Bazar

Chakrikom Bazar was established in the year 1994 and located in the northern side of Session Court, Imphal. The numbers of sheds available in this bazar are 5 having 140 seat capacity. This market deals with mainly fresh coconuts and seasonal fruits. The details of this market are shown in Table 5.

Bazar in the East of the Session Court

The Bazar in the east of the session court was established in 1994. There are only 3 sheds with 220 seats capacity. This market deals with the selling of seasonal fruits, sweets, vegetables etc.

Table 5
Main Items of Chakrikom Bazar

Sl. No.	Main Items	Shed No.	Seat capacity
1	Fresh coconut	1	24
2	Seasonal fruits and fresh coconuts	2	24
3	Seasonal fruits	3,4,5	28+32+32 =92
	Total		140

Source: Imphal Municipal Council and Personal Survey.

Naga Nullah

The bazar in Naga Nullah was established in the year 1997. The number of sheds available in this market is 9 with 721 seats capacity. The main items deals with in this market are seasonal vegetables and fruits. Women sell sugar-cane in large number in this bazar. Fresh vegetables, fruits, occasional fishes, sweets etc. are also available. There are also tribal women dealing with various kinds of vegetables and banana leaves.

Financial Support of Women Market

Finance is the lifeblood of any business. The survey covers all the main women markets of Khwairamband Bazar. The women businessmen of Purana Bazar are the most experienced businessmen. Only 35% of the women businessman had taken loan for their business and remaining 65% of the women businessman conducts their business without loan from banks and funding agencies. Those women who take loans for their business face the problems in repayment of loans amount. Most of them are not interested in getting loans from the private financer. Most of the women were not getting any loans from the nationalised banks because of strict procedure in getting the loan from such banks. Women businessman getting financial support from their families' member like husbands, children, parents, friends, relatives etc. They also share the financial responsibilities of their families specially children. Some of the family members depend on them for financial support. The same trends are also found in New Market, Linghoinganbi Market, Laxmi bazar, Eastern part of the Session Court and Naga Nullah.

More than 80% of women entrepreneurs of Chakrikom Bazar had taken loan from the private agencies or financer for running their trade and business and it is because of awareness among the women businessman for taking loan from this financer. For them, it is easy to repay the loan amount on instalment basis daily. Majority of them take the loan amount on varying amount i.e. between Rs. 3,000 to Rs. 10,000. 20% of women businessman runs their business with own capital investment.

Earning of Women Traders

Women traders are having independent source of income as they got success in their business. More than 90% of women traders responded that they have independent source of income. It means that they are success in their business. Remaining 10% of the women traders responds that they are having problems for conducting their business. It is because of loss in their business and the problem of interest payment on borrowed loans from the private financers.

Saving of Women Traders

About 70% of the women traders in Purana Bazar do not save any amount from their income and remaining 30% have saved some amount from their income. In New Market, about 80% do not save from their income and 20% save some amount from their income. The same is happened to the women traders of Lingthoinganbi Bazar, Laxmi Bazar, Chakrikom and Naga Nullah. The women businessman in the east of the Session Court does not have the habit of saving. 80% of women respond that saving is not required for their old age and 20% save money from their income for their old age.

The young women group of the different markets are interested in making plans for future growth and development of their families. 87% in Laxmi bazar, 83% in New Market, 75% in Purana Bazar planned for growth and development of their families. The remaining traders also are equally interested in financial planning and development of their families. It shows that women traders of different markets of Khwairamband bazar occupy permanent seat plan in advance to run their families. They save their money by joining to Marup. Most of the women traders joins different kinds of marups. This helps them in saving their income in a very useful manner. They get various commodities like utensils, clothes, gold and other luxurious items from their marups.

Conclusion

From the above study it may be concluded that majority of the women traders in the different markets bear the financial responsibilities in the maintenance of their families. Only a small percentage of the women are having sound financial position in their families and majorities of them are depends to the private investor/ financers. Some of rich women traders purchased more seats and rent for earnings. About 90% of the women traders belong to poorer section. They performed their business for financial responsibilities of their families. They take loan from private financer earn profit as well as the repay of loan amounts in instalment.

In economical terms, the women traders can be divided into three groups as (i) Higher Income Group (ii) Middle Income Group and (iii) Lower Income Group.

The women belonging to the higher income group purchase more seats and rent for earning. The middle-income group gets financial support from their husband, sons, daughters, parents etc. The lower income group get financial support from private financers or agencies to run their business and earn their livelihood as well as managed their families with great difficulties.

The study of the women businessman of Khnwairamband indicate the following observations:

1. The women traders contribute towards the financial support of their families.
2. The women traders markets with the exception of a few deal with mainly in home products.
3. The women as a collective body always act as a force on issues concerning economic life of the people of Manipur. They try to protect not only the interest of their families but also the interest of the state at large.

NOTES AND REFERENCES

1. *Administrative Report* (1891-1946), Manipur State Political Agency.
2. Imphal Municipal Council (1956-1994), *Proceedings of the Imphal Municipal Board.*
3. Imphal Municipal Council (1962-2003), Records and Documents relating to *Khwairamband Markets*.

4. Government of Manipur (1997), (Law and Home Department), Records relating to Khwairamband Market.
5. Government of Manipur (1980-2002), *Manipur Gazette.*
6. Government of Manipur (1996), (Manipur State Archives), *Select Documents of Jananeta Hijam Irabot*, Vol. I.
7. *Encyclopaedia Britannica* (1971), Vol. 22, William Brinton.
8. Khelchandra, N. and Ibungohal, L. (1967), *Cheitharol Kumbaba*, Imphal.
9. Bhuyan, S.K. (1954), *Assam and Manipur*, Bhusan Khonjenba.
10. Brown, R. (1975), *Statistical Account of Manipur*, Mittal Publications, New Delhi.
11. McCulloch, M. (1980), *Valley of Manipur*, Delhi.

22

WOMEN ENTREPRENEURS AND SELF-HELP GROUPS

KH. SOMORENDRO SINGH

Introduction

The entrepreneur is a key to economic development. The emergence of women entrepreneurs in a society depends to a great extent on the economic, religions, cultural, social, psychological and other factors.

Women Entrepreneurs are the women or a group of women who initiate, organise and operate a business enterprise. The Government of India notes women entrepreneurs as

> "An enterprise owned and controlled by women saving a minimum financial interest of 51 per cent of the capital and giving at least 51 per cent of the employment generated in the enterprise to women".

Plight of Rural Women

The World Bank Report (1991) has observed "women are central to success of poverty alleviation effort in the short and medium as in the long run".

The 9th Five-year Plan of India was very clear about the larger scope for SHGs and the need for infusion of professionalism. The plan document observes:

"The SHGs would be given 'Pattas' for development of wasteland, social forestry, soil conservation and watershed project. Common property resources would also be allocated to SHGs in the villages on a long term basis for eco-sensitive reserve management. There is also a potential for allotting nurseries of the forest department to these groups for management. In all these, the interest of women's group would have to be protected".

Plan document further observes:

"A cadre of para-professionals from within the community would be created to enhance the capability of SHGs and help the community to access the facilities and services meant to them". (GOI, Planning Commission, 9th Five-Year Plan, 1997-2002, Vol II-P. 30).

Self-Help Groups (SHGs) - A New Lease of Life for Rural Masses

Now-a-days SHGs are gaining popularity in rural areas. The SHGs are considered a new lease of life for the women in villages for their social and economic empowerment.. SHG is a suitable means for the empowerment of women. The SHGs started playing an important role in the rural development. It is a voluntary group in a particular village. Those who are below the poverty level joined together under one banner. They pay some subscription towards savings and with this accumulated amount, credit is given to group members at a very low rate of interests for starting new business.

Keeping this in mind the present study "Women Entrepreneurs and Self-Help Groups" made an attempt to study about the SHGs and Women Entrepreneurs in Imphal East District of Manipur State. In this study an attempt has also been made to study the attitude of SHGs members towards their SHGs by selecting 85 members randomly from SHGs formed in Imphal East District.

Measurement of Attitude of SHGss Members

Attitudes are evaluative statements or judgements concerning objects, people or events. Hence, the attitude may be positive or negative. The attitude scale has been used in this study to measure the overall attitudes of the sample respondents.

Formation of SHGs

The SHG is an association of people belonging to similar socio-economic characteristic, residing in same locality. The SHGs are voluntary association of people formed to attain some common goals. These are groups which have similar social identity, heritage or traditional occupations, and come together for a common cause and manage resources for the benefit of the group members.

SHGs are presently promoted by Women Cooperative Education Project, NCUI, New Delhi located at ICM, Imphal; Institute of Cooperative Management, (ICM), Imphal, Lamphelpat; Manipur State Cooperative Union (MSCU); Cooperative Education Field Project, NCUI, New Delhi, located at Nambol, Bishnupur District, also other voluntary agencies with a Focus on social and economic issues, mainly thrift and credit programmes. They are also taking up issues relating to rural industries and modernisation of agriculture.

Working of SHGs

The SHGs usually generate a common fund out of small savings from persons of groups collected on a regular basis by curtailing unproductive expenditure. Also the internal savings generated are supplemented by external resources loan from financial institutes and donated by any voluntary agencies involved in promoting and strengthening the SHGs.

Apart there, Institute of Cooperative Management (ICM), Manipur State Cooperative Union (MSCU), Women Cooperative Education Project (WCEP), and other agencies provides formal training through which the women entrepreneurs acquired skills for managing the small scale enterprises such as fruit preservation, toy makings, papad making, agarpathy making, poultry, diary, piggeries, and allied operations etc. Though the intervention of micro-credit, the women entrepreneurs has benefited many things and shifted even their lives from rural areas into semi-urban lives.

The Institute of Cooperative Management (ICM), Manipur State Cooperative Union (MSCU), and Women Cooperative Education Project (WCEP), Imphal recommended to financial institutes for providing financial support to start micro enterprises and also suitable place for marketing the produces of women entrepreneurs. In order to activate the system of rural marketing Kanglei Agro Business Services (KABS) and other Marketing Voluntary agencies are acting as internal agency for selling the products produced by women entrepreneurs. From time to time ICM along with other agencies insist the SHG members to undergo training for technology upgradation and to give uptodate market information for creating awareness on the matters pertaining to price trend of commodities in the marketing system in rural areas, the SHGs members may easily sell their products in the villages which paver the ways for self-sustainability among women entrepreneurs.

Findings of the Study

From the analysis it is found that SHGs are organised to manage their economic activities better and are gaining empowerment in directions, which are appropriate to their needs, interests and constraints. They gained confidence from an increase in their relative financial independence and security. The increase in the literacy skills of the SHG members is another indicator of empowerment, some of them learned to sign, to read and write and could do simple arithmetic work.

The new instrument namely SHG has been so designed as to develop the sense of mutual help and self employment, a new work culture to strengthen the human and capital base collectively and also to develop rural entrepreneurship.

Now, the SHG as a collective entity has a look beyond mere frontier of production and income to the development of input and output market and also to the possibility of tapping the available resources in and around the area.

Market interaction is key to productive process. In fact the advantage of division of labour for that matter the large scale production "is limited by the extent of the market" (Adam Smith). Therefore, production is going to be driven and directed by the structure and extent of demand, perform or perish.

The SHG members are sensitized in acquiring an attitude of protest against various abuses, knowledge about their rights, and other social issues. Decision-making is the ultimate level of empowerment and equality. It signifies that women have started taking control of their lives and situation through attending group meetings, public functions, involvement and income generating activities, joining other women in social causes. The collective and integrated activities of the SHGs are presumed to have helped them in sustaining their family economically, giving better education to their children, meeting financial crisis in the family, meeting every crisis independently.

Communication skills is very important to overcome any possible communication gap. Better Communication Skills is also another indicator of empowerment of women. Most of the group members of SHGs in Imphal East District of Manipur are attending the group meetings and meets regularly. In this way they develop their ability to interact and communicate with each other.

It is evident from the study that many SHG women members are currently involved with some additional economic activities such as making agarpathies, production of candles, soap, readymade garments, pickles, papad, toys, bags, Handloom and Handicraft products etc. Majority of the SHG members are earning not less than Rs. 1,000 per month as their income particularly those SHGs promoted by ICM and WCEP, Imphal.

Some of the successful SHGs in Imphal East District are :

(a) Kiyamgei Lairam Wangma SHG located about 14 kms. away from Imphal under Keirao Assembly Constituency.

(b) Twenty Smart Women SHG and Women 20 Star SHG, Khabam - which is situated 11 kms. away from Imphal at Kontha Khabam Village.

(c) Leima Women SHGs - which is located at Mokhanglambi, Singjamei Kshetri Leikai about 7 kms. from Imphal.

(d) Asha Women SHG - which is located at Thongju, Imphal East, around 12 kms. from Imphal and

(e) Kabok Pokpi women's SHG - which is located at Larikyengbam Leikai, 7 kms. from Imphal

And many more SHGs are also there which are working very well. Interestingly a new linkage has also developed. Now, by and large, with a new initiative of NABARD, actualised through agencies like Manipur Rural banks and other commercial Banks, a good linkage has been established.

It is also observed that how Self Help Group(SHG) develops rural Women Entrepreneurship and linkage of financial assistance from banks and various other aspects and features of SHGs in terms of economic benefits, as well as social benefits. They become alert to take advantage of "project-opportunities" that develop in the market from time to time.

The main focus of activity of the SHGs is to generate savings for income-generating projects in the village. This has pioneered a unique participatory method for the identification of ventures as well as beneficiaries at the grassroots level in the spirit of planning from below : Although the entry point of the project is mainly credits and saving, the SHGs benefit the people in every aspect of life in a village community.

Women Cooperatives and SHGs

As on 31-03-2005 11 Women Cooperatives have been formed in Imphal East District of Manipur by WCEP, Imphal. All the women cooperatives are converted from SHGs. Because women should be encouraged to join in the management and administration of the cooperative affairs. Women can play an important part in the management and working of cooperative societies by being elected representatives. They can participate in the decision-making process and formulate new programmes and policies. In addition to strengthening the existing programmes as elected members of Board of Directors (BODs). This will help in developing a new stream of professional leadership in the women cooperative sectors. The participation of women in cooperative is necessary for entrepreneurial development. By opening a large number of small industrial ventures women entrepreneurs can strengthen the industrial base, provide employment opportunities and achieve balanced growth through cooperatives.

Some Constraints

A few constraints discourage the SHGs in Manipur particularly Imphal East District. Mention may be made of operational constraints, financial constraints, organisational and management constraints, marketing constraints and viability constraints.

In the course of investigation and also interaction with the members of SHGs in Imphal East District, the members feel free to point out various aspects of operational constraints covering lack of proper workshed, lack of availability of sufficient quantity of inputs including credit, power, equipments and lack of family support.

Conclusion

It is observed from the study that revolution is taking place in rural areas because of formation of many Self-Help Groups (SHGs) in rural areas particularly in Imphal East District. It is also further observed that the rural women are really empowered socially and economically after having become members of the Self-Help Groups. Hence, it is duty of the Government, cooperative organisations, voluntary organisation and allied agencies to assist the women in formation and management of many more SHGs covering the all rural areas in Manipur. What they need is encouragement and support from the family members, Government Society, male counter part. These benefits indicate the worthiness and viability of assisting entrepreneurial women in Manipur through multiple challenges still exist. Greater and continuous support for entrepreneurial activities is needed to further improve the lives of these women and the condition of their communities. Thus the formation of quality SHGs both in rural and urban areas make the women empowered socially and economically. Such a joint effort will help them to go for producing value added Industrial products which will fetch more income to the women entrepreneurs of such Self-Help Groups.

ANNEXURE-I

THE ACTIVITIES UNDERTAKEN BY THE WOMEN COOPERATIVE EDUCATION PROJECT (WCEP), IMPHAL EAST FOR THE MEMBERS OF SHGS AND COOPERATIVE SOCIETIES SINCE INCEPTION AUGUST 2000 TO DECEMBER 2004

Sl. No.	Activities	Target		Achievement	
		No.	Participant	No.	Participant
1.	Education Activities Motivation Meeting for Formation of Self Help Group	625	5000	684	14228
2.	Social Development Activities - Adult Education - Health and Family Welfare - AIDS Awareness	640	8075	650	11432
3.	Deposit Mobilisation and Recovery of Loan	360	4500	379	6558
4.	Income Generating activities	315	4650	342	6098

Source: Annual Report, NCUI-Women Coop. Education Project, ICM, Imphal.

ANNEXURE-II

THE POSITION OF SELF-HELP GROUP SINCE INCEPTION UNDER VARIOUS HEADS (SINCE AUGUST 2000 TO DECEMBER 2004)

No. of SHG Formed since Inception Aug. 2000	No. of Member	Thrift Collection (Rs.)	Disbursed (Rs.)	Loan Recovery (Rs.)	Recovery Rate %	No. of Benefi-Ciarles	Credit Linkage with NABARD through Manipur Rural Bank	Credit Linkage with State Bank of India. Imphal Branch
136	2538	20,74,508	91,05,068	32,44,670	100	4069	50 SHGs Rs. 68,400	30 SHGs Rs. 58,73,000

Source: Annual Report, NCUI-Women Coop. Education Project ICM, Imphal.

ANNEXURE-III

INCOME GENERATING ACTIVITIES CONDUCTED BY NCUI, WOMEN PROJECT, IMPHAL EAST FOR THE MEMBERS OF COOPERATIVE SOCIETIES AND SHGS IN COLLABORATION WITH OTHER DEVELOPMENT AGENCIES (SINCE INCEPTION AUGUST 2000 TO DEC. 2004)

Sl. No.	Activities	No. of events/ group benefitted	No. of members trained/	Name of the collaborating agency
1	2	3	4	5
1.	Fruit and Vegetable Preservation Training	19	547	Community Food and Nutrition Extension unit, Chingamathak, Ministry of HRD Govt. of india
2.	Complementary Food Production Training	1	27	-do-
3.	Shawl Embroidery Training	14	359	ICM, Imphal and NCUI, New Delhi and Private Instruction
4.	6 Months Embroidery/ Tailoring Training	3	7	Border State Development Programme of NCCT, New Delhi and NEC Shillong
5.	6 Months Weaving and Design Training	3	7	Border State Devt. Programme of NCCT, New Delhi and NEC Shillong and Manipur Devt. Society, Imphal

(*Contd.*)

1	2	3	4	5
6.	Establishment of Homescale Silk Reeling and Spinning Unit	3	36	Tasar Research Station Central Silk Board, Government of India, Mantripukhri
7.	Distribution of HYV seeds 150 kg of Peas (Rachana)	1	20	Manipur Development Society, Imphal (A Govt. of Manipur undertaking)
8.	Waste Minimisation and Cleaner Production in Hosiery Garments Bleaching	1	15	Small Industries Service Institute Takyel (SISI)
9.	Silk Dyeing Training	5	204	NCUI, Handloom Project and Weavers Service Centre, Ministry of Textile, Government of India
10.	Incensed Dhoop Making	35	763	Integrated Socio Devt. Organisation, Lily Enterprises, Nongmeibung ICM, Imphal and NCUI-New Delhi and other Private Instructor
11.	Papad Making Training	17	545	ICM, Imphal and NCUI, New Delhi and Other
12.	Recycling of Waste Plastic/ Cement Bags into different Income Generating Items	11	383	ICM, Imphal and NCUI, New Delhi and Private Instructor by a trained SHG member under Cooperation
13.	One month Training on Block Printing and Designing and Weaving	1	8	Weavers Service Centre, Takyel,Ministry of Textile, Govt. of India
14.	Five Days Bed Sheet Embroidery in Traditional Motif (Sagol Samu)	1	40	Private Instructor by a trained SHG Member under cooperation among SHGs scheme
15.	Five Days Plastic Bag	3	90	-do-

(*Contd.*)

1	2	3	4	5
16.	Five Days Bory Making	2	60	Private Bory Making Firm, B3amon Leikai
17.	One Month Block Printing and Rubber Stamp Making	1	7	Small Industries Service Institute Takyel (SISI), Govt. of India
18.	Three Months Leather Bag Making	5	111	NCUI, New Delhi and ICM sponsored by NEC, Shillong
19.	One Month Leather Bag Making	2	13	ICM, Imphal Sponsored by NCCT, New Delhi and SISI, Takyel, Govt. of India
20.	One/Two Month Kouna Bag	2	20	ICM, Making Imphal sponsored by NCCT, New Delhi and SISI, Takyel, Govt. of India
21.	Demonstration-cum-training Programme on Besan Making with Electric Grinding Machine	1	20	Private Firm/Trained SHG
22.	Tie and Dye Training	1	30	-do-
23.	Hand Embroidery Training	1	20	-do-
24.	Soap Making	1	40	-do-

Source: Annual Report, NCUI-Women Coop. Education Project, ICM, Imphal.

ANNEXURE IV

REGISTRATION OF SUCCESSFUL SELF-HELP GROUPS

During the month of December, 2002, the following successful SHG heave been register as Cooperative Societies

Sl. No.	Name of SHG/Address	Name of Coop. Society	Regn. No.	No. of Membership
1.	Thongju Part-II Women SHG, Pheijaleitong	The Progressive Sericulture Coop. Society Ltd.	54/2002	20
2.	(I) Asha Self-Help Group (ii) Luxmi Self-Help Group, Thongju Nameirakpam Leikai (iii) Saraswati SHG, Thongju	Asha Luxmi Handicraft	58/2002	60
3.	Kongba Weavers Self-Help Group, Kongba Laishram Leikai	Kongba Handloom and Handicraft Cooperative Society Ltd.	59/2002	20
4.	(I) Sileima Sintha SHG, Khabam (ii) Women 20 Star SHG, Khabam (iii) 20 Smart Women SHG Khabam	The Elite Women Multi Coop. Society Ltd.	61/2002	46
5.	(I) New Checkon Women SHG (ii) Chingnang Leikai Women SHG (iii) Checkon Mayai Leikai SHG (iii) Mandop Leirak WSHG	Luxmi Women Multi Industrial Coop. Society Ltd.	62/2002	67

6. (I) Kiyamghei Lairam Wangma Women SHG (ii) Kiyamgei Lairam Wangma Leishabi SHG	Progressive Handicraft and Allied Industries Coop. Society Ltd.	66/2002	35
7. Kongpal Laishram Makha Leikai Women SHG	The Pioneer Handloom and Handicraft Coop. Society Ltd.	67/2002	25

Source: Annual Report, NCUI-Women Coop. Education Project, ICM, Imphal.

23

PROBLEMS OF WOMEN ENTREPRENEURS:

A Case Study of Imphal and Kamrup Districts

TH. PRABHA DEVI

Introduction

During the last seven years of my career as a research scholar, I got the opportunity to visit a number of small scale industries and interact with a number of small industrialists in both inside and outside the state of Manipur (in the North East Region). Out of these large numbers of industries I have visited, a considerable number of units are owned by women. Majority of units owned by women I have visited so far have mentioned various constraints, out of which a large number of them have mentioned customary problems, managerial problems, production problems, marketing problems, financial problems and problems of government assistance etc.

In recent years, women are making their mark even in the field of business and industry. The problems faced by women entrepreneurs are more serious and different in many respects than the problems faced by the men entrepreneurs. Men are comparatively has access to better education, better facilities and a variety of opportunities when compared to women in our society up till now.

The present study aims at analyzing and critically examine the problems faced by women entrepreneurs of north-east region in particular and women entrepreneurs of India in general and to suggest different remedial measure in helping and promoting women entrepreneurs.

Methodology

The present study was carried out in Kamrup district of Assam and Imphal district of Manipur randomly selecting 20 women entrepreneurs, each engaging different types of business. The data for the study were mainly collected through a structured questionnaire and personal interviews.

Problems

Development of a country is a reality only when women are developed. Women entrepreneurs face certain problems not as an entrepreneur but as a woman. Therefore, when compared to men the problems of women entrepreneurs are more in number. Problems faced by women entrepreneur were:

1. Customary problems
2. Managerial problems
3. Production problems
4. Marketing problems
5. Financial problems
6. Problems of Government assistance

Customary Problem

Women in general face a lot of problems in the male dominated society. I rural tradition, women are still subjected to discriminative treatment form childhood some parents are less bother about their female children's educations and less worried if she is dropped out of school. But women take more socio-economic responsibilities in the society especially in Manipur. Though Manipur society is not a male dominated society, there are many unwritten rules which our society scrupulously follows. Most of these rules pertain to woman and encompass a wide variety of social activity like she is trained and brought up to be a good housewife, expert in doing household works to play subservient, dependent role in the family, her interaction with others, dress outing and the like. Women can interact with only known persons. The society talks ill of a woman who moves freely with outsiders. Women find it difficult to have even business relationship with others due to this environment. Thus, women are so conditioned by this value system that they too unquestioningly accept this view of themselves. This restricts woman from acquiring traits such as self confidence, independence need for achievement which are very much essential for entrepreneurial ventures. Hence, these customary problems directly or indirectly are responsible for personal problems. Lack of experience, lack of business exposure and conservative attitude towards risk taking are some of the personal problems of women entrepreneurs. Women have been traditionally doing service jobs in business enterprises. Back home, they have been involved only is activities concerning home making. A majority of the households do not consult women in major decisions resulting in a situation where women lacked experience in managing major problems individually. Another related problem is the lack of adequate technical knowledge on the part of women. Women are of less encouraged to take up opinion that the women are not suitable to such programmes. Women in general in rural areas, seem to have a conservative attitude towards family and business. It is hard to convince an average woman to accept to changes. Above all these problems, are the physiological problems women face. The fragile structure of the body, menstruation pregnancy, need to tender infants and the likes are some of the problems specific to women. Working women have the option of taking have subject to limitations -- when they face such problems. But women entrepreneurs cannot afford to go on leave during the crucial phases of the ventures. Women entrepreneurs of north eastern and personal problems. These problems can be seen from Table 1.

Table 1
Customary Problem

Sl. No.	Problems Parameters	Number	Percentage
1	Lack of family and community support	25	62.50
2	Lack of confidence to start business	14	35.00
3	Male dominated society	10	25.00
4	Lack of education and information network	20	50.00
5	Low risk bearing nature	15	37.50
6	Economic backwardness	20	50.00
7	Suppressed need for achievement	10	25.00

Source: Personal field survey, Data indicate multiples responses.

Managerial and Technical Problem

Though business is the best occupation for women to north-east since it gives them a chance to apply their creativity, earn additional income for the family, maintain self respect, flexibility of working hours etd. Women particularly rural women entrepreneurs are facing managerial and technical problems because of low level of education among the rural women in the concern field. Even if an entrepreneur is functionally well versed and possesses good entrepreneurial qualities, it would be desirable that she has prior exposure to basic managerial functions. Most of the respondents did not have knowledge of General Management and labour administration. And majority and labour administration. And majority of the respondents did not have clear cut objective and did not maintain proper accounts of their enterprises. These problems could be seen from Table 2.

Table 2
Managerial and Technical Problems

Sl. No	Problems Parameters	Number	Percentage
1.	Lack of knowledge of general management and experience	25	62.50
2.	Lack of skilled labour	21	52.50
3.	Poor record keeping and control	20	50.00
4.	Labour absentiesm and labour turnover	22	55.00
5.	Lack of clear-cut objectives	18	45.00
6.	Transportation problem as women	21	52.50

Source: Personal field survey, Data indicate multiple responses.

Production Problems

The women entrepreneurs encounter these problems during production process. These problems can be seen from Table 3.

Marketing Problems

Collecting the data and information on the market is very essential for marketing decision on what products to make and sell? What is the likely trend of demand in the future, what production techniques to adopt, pricing place, packing, potential and credit policy etc. Marketing as all we know that is one of the crucial factors affecting the fortune of any enterprise, whether it is micro, tiny, small or large scale enterprise and whether it is located in backward states or not. It does not matter what type of enterprise it is and where it is located but it is mainly concerned with the products and services it is provided as per need and satisfaction of the customers. The biggest handicap for women entrepreneurs is lack of mobility which forces them to approach middlemen to arrange for the sale of their goods and services who try to exploit them. This also prevents them from expanding their markets since they are not in direct contact with the market and are unaware of the opportunities and threats in the market. Now-a-days marketing problem is common to all entrepreneurs in general and women entrepreneurs in particular. The marketing problems that encountered by women entrepreneur of the selected units can be seen from Table 4.

Table 3
Production Problems

Sl. No	Problems Parameters	Number	Percentage
1.	Inadequate availability of land for the business	30	75.00
2.	Non-availability of required inputs	28	70.00
3.	Non-availability of adequate technical support	23	57.50
4.	Non-availability upgrading technology & R & D	20	50.00
5.	Poor inventory management	19	47.50
6.	Irregularity of power supply	35	87.50

Source: Personal field survey, Data indicate multiple responds.

Financial Problems

Availability of adequate funds is a major constraint for women entrepreneurs. Women entrepreneurs are more pronounced because in most of the cases they do not have any property in their name, which can be sold or offered as tangible security for securing credit in the money market. Thus financial problem is also a major problem faced by all women entrepreneurs. Most of the women entrepreneurs are facing financial problems at the time of starting as well as during the operation of their business enterprises. These problems can be seen from Table 5 for the selected units.

Table 4
Marketing Problem

Sl. No	Problems Parameters	Number	Percentage
1.	Lack of knowledge of how and whom to contact	28	70.00
2.	Heavy competition with big enterprises	25	62.50
3.	Exploitation by middlemen and difficulties in collecting dues	20	50.00
4.	Inadequate sales promotion avenues	22	55.00
5.	Lack of export marketing support	20	50.00

Source: Personal field survey, Data indicate multiple responses.

Table 5
Financial Problems

Sl. No	Problems Parameters	Number	Percentage
1.	Problem of getting loan and subsidy	32	80.00
2.	Insistence or collateral and margin money requirement	27	67.50
3.	Time taken to process loan	22	55.00
4.	Tight repayment schedule	21	52.50
5.	Poor financial management and maintenance of accounts	18	45.00

Source: Personel field survey, Data indicate multiple responses.

Problems of Government Assistance

Both Central and state Government are implementing various assistance schemes for promotion of women entrepreneurship. But in practice selected women entrepreneur have complain many difficulties in obtaining various government assistances and the same can be seen from Table 6.

Table 6
Government Assistance Problems

Sl. No	Problems Parameters	Number	Percentage
1	Inadequate Govt. assistance	30	75.00
2	Red Tapism at various levels	26	65.00
3	Advisory organisations become exploitive and dishonest	23	57.50
4	Complicated and time consuming procedures for getting assistance	20	50.00
5	Government policies are not favourable	18	45.00

Source: Personel field survey, Data indicate multiple responses.

Suggestive Measures

- To solve financial problems, Government and Financial institutions should draw attention and implement special lending policies. Government and other voluntary organisations should conduct financial management training programme for women entrepreneurs.
- To solve the marketing problems Government and non-Government organisation should conduct elaborate training to women entrepreneurs. Government must give subsidies and concessions to women entrepreneurs. Government must make reservation of certain products to women entrepreneurs. Women entrepreneurs association for every state must be formed and should make arrangement for conducting exhibitions and conferences in collaboration with the concerned state Governments.
- Government must rectify the production problems by allotment of factory shed and land in Government industrial areas on priority basis, supply of raw material and power and other inputs regularly at subsidies rates, giving assistance for upgradation of technology, research and development and giving production training to women entrepreneurs.

- Government and the voluntary organisations need to draw their attention to rectify the customary problems. A special programne can be conducted against the social evils. Liberal assistance and gearing up of various facilities should be done for enhancement of the status of women entrepreneurs.
- To solve the problems of getting government assistance, it is recommended that adequate assistance should be given to the right person at the right time. Governme not must be able to identify the right person.

Conclusion

Development of entrepreneurship among women in our region heavily depends on reducing all the above problems. Most of the problems could not be solved within a short period since they involve little changing the customary values and tradition with respect to women. The government can take up some of the financial problems immediately for their redressal. The society and the government have to undertake various efforts before enabling environment is created for developing women entrepreneurs in large extent. Last but not least active and dynamic participation of women is indispensable in fighting against these problems.

ENTREPRENEURSHIP DEVELOPMENT IN THE NORTH EASTERN REGION OF INDIA

24

ENTREPRENEURSHIP DEVELOPMENT IN THE NORTH-EASTERN REGION OF INDIA

(Experiences and Prospects)

S.S. KHANKA

Introduction

The 'Eight Sister States' of India viz. Arunachal Pradesh, Assam, Sikkim, Manipur, Meghalaya, Mizoram, Nagaland, and Tripura constitute the North Eastern Region (NER) of India. The entire NER is spread over 2,55,089 sq. km area which is 7.8 per cent of the total geographical area (3,287,263 sq. km) of the country. As per the Census of India 2001, the total population of North East India is 3,65,00,108 persons which is 3.5 per cent of the total population of India. Speaking alternatively, about 3.5 per cent population of India lives in its 7.8 per cent area in the North East India.

The NER enjoys a unique geographical location. While China and Bhutan fall on its north and north-west, Myanmar and Bangladesh on its east, south and south west. Thus, the NER is characterized by its unique geo- political entity. It shares quite longer border (98%) with these four neighboring countries than with India (2%). It is connected with ' mainland' India by a very narrow land corridor often called 'Chicken Neck' having an approximate width of 33 km on the eastern side and 21 km on the western side. As such, the narrow corridor is bound to be overburdened and constricted.

Such geo-political situation of the NER is very important from two standpoints. One, strategic and two, the feeling of alienation. The NER is not only geographically far from the mainland India, but also lagging far behind in economic development from the mainland India. This indicates that a lot still remains to be done in the NER. Various indicators given in Table 1 confirm it.

Table 1
NER Lags Far Behind the Country

	Indicators	NER	India
01	Literacy Rate, 2001	68.63	65.38
02	Urban Population (in %), 2001	15.51	27.78
03	Sex-Ratio (Females per '000 Males), 2001	937	933
04	Population Density (Persons Per sq. km), 2001	147	324
05	Percentage of workers engaged in Household Industries to Total Workers, 2001	3.48	4.07
06	Percentage of Gross Cultivable Area to Total Geographical Area, 2001	24	59
07	Land-Man Ratio (ha/man), 2001	0.66	.32
08	Percentage Utilization of Agricultural Land, 2001	58.74	73.05
09	Per Hectare Use of Chemical Fertilizers (in kg), 2001	26.59	87.12
10	Foodgrain Production (kg per ha), 2001	1367	1630
11	Average Population per Bank (in '000), March,1999	19	15
12	Credit-Deposit Ratio (in%), 2001	28.31	57.20
13	Percentage of Electrified Villages to Total Villages 1999-2000.	80.87	86.30
14	Length of Roads per 100 sq km area (in km), 1997	54.80	74.90
15	Percentage of Roads to Total Length of *Pucca* Roads, 1997	24.96	58.68
16	Area Per Post Office (in sq. km), 2001	41.91	22.33
17	Per Capita Income (At Current Prices in Rupees), 2000-2001	12,202	16,487

Source: Basic Statistics of NER, E and M Cell, Government of India, North Eastern Council Secretariat, Shillong, 2002.

The economic backwardness of the NER has given genesis to the feeling of alienation which, has got manifestations in the forms of militancy and terrorism. These problems over the years have become a headache, or, say, cancer for the whole country. Because poverty anywhere is dangerous for prosperity everywhere. Therefore, the problem warrents earliest solution.

Then, the million dollar question arises is what is the solution to the problem? The obvious answer to this question is to remove economic backwardness of the region by judicious harnessing of available resources in the region. Evidences abound in both at world and national levels confirm that entrepreneurship development by harnessing resources promotes economic development. The regions/states like Gujarat, Maharashtra, Panjab and Haryana where entrepreneurship has developed are developed. On the country, the regions/States like Bihar, Madhya Pradesh and North Eastern States with lack of entrepreneurship development have remained backward. Economic history is witness that entrepreneurship development is pre- requisite for industrial / economic development. That is why it is said that "an economy is the effect for which entrepreneurship is the cause."

It is evident that the NER is endowed with various resources such as forests, minerals, oil, water, medicinal plants, huge bio-diversity, natural beauty, human resources, etc. But it is unfortunate that, the NER even after five decades of country's freedom, is plagued by the predicament of "poverty amidst plenty." Given such condition, entrepreneurship development can play a very significant role in removing poverty and unemployment by utilizing available local resources. Keeping these in view, an attempt has been made in this paper to delineate the entrepreneurship development in the NER. For the convenience of the study the topics considered coalesced around four main themes: I) Entrepreneurship Development Programmes in India : A Historical Perspective, II) Entrepreneurship Development Programmes in the NER: Efforts and Experiences, III) Development of Small- Scale Industries in the NER: An Overview, IV) Prospects for Entrepreneurship Development in the NER.

I

Entrepreneurship Development Programmes in INDIA: A Historical Perspective

It will not be less than correct to say that India got the political freedom on 15th August 1947, but not the economic freedom. And attainment of economic freedom i.e., emancipation from poverty and unemployment was the biggest challenge before the country. The war for economic freedom started in 1950 in the form of planned development. Then, it was realized that the way to get rid of poverty and unemployment lies in the effective exploitation of hidden potential in the country. For this the policy maker started advocating the promotion and development of small-scale industries in the country. As a result, small-sector was recognized as employment-oriented sector during the early sixties. The employment-oriented thinking for small sector underwent changes by the end of sixties and now small-sector was recognized as an effective instrument to utilize the entrepreneurial potential remained hitherto dormant in the country.

Realizing the various problems faced by the entrepreneurs in establishing enterprises, the Government decided to offer promotional package to the entrepreneurs. Promotional package included financial help and incentives, infrastructural facilities, and technical and managerial guidance provided through various supporting organizations of the Central, State and local levels. This experience made the planners and policy-makers realize that facilities and incentives are, of course, necessary for establishing enterprises, but are not sufficient to solicit adequate response from the entrepreneurs. Hence, now it was realized that emphasis on human development is a necessary condition for entrepreneurship development. As such, the serious thinking on entrepreneurship development began from here.

Entrepreneurship development in India started with the establishment of Small Industry Extension and Training Institute (SIET) in 1962 in Hyderabad. SIET got an opportunity with support from Harvard University to do pioneering work in entrepreneurship development in India-SIET in collaboration with Prof. David C. McClell and[3] of Harvard University conducted[3] months training and research programmes in Rajamundi, Kakinada and Vellur towns of Andhra Pradesh and Tamilnadu. McClelland proved that, through proper education and training, the vital quality of an entrepreneur, which McClelland called 'need for achievement' (n'ach) can be developed[1]. The fact remains that McClelland's this successful experiment proved to be a seed for entrepreneurship development in India which has become popular today as EDP (Entrepreneurship Development Programmes).

It is against this background now the Government and financial institutions started thinking to develop entrepreneurship in the country through training programmes. It was the Gujarat Industrial Investment Corporation (GIIC) who for the first time started a three month training programme on entrepreneurship development in 1970. This programme was designed to unleash the talent of potential entrepreneurs and some selected entrepreneurs. Special emphasis was given on three aspects: 1. Establishment of a small-scale enterprise, 2. Its management, and 3. To earn profits out of it. By the latter half of 1970s' the news of GIIC's EDP spread to the other parts of the country also. As a result, SIET and Small Industry Development Organisation (SIDO) through Small Industry Services Institute (SISI) and Industrial Development Bank of India (IDBI) through Technical Consultancy Organisations (TCOs) started organising EDPs. The encouraging results of these efforts culminated to the establishment of 'Centre for Entrepreneurship Development (CED), Ahmedabad in 1979. Here, it is noteworthy that CED, Ahmedabad was the first centre of its kind wholly committed to the cause of entrepreneurship development. Inspired and influenced by the success of CED, Ahmedabad, the national level financial institutions such as IDBI, IFCI, ICICI and SBI with active support from the Gujrat Government sponsored a 'Nation Resource Organisation', called 'Entrepreneurship Development Institute of India (EDI), Ahmedabad, in 1983. This instituted was entrusted with the responsibility of extension and institutionalization of entrepreneurship development activities in the country which the Institute has been discharging successfully. Almost at the same time of establishment of EDI in 1983, the Government of India established 'National Institute for Entrepreneurship and Small Business Development' (NIESBUD) to coordinate entrepreneurship development activities in the country. In course of time, some State Governments with the support from national level financial institutions. By now, the twelve States, viz., Bihar, Goa, Gujrat, Himachal Pradesh, Jammu and Kashmir, Karnataka, Kerala, Madhya Pradesh, Maharashtra, Orissa, Tamil Nadu, and Uttar Pradesh have established CED or IED. EDPs in these states were conducted by the TCOs before the establishment of CEDs or IEDs. According to the study of NIESBUD, some 686 organisations are involved in conducting EDPs in the country which have imparted training to thousands of people by conducting hundreds of EDPs. Today EDP has emerged as a nation-wide campaign in our country.

II

EDPS in the NER : Efforts and Experiences

The relatively more backward NER has been attracting the attention of development advocaters of India since Independence. However, the first sincere effort for economic development of the NER took place with the establishment of the North Eastern Council (NEC) in 1972. The main objective of the NEC was to promote economic development of the NER through inter-state plans and bring the NER to the mainstream of the country, This is a matter of great satisfaction that the NEC has since been seriously involved in its task of regional development. Two more significant efforts were intiated in 1973 with an objective to remove the economic backwardness of the region. One, the establishment of the North Eastern Industrial and Technical Consultancy Organization (NEITCO) to impart training on entrepreneurship development, and second, the establishment of the Enterpreneurial Motivation Training Centres (EMTCs) in its six district headquarters of Kokrajhar, Mangaldai, Diphu, Dhimaji, Jorhat and Silchar. With a view to extend and promote this idea, the State Government opened the EMTCs in the districts headquarters of three more districts namely, Nalbari, Nagaon and Dibrugarh in 1979. The EMTCs have been engaged in entrepreneurship development training since beginning. During 1973-97, these have imparted training to 30,485 candidates of which 4,767 (15.6%) got seed money to start their enterprises. The biggest strength of the EMTCs was that, being the district-level organization, these were well versed with the regional needs, expectations, possibilities and problems. But inadequacy and non-availability of necessary resources and facilities was their major weakness.That is why the EMTCs could not achieve expected success in the field of entrepreneurship development and by now are almost fizzled out.

With an objective to bring the EDPs in the NER at par with the national level, the North Eastern Regional Centre of SIET was established in Guwahati in 1979. The main task of this regional centre was to develop and promote entrepreneurship and small - scale industries in the NER. The name of SIET was also changed as the National Institute of Small Industry Extension and Training (NISIET) in 1984 and the Regional Centre of SIET in Guwahati became the North Eastern Regional Centre (NERC)of the NISIET. The NISIET has played a significant role in the regional development of the NER. In 1984, the NERC of NISIET was converted into a fullfledged institute, named, Indian Institute of Entrepreneurship (IIE), Guwahati. The IIE, Guwahati has been seriously involved in the entrepreneurship development in the Region and has by now emerged as one of the premier institutes in entrepreneurship in the country.

Having discussed the government approach toward entrepreneurship development, now it seems pertinent to delineate the so far progress made and experiences gained in the field of entrepreneurship development in the NER.

Human development is essential condition for economic development. Recognizing this fact, the NEC has shown keen interest in human development in the NER and has done some appreciable job in this regard. For example, the NEC sponsored one study on " Entrepreneurial and Managerial Needs of the North East Region" to the SIET in 1976. The study was completed in 1978. The SIET combined this study along with the similar efforts going on in another six countries. Thus by integrating the researches of eight institutions in seven countries SIET under the auspices of the 'Asian Association of Development Research and Training Institute' published a significant publication entitled *Small Industry Development in Selected Asian Countries 1979*[2]. For the NER, a separate detailed study was brought out by the SEIT in 1978 [3]. Among other aspects, this study perspicaciously analyzed the existing and potential entrepreneurship development in each state of the NER and also suggested a working strategy for entrepreneurship development in the region. NEC has since beginning taken the onerous responsibility of entrepreneurship development in the NER. The EDPs sponsored by the NEC are oriented towards three directions: (1) Create awareness about entrepreneurship development, (2) Organise EDPs for 6-8 week duration, and (3) Organise some special EDPs for the existing entrepreneurs. None theless, development of new generation entrepreneurs has been the main focus of the EDPs conducted by the NEC.

The NEC set a target to impart EDP training to develop some 5,000 entrepreneurs during the seventh plan period. However, the NEC through four training organizations, could impart training to 3609 candidates only as against its target of 5000 candidates[4].From April 1990 to March 1996, the NEC in collaboration with the SIDBI and the IDBI, sponsored a total of 212 EDPs to five training organizations. The number of EDPs with their types and number of participants organised by these organizations is given in Table 2.

Table 2
Training-Organisationwise EDP's Number and the Participants

Training Organization	General EDPs	Women EDPs	Rural EDPs	Total	Number of Participants
NISIET	24	4	10	38(18%)	940
IIE	12	4	8	24(11%)	591
NEITCO	41	11	13	65(31%)	1,715
NSIC	16	4	6	26(12%)	524
NECON	30	7	22	59(28%)	1,605
TOTAL	123(58%)	30(14%)	59(28%)	212(100)	5,375

Source: North Eastern Council, Shillong.

It is seen from figures in given Table 2 that the maximum number of EDPs organised are general ones, but women EDPs have also been given importance, As regards organization- wise EDPs, NEITCO (41) and NECON (30) have organised the maximum number of EDPs.

The state-wise distribution of these EDPs is presented in Table 3.

Table 3
State-wise Number of EDPs and Participants

State	No. of EDPs	No. of Participants
Arunachal Pradesh	23(10.8)	598(11.0)
Assam	74(34.9)	1,807(33.6)
Manipur	27(12.3)	693(12.9)
Meghalaya	26(12.3)	653(12.2)
Mizarom	13(6.1)	340(6.5)
Nagaland	27(12.7)	694(12.9)
Tripura	22(10.5)	580(10.8)
Total	212(100.0)	5,375(100.0)

Note : Figures in parentheses denote percentages to total.

As seen from Table 3, Assam has conducted the maximum EDPs and Mizoram the minimum (6%). The three states of Manipur, Meghalaya and Nagaland have conducted 13% EDPs each.

In fact, entrepreneurship development is a dynamic activity which needs to be revised and improved as per the requirement of the target group. Since conducting EDPs involves much resources such as money, time and human efforts which are always scarce in supply, it becomes imperative to know whether the EDPs are beneficial or not. In other words whether the objectives for which EDPs are conducted are achieved or not or achieved to what extent, is known by studying the effectiveness of EDPs. So far, several studies have been conducted on the effectiveness of EDPs in the country[5]. Such studies on the effectiveness of EDPs are conducted in the NER also[6]. One such recent evaluation study titled *A Critical Study of the Effectiveness of Entrepreneurship Development Programmes in the North East* was conducted by the IIE, Guwahati for the aforesaid 212 EDPs conducted under the auspices of the NEC, Shillong. Here, a mention about the main result on the effectiveness of EDPs as reported by the said, study seems pertinent.

In the first phase of the study, structural questionnaires were sent by mail to a total of 3717 trainees which resulted in response from,1097 (40%) participants only. Due to quite low response received, it was decided to obtain some more responses by sending investigators to the different states of the NER. This effort could generate response from 2,616 trainees. Thus, the study could cover a total of 3,713 (69%) trainees out of 5,375 trainees. The main reasons for intractability of around 31 per cent were non-availability of proper address,migration to other places, inaccessibility etc. The study revealed that only 935 (25%) trainees could establish any industry out of 3,713 EDP participants (Table 4).

According to a national level study on effectiveness of EDPs, the success rate of EDPs is reported at 25.94%[7]. Relatively speaking, out of every 10 trainees, only 3 started their enterprises.

In its above study, IIE classified its respondents into three categories: achievers, dreamers and duds. Here, it is worthmentioning that obtaining such information through mail was virtually impossible, hence the above classification relates to 2,616 trainees only those who were contacted directly. Their category-wise distribution is given in Table 5.

Table 4
Success Rate of EDPs

Sl. No.	Items	Number	Per cent
1	Total Number of Trainees	5,375	100.0
2	Respondents:		
	(a) Contacted via Mailed Questionnaire	1,097	20.4
	(b) Contacted Directly	2,616	48.7
3	Total Number of Respondents	3,713	69.0
4	Successful, i.e. who established industry	935	25.2

Note: Rate of success calculated on the basis of 3,713 respondents.

Table 5
Category-wise Number of Respondents

Sl. No.	Classification	Number	Per cent
1	Total Number of Trainees	5,375	
2	Respondents contacted directly	2,616	100.0
3	Achievers contacted directly	569	21.8
4	Dreamers	541	20.6
5	Duds	1,506	57.6

It is starting to note that of the 78 per cent trainees who did not start their enterprises, 58 percent were duds, i.e. who have altogether given up idea to establish any enterprise. It other words, training interventions could not motivate around three fifths of trainees at all to start their enterprises. This, in turn, underlines the relevance of training interventions to motivate people to become entrepreneurs. Attempt were also made in the study identify the reasons for not establishing enterprises by the trainees. Following were the major reasons reported in Table 6.

It is seen from figures given in Table 6 that problems of fund,raw material, government policies, family problems, and legal formalities are the major reasons in that order deterring the trainees to start their enterprises.

Table 6
Reasons for Not Establishing Enterprises

Reasons	Dreamers	Duds
Problem of fund	483(89.2)	1,107(73.5)
Lack of Encouragement	192(35.4)	286(19.1)
Government Policy	206(38.0)	—
Legal Formalities	168(31.0)	—
Problem of Marketing	173(32.0)	182(12.1)
Family Problems	—	560(37.3)
Problem of Row Material	143(26.4)	156(10.4)
Problem of Electricity	152(28.00)	—
Factory Land/Shed	100(22.00)	218 (14.5)

Note: Most of the respondents reported more than one reason for not establishing their units.

III

Development of Small-Scale Industries in the NER: An Overview

Entrepreneurship precedes enterprise. Thus entrepreneurship gets its reflection on small-scale enterprises entrepreneurship development a mention about the development of small-scale enterprises. Hence, in any discussion on enterpreurship development,a mentioned about the development of small-scale industries is inescapable. In fact, development of industries is already limited in the NER, but much more limited is the availability of data on whatever industries exist there. Nonetheless, based on available data, an overview of development of industries in the NER is presented Table 7.

The already very small number of industrial units are highly unevenly distributed among the states in the NER (Table 7). For example, while around 54 percent industrial units are concentrated in Assam alone, industrial activity in Nagaland and Tripura is almost in non-existence. Manipur and Arunachal Pradesh come next to Assam in terms of number of industrial units working over there. Figures in Table 7 like that of Table 1 also indicate that the entrepreneurship or industrial development is still at a very low level in the NER.

Table 7
Industrial Development in the NER (An Overview)

States	Large and Medium Scale enterprises	Small-Scale Enterprises
Arunachal Pradesh	17(9.55)	4,520(10.22)
Assam	129(72.48)	23,637(53.47)
Manipur	12(6.74)	6,000(13.58)
Meghalaya	10(5.62)	2,629(5.92)
Mizoram	1(0.56)	4,333(9.80)
Nagaland	7(3.93)	982(2.23)
Tripura	2(1.12)	2,114(4.78)
Total	178(100.00)	44,207 (100.00)

Source: Indian Institute of Entrepreneurship, Guwahati, 2000.

This is also a matter of great concern that not only the number of industrial units is small in the NER, but most of them (53 %) are plagued by sickness also. In most of the cases, the sickness has advanced to such an extent that it has rendered them unviable.

To quote, in March 1999, out of a total of 23, 506 sick small-scale industries in the entire North-East Region, as many as 20,063 units (85 %) were termed as non-viable. Speaking alternatively, out of every 10 sick small-scale industries, 8 were non-viable. These are at the brink of their death. Sooner or later their closure is sure; The scenario of state-wise sick small-scale industries in the NER is presented in Table 8.

The main evil effects of industrial sickness on an economy have been locking up the economy's financial resources, wastage of scarce capital assets, loss of production, and loss in employment or increase in unemployment.[8] Thus, sickness benefits none and industrial sickness is a bane on the Indian economy. According to a study of the Indian Institute of Entrepreneurship, Guwahati, about 24 per cent of small-scale industries have already been closed by now in the entire NER and another about 85 per cent are at the brink of their closure (see Table 8) Then, it is sure that it is going to aggravate the already prevalent mass unemployment hoving in the region. The fact remains that the problem of unemployment has been the root cause of disturbances in the NER whose manifestation in various forms has become a threat for the NER and the country as well. Increasing incidence of industrial sickness also presents an unhappy example for the prospective entrepresenurs that there in no scope for career for them in industry. Possibly, this is one of the important reasons why the local unemployment youth are not coming forward to start their enterprises in spite of the Government's pronouncements to offer various incentives and concessions to establish industries in the NER. Here, it seems pertinent to make a mention about the various incentives and concessions the Government offers to entrepreneurs to establish industries in the NER.

Table 8
State-wise Sick Small-Scale Industries in the NER (March 1999)

States	Viable	Non-viable	Viability not Decided	Total Sick Units
Arunachal Pradesh	6	102	8	116
Assam	581	9,003	705	10,586
Manipur	391	4,367	479	5,237
Meghalaya	21	401	25	447
Mizoram	—	40	0	40
Nagaland	3	160	3	166
Tripura	549	5693	672	6,914
Total	1,551	20,063	1,892	23,506

Source: Indian Institute of Entrepreneurship, Guwahati.

It is evident by now that whatever industrial development has so far taken place in the NER, it is mainly concentrated in Assam. Hence,it seems pertinent to present the incentives and concessions offered by the Government of Assam to the entrepreneurs to establish industries in the State. The Government of Assam has so far announced its five Industrial Policies in 1982, 1986, 1991, 1997 and 2003. The Industrial Policy 2003 is effective from 1st October 2003 and will be valid for a period of 5 years i.e.up to 30th September 2008 unless modified/ terminated whichever is earlier. The main provisions for fiscal incentives for industrial/entrepreneurial development under the Industrial Policy 2003 of the Government of Assam are produced here:

State Capital Investment Subsidy (SCIS)	The State Capital Investment Subsidy @30% on Investment in Plant and Machinery subject to a ceiling of Rs.20.0 lakhs will be provided to eligible industrial units. For Export oriented units the ceiling is Rs. 25.0 lakhs.
Interest Subsidy on Working Capital Loan (ISWC)	Interest subsidy shall be provided @ 30% of the amount of interest charged by paid to the banks on working capital loan/cash credit to the eligible industrial units for a period of 5 (five) years from the date of commercial production subject to a ceiling of Rs. 5.0 lakhs per unit or 20% of the turnover whichever is less during the entire period of claim.
Power Subsidy (PS)	Power subsidy will be provided to the eligible industrial units on the power tariff paid against the actual units consumed for a period of 5 (five) years subject to a celling shown below : Connected load rate of subsidy celling of subsidy per annum up to 1.0 MW 50% Rs. 10.0 lakhs above 1.0 MW 30% Rs. 20.0 lakhs
Subsidy on Captive Power Generation(SPG)	Subsidy @ 50% of the cost of Generating Set to the eligible industrial units will be provided subject to a ceiling of Rs. 10.0 Lakhs per unit. The installed generating set capacity should be at par or above of the ASEB sanctioned load.
Subsidy on Feasibility Study Cost (SFC)	The cost of preparation of the feasibility report prepared by agencies approved by the Udyog Sahayak of AIDC/ Director of Industries and Commerce will be subsidized to the extent of 100% subject to a ceiling of Rs. 1.0 Lakhs

per scheme of the unit. The cost of preparation of feasibility report / project report should not exceed 1% of the Project Cost. The claim will be entertained only after the unit goes into commercial production.

Subsidy on Quality Certification/ Technical Know-How

The fees payable for obtaining BIS/ ISO/ FPO/ AGMARK and fees payable for getting the technical know-how from approved and recognized organization like Research Laboratories/ CFTRI etc. by the eligible industrial units will be subsidized to the extent of 75% subject to a ceiling of Rs.1.0 Lakhs per unit.

Subsidy On Market Assistances (SMA)

Eligible industrial units specially approved for this purpose will be provided the following support under marketing assistance scheme. 50% of the rent /fee payable by the unit in participating in trade fair/ exhibitions sponsored or recognized by the Government against rent /fees rates approved by the government will be subsidized subject to a ceiling of Rs. 50,000/- per unit per annum within India and Rs. 1.0 Lakhs per unit per annum in case of participating abroad and with prior approval of Government. 50% of the cost of advertisement through Cinema Hall/ Any electronic media will be subsidized up to a ceiling of Rs. 20,000/ - per unit per annum subject to prior approval of the Government. 50% of the transportation cost on exhibits for participation in Government sponsored/ recognized Trade Fair/Exhibition etc. will be subsidized upto a ceiling of Rs. 20,000/- per unit per annum subject to prior approval of the Government.

Subsidy on Drawal of Power Line (SDP)	20% of the cost payable to ASEB for drawal of power line from HT/LT power line up to the factory premise including the cost of transformer will be subsidized subject to a celling of Rs. 1.0 Lakhs.
Special incentaives for Food Processing/Electronic/Agrobased/ Biotech Industries	Special incentives will be provided to the above category of eligible industrial units as additional SCIS @10% subject to a ceiling of Rs. 5.0 Lakhs.
Special incentives to women/ Physically Handicapped Enterpreneurs	Special incentives will be provided as additional SCIS to industrial units set up by women or physically handicapped entrepreneur @10% subject to a ceiling of Rs. 5.0 Lakhs.
Special Incentives to sick PSUs	The management of Sick Sector Undertakings it taken over on joint holding /lease by any party from State Financial Corporation/ any Central or State Govt. Agencies will be treated as a new unit for the purpose of incentives under this sector. However the value of plant and machinery in the sale deed will be considered for the purpose of computation of the incentives.
Special incentives for major/ heavy industries and industries set up through Foreign Direct Investment	Priority clearance of various permissions, allotment of lands, power sanction etc will be made through high power single window clearance committee at Government level. The major/heavy industries and industries set up through foreign direct investment who have own generation facilities will be provided special incentives as follows: Further the ceiling limit of some of the incentives for such type of industries will be increased to: i. SCIS 30% Rs. 25 lakhs ii. Gen. Set Subsidy 50% Rs. 20 lakhs

iii. Power Subsidy
Up to 1 MW 50% Rs. 10 lakhs,
For 5 years between 1 MW to5MW 30 % Rs. 20 Lakhs, for 5 years Above 5 MW 20% Rs. 30 Lakhs, for 5 years
iv. Development Subsidy
(for drawal of H.T/ L.T lineup 10% Rs. 20 Lakhs
to permises of the unit/ Installation of pollution control equipment).

Source : www. assamgov. Org.

Problems of Entrepreneurship Development

We have seen so far that, in spite of various incentives and concessions, there has not been any perceptible development in entrepreneurship and, in turn, small -scale industries in the NER. An enquiry into it reveals the following major reasons for it.

Inadequacy of Infrastructural Facilities

It is a well established fact that the availability of infrastructural facilities facilitates and accelerates industrial development and its absence restrains it. The early ledger of Indian industrial development reveals that the lack of inception of industrial growth in India was not due to lack of entrepreneurial motivation, but due to lack of infrastructural facilities termed as ' supporting conditions'[9]. There is need for a minimum level of prior built -up infrastructural facilities before starting any economic activity like industry. It is quite evident from figures in Table 1 that the development of infrastructural facilities like transport, communication, banking, power, etc. is still quite inadequate in the NER. Thus, the inadequacy of basic infrastructural facilities holds back the Region from taking benefits of whatever advantages it has in terms of forests, minerals, and climatic conditions, on the one hand, and makes the products of NER costlier than those of outside, on the other. Here, it is also worth mentioning that the Government incentives and concessions available to start industries can not duly offset the inadequacy of infrastructural facilities[10].

Unstable and Uncertain Law and Order Situation

The economic history of many countries including India well evidences that the unstable and uncertain law, order and political situation hampers development efforts of the country. The NER has been plagued by the disturbing law and order situation for quite some years. The fact remains that the unstable and uncertain law and order situation has derailed and shattered the developmental process of the region. While this is adversely affecting the running of industries in the NER, on the one hand, it is developing the negative attitude among the local people toward the entrepreneurial career, on the other. According to a study conducted by the Indian Institute of Entrepreneurship (IIE), Guwahati, about 24 per cent of industrial units have been closed in the entire NER in 1998 and 85 per cent of sick small scale industries are non-viable, i.e these are on the verge of their closure. The plight of industries in the region is dismal and prognostic.

Lack of Required Human Resources

The problem of unemployment and uncertain law and order situation hovering the Region has propelled mainly the males to migrate to outside the NER in search of education and job. Absence of many young men from the region results in increase in the proportion of other groups, namely, women, children, or the old in the population. A higher sex-ratio in the NER (for example, 978 in Manipur and 975 in Meghalaya) is well indicative of it. (see Table 1). In nustshell,out -migration of males results in denudation of population with such qualities as skills, education, entrepreneurship and beacon of new orders.[11]

Complex Procedure

An entrepreneur has to follow a prescribed procedure in establishing his/her enterprise. The entrepreneur has to approach to the officials of different Departments which are often located at different places. The money, time and energy of the entrepreneur to be spent in the process lowers his enthusiam to establish an industry. So much so, the entrepreneur being so much fed up or puzzled with the complex and cumbersome process gives up idea of establishing any industry. Besides, the time-consuming procedure leads to cost overrum. The result is the enterprise falls prey to the inadequacy of funds, or say, suffers from malnutrition since birth. M/s Saraswati Woollen Mills (P) Ltd., Ranikhet (Uttaranchal) represents the classical example of cost overrun and time overrun on account of procedural delays[12]. This mill was registered in 1973 and it got an industrial license two years later, it took about 9 years for it to build the factory shed, instal the machinery and go into production. The evil effects of the procedural delays were seen in the cost escalation of the project from Rs. 32 lakhs in 1973 to Rs. 56 lakhs in 1981.

The same problem of procedural complexities applies to availing of government subsidies and concessions for establishing industries. Research studies[13] report that many times the complexities of procedure causes more costs than the value of subsidies and concessions to be availed by the entrepreneurs. That is why the majority of the entrepreneurs are not found in favour of availing these concessions and subsidies.

Prospects for Entrepreneurship Development

The remote and undulating topography of the NER not only poses problems for economic and entrepreneurship development, but also possesses plenty of prospects within its fold for its development [14]. Thus, the trite saying of " blessings in disguised" squarely applies to the NER. There are few regions in the world that can boast of the treasure house of resources that North East India possesses. Here is an overview of the same:

- The region has about 8 per cent of the country's total land space with 4 per cent of the country's population. Thus, NE enjoys a distinct demographic edge over the rest of the country.
- It is an emergency market of 400 million people.
- It has potential to be India's future power house. Has 38 per cent of hydropower potential of the country because of the presence of the country's largest perennial water system, natural gas reserves of 190 billion cubic metres, coal reserves of 909 million tonnes, hydroelectric potential estimated at 49,000 MW, oil reserves of 513 million tonnes.
- Large mineral resources including limestone reserves of 4,933 million tonnes and a forest cover which is 25 percent of the country's total forest area.
- Enjoys phenomenal bio-diversity be it the forest wealth, agro-base, fruit and vegetables, herbs, aromatic, plants, exotic flowers, other flora and fauna.

- Almost 98 per cent of its boarders form India's international boundaries - a veritable gateway to the South East and, in turn, to the world. China to the North, Bangladesh in the South West, Myanmar in the East and Bhutan in the North West share borders with the North East Region (NER) of India. Thus, the NER possesses strong potential to be a future international trading hot spot and a strategic base for foreign and domestic investors to tap the vast contiguous markets of Mynmar, China, Malaysia, Thailand, Singapore, Philippines, Indonesia and other East and South East Asian countries. It is this vast potential that the Government of India is giving increasing emphasis on its "Look East Policy through North East"
- It has also proximity to SAARC countries like Bangladesh, Nepal and Bhutan offering enourmous possibilities for trade and investment.
- It's a region with very high literacy rate of over 68 percent. It has more people who are fluent in English than any other region in the country. Thus, it has a strong potential for growth of information technology enabled services.
- It's also a region of virtually tax-free fiscal package.
- The NER is also blessed with breath taking beauty, and has in its fold, some of the most scenic spots in the country, prompting many comparisons like the "Scotland of the East" and "Switzerland of India". Be it wild life sanctuaries, adventure tourism, eco-tourism, hill stations, lakes, cultural and historical heritage- the NER has it all in full and plenty. Recognizing the vast potential for tourism development, the Government of India has notified the NER as "Hot spot in Tourism" like "Hot Spot in Bio-Diversity".

Thus, it is clear and evident that the NER is a region in India waiting to things happen because vast opportunities are yet unexplored and unexploited which, in turn, means ample possibilities for entrepreneurship development and, in turn industrial / economic development of the region.

Conclusion

The wholesome process involved right from the conception of an idea to the establishment of a business enterprise is a daunting task.

Enterprise establishment and/or entrepreneurship development has never been an individual's task but outcome of the combined efforts of various people involved in the process. An integrated view indicates that entrepreneurship emerges, develops, declines and dies in a given contextual setting. Entrepreneurial history bears evidence that the economic, social, cultural, and political conditions prevalent at a particular point of time create the entrepreneurial context and the presence of a favourable context has been a necessary conditions for entrepreneurship development. The preceding description clearly indicates that there has so far been absence of such positive / favorable contextual setting for entrepreneurship development in the NER. Hence, the creation of a favourable context is the urgent need of the time for entrepreneurship development in the NER. Sooner it is created, better for the entrepreneurship development in the NER.

NOTES AND REFERENCES

1. David, C. McClelland and D.G. Winter (1969), *Motivating Economic Achievement* (New York: Free Press,).
2. Sharma, S.V.S. (1979), *Small Industry Development in Select Asian Countries* (New Delhi: Light Publishers).
3. Sharma, S.V.S. and M.M.P. Akhouri (1978), *Small Entrepreneurial Development: Indian Experiences in the North Eastern Region* (Hyderabad: SIET Institute).
4. Mali, D.D. and R. Bandopadhyay (1993), *Small Industry Development in North East India- Status and Strategy* (New Delhi: Omsons Publications).
5. Awasthi, Dinesh N. and Jose Sebastian (1996), *Evaluation of Entrepreneurship Development Programmes* (New Delhi: Sage Publications); *Entrepreneurship Development Programmes of SBI: An Evaluation* (Bombay: State Bank of India, Central Office 1978); Gaikwad, V.R., H. Gor, U. Pareek, T.V. Rao, H.C. Shah, B.G. Shah and M.C. Shetty (Eds.) (1974), *Entrepreneurship Development Programmes : An Evaluation* (Research Report) (Ahmedabad: Indian Institute of Management).
6. SIET Institute (1974), *Evaluation of Entrepreneurial Motivation Training Programmes in Assam* (Research Report) (Hyderabad :Small Industries Extension and Training Institute); NISIET, *Entrepreneurship Development in North Eastern Region: Planning, Implementation and Evaluation* (Guwahati: North Eastern Regional Centreof the National Institute of Small Industry Extension and Training Institute, 1990); NEITCO, Review of *Entrepreneurship Development Programmes* (Internal Report)

(Guwahati North-Eastern Industrial and Technical Consultancy Organisation, Ltd. 1991).

7. Awasthi, Dinesh N. and Jose Sebastian, *Evaluation of Entrepreneurship op. cit.*
8. Khanka, S.S., 'Industrial Sickness in India', *Indian Management*, 31-5,
9. Medhora, Phiroze B. (1965), 'Entrepreneurship in India,' *Political Science Quarterly*, L30.
10. Papola, T.S. and R.T. Tiwari (1981), *Impact of Concessional Finance on Industrial Development of Backward Areas: A Study in Uttar Pradesh* (Lucknow: Giri Institute of Development Studies).
11. Oberai, A.S. and H.K.M. Singh (1983), *Causes and Consequences of Internal Migration: A Study in the Indian Punjab* (New Delhi: Oxford University Press), Also Khanka, S.S. (1984), 'Migration from Kumaon Region: Some Findings Based on the Sample Study of Pithoragarh District', *The Indian Journal of Labour Economics*, 26-24.
12. Khanka, S.S. (1990), 'Entrepreneurship Development in a Notified Backward Economy,' *Decision*, 17(2).
13. Papola, T.S. and R.T. Tiwari, *op. cit.*
14. Department of Development of North Eastern Region (2000), *N.E. Newsletter*, Ministry of Home Affairs, Government of India issue, 4 July 2002.

25

SUSTAINABLE DEVELOPMENT OF TOURIM ENTREPRENEURSHIP IN THE NORTH EAST INDIA:
An Appraisal of Tourism Entrepreneurship Incubator

ANJAN BHUYAN

Introduction

Tourism, the service oriented industry, has emerged as a revolutionizing phenomenon, especially in the second half of the last century having the distinctive effect of income and employment multiplier in the development process of a nation. It is multidimensional in perception and implies divergent interpretations. For a tourist it is travel, relaxation, a holiday, an exposure to alien cultures and traditions etc. But, those who trade in tourism, it is an industry, a source of income with stable establishments. Thus, conceptually, tourism is an amalgamation of dynamic (e.g., travel) and static elements (e.g., stay/ settlement).

> "It is a composite product involving, transport, accommodation, catering, natural resources, entertainments and other facilities and services, such as shops and banks, travel agents and tour operators. Many businesses also serve other sectors and consumer demands,

thus raising the question of the extent to which suppliers can be considered as primary supplier of tourism. The many components of the product, supplied by variety of business operating in a number of markets, create problems in analyzing tourism supply. It is, therefore, convenient to consider it as a collection of industries and markets (Sinclair and Stabler, 1997:58)."

As commonly accepted, tourism as a word appeared in 1811 and was associated to 'mobility' for recreation (Lundberg, 1972). According to Hunizkar and Kraw it is "an entity of relations and facts constituted by travel and sojourn of person out of their normal place of domicile, as far as this sojourn and travel are not motivated by any lucrative activity". This concept has been adapted by International Association of Scientific Experts (IASE) in tourism for international compatibility and the formation of domestic policies for the promotion of tourism. It is noteworthy that during 1970s the popular notion of nominating tourism as an industry, more specifically the 'smokeless industry' was started which became a cliché in these days. European and American leisure tourists are chiefly credited for this 'tourism festivity' known to be mass tourism. However, indiscriminate rise in tourism in many corners of the globe compelled world community to realize that development of tourism is a two-way phenomenon. On one hand, it has been identified as an economic saviour while on the other; it is characterized as an exile. In fact, tourism like any other economic component has the basic aspects of the supply of services based on the resources of the destination area and demand designing a certain tourism pattern. However, this is only a spatial or temporal incidence of tourism. The reality lies in its long term application in an economy which may prove fatal as cultural tumbles and dilapidation of ecological sustenance with bio-diversity threats. At the same time, it was also realized that if used properly, tourism resources of a region can contribute a great deal in enhancing income and employment. The global tendency of the late twentieth century was therefore to internationalize the concept of tourism industry and consequent commoditization of tourism resources along with the most popularized idea of alternative tourism.

Liberalization in the world-economy during 1990s opened up new possibilities for service sector development and tourism poised itself as a competent sector in it. Most of the Third World developing countries including India initially rejected the idea of liberalizing service sector due to its vulnerability towards competitive international environment. It is evident from the fact that India and Brazil initially opposed to agree with the World Trade Organization's (WTO's). General Agreement on Trade in Services (GATS, 1994) which scheduled twelve service sectors including travel and tourism for extensive global participation. However, at the end, India had to comply with GATS by submitting nine sectors including tourism and related services (USAID, 2004). Moreover, the attachment of the principle of sustainability in tourism during late 1990's created a new order in world tourism.

It is experienced that a good number of developing countries have experienced steady rise in the Gross Domestic Product (GDP) contribution in recent times. To quote, the contribution of tourism sector in the national income of developing countries like Singapore, Malaysia and Thailand is more than 65% (ILO, 2003).

India plunks huge potentiality of developing tourism as a leading component of service (tertiary) sector with its high percentage of unused natural resources as well as human expertise. However, the contribution of tourism in the national income of India is so far dismally low at 2.5%. The country accounts for only 0.38% share in the world tourism market (WTO, 2003). Nevertheless, it shelters 15% of world population with 2.5% of the topography of the world (Rajasthan Tourism Policy, 2002). These facts well reflect the very low level of tourism development in India. Considering the North Eastern Region of India, presently comprising eight states viz., Arunachal Pradesh, Assam, Meghalaya, Mizoram, Manipur, Nagaland, Sikkim and Tripura the contribution is much negligible. The average contribution of all these states is insignificant being lower than 0.25%. This seems to discourage tourism research by considering it as an immature sector. It is said that the interpretation of high performance of tertiary sector has not been significant in India over the decade of 1990s.On a trend basis, the primary and tertiary sectors, like GDP, have grown at the same rates as in the 1980s. However, there has been a symptom of reduction in the employment elasticity of output by this industry. Kelkar, admitting the fact that there had been some sporadic growth process during the decade of 1990s states, "As we enter the new century, the economy stands at the crossroads. It can take either the 'business as usual' road which means continued poverty and the low growth trap or the high road through accelerated reforms (Kelkar, 1999)."

It is worth noticing that the World Travel and Tourism Council (WTTC) predicted: "India has potential to become number one tourist destination in the world with the demand growing at 10.1% per annum (2000)." World Tourism Organisation has identified India as an attractive destination with ample promise for tourism development in terms of annual net revenue contribution (an average of Rs. 13,000 Crores) and average stay of tourists in India for 30 days (2002). These augur well for Indian tourism. Moreover; the necessity of tourism sector development can never be discarded for some strategic reasons: *First,* it has a strong multiplier effect. Income and employment enhancement are of immense necessity in a capital poor country like India. Tourism, by virtue has high labour absorption capacity with varying levels of capital requirements and partial or no industrial gestation period. *Secondly,* sustainability considerations of tourism are mainly designed to attract 'common man approach' of preserving natural and cultural heritages, maintenance of bio-diversity and long-term ecological sustenance. It is believed that generation of peripheral sentiments of preserving eco-bio surroundings through the active participation of the stake-holders and creation of a class of ethical tourists may be bold steps towards an eco-friendly nation.

It is to note that modern tourism in India dates back to 1945, when Bhatia Committee favoured tourism as an exclusive state subject (Bhattacharyya, 2004). But, more than sixty years of tourism experiences of the country could arrest a slow pace of development in the sector. The NER suffers more or less insignificant rate of development and that too erratic in nature although the region started tourism policy planning way back in 1958 with the establishment of the state department of Tourism in Assam.

Given such backdrop, some obvious and vexing questions arise are: What holds the Indian tourism back in development? Is there the lack of supportive facilities for tourism development? Are there the cultural and ecological inhibitions rooted in the society towards tourism development? Is there the lack of entrepreneurial spirit in the countryside? Each of these questions is quite evolving and embracing. Recognizing that entrepreneurial spirit is the pre-requisite for any economic activity including tourism, the present study, therefore, proposes to study the problems and prospects of tourism entrepreneurship the NER with a policy suggestion of tourism entrepreneurship incubator for generating tourism based entrepreneurship in the region.

I

Sustainable Tourism: The Concept and Determinants

The concept of 'sustainable tourism' has become a strategic phenomenon of tourism development throughout the globe. To be specific, sustainability in tourism development was rooted in the Agenda 21 of the United Nations Conference on Environment and Development (the Earth summit) in Rio De Janeiro, Brazil in 1992 (UN Report, 1992). Sustainable development was defined in the summit as it was in the Brundtland Report in 1987 as "meeting the needs of the present generation without compromising the ability of the future generations to meet their own needs" (Brundtland Report, 1987). This may also be regarded as the starting point of a new world economic order of a 'Globalized Economy'. For some, sustainability may sound like a political slogan being more holistic in connotation, but for the interest of world tourism it is the inevitable course of action. Ironically, sustainability considerations for tourism sector development were not determined in that summit. However, in the summit at Rio-de-Janeiro, Brazil, 1997, World Tourism Organization declared the principles of sustainability in tourism. It is felt that planned development is essential for sustainability in tourism. This realization actually reflects a dimensional shift of mass tourism culture towards segmented tourism markets, popularly designated as 'alternative tourism'. The idea was the upshot of the declaration of 'ambivalent modern tourism development' by the World Tourism Organization and characterizes 'new tourism paradigm' (WTO, 1989). Following the definition of WTO, sustainable development in tourism may be referred to as the policy of satisfying the needs of the present tourists and host regions at the same time enhancing opportunity for the future (WTO, 2003).

The common indication of ascribing sustainable tourism is the projection of tourist flow to a particular region based on past trend. It is in fact demand projection of tourism infrastructure. This is for the main reason that, so far tourism has been designated as a demand-centric service industry. World Tourism Organization has so far adopted 10 core and 3 composite indicators of sustainable development of a tourism structure (Table 1).

Table 1
Core Indicators of Sustainable Tourism evolved by World Tourism Organization

Indicator	Specific Measures
1. Site Protection	Category of site protection based on IUCN index
2. Stress	Tourist numbers visiting site (per annum/peak month)
3. Use Intensity	Intensity of use in peak period (person/hectare)
4. Social Impact	Ratio of tourists to locals (peak period)
5.Development Control	Existence of environmental review procedure for formal controls over development of site and use density
6.Waste Management	Percentage of sewage from site receiving treatment (additionalindicators may include structural limits of other infrastructural capacity on site, such as water supply)
7.Planning	Existence of organized Process regional plan for tourist destination region (including tourism component)
8.Critical Ecosystems	Ecosystems Number of rare/endangered species
9.Consumer Satisfaction	Level of satisfaction by visitors (questionnaire-based)
10.Local Satisfaction	Level of satisfaction by locals (questionnaire-based).
	Composite Indices
A. Carrying Capacity	Composite early warning measure of key factors affecting the ability of the site to support different levels of tourism
B. Site Stress	Composite measure of levels of impact on the site (its natural and cultural attributes due to tourism and other cumulative stresses)
C. Attactivity	Qualitative measure of those site attributes that make it attractive to tourism and can change over time.

Source: Adapted from the Report on Contribution of the World Tourism Organization to the World Summit on Sustainable Development (Johannesburg, 2002).

As Table 1 reveals, the WTO declaration of the sustainability indicators are designed to sort out technical feasibility of sustainable tourism. From such a perspective, it is reason based to say that sustainable development in tourism has higher applicability in its supply side than the tourism demand pattern. Thus, the resource base, socio-economic development, environmental concerns and like factors should be the guiding lines for the development of tourist infrastructure and promotion of new areas as potential tourist destination. Tourism potentialities can be best enumerated and estimated in a developing economy where there is high unemployment with a relatively unskilled labour force and few or a very few alternative sources of employment. Under such a situation, stimulation of the tourism sector may be a better course of action. But, the next stage of economic development (characterized by reduction in unemployment and under-employment along with better education and enhanced standard of living) creates the problem of furthering tourism development. This happens due to the common tendency of movement of labour to a higher standard of occupation (Agarwal, 2003). However, Agarwal's idea seems to support the quality of employment in the mass tourism culture where enterprise specialty is not maintained as it is required under alternative tourism. Sustainability conditions also vary regarding the size of enterprises. Micro- and small enterprises in the tourism industry tend to be less sustainable than medium-sized enterprises. This is important for developing countries like India because they need more sustainable jobs, especially in tourism. Micro- and small tourism enterprises tend to be less sustainable than medium tourism enterprises and seem to be much more influenced by external factors, for example the weather. If it rains for a couple of days, these enterprises are hampered in doing business, which leads to a loss of revenue. Medium-sized tourism enterprises create more job opportunities than small and micro-enterprises, although they cost considerably more to develop (Saayman & Slabbert, 1998: 9)

II

Tourism Enterprise, Entrepreneur and Entrepreneurship

Tourism enterprises refer to the different forms of tourist related business ventures permitted within of national constitution. Like any other enterprise tourism enterprises are also business ventures having similar preparative principles, but working on a very wide scale. Sinclair and Stabler (1997) have defined tourism enterprise as "a composition of products involving transport, accommodation, catering, natural resources, entertainments and other facilities and services, such as shops and banks and other tour operators."

A 'tourism entrepreneur' may be defined as a person or a group of persons producing and managing tourism products. In this process the entrepreneur must have the commonly prescribed entrepreneurial traits along with service sector specialties. As revealed by Shaw and Williams (2002) service sector specialties arouse two fundamental things: "*One* concerns the commercial structure of the industry (especially the dominance of certain activity components and ownership groups), while the *second* relates to an understanding of the general organization of economic power structures."

Entrepreneurship in tourism, or say, tourism entrepreneurship refers to the activities of the major group of stake-holders of this service sector primarily designed for the effective and profitable interaction of demand for and supply of tourism products; at the same time assuring competitive professionalism and gainful socio-economic status. In simple words, it embraces all sorts of activities involved in creation and operation of a legal tourism enterprise. By the phrase 'legal tourism enterprise', all forms of tourism or tourism like activities, which are against the generally accepted laws of the Land, are excluded. For example, in India, wildlife hunting, flesh-trading (prostitution), drug trafficking etc. are considered as illicit and therefore illegal.

III

Prospects of Tourism Industry in NER

Covering a stretch of 2, 55, 089 sq. kms. which is 7.8 per cent of the total geographical area of the country (3,287,263 sq. km), the North East Region (NER) of India has been a strategically important corner. The total population of North East India is 3, 65, 00,108 persons which is 3.5 per cent of the total population of India (Census, 2001). Geo-politically, the North East covers 98% of international boundary of India. It shares its boundary with China and Bhutan through its North and North-West, Myanmar and Bangladesh on its East, South and South West. The region is attached to the mainland India through a small corridor extended 33 kms on the eastern side and 21 km on the western side. Such uniqueness poses the region internationally sensitive, nationally strategic and regionally estranged. The North-Eastern region comprises eight states namely, Arunachal Pradesh, Assam, Manipur, Meghalaya, Mizoram, Nagaland, Sikkim and Tripura. All the states have individual administrative structures. But physiologically, the states are so close to each other that it becomes difficult to maintain their individual differences. Not only cultural similarities are experienced, but also economic and political structures are closely tied. This may be for the reason that the entire area was administratively under a single entity up to 1960's. The early Assam, better known as 'Bor-Axom' was a common entity of all the present North-Eastern divisions (excluding Sikkim). The 'Bor-Axom' was characterized by agrarian tribal culture (Baruah, 1988).

Area-wise Arunachal Pradesh has the largest state immediately followed by Assam; other states being comparatively smaller. Mizoram is declared a state of cent percent literacy while Assam is the state of highest density population.

The Northeastern states are still agricultural in nature. The traditional agricultural practices and low rate of industrialization keeps the state income at a lower level. At current prices, the primary sector in Assam contributes about 42.12 per cent of NSDP while the secondary sector contributes 18.33 percent of NSDP. It is remarkable to note that the tertiary sector including transport, storage and communication; trade, hotels and restaurants; banking and insurance; real estate; public administration; and other services contribute 39.56 per cent of NSDP (Statistical Handbook Assam, 2002). This shows an increasing rate of contribution of the service sector. The direct contribution made by the travel and tourism sector has not been separated and is included in the head 'other services'. This is a clear indication that either the state has not accorded higher importance to tourism or this sector does not have much significance.

Considering tourism, the North East is said to be the 'unexplored paradise for the tourists' for its rich natural resources and ethnic diversity. Indian Tourism Development Corporation (ITDC) elaborates the intricacy of North Eastern tourism as following: "Connected by an infinite chain of pearly threads, intricate as a spider's web, the Northeastern states of Arunachal Pradesh, Assam, Manipur, Meghalaya, Mizoram, Nagaland, Sikkim and Tripura offer visitors a rare feast – a kaleidoscopic fiesta that lures you with its magical richness and stunning variety. The raw natural beauty, rare orchids and butterflies, brightly painted monasteries, challenging rivers, intricately woven tribal shawls, indigenous sports......each one has its own special message to the traveller as he passes from one state to another - mesmerized by its dazzling variety and compelling appeal (*Traveller's Companion*, 2003)."

Indian tourism has rated the Northeast as a key tourism priority to make the region a prime tourism destination. The initiative includes a heightened presence of North-Eastern states' tourism representatives in international tourism events as well as a renewed share in the nation's overall tourism allocation to develop infrastructure and fund special interest tourism projects. According to Gour Kanjilal, Regional Director (Western & Central India), Indiatourism (Mumbai), "The North Eastern region has been a tourism priority for the government since the early 80's and was mentioned so in the five year plans. There were real concerns at the Centre regarding the fact that these states felt isolated from the rest of the country. Tourism promotion is a wonderful antidote to such a misgiving. So, in this direction, the Centre has ensured prime and complimentary visibility for North Eastern states at trade fairs in India and abroad. "

Modern tourism in India passed a phase of slow development since 1945 when Bhatia Committee favoured tourism as an exclusive state subject. Since than a part of country-wide programme, several developmental activities took place in the tourism sector of the NER. However, all such moves were irregular and routine type. As such, the outcome has not been much encouraging. It should be noted that after 1997, a new tendency is observed in the NE economy favouring radical changes in its existing status. But, it may not be the spontaneous action of the indigenous population; a majority of it, being simply exaggeration of facts.

Last decade showed a typical global restructuring process in Indian tourism. Some of the significant altercations are mentioned below:

- Tourism was made a priority sector for foreign direct investment in 1991 making it eligible for automatic approvals up to 51% of the equity.
- A National Strategy for Tourism Development was evolved in 1996, which advocated the strengthening of an institutional set-up in human resource development, setting up of an Advisory Board of Tourism Industry and Trade (which has since been set up), the integrated development of tourist

destinations and the promotion of private sector in tourism development.

- In order to take advantage of the *liberalized economic regime* and the developments taking place around the world, a new National Tourism Policy is under consideration of the Government.
- *Declaration of Export House Status* to tourism industry. Specifically, Hotels, Travel Agents, Tour Operators and Tourist Transport Operators are give the status vide Notification No. 33 (RE-98) 1997-2002 dated 26.11.98 of the Ministry of Commerce, Government of India.
- The draft of *National Tourism Policy* was prepared and submitted to the Cabinet Secretary in November, 1997 after the thorough discussion of Indian Tourism Policy in the meeting of the State Tourism Ministers on 27th June, 1997. The draft highlighted six broad (Six-Ss) areas of tourism policy comprising Welcome (*Swagat*), Information (*Suchana*), Facilitation (*Suvidha*), Safety (*Suraksha*), Co-operation (*Sahyog*) and Infrastructure Development (*Samrachana*). In 2002, the New Tourism Policy has been adopted by the Indian Planning Commission.
- Signifying tourism as a *multi-dimensional activity* of linkages between public and private sectors.
- *Confederation of Indian Industry* (CII) and the Task Force on Infrastructure for Tourism suggests in their reports that tourism should be declared as the infrastructure industry of the country.
- Proposal for the inclusion of tourism in the Seventh Schedule of the Indian Constitution by including it in the concurrent list.
- Sustainable policy determination, popularizing the concept of 'New Tourism Paradigm', openness for foreign direct investments, financial assistance to the private tourism entrepreneurs etc. are also remarkable in this regard.

It is striking to note that even though Indian planners and policy makers assign high priority to this sector, the experiences of the last thirteen years (1991-2003) have not been very much significant.

Presently, India is ranked 44th in the top 60 destinations of the world. However, according to *World Tourism Organisation*, India experiences hopeful signs of tourism industry development in the form of foreign exchange earning and tourist choices. "...the number of tourists who crossed international frontiers during 2002 exceeded 715 million. Of them only 2.4 million came to India while some 80 million went to France, the world's number one destination, followed by more than 50 million each to the US and Spain. China with its 37 million arrivals now occupies the fifth place among the top destinations. Even smaller countries like Malaysia and Thailand have crossed the 10 million mark in the visitor count. India's 0.38 per cent share of the world market has remained stagnant for decades. It needs, however, to be pointed out that in spite of the miniscule market share there are a few significant factors of the Indian scene.

Howsoever be the reality; there have been a positive tendency towards change. During the period, the widely dispersed tourism resources were tried to be linked to the national mainstream. A brief account of some of such activities is shown in Table 2. The table indicates that so far a total of 21 tourist circuits have been selected in the North East for their extensive presentation in the national tourism map. However, the number of accommodation facilities nominated is much lower than necessity. As the table shows Assam has the highest number of approved accommodation units with a total of 41 different units. All other states jointly possess only 65 such units. Development of properly standardized accommodation units is essential for a region to experience influx of tourists. At the same time it is a major determinant of tourist carrying capacity of the concerned area.

Although, the entire NER has tremendous potentiality of the tourism sector development and even though a series of measures have been taken at different levels, the region has not been able to attract considerable amount of tourists to the region. Particularly, since 1997 India has been experiencing a positive tendency of tourist traffic in the country. So far the NER is concerned; the tourist traffic has not experienced any significant change over the years (Table 3).

It is observed that Assam receives the highest number of tourist inflow among the NorthEastern states (Table 3). This establishes a promising future of Assam tourism in respect of revenue generation and employment creation. But, at the same time it should also be noted that the quantitative increase of tourists over the years has certain special features:

Table 2

ITDC Recommended Tourist Circuits and Accommodation Units in North East India

State	Tourist Circuits	Popular Tourist Centres/Spots	Tourist Season	Units			
				Hotels	Lodges	Others*	Total
A.P.	1. Bhalukpong–Bomdila–Tawang	Itanagar, Bhalukpong, Bomdila,					
	2. Itanagar–Ziro–Daporijo - Pasighat	Tawang, Ziro, Pasighat, Tipi,	October to May	03	03	02	08
	3. Tinsukhia – Parasuram Kund	Parasuram Kund etc.					
	4. Miao – Namdapha						
	5. Dibrugarh – Roing – Anini	Wildlife Sanctuary: Nampada					
	6. Dibrugarh – Tezu – Hayuliang						
	7 Pasighat – Yingkiong						
Assam	1. Guwahati – Phulbari/ Jakhalabandha	Guwahati, Hajo, Sualkuchi,	October to May	15	16	10	41
	– Kaziranga – Sivasagar.	Tezpur, Sivasagar, Haflong, Majuli Island, Dibrugarh etc.					
	2. Guwahati – Barpeta – Baroma – Manas	Wildlife Sanctuary: Kaziranga, Manas, Nameri, Pobitora, Orang					

(Contd.)

Table 2 (*Contd.*)

State	Tourist Circuits	Popular Tourist Centres/Spots	Tourist Season	Units			
				Hotels	Lodges	Others*	Total
Manipur	1. Imphal – Moirang – Loktak Lake – Keibul Lamjao National Park. 2. Imphal - Ukhrul – Imphal	Imphal, Langthabal, Kangchup, Waithou, Kaina, Khongjom, Tengnoupal, Loktak Lake, Sendra Island, Bishnupur, Ukhrul etc.	October to March	05	N/A	01	06
Meghalaya	1. Kajiranga - Guwahati - Shillong - Cherrapunji - Shillong. 2. Shillong - Mawphlang - Weilloi - Mawsynram - Shillong. 3. Shillong – Smit - Nartiang - Jowai – Thlu Umwi - Shillong 4. Guwahati – Dudnai – Bejengdoba - Annoggre - Tura – Berangapara – Baghmara – Siju – Balpakram – Shillong	Shillong, Umiam Lake, Cherrapunji, Mawphlang, Tura, Nartiang, Ranikor, Dawki etc	Sept. to April	07	N/A	N/A	07
Mizoram	1. Aizawl and excursions in the areas around	Aizawl, Bang, Patkhai, Tamdil, Vantawang, Champhai, Phawngpui etc. Wildlife Sanctuary: Dampa	October to March	06	11	01	18

Nagaland	1. Dimapur – Kohoma – Wokha – Mokokchung - Zunhebeto - Kohima.	Kohima, Khonoma, Dimapur, Mokokchung, Wokha, Phek, Zunhebeto Wildlife Sanctuary: Intanki	November to March	04	01	N/A	05
Sikkim	1. Pemayangtse – Yuksam - Kewzing – Ravangla – Timitarku Gangtok – Singtam – Rangpo – Teesta – Siliguri 2. Namchi – Nayabazar – Chakung – Soreng – Buriakhop - varsey – Hilley – Uttareya – Dentam – Burmoik - Legship – Tayopani – Sikip – Namchi.	Gangtok, Tsomgo Lake, Nathu -La- Pass, Bakkhim, Dzongri, Pemayangtse, Yuksam, Khangchendzonga View Points. Monasteries of Rumtek, Tashiding, Zurmang Kagyud etc.	March to May	07	N/A	02	09
Tripura	1. Agartala – Sipahijala – Neermahal – Udaipur – Matabari – Pilak – Mahamuni. 2. Agartala – Dumboor Lake – Unakoti – Jampui Hills	Agartala, Kamalasagar, Udaipur, Bhubaneswari Temple, Matabari, Pilak,Mahamuni, Dumboor, Jampui Hills, Unakoti Wildlife Sanctuary: Sipahijala, Trishna	Sept. to Mar.	09	08	05	22

Source: www.indiatourism.org and www. Incredibleindia.org

Table 3
Tourist Arrival in the Northeastern States during 1996-2003

STATE	VISITORS	1996	1997	1998	1999	2000	2001
Arunachal Pradesh	Domestic	2283	2912	1222	1008	9932	6349
	Foreign	9	52	93	48	2044	323
	Total	**2292**	**2964**	**1315**	**1056**	**11976**	**6672**
Assam	Domestic	3,27,260	8,42,656	9,39,721	9,64,939	10,01,577	10,10,652
	Foreign	5,885	4,194	3,843	5,218	5,959	6,171
	Total	**3,33,145**	**8,46,850**	**9,43,564**	**9,70,157**	**10,07,536**	**10,16,823**
Manipur	Domestic	86749	909704	87667	97523	105167	76527
	Foreign	241	215	261	227	429	183
	Total	**86990**	**91189**	**87928**	**97750**	**105596**	**76710**
Meghalaya	Domestic	136183	115559	136952	159730	169929	178697
	Foreign	1573	1071	1055	1971	2327	2390
	Total	**137756**	**116630**	**138007**	**161701**	**172256**	**181087**
Mizoram	Domestic	23434	29713	23945	27139	28221	18771
	Foreign	93	90	126	216	235	152
	Total	**23527**	**29803**	**24071**	**27355**	**28456**	**28923**

Nagaland	Domestic	13139	39139	15940	21041	13272	9948
	Foreign	54	228	60	119	451	920
	Total	**13193**	**39367**	**16000**	**21160**	**13723**	**10868**
Tripura	Domestic	206229	202659	291978	246507	231902	254912
	Foreign	156	192	846	335	NA	NA
	Total	**206385**	**202851**	**295824**	**246842**	**231902**	**254912**

NB : Arnachal Pradesh figures represent the financial year i.e. 1996-97, 1997-98 and 1998-99 respectively and rest represent calendar year. The table excludes tourist traffic in Sikkim

Source: 1. The figures of Assam are taken from Department of Statistical Records, Directorate of Tourism, Assam.
2. The figures other states are compiled from 'Basic Statistics of North Eastern Region, 2002' of the North Eastern Council.

- The tourists normally prefer Assam as a central location for visiting NER. Their motive may not be associated with Assam tourism.
- As compared to other states of the NorthEast, Assam possesses better tourism infrastructure.

IV

Tourism Policy Measures in NER

In India, tourism accords a major service sector industry contributing a great deal of contribution in national income. So far, 14 States namely Arunachal Pradesh, Assam, Meghalaya, Himachal Pradesh, Uttar Pradesh, Andhra Pradesh, Kerala, Haryana, Tamil Nadu, Manipur, Bihar, Tripura and the union Territory of Andaman and Nicobar Islands have declared tourism as indystry. Dadra, Nagar Haveli and Lakshadweep. States like Punjab, West Bengal, Orissa and Rajathan have declared 'Hotels' as an industry. The governments of the States and Union Territories have also set up Directorate of Tourism Development. The National Tourism Policy, 2002 is considered to be a visionary statement of tourism in the context of new world economic order in emphasizing the service sector development. The new approach of the policy signifies tourism as a multi-dimensional activity of linkages between public and private sectors and highlights six broad (Six-Ss) areas of tourism policy comprising Welcome (*Swagat*), Information (*Suchana*), Facilitation (*Suvidha*), Safety (*Suraksha*), Co-operation (*Sahyog*) and Infrastructure Development (*Samrachana*). The Union Government attaches great importance to the development of tourist infrastructure in the North-East region in view of immense tourist potential of the region. Tourism has been identified as one of the most important segments, which could accelerate developmental activities in this area. The thrust has been on development and up- gradation of various tourist facilities namely tourist accommodation, wayside amenities, budget adjustments, beautification and refurbishment of historical monuments/monasteries etc. However, the North Eastern states including Sikkim have so far no comprehensive regional policy statement for tourism sector development. Except, Meghalaya no other NER state has an updated tourism policy in line with the national plan. Meghalaya Tourism Policy, 2001 considers tourism sector as 'gateway to economic development of the State' and determines the following thrust areas:

(a) Nature Tourism (Flora & Fauna)

(b) Adventure Tourism

(c) Cultural and Socio-cultural Tourism (Fairs and Festivals)

(d) Health Resort Tourism

(e) Golf Tourism

(f) Conferencing and Convention

(g) Sports Tourism

(h) Casino Tourism

(i) Travel/Transportation and Communications

(j) Arts & Crafts promotion Tourism.

Moreover, the state plan envisages that a close co-coordination is urgently required for tourism sector development. For attracting private sector participation, different schemes have also been developed. Subsidies on investment on tourism projects, maintenance and up keep tourist attractions, publicity drives, power generating set, telephone connection, cost of feasibility studies and project reports, interest on loans; sales tax exemption etc are some of the salient features of the state plan on tourism in Meghalaya. However, only projects approved by the Department of Tourism after 1997 would be eligible for incentives and concessions.

The initiation of policy measures for tourism sector development in the North East was initiated by Assam by setting up State Department of Tourism in 1958. In 1959, Directorate of Tourism was also established. Astonishingly enough, since then no significant works have been done in the state except certain sporadic programmes like establishment of Kaziranga tourist information office in 1962, opening of tourist lodge at Sivasagar in 1965 and some other tourist lodges at Tezpur, Bhalukpong, Barpeta Road, Háflong, Diphu, Nagaon, Silchar, Jorhat, Chandubi etc. In 1987 (During the 7th Five-Year Period), the first ever Tourism Policy was notified and subsequently the Assam Tourism Development Corporation (ATDC) was instituted in 1988 with a paid up capital of Rs.24 Lakh. Since then no initiatives have been taken by the state government of Assam in this direction.

Section 10.0 of the Manipur Industrial Policy, 2002 considers hotel and tourism related industries in the list of high priority industries. This is a sector with immense possibilities for foreign investment. State

Government shall have to notify the modalities in this regard. According to the policy statement, "the term "Hotel", includes restaurants and other tourist complexes providing accommodation and / or catering and food facilities to tourists. It may further be clarified that "Tourism related Industry" includes amongst other the following:-

i) Travel agencies, tour operating agencies and tourists transport operating agencies.

ii) Units providing facilities for Cultural, adventure and Wild life experience to tourists.

iii) Surface, air and water transport facilities to tourists.

iv) Leisure, entertainment, amusement, sports and health units for tourists; and

v) Convention/seminar units and organisations."

It is no denying that each of the North Eastern states considers tourism as a vital sector of economic development. But avoiding few instances, the region lacks a comprehensive tourism policy statement to adhere to.

It is strongly believed that the NER tourism development should essentially be a collective approach. The region's unique topographic similarity, socio-economic traditions, inter-dependent resource variety, common entrance to the states and possibility of common international route for ASEAN countries evidently establish the justification of this prerogative:

Considering all matters, it is proposed that social entrepreneurship development may be a feasible strategy of enhancing tourism sector development in the NER.

V

Tourism Entrepreneurship Incubator (TEI): A Simplified Model of Social Entrepreneurship

Social entrepreneurship, in essence, represents collective entrepreneurship. It revolves round the holistic approach of an enterprising society in combining and managing productive resources to ascertain maximum socio-economic advantages. "If we are to compete effectively in today's world, we must begin to celebrate collective entrepreneurship, endeavours in which the whole of the efforts is greater than the sum of individual contributions. We need to honour our teams more, our aggressive leaders and maverick geniuses less (Reich, 1987:78)."

Social entrepreneurship differs from conventional aggressive business leaders in a number of ways. Herlau & Tetzschner (1999:38) provide a comprehensive idea of social entrepreneurship as shown in the following table Table 4.

Table 4
From Individual Entrepreneurship to Social Entrepreneurship

From: Individual Entrepreneurship	To: Social Entrepreneurship
Individuals	A participant or an agent such as a network or a team
An action	A holistic process
Innovation and favourable opportunity	Societal innovations create favourable opportunities
Risks may be taken	Minimizing uncertainty and risk

Based on these basic specialties, social entrepreneurship may be defined as a participatory process of enterprise development in which a team of enterprising participants perform different tasks of a conventional heroic entrepreneur by minimizing risks and opening up opportunities. Both the approaches mentioned above are relevant to the growth of entrepreneurship in a society. Social entrepreneurship in rural tourism is comparatively a new phenomenon in Indian tourism industry. It is similar to the principle of community participation in production. However, it should not be confused with co-operative structure of an organization. It is in fact sharing of tourism avenues among local stake-holders according to efficiency and expertise in a motive to create an enterprising society. This enterprising society rests on the principle of active mutual dependence, but every entrepreneur is individually responsible for their destiny.

However, considering the inherent appeal and charisma of the sector in enhancing sustainable entrepreneurship, high level employment multiplier and above all, generation of a social consciousness for the preservation and maintenance of local bio-diversity and traditional value system; a comprehensive strategy of generating entrepreneurship is urgently felt.

The process of generating social entrepreneurship follows a distinct pattern under three major stages. (Fig 1).

Initial Stage

Determination of core potential of rural tourism base of a region is the primary task. This task may be fulfilled by the Government by adopting independent or joint spatial surveys in co-ordination with local non-governmental organizations (N.G.Os.). At every stage of the survey, participation, recommendations and preferences of the local stakeholders should be given high priority. The survey should also concentrate on the following aspects:

1. The possibility of increasing tourist carrying capacity of the region, physically as well as culturally.
2. The possibility of developing proper transport and communication facilities.
3. To measure the possibilities of long term damage to the aboriginal culture and heritage due to its exposure to the market.
4. To census the growth of human population of the region to measure possibility of socio-cultural clashes. It is found that lower the rate of the growth of human population of a region, higher is the rate of tourism development.
5. The history of any form of threat to the aboriginality of the region and retaliation of aboriginal culture against such attacks.

The Second Stage

This phase is associated with the preparations to establish the potentialities of the region as a major site of tourist attraction. Community Entrepreneurship generation is the major course of action during this stage. This stage depends upon the coherent approach of a series of formal and informal institutions forming a sort of 'Tourism Business Incubator'. The idea of the incubator in social entrepreneurship revolves round the following major aspects:

- ✓ Technical assistances in the form of dissemination of tourism based expertise provided by education and training institutions, N.G.O.s and Government.

Fig-1: A Model for Social Entrepreneurship Development in Rural Tourism

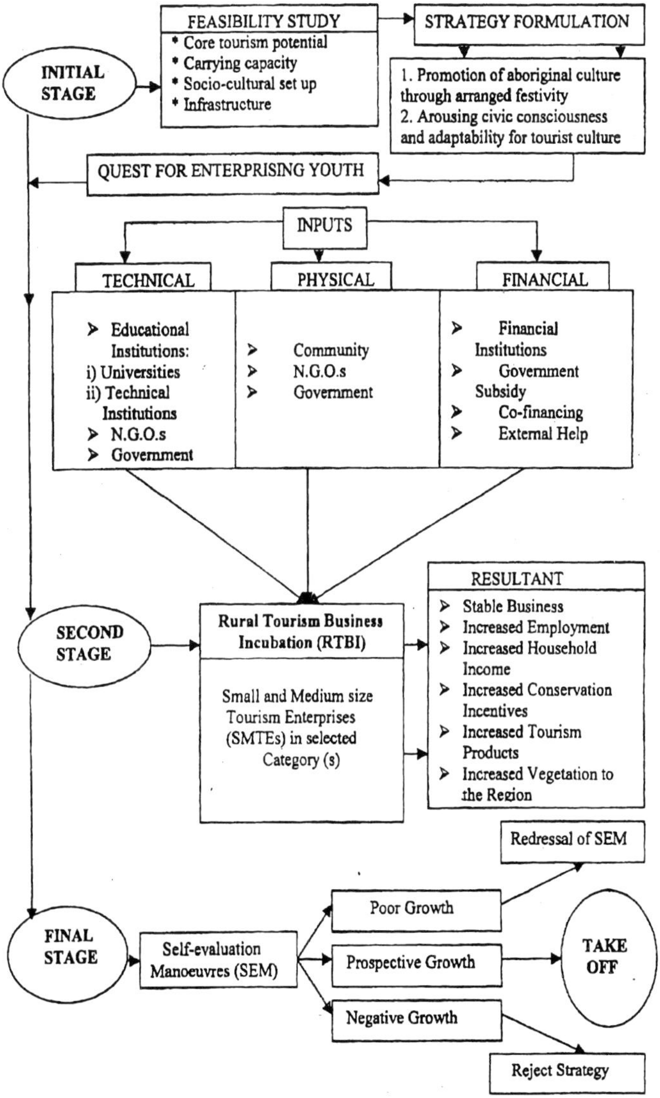

- ✓ Physical assistance and co-operation of the local stakeholders in tourism business.
- ✓ Financial assistance in the form of subsidised borrowings from the financial institutions. This can also be done on participatory basis of partnership between the government and groups of local stakeholders.
- ✓ Continuation of aboriginal culture is a must which can be maintained through the generation of strong desire among the stakeholders to maintain originality.
- ✓ Assessment and monitoring.

The Final Stage

The final phase is divided into two sub-stages, viz., *Self-evaluation Manoeuvres* and *Take Off/Open Competition*. Self-evaluation is essential for the attainment of clarity of sustainability conditions, on one hand, and assurance of strict adherence to the sustainability ethics, on the other. If it is found during the evaluation period that in a designated area the stake-holders are contributing negatively to the process of change, it is advisable that the strategy of social entrepreneurship should be withdrawn systematically. Otherwise, it will prove dangerous for the continuation of native cultural values. The concept of open competition is attached to the exposure of the local market for tourism to the national as well as international markets. Open competition is possible only when the stake-holders practically realise the economic as well as non-economic conditions of sustainable growth in tourism sector.

The Consequential Actions

SMEs in rural tourism suffer from the greatest drawback of entrepreneurial shifts to other sectors of the economy. Increased social status and less service-variant manufacturing sector attract most of the tourism entrepreneurs especially in case of second generation entrepreneurs (Agarwal, 2003). It is believed that sustaining social entrepreneurship becomes pertinent in rural tourism for greater sustainability of regional tourism segments. To achieve a self-propelling growth in rural tourism, the following should be maintained after tourism take off:

1. Demarcation of the rural tourism sector as a special tourism segment and allowing only focused tourists in the sites.

2. Creation of an environment for innovative tourism services. Exposure of local entrepreneurs to developed regions in different forms (inbound and outbound tours, exhibitions, fairs and festivals, competitions, symposium etc.) may help in this direction.
3. Encouraging the growth of tourism ancillary product units at a reachable distance of the major attraction.
4. Developing a special armed professional tourism protection force (Non-voluntary) with sufficient calibre to prevent physical assaults to the tourists as well as to the tourism resources of the region.
5. Imposition of penalty charges on the stakeholders as well as the tourists by the local authority on wilful damages to the tourism resources.
6. Determination of tourist carrying capacity of the area and not allowing tourists above the determined capacity.
7. Imposition of strict, punishable ban on illicit activities like prostitution, drug trafficking and any activity that disturbs traditional culture and heritage.
8. Preservation and adherence to the 'Codes of Ethics' of tourism development as prescribed by the World Tourism Organisation (WTO) in 1999.

Limitations of Social Entrepreneurship in Tourism

The idea of social entrepreneurship is theoretically admirable as a competent strategy of tourism sector development in Assam. However, there has been a perplexing doubt that in real time application the strategy may face certain limitations due to the inherent maladjustments in service sector economy, especially tourism.

First, it is difficult to infuse cultural consciousness within a community by any external organization from outside, if it is not arising out of a strong sense of the local stakeholders. It is a world-wide experience that tourism activities are most closely contagious to the local tradition.

Secondly, seasonality of tourism business may adversely affect local entrepreneurs as secondary options of business will be limited for them.

Thirdly, being a community aspect, social entrepreneurship may develop a sense of misgivings relating to the concept of community participation in business. This may create a lethargic and innovation-less atmosphere.

Last but not the least, if the public participation in social entrepreneurship is not genuine and politically motivated, the benefits of this branch of entrepreneurship will not be realized.

VII
Conclusion

Social entrepreneurship is in fact a community requirement in the less developed peripheries in tourism trade. Apart from socio-cultural impacts, it has vast economic possibilities in all its forms. However, infusing social entrepreneurship in the development process of tourism trade in the NER experiences a great deal of hindrances. These hindrances may be overcome by a concerned regional tourism policy of the state setting-off the strategy of social enterprise development.

NOTES AND REFERENCES

1. Acharyya, N.N. (1985), *North East as Viewed by Foreigners*. New Delhi: Omsons Publication.
2. Agarwal, S. B. (2003), *Tourism for Sustainable Development.* New Delhi: Reference Press.
3. Bhattacharya, P. (2004), *Tourism in Assam: Status and Potentialities, Dibrugarh,* Assam: Bani Prakash.
4. Baruah, K. L.(1988), *Early History of Kamrupa* (3rd Ed.). Guwahati: Lawyers. pp. 4-6.
5. Herlau & Tetzschner (2003), Innovation and Social Entrepreneurship in Tourism-A Potentional for Local Business Development?.http:/ www.hl.lp.dk/imeworking paper/no.49/03.html.
6. *International Labour Statistics*. (2002), Jeneva: ILO.
7. Kelkar, Vijay. (1999), India's Emerging Economic Challenges. *Economic and Political Weekly*, 24(33), August 14-20.
8. Lundberg, D.F. and Lundberg, L.B. (1993), *International Travel and Tourism*. John Wiley, Chichester, U.K.
9. Reich, R. (1987), Entrepreneurship Reconsidered: the Team as Hero. *Harvard Business Review*, May-June, 77-83.
10. *Rajasthan Tourism Policy*, 2002.

11. Sinclair, M.T. & Stabler, M. (1997), *The Economics of Tourism*. London: Routledge. p. 58.
12. Saayman, M. and Slabbert, E. (1998), *Tourism Entrepreneurs: Opportunities and Threats. A South African Perspective*. http://www.puknet.puk.ac.za/ enterprise/alpapers.htm. Retrieved on 09.12.2003.
13. Shaw, Gareth and Williams, Allan M. (2002), *Critical Issues in Tourism, A Geographical Perspective*: Blackwell Publishers Ltd. p. 112.
14. *Statistical Handbook Assam*, 2002.
15. *USAID Research Report*, 2004.
16. UN Report. (1992), *Report of the United Nations Conference on Environment and Development*, Rio de Janeiro, 3-14 June 1992, vol. I, Resolutions Adopted by the Conference (United Nations publication, Sales No. E.93.I.8 and corrigendum), resolution 1. annex II.
17. World Commission on Environment and Development (1987), *Our Common Future* (Brundtland Report). Oxford: Oxford University Press.
18. World Travel and Tourism Corporation (2002), *High Hope for Indian Tourism*. http:www.tourismof India.com/archive. Retrieved on 22.06.2004
19. World Tourism Organisation. (1993), *Annual Report*. Madrid: World Tourism Organisation
20. World Tourism Organisation. (1993), *Sustainable Tourism Development: Guide for Local Planners*. Madrid: W.T.O.
    a. (2003), *Traveller's Companion*. New Delhi: ITDC.
    b. (2001), *Census Report*, Government of India.
    c. (2002), *Tourism Policy of Rajasthan*, Government of Rajasthan.
    d. (2002), *Statistical Handbook*, Assam. Guwahati: Directorate of Economics and Statistics, Assam.
    e. (May, 2004), *Trade Capacity Building in the Services Sector (A Resource Guide)*, U.S.A.: Nathan Associates Inc.
    f. (1989), *WTO Annual Report*. Madrid: World Tourism Organisation. Madrid: W.T.O.
    g. (1993), *Annual Report*. Madrid: World Tourism Organisation
    h. (1993), *Sustainable Tourism Development: Guide for Local Planners*. Madrid: W.T.O.
    i. (2000), *Annual Report*. Madrid: World Tourism Organisation.
21. (2000), *Annual Report*. World Travel and Tourism Council. New Delhi: WTTC.
    a. (2001), *Census Report*, Government of India.

26

ISO-9000 AND TQM IN SSI UNITS: Issues and Challenges

CH. IBOHAL MEITEI

Introduction

The Small Scale Industries (SSI) sector has emerged as dynamic and vibrant sector of Indian economy and it contributes substantially to industrial production, export and employment generation. Globalization and market reforms have opened up the Indian small scale industries to the global competition. During 2002-03, SSI sector accounted for almost 39% of the industrial value added and 34% of the total exports of the country. This sector with 3.57 million units produced over 8000 items and provides employment to about 20 million people. Dr. S.P. Gupta Study Group (2002) on "Development of Small Enterprises" identified the importance of SSI sector in the Indian economy and also stressed on the problems relating to inadequate credit flow from banks and Financial Institutions, inadequate infrastructure facilities, low quality standard of products, use of obsolete technology, plant, machinery and equipment and inefficient management techniques.

Moreover, globalisation and increasing domestic competition have brought a sense of urgency in inducting highly successful quality management techniques in the operation of companies and organisations. To survive in such a competitive business environment organizations make all possible efforts to produce the products which satisfy their customers to the fullest extent. The image attached to an organisation for the quality of its products and services is accepted as a key to its success and the future of its employees.

To prosper in today's highly competitive and rapidly changing business climate any organization and its suppliers must be dedicated to continuous and never ending improvement and more efficient ways to obtain products or services that consistently meet customer's requirement and expectations. In the tough present day business environment the development and implementation of a comprehensive quality policy is not merely desirable but it is essential.

Thus, quality is often used to signify excellence of a product or service and if we are to define its quality in a way, which is useful in its management, then we must recognize the need to include in the assessment of quality, the true requirements of the customers. The International Organisation for Standardization (ISO) defines quality as "totality of features and characteristics of a product or service that bears on it ability to satisfy stated or implied needs". Quality is expressed by Feigenbaum (1983) too as "the total composite product and service characteristics of marketing, engineering, manufacturing, and maintenance through which the product and service in use will meet the expectations by the customer". In determining the quality of a product, the customer's expectations about the product will be given the utmost priority. In fact, quality is something we all think we understand; a quality car, a quality toothpaste etc. It means different things to different people. Different quality movements have focused on different aspects of quality but what is inevitable is the fitness for use at a given time and given price. Fig. 1 shows the dimensions of quality.

Earlier companies used to set their own standards according to their resources which were not necessarily comparable with competitors abroad. The provision made by ISO in 1987 of issuing certificates (ISO 9000) to companies having a standard quality system is a breakthrough in the direction of globalization quality systems. Beginning in 1993, all companies exporting products to the European Community are required to comply with ISO norms. They must certify their products and quality control systems meet ISO 9000, the minimum quality standards.

Quality, today has become one of the most vibrant buzzwords of the business world. Since the mid 1980, companies around the globe have embraced some or all the percepts of the so called quality movement aimed at improving productivity, lowering costs, attracting and retaining valued employees and achieving top performance.

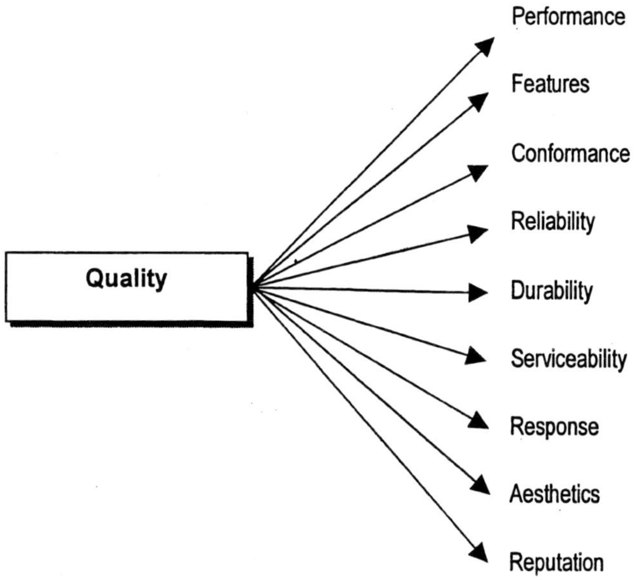

Fig. 1 : Dimensions of Quality

In Indian context, till recently concept of quality and the activities related to its control in organizations used to be confined to only a small group of personnel called the quality control group. By employing quality principles in controlling process waste, it was realized consequently that quality could not be restricted any longer to a designated quality department but it was to spread across the company.

With the increasing quality consciousness among customers and changing scenario of the global market, the scope of the quality is being broadened and the focus has now been shifted from 'quality to total quality'. This has given birth to the concept called Total Quality Management (TQM), a comprehensive and customer oriented approach to quality management. Today, TQM has got its formal recognition by way of ISO 9000. In order that companies may compete with world class leaders it is imperative to look at and be prepared for quality way beyond the ISO 9000.

ISO 9000 in India

Indian industries started facing stiff competition both in domestic and international markets due to liberalization of trade and industrial policies. By 1992-93, quality movement with ISO 9000 tag had started in India, and mainly large companies had got this certification. It was then perceived that ISO-9000 being a complex exercise involving lot of documentation, control checks and voluminous records etc. can be obtained only by well organized large sized companies.

The Small Industries Development Organization (SIDO) took the initiative to motivate SSI sector for ISO 9000 quality system. Various programmes on ISO-9000 quality systems were launched through their network Small Industries Services Institute for SSIs to adopt the international quality system. The total number of ISO 9000 certified companies for both large and SSI units is estimated to 6500 nos. and of which around 25% are SSI enterprises by the end of 2002. Now, we can have a brief overview of the ISO 9000 as such.

ISO means International Organisation for Standardisation. Its purpose is to provide common world wide standards. It is made up of national standards institutes from countries large and small industrialized and developing in all parts of the world. ISO develops voluntary technical standards which add value to all types of business activities. It is not mandatory to use ISO standards except in some cases where governments and regulatory authorities impose them for public security reasons or where they are required in contractual terms. However, the demand for these standards has been increasing in the market and avoiding them will become impossible.

The working of ISO is carried out through technical committees and working groups. Developing and maintaining the ISO family of standards are responsible by a technical committee called ISO/TC 176. The scope of ISO 9000 series is standardization in the field of generic quality management including quality systems, quality assurance and generic supporting technologies such as standards which provide guidance on selection and use of these standards.

The ISO 9000 family based on the revision in 1994 is a set of five individual but related standards (Table 1). The series set out generic standards that are applicable to any industry such as manufacturing, services sector, software houses, small and medium enterprises etc.

Table 1
ISO 9000: 1994 Documents

❖ ISO 9000:	Quality management and quality assurance Standards - Guidelines for Selection and Use.
❖ ISO 9001:	Quality Systems – Model for Quality Assurance in Design/Development, Production, Installation and Servicing.
❖ ISO 9002.	Quality Systems – Model for Quality Assurance in production and Installation.
❖ ISO 9003.	Quality Systems – Model for Quality Assurance in final Inspection and Test.
❖ ISO 9004.	Quality Management and Quality Systems Elements – Guidelines.

The most critical challenge facing Indian quality movement today is the development and implementation of quality focused management system that achieve the coherence, integration and comprehensiveness of quality practices. In India quality of the 90s as a consequence of economic liberalization was almost synonymous with ISO 9000 certification. In fact, organizations need to create a corporate culture where quality products and services, business processes and people are central.

The ISO 9000 series specifies the required elements to a quality system. However, it does not set out how a quality system is to be implemented. Thus, ISO released the new version of the ISO 9000:2000 series of standards on 15th December, 2000 (Table 2). This new version is based on eight quality management principles such as consumer focus, leadership, involvement of people, process approach, systems approach to management, continual improvement, factual approach to decision making and mutually beneficial supplier relationships. It is more of management standards and in this version the earlier ISO 9002 and ISO 9003 had been removed. The focus has also moved more towards the customer requirements.

The change in title itself signifies a paradigm shift and evolution of managing quality from inspecting quality to build quality but to quality products and services through Quality Management System. From management point of view, TQM approach has emerged in response to the challenges of implementing a quality system in organizations conforming various quality standards. As a result, a working understanding of TQM among the employees (managers plus workers) of the organization is called for.

Table 2 ISO 9000:2000 Main Documents

❖ISO 9000: 2000	Quality Management Systems – Fundamentals an Vocabulary
❖ISO 9001: 2000	Quality Management Systems – Requirements
❖ISO 9004: 2000	Quality Management Systems – Guidelines fo performance improvements

TQM for ISO 9000 Quality Management System

The term TQM was inspired by W. Edwards Deming and Joseph M. Juran in 1950s. Initially these ideas and techniques were not accepted in the United States but were enthusiastically embraced by Japanese companies and as a result, Japanese manufacturers began beating out US competitors in quality comparisons. Now, managers in the western countries too have started a serious look at TQM system. Today, the ideas of Deming and Juran became the basis for organizational quality management programme.

TQM is not a new concept, but it is a new management philosophy pervading our approach to joining business. It envisages integrating people with organization through continuous system development and a change in attitude. The job of quality management is not just advising a sample plan for the acceptance/rejection of the supplied materials and controlling manufacturing process conditions. In fact, it is a job at every stage of the organization's activities. It is an organization wide activity involved the combined efforts of various departments such as design, engineering, purchase, production, inspection etc. in different phases with a view to achieving the desired quality of the output. It encompasses all activities in an organization and involves everyone.

TQM programme though it is known to different companies by different names must try to view company operations as an integrated system rather than a series of independent parts and company itself is a larger societal system involving customers, suppliers, communities, stockholders and others etc. TQM movement has become a cornerstone and a guiding force in virtually every organization in the globe.

In fact, TQM is a blend of technology focused on four dimensions such as defect, prevention, continuous improvement, the customer and a philosophy that quality is the responsibilities shared by *al.* TQM techniques can improve any organization which has a sequence of activities directed towards a defined end result and has business processes. Fig. 2 depicts the dimensions of TQM.

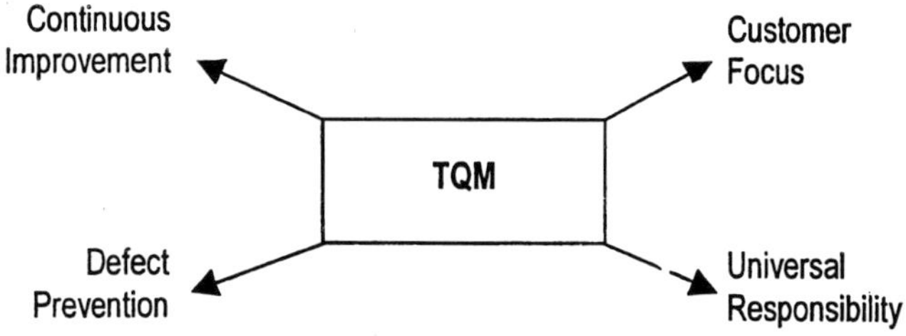

Fig. 2. Dimensions of TQM

There are several concepts that are inherent to TQM, but all will fall on these four dimensions. Let us take a brief overview of the key dimensions of TQM.

Customer Focus

Quality is based on the idea that everyone has a customer (internal and external) and that the requirements, needs and expectations of the customer must be met every time. Satisfying customer has to be a permanent concern as dissatisfied customers represent major lost opportunities. Research studies confirm that developing new customers to replace dissatisfied customers costs in an average of five times more than it does to retain a satisfied customer. Moreover, dissatisfied customers express their dissatisfaction to an average of eleven other potential customers. However, all business, no matter how hard they work to satisfy their customer, face the problem of dissatisfied customer from time to time. Prompt rectifications the source of dissatisfaction of dissatisfied customers will provide an opportunity in disguise. Neither organizations nor individuals can afford to be passive when the subject is defining sources of customer's dissatisfaction. A strong proactive stance is a must. Lee Iacocca once advertised that Chrysler had only three rules: satisfy the customers, satisfy the customers and satisfy the customers. From TQM perspective, satisfying the customers is a golden set of rules to run an organization successfully.

Universal Responsibility

A basic percept of TQM is that the responsibility for quality is not confined to a company's quality control department but is instead a guiding philosophy shared by everyone in the company. It represents a significant shift in thinking for most of manufacturing companies which have traditionally relief on inspection to assure quality. By relying on inspection i.e., detection defects rather than prevention, organizations of such type have unknowingly and unwittingly instilled a deep belief in the people who actually manufacture products that they are no longer responsible for the quality of their output. From TQM point of view, this thinking is reversed and everyone takes responsibility for quality. If everyone is responsible for the quality of the output, the need for quality assurance function vanishes. This espouses a philosophy of creating a quality culture with total employee involvement from all areas of an organization.

Defect Prevention

TQM is a management philosophy of doing right first time and every time with zero defects. It seeks to prevent poor quality in products and services, rather than simply to detect and sort out defects. As the saying goes "an once of prevention is worth a pound of cure". Another basis TQM precept is that prevention rather than detecting defects makes no defects in the output. Cost of a register in a PC is hardly Rs. 10 but a substandard register may cost us many folds in repairing. Moreover, the likely loss of image of the company is again costlier which is detrimental to the success of the business. The worst ever industrial accident in history, "Bhopal Gas Tragedy, 1984" are not accident because of human error but a part of flawed business processes where quality is ignored. The tragic explosion of space shuttle Challenger of NASA can be sited as another similar example.

Continuous Improvement

If a single characteristic is most strongly attached to the TQM philosophy, it is continuous improvement. It consists of measuring key quality and other process indices in all areas and taking actions to improve them. The customers' need and expectations vary from customer to customer and the needs are also constantly changing. This requires us to look for improvements and innovations continuously. Continuous improvement should be focused on processes including the output of a manufacturing process, customer satisfaction, and warranty returns etc. and pursued in all these areas which are used to characterize a process. It takes up on findings shortfalls and sources of variability in administrative, manufacturing and service processes that can detract from a quality output, and improving the process to eliminate undesirable output. An understanding of on-going continuous improvement as a part of quality management system will determine the future of an organization. Eicher Tractor introduced Japanese system of workers' participation such as Kaizen (continuous improvement) and Poka Yoke (zero defects) in its Alwar plant. In three years, their production jumped up by 45 per cent, productivity by 27.4 per cent and manpower requirements reduced from 320 to 277.

Quality does not happen as an accident. It is always the outcome of high intentions, sincere efforts intelligent directions and skillful executions. For successful implementation of TQM some specific managerial skills, tools and technique are required to work in a totally new environment.

Important Techniques of Implementation

Some important techniques of implementing TQM are as below:

1. **Supplier Relationship**: Developing a long term relationship with a few high quality suppliers, rather than simply selecting those suppliers with the lowest initial cost should be a principle of the TQM philosophy. It is advantageous to both the customer and the supplier to have a long term agreement with fewer quality suppliers and provides less variability in supplies. Company adopting TQM must extend its philosophy to their suppliers too. Rolls Royce and IBM computers came out ads with messages exclusively for their suppliers telling that they are way to the corporate successes. This creates an image of quality conscious companies heavily dependent on quality supplies.

2. **Employees Involvement and Empowerment** : One of the most important underlying factors in the success or failure of any organization is the power of its people and how judiciously that power is focused towards achieving the organizational objectives. Every employee should be regarded as a unique human being not a just a cog in a machine and each employee

is involved in making the organization function successfully. Hence, each employee's input must be solicited and valued by the management. Employee empowerment means that management recognize the ability, and provides employees with tools and authority required to continuously improve their performance. It means that management states its expectations about employees, recognizing and solving problems and empowers them to do so. However, motivating people to work is a major concern for any management team. Demotivators are stumbling blocks to the organizational growth. Understanding what makes to motivate people is an important aspect of managing people in the organization.

3. **Team Work:** "one plus one is always greater than two", the underlying idea is the concept of synergies available through team work. Team building is a concept used as a powerful tool for solving problems and meeting continuous improvement objectives. The essence of a team is mutual trust, openness and a feeling of interdependence and interrelationship among the members. Companies adopting TQM must ensure that communication moves in all directions up, down, and across internally and externally. From TQM perspective, team building concept has enabled the management view the functioning of organization in a holistic manner. Concerned effort of team members are of immense importance in developing TQM culture.

4. **Benchmarking :** Benchmarking consist of identifying other organizations that perform well and incorporating their wisdom into our organization. It is a continuous process of measuring one's products, services and practices against toughest competitors. Benchmarking includes defining competitions best features from both internal and customers perspectives and then adopting the best practices of these organizations to our company.

5. **Quality Function Deployment :** It is a basic TQM tool that identifies and develops customers need and wants. The tools provides a graphic methodology for detecting a customer's requirements and expectations for making decisions in cases where these needs and wants conflict and for converting these customer requirements and expectations into the product

development and manufacturing process. Today, business is customer driven oriented. Using the quality function development companies achieve notable success in satisfying the needs and expectations of its customers. As such, the technique is described as "developing the voice of the customer".

In fact, if an organization is serious about implementing TQM, top management's commitment to quality becomes inevitable. It is the responsibility of management which have to develop a total quality culture to achieve the desire goal of satisfying customer needs and expectations and finally the objectives of the organization as well. If management is willing to let a defective product go out the door in order to make sales, all the talk in the world about quality won't make a difference to the people making the product.

There are certain other techniques which will support in the effective implementation of TQM, such as quality measurements, value improvement, corrective actions, problem solving skills, thinking strategically and training etc. However, this paper gives more emphasis on the behavioral and attitudinal aspects of the people working under TQM system with a view to developing a desirable work culture.

Creating a TQM Culture

Culture is the set of important understandings (often unstated) that members of a community share in common. In management circles too, corporate culture is widely used denoting the culture of the organization as a whole or the culture of any community/unit within the corporate context. Culture is deeply rooted in organizations and has profound influence on organizational life. Creating a total quality corporate culture is one of the biggest challenges of a TQM programme. For managerial action, culture according to Vijay Sathe (1983) generates four aspects for manifestation such as shared things (objects), shared saying (talk), shared doings (behavioural) and shared feelings (emotion) through which culture is to be built around.

Culture is both an asset and liabilities. It becomes an asset when shared beliefs provide ease and economized communications and shared values generate higher levels of corporation and commitment. Culture becomes a liability if the shared values and beliefs are not keeping with the needs of the organization, its members and its other constituent elements. When we take a closer look at the pattern of communications, cooperation, commitment and decision making in organization, culture influences behaviour. The challenge for managers is to create quality the central shared value in a TQM/ISO 9000 programme and everything else will flow from it.

Incentives for ISO Certified SSI units

The Ministry of Small Scale Industries, Government of India has been operating an incentive scheme of reimbursement of expenses of acquiring ISO-9000 certification in SSI sector to the extent of 75% of the amount limited to Rs. 75,000 to each unit. This scheme was launched during 1994 and has been extended up to the end of Tenth-Plan (i.e., up to 31.3.2007). Moreover, the scope of the scheme now has been extended to provide reimbursement of expenses of acquiring environment Management System, ISO-14001 certification. There are concessions in the application fees too for SSI units when they apply for fresh/renewal of ISO certification.

In India more than 2375 SSI and ancillary units have already been benefited from the incentive scheme of ISO-9000 certification till 31st March, 2002. However, of the total of 5779 SSI units registered in Manipur in 2001, no unit has got ISO-9000 certification till date. It is felt that they are not familiar with these terms like ISO 9000 and TQM etc. Concern authority should come forward to the introduction of the Short term courses for awareness of ISO certification and Quality Management Systems in the SSI sector and Quality Movement Campaign so that the survival of these units can be strengthen. At the same time, the SSI units in the state will be globally competitive as well.

Precautions

ISO 9000 certification and Total Quality Management is not an overnight cure for a company's quality problems. Implementation effort of TQM has a beginning but if implemented successfully it does not have an ending. Its implementation process is not a time bound programme. The continuous improvement process continues and has never ending. Implementing a TQM culture takes years. There will not be immediate return on TQM investment. We cannot expect prompt result as it is a long term pay off.

However, no organization can afford to overlook customer, competition and change, the three vital forces of today's competitive business environment. To retain the competitive position, companies should change their traditional ways of working to their customer's mind. To be successful in TQM/ISO certification programme the commitment of the top management is utmost necessity and we should focus not on specific technique but on the whole system.

Conclusion

In the context of fast changes taking place in the economic and business environment in the country, companies need to perform themselves radically in order to capture new opportunities. Today, with more and more companies going in for the ISO-9000s tag, manufacturers and service providers in India are realizing the economic advantages of an effective quality management system.

Compliance with the ISO quality standards will help the organizations to stay competitive in the global market place as it will bring many benefits to them such as enhancing the organization's reputation and public image, developing good relations with government, establishing quality leadership and creation of competitive advantage. However, the certificate ISO 9000 is no guarantee of being world class in quality as this only certifies establishment of a standard quality system.

The important challenge facing quality movement in the SSI sector in the present context is the development and implementations of quality focused management system that may enable the units excel in the competitive market place. It is inevitable for small scale sector to have a quality focused management system to face the challenges in the market front.

To be competitive in both domestic and global market place, SSI units first have to reorient the mindset with attitude and outlook and create a total quality culture. For creating such an environment top management's commitment to the quality culture is of pivotal importance. Moreover, Government has to come out various programmes on ISO 9000 and TQM area to enthuse the SSI sector in developing and adopting the internationally acclaimed quality management system. TQM a holistic concept encompasses a number of precepts which all support the philosophies of customer focus, continuous improvement, defect prevention and recognition that quality responsibility is an organization wide activity. For effective functioning and globally competitive of SSI sector, creating an organizational culture with quality the central shared belief in being the 'best' is the need of the hour.

NOTES AND REFERENCES

1. Denis, L. and Rodney, M. (2002), The Strategic Impact and Implementation of TQM, *TQM Magazine*, 14(1).
2. Diwan , P(1998), *Total Qouality Management in Small Scale Industry*, New Delhi, Deep and Deep Publications.
3. Feigenbaum, A.V. (1983), *Total Quality Control*, New York, McGraw Hill.
4. Joseph and Susan Berk (1985), *Total Quality Management, Implementing Continuous Improvement*, New Delhi, Excel Books.
5. Juran, J.M. (1989), *Juran on Leadership for Quality, An Executive Handbook*, New York, The Free Press.
6. Kishore, S & Naik, R (2003), *ISO-9000:2000 for Software Organisations*, New Delhi, Tata McGraw-Hill.
7. Lulla, S. (2002), Quality is n't about Superhuman Effort, *Indian Management*, May.
8. Oakland, J.S. (1989), *Total Quality Management*, Oxford Buttlerworth Heinemann, Professional Publishing.
9. Sathe, V. (1983), *Some Action Implications of Corporate Culture: A Manager's Guide to Action*, Organizational Dynamics, Autumn.
10. Shukla, M. (1996), *Understanding Organizations; Organizational Theory and Practices in India*, New Delhi, Prentice-hall of India.

Websites:

1. http://www.ficci.com
2. http://www.iso.ch
3. http://www.skyenet.net
4. http://www.tqvision.com

27

ROLE OF ENTREPRENEURSHIP IN FRUIT AND VEGETABLE PROCESSING SECTOR: Perspectives of North Eastern Region of India

R M PANT
P K NEMA
RITUPARNA DATTA

Food Industry is one of the fastest developing industries in India, which is totally dependent on agriculture and contributes in the country's economy quite significantly. In the recent years the importance of this industry is being increasingly recognized both for the generation of income and employment. The employment generated by this industry is approximately 1.5 million, which constitutes 19% of the country's industrial labour. The industry also contributes 19% of the total number of manufacturing units, 13.5% of the total output 6.5% of the value added. Moreover food industry accounts for only 5.2% of the total investment in the industry in the whole of the country yet contributing 18% to India's GDP.

Food processing as technological activity covers the application of scientific principles to slow down the natural processes of food decay caused by micro-organisms, enzymes in the food or environmental factors such as heat, moisture and sunlight and so preserve the food. Much of this knowledge is known traditionally and put into practice by experience and information handed down through the generations. In most developing countries food processing is also a method of generating employment and family incomes. Under these circumstances, producers must compete with others in the same country and with imported products. With some important exceptions, traditional processing methods produce foods that are usually inadequate to compete with the 'newer' products. This is particularly important with respect to packaging and presentation of the processed foods.

The food processing industry covers a wide spectrum of product, of which the fruits and vegetables (F&V) based products cover a unique position. This industry plays a vital role in the effective utilization of horticultural products. North East Region (NER) of India is mainly an agricultural area. The main occupation of the rural people of the region is agriculture. Moreover horticulture bears a bright future here as this region of northeast India is endowed with a wide range of horticultural products due to its unique geographical and climatic condition. Yet the growth and development of F&V based units are not proportionate to supply the raw materials and a 'big push' in terms of entrepreneurial efforts is needed to tap the potentials of this promising sector for the development of the region..

F&V Production in India

At present, India is the largest producer of fruits and the second largest producer of vegetables in the world next to China. It's share in the world production of fruits is 11% and in vegetables 7%. India can produce a wide variety of F&V because of its varied agro climatic conditions as temperate, sub tropical and tropical. The major fruits grown in India include mango, banana, papaya, orange, *mosumbi*, guava, grapes, apple, pineapple, sapota, *ber*, pomegranate, strawberry, litchi etc. The major vegetables grown are onion, potato, tomato, okra, chilly, brinjal, green peas, cabbage, cauliflower, carrot, radish, turnip, pumpkin, gourd, cucumber, french beans etc. Presently India produces about 70 different varieties of leafy, fruity and starchy tuber varieties of vegetables. The per capita annual consumption of vegetables in India is only about 63 kg as against 220 kg in South Korea, 115 kg in China and 105 kg in Japan.

As advised by the diet advisory committee of the ICMR, the availability of 120 grams of vegetables and 40 grams of fruits in India, against the recommended 280 grams of vegetable and 120 grams of fruit respectively per day per capita are far below the desired level. Therefore the need of the hour is to ensure the minimum nutritional level of diet for every common man. Besides usual diet, F&V are also very important for human being in view of their nutritive value.

F&V Processing in India

Despite being worlds largest producer of fruits and second largest producer of vegetables only 0.5 to 1.0% is processed as against 83% in Malaysia, 80% in South Africa, 78% in Philippines, 70% in Brazil and 65% in the USA. Some of the popular processed F&V foods produced in the country includes potato and banana chips; dried onions and garlic powder; ginger and garlic paste; jams of mixed fruits, pineapple and strawberry; juice and concentrates of apple, pineapple, orange and litchi; squash of orange, lemon and mango; canned pineapples, canned beans; frozen peas, cauliflower and okra, pickles of mango, lime, chilies and mixed fruits and vegetable; tomato ketchup and puree; mango fruit drink and nectar; chilly sauce; mango chutney etc. Recently the production of frozen vegetables has also been taken up in the country for both domestic and export markets. Freeze dried and individually quick frozen vegetables are mainly produced for export.

Indigenous Market for Processed F&V Products

At present 40% of the processed F&V produced in terms of value are bought by institutional buyers like hotels and restaurants, defence services and catering departments of railways and airlines, 40% by the housewives and household and 20% are exported. The buyers of exported product are also mostly ethnic Indians living aboard. In recent years the highest growth in the domestic market has been in fruit drinks, tomato ketchup and jams. At present jams and ketchup have as Rs. 600 crore market in India and frozen vegetables Rs 100 crore.

Export Market for Processed F&V Products

The main items exported from India are dried and preserved vegetables, mango pulp, pickles, chutneys and other processed fruits and vegetables. After liberalization a number of 100% export oriented units were setup but have failed because of high cost of production and a severe competition in this section in the world market. India has a share of about 1% in the world fruit juice and concentrate market, which is to the tune of 6 billion. India has a presence only in mango, guava and banana pulp, while in the world market the main trade commodities are fruit juices of orange, apple and pineapple.

Future prospects for Processed F&V Products

The fruit based beverage market in India accounts for 25% of the total market for all beverages. It is growing @ 20-25% against synthetic beverages which are growing at 10% The demand for fruit based drink is expected to grow up by 150% in the coming few years from 9.5 crore packages per annum at present to 25 crore packages. The present market for fruit drink nectar is estimated at about Rs. 300 crore and for fruit juice at about Rs. 80 crore. The market for frozen vegetables in India is expected to go up to $ 100 million in 2005. Market for jams, sauces and purees is expected to rise to $ 30 million & for fruit drinks to $ 550 million. The DFPI has set a target of increasing the processing capacity to 10% by 2010. This would require an investment of Rs. 1,40,000 crore and will generate direct employment to about 77 lakh persons and indirect employment for about three crore. This would also reduce wastage by about Rs. 8,000 crore. The value addition of food products will go up from 7% to 35%.

F&V Status with Respect to Food Processing Prospects

In general terms, following points can be considered in favour of the benefits of small-scale F&V processing industry for people in India as a whole and NER in particular:

- Various F&V raw materials are readily available, often in surplus
- Most technologies are available, accessible and affordable at scales that are suitable for small operations
- Equipment can often be manufactured locally, creating additional employment
- The products, if chosen correctly, have a widespread demand
- Most processes have few environmental impacts.

However, the selection of suitable products for small-scale manufacture and the processes chosen to make them, require very careful consideration. There must be a demand for the processed food, in general the types of products that are suitable for small-scale production are those for which there is a high demand, and a higher value can be added by processing. Typically F&V have a low price when in their raw state, but can be processed into a range of snack foods, dried foods, juices, pickles, and chutneys etc., which have a considerably higher value.

Dried F&V do not allow microorganisms to grow, provided that drying is carried out correctly and the food is kept dry. However, if the food is heavily contaminated before drying, or if it is allowed to get damp during storage, these microorganisms can grow again before the food is eaten. In addition to the actions of microorganisms, naturally occurring enzymes rapidly change the colour, flavour and texture of F&V after harvest. In general, these changes, due to both microorganisms and enzymes, produce a characteristically short shelf life and rapid processing after harvest is therefore necessary.

Importance of Development of F&V Processing in NER

The establishment of agro-based industries in the rural areas will not only reduce the migration of people from rural to urban areas but will also be used as one of the effective tools in bringing prosperity in rural areas. As the shifting cultivation in North Eastern region of India is no more a profitable and self-sustaining scheme, the agro-based industries can bind the people to rural areas. Their establishment may lead to improve the infrastructure facilities in backward areas and may create potential for more industries.

Development of agro-based industries will help in tackling exploitation (to a reasonable extent) of farming community by traders and middleman. Agro-based industries should be encouraged to achieve the balance growth between industry and agriculture. In order to keep rural economy at par with urban community's economy, rural industrialization through agro-based industries is one of the important means. Income generation through agro-based industries may improve the purchasing power of rural people; thereby creating potential for demand based industry and increasing the standard of living of rural people.

The agro-based industries should hopefully bring down the indiscriminate felling of tree in jungles. These industries will bind the local populace with socio-economic, legal and moral responsibility.

Table 1
Agro-climatic zones of NER and the F&V grown in these zones

Agro-climatic Zone	Area	Crops
Temperate zone	**Arunachal:** Tawang, Dirang, Bomdila, Shergaon, Diban valley, Upper subansiri, Anini, North eastern part of Lohit and Northern part of east Siang **Meghalaya:** Upper Shillong, Mawphlong and Mairang **Mizoram:** Blue mountain, Halkhan, Turpang, Nauzuarzo, and Tiang **Nagaland:** Tuensong and Zunebota, Vangkung and higher areas of Mokachung **Sikkim:** gnathing, Chhangu, Serrathong, Lima, Zema, Karponag, Bordong, Resi, Kangdem, Melli param, Lachem Hilley and Yaksum	**Fruits:** Apple, pear peaches, plums, cherries, pistachio, almond, apricot, walnut, chestnut and kiwifruit. **Vegetables:** Cabbage, cauliflower, knoll-khol, broccoli, radish, turnip, beetroot, carrot, garlic, onion, spinach, cucumber, tomato, brinjal, okra, French bean, aspergus, bean, capsicum and peas
Subtropical zone	**Arunachal Pradesh:** Changlang district, Naga, Khonsa areas of tirap district, Basar area of Siang district **Manipur:** Imphal valley **Meghalaya:** Jawai, Nongstonin, Nokrek, Kailash area of west garo hills, western part of east Garo hills and Umkeang area **Mizoram:** As whole except lower valleys, adjoining area of Cachar and lower parts of Chhimtuipuii	**Fruits:** Mango, guava, citrus, litchi, low chilling peaches, pears, plums, almond, aonla etc. **Vegetables:** Brinjal, tomato, okra, beans, peas, all cucurbits, carrot, radish, turnip, cole crops, leafy vegetables, onion, garlic, chillies and capsicum etc. **Tuber Crops:** Potato, sweet potato, colocasia,

(Contd.)

Table 1 (*Contd.*)

	Nagaland: Mokachung district, lower parts of Kohima, Wokha and Monbhagti and Longhak valley. **Sikkim:** Namchi, Gayzing, Rongli, Rehnok, Mangan, Changthong, Uttre and Gangtok	yams, alocasia **Ornamentals:** Rose, gladiolus, orchids, chrysanthemum, carnation, marigold, petunia, large number of other ornamental and foliage plants.
Tropical zone	**Arunachal Pradesh:** Southern part of lower Subansiri, Pasighat, Singhthow and lower part of Lohit **Assam:** Whole Assam except Karbi Anglong and North Cachar hills **Meghalaya:** Southern part of Jawai, adjoining part of Karimganj, Cachar, North Cachar Hills of Assam, southern part of Nongpol, eastern part of east Garo hills and west Khasi hills, lower part of west Garo hills **Manipur:** Manipur west district including Juibair area,Chrachanpur and Thallour of south district, Marera area **Mizoram:** Northern and western part, Chhimheipuii district **Nagaland:** Medzephena area of Dimapur sub division, sourthern part of Dimapur and Jampuii area **Tripura:** major part of Tripura **Sikkim:** Rongpoh area of east district	**Fruits:** Mango, citrus, banana, pineapple, papaya, grape, sapota **Vegetables:** Brinjal, tomato, okra, beans, gourds, amaranthus etc. **Tuber crops:** Cassava, sweet potato, amorphophallus, dioscorea, yams, coleus, colocasia etc. **Plantation crops:** Coconut, arecanut, cashew, oilpalm, rubber, coco **Spices:** Turmeric, ginger large cardamom, pepper etc. **Ornamentals:** Rose, chrysanthemum, jasmine, marigold, zenna, balsum, orchids etc.

Although northeastern region is endowed with plenty of natural resources yet the big industries have not to able to come on a big way. The main reason behind this is the difficulties experienced in transportation and communication. Agro-based industries on other hand, mostly based on local resources have greater potentialities for development.

Present Status of F&V in NER

About 362841.7 hectares area was brought under cultivation of fruit crops during 1995-1996, which indicates 49.42% increase in area coverage over 1993-1994. However in vegetables, 354690 hectares area was put under cultivation, which was 15.55 per cent higher than that of 1993-1994. The production of F&V increased by 28.18 and 20.84 per cent respectively in 1995-1996 over 1993-1994. The highest increase in area (115.60%) and production (63.28%) of fruit crops were noticed in Assam and Mizoram, respectively over 1993-1994. However production of fruit crops decreased in Nagaland (8.42%) and Sikkim (44.33%) over 1993-1994. In vegetables, maximum increase in area and production was noticed from Mizoram (120.83 and 75.72%), whereas area and production decreased in Nagaland (6.46 and 19.04%, respectively) and Meghalaya (12.36 and 11.18%, respectively).

F&V Based Units in NE Region

Some of the feasible areas of agro-based industries that can be effectively developed in NER are suggested below:

Food and Vegetable based industry can be considered as one of the important agro-based industry in the region. The most common and widely cultivated fruits in the region are mandarin, pineapple, banana etc. while some others are also covered under fruits like apple pear, stone fruits, coconut papaya, litchi, lemon, mango, guava and jackfruit.

Despite the well-established and distinctive quality character of *Khasi* mandarin, the annual production of fruits is progressively declining. One of the reasons given is the lack of marketing facility. If preservation industries, such as orange squash industry come up near the producing orchard, it will lessen the burden of quick disposal and at the same time fetch a high price

Pineapple occupies the second largest area under fruits cultivation in this region favors its tremendous growth. The pineapple juice extraction units and other allied preservation activities will give a further boost to the pineapple cultivation. At present, the pineapple is consumed in it's raw form withour any value addition within the region. Recently the Nagaland government invited some experts in food preservation from Chezoslovakia and they decided to set up joint ventures in the processing and preservation of pineapples.

Among the temperate fruits, apple has shown great sign of development in Arunachal Pradesh. But difficulties in transportation is the major bottleneck and this problem could be solved to a great extend by establishing food processing units.

Cultivation of off-season vegetables offers a splendid scope in the mid and high hill areas of NorthEastern region. The region being in high rainfall areas with more or less better distribution pattern provided ideal condition for production of off-season vegetables under rain fed condition. At present only a small area, with no consequence, is under off-season vegetable cultivation and a vast potential areas are unexploited. It is quite imperative that major thrust has to be given for economic utilization of areas suitable for off-season vegetable production. This will meet various objectives like improving the economy of growers; create employment opportunities, effective utilization of land resource, meet nutritional need of population, provide raw materials from processing industries.

The fruit and vegetables based units of the region is still in infant stage. Even through the region has tremendous treasure of horticultural products yet the growth of this industry is too commensurate to the raw materials available for this industry in the region. Followings are some of the problems of the fruit and vegetables based units in general on the basis of the reports of extensive personal survey of entrepreneurs.

Problems and Prospects of F&V Industry in NER

Problems

The stunted growth of entrepreneurship in the fruit and vegetable sector in North Eastern region is due to various bottlenecks that come in the way of its growth. Some of them are discussed below: -

1. The F&V industry depends upon the local markets for the supply of raw materials. The quality, quantity and the price of the raw materials are constantly fluctuating and unpredictable. Moreover, the raw materials are seasonal in supply. Hence the production of the F&V industry is confined

to the seasonal availability of fruits and vegetables. The crops are also destroyed by the natural calamity which is a major problem faced by the agriculture of the region.

2. Another primary problem faced by this industry is finance. No adequate financial support is available from the government or from any private sector. It is also seen that the entrepreneurs suffer because of the 'not so hospitable' attitude of the banks and the other financial institution towards this industry.

3. Most of food processing units of the region are run on individual proprietary basis, which is not a favourable condition to gain the advantage of economies of scale.

4. Lack of availability of packing materials is another problem of this industry. Containers and packaging material, which can be used for packing are not available within the region and are to be purchased from outside which increases the cost.

5. The units also face difficulty in labeling their products. Most of the units resort to ordinary labeling as the rate of offset printing of labels being high and cannot be afforded by the local units. Moreover, the standard of offset printing of labels within the region is also not attractive. As a result, the products from outside the region are more attractively presented so far as packing and labeling is concerned and this attracts the local people to the products from outside the region.

6. Another major problem is the problem of warehousing of the finished products and the raw materials. The raw materials of this industry are mostly perishable and seasonal in nature and are to be preserved in cold storage but the entrepreneurs cannot afford the cold storage facility due to the lack of finance. Moreover there is also lack of space to store the finished products. Most of the units started by the entrepreneurs in their own sheds, which are very small. Even the sheds allotted by the government in the industrial complexes are not sufficient for the units to store huge quantities of the finished products and raw materials.

7. There is also a dearth of skilled and semiskilled labour within the region.

8. There is no adequate research and development activities initiated by the local entrepreneurs to develop their products neither the government has shown much enthusiasm in this regard. No step has been taken for the upliftment of the quality of the products. Moreover, there is lack of FPO (Food processing order) facility in the region (the nearest office being at Calcutta).
9. Another major constraint as to why the local products do not get a bright response from the consumers is due to the lack of advertisement. The entrepreneurs pay least interest to advertise their products and as a result people are less aware of the locally manufactured products.
10. The units are mostly ill organized and are started by the entrepreneurs in small scale at their own homes. Therefore the productions of these units are not sufficient to cover a huge market.
11. Various taxes and duties both by the central and state government cause hurdle on the market expansion and creates problem in production especially for small units.
12. The local dealers and wholesalers do not give patronage to the local products because there is no suitable selling scheme for these products. The costs of production of the locally made products are quite high because of the increase in labour cost, hike in transportation rates and also due to the production processes.
13. Last but not the least, the psychological attitude of the local people that the local products are not adequate in comparison to the out side products creates hindrance in the development of the fruit and vegetables processing industry in the region.

Prospects

- Though the fruit and vegetables processing industry of the region is surrounded by many hurdles, which create problems in its development, yet it holds promises for the overall development of this region.
- Abundance of raw materials within the region and the climatic condition suitable for setting up of F&V industry.

- The frequent change of food habits by the consumers increases production.
- Large scale expansion of tourism and hotel industry in the region shows bright prospects for this industry.
- The processing is restricted to only few fruits and vegetables. There is a vast potentiality to tap under-exploited F&V potentials in the region
- Moreover the bright response secured by the entrepreneurs in the national and international fares and exhibition outside the region shows that if a little bit of regard is paid by the entrepreneur and the government towards the development of this industry it is certain that this industry will reach it's highest peak and earn a fair amount of revenue for the region.

Strategies and the Measures

- There is a dearth of modern technology used by the industry inorder to increase productivity and meet consumer demand it is necessary to upgrade the technology
- To increase the horticulture productivity the government should provide improved seed at subsidized rate along with other inputs like pesticides, fertilizers agricultural implements. The government should also provide crop insurance scheme to safeguard the farmers in case of loss by atleast foreseeable risks.
- Periodic market surveys should be carried out by the entrepreneurs and other market agencies to find out the trends i.e. change of taste, price and competitions etc.
- Banks and financial institutions should liberalize the loan formalities and speed up the disposal of the loans
- Cold storage facilities should be provided by the government in various localities and private investment in these areas is to be encouraged.
- Multipurpose food testing centers and training is highly required, moreover research and development facilities need to be strengthened.
- The government should take initiative in the establishment of FPO (Food processing order) office in the state vis a vis NE region.

- The local entrepreneurs should visit the industrially developed states to get a first hand knowledge.
- Both the center and state government need to provide the further reduction in taxes and duties particularly for packing materials since the whole of the NE region is industrially backward.
- Efforts should be made both at government and private levels for the export of the products to other countries.
- Fairs and exhibitions should be arranged by the government and other business agencies i.e. Chamber of Commerce etc. to popularize the local products through displays.
- Preferential purchase order should also be strictly observed in case of any purchase by the government or state undertakings.
- Production technologies in fruit crops like pineapple, banana, orange and rejuvenation technologies for declined mandarin, orange orchard, etc., are some useful technologies for dissemination among farmers so as to increase the productivity and quality of produce. Area should be increased under *amla*, papaya, pomegranate, and jackfruit at low to mid altitude and walnut, chestnut, cherry, almond and kiwifruit at higher altitude of the region.
- Few crops such as banana, citrus, pineapple, jackfruit, potato, cassava, sweet potato, ginger, turmeric, large cardamom, coconut, arecanut and good number of vegetable crops are well adopted in larger parts of the region. These crops need priority research attention for increasing the productivity and quality of the produce. Certain other fruit crops like litchi in Tripura, kiwi and avocado in Sikkim and Arunachal Pradesh, gauva and low chilling peaches in Meghalaya and Arunachal Pradesh have shown good potential and needs research support for their commercial scale cultivation. Among the spices, black pepper and cinnamon have good potential. Potato is the most important crop and its yield is quite high in Tripura (17.10t/ha). The yield of potato in Meghalaya is about 6.78t/ha against 24.4t/ha in West Bengal. The advantages of off-season cultivation have to be exploited to the maximum and potato cultivation should be increased in mid hills of the region.

- Orange is a unique horticulutral crop of NER and need priority research attention for increasing its productivity and quality of the fruits. Organic cultivation of oranges can pave the way for successful venture.
- Since the productivity of vegetables per unit area is much low in this region, there is ample scope for adopting plasticulture applications like polyhouse cultivation, drip irrigation and mulching. Low cost plastic house technologies have potential and opportunities in various agro-climatic zones of India for commercial vegetable production. These polyhouses with environment control facilities can be used for successful cultivation of high value crops like tomato, capsicum, broccoli, brussels sprout, lettuce, celery and cucumber, etc.
- Production of vegetable nursery under protected condition is becoming popular through out the country especially in hilly regions. Management of vegetable nursery in protected structure is easier and early nursery can be raised. Needless to emphasize that this practice eliminates dangers of destruction of nurseries by hailstorm, rain, etc., and protects from biotic and abiotic stresses. As a result cultivation of vegetables like cabbages, cauliflower, knol khol, tomato and onion has become commercial in cold desert region of the country.

Technologies for North Eastern Region

Several organizations have made studies on investment potentiality of the North Eastern Region where they have suggested several viable industries for the region based on its resources. Organizations like Council of Scientific and Industrial Research (CSIR), Assam Productivity Council (APC) & Small Industries Development Bank of India (SIDBI) have developed quite a number of viable technologies as well as project profiles for the region. They have suggested food & agro based technologies, technologies on cultivation & processing of economic plants, leather and animal waste based technologies etc. The North Eastern Region has a vast potential to become an important player in the processed food sector. So there is requirement of technologies for post harvest processing and production of useful products. CSIR is developing technologies for the storage and preservation of resources and their processing to make value added products as well as to meet substantial needs. A number of CSIR laboratories contribute in this area, with the Central Food Technological Research Institute, Mysore playing the premier role.

The technologies presented here imply establishments of small scale units which needs raw materials like cereals, pulses, fruits, vegetables, oilseeds, spices, condiments etc., besides meat, fish and poultry. There is an increase in demand of natural plant materials for use in the manufacture of drugs, pharmaceuticals, cosmetics, food flavour, perfumes & other industrial products. For these purpose CSIR has developed technologies for cultivation and processing of various F&V that are cost effective, acceptable and appropriate to the climatic conditions of the region. These technologies focus on materials of higher quality, substitutes for scarce materials and items based on wastes to increase the earning capacity.

A number of useful technologies have been developed and are also in the process by various scientific and technological institutes/ laboratories in the country based on which viable units on commercial scale can be set up in the region. In the studies done by Assam Productivity Council and SIDBI, they have given the outline of the projects and also information on the improved technologies. These can be exploited for new industrial set up in the region. While selecting the projects, due consideration is to be given to the resource availability, easy accessibility of raw materials, technology levels, quantum of investment and market potentials.

Conclusions

The F&V processing industry of region is still in it's developing state. Though there are enough potentialities within the region for development of this industry in terms of raw materials etc. yet the industry has to undergo a long process to establish itself in the national market. One of the major hurdles in the way of this potential industry is the lack of entrepreneurial spirit and adequate infrastructure that is a prerequisite for the development of entrepreneurship. The various problems faced by this industry are to be collectively solved by the government and private sector along with the semi government institution to make the F&V industry a landmark in the industrial scenario of region.

There is a need to create awareness about the importance of entrepreneurship in the region and make the farmers receptive to the new ideas, technology through farmer's participation in demonstrations and training programmes. Training facilities with respect to growing of horticultural crops and raising nursery has to be made available as per requirements. Therefore, there is a need for establishing a sound marketing system with forward and backward linkages so that vast potential of horticulture crops can be exploited through adoption of improved production technology. Transforming subsistence level farmers into entrepreneurs will go a long way in bringing about a complete turn around in the economy of North Eastern Region of India.

NOTES AND REFERENCES

1. Anonymous, (1999). *Annual Report*, ICAR Research Complex for NEH Region, Barapani
2. Borthakur, D.N. (1984), *Potentials of Agriculture in the N E Region.* Meghalaya Science Society, Shillong Vol II pp. 2-3.
3. Borthakur, D.N. (1992). *Agriculture of the North Eastern Region*, Bee See Prakasan Guwahati
4. Choudhury, Monalisa and Barua Nayan (1999) Strategy for Development of F&V Based Industry in Assam, *J. North Eastern Council*, 19(3).
5. Dubey, A.K., K. Babu Dhinesh and Yadav D.S., Status and Prospects of Horticulture in NEH Region, *ENVIS*, 10(2).
6. Kual, G.S. (1984) *Horticulture in NE Region Resources Potentials of North East India*. Meghalaya Science Society, Shillong Vol II pp. 51-53.
7. Nema, P.K. and Pandey Ashish (2003), Prospects of Ginger Processing in North Eastern Region of India. *Beverages and Food World.* Vol 32.
8. Prasad, R.N. (1998). Soil and Water Conservation in NEH Region lecture delivered in *National Seminar on Management Strategies for North Eastern Hill Ecosystem.*
9. Sheo, Govind and Ghosh S.P. (1997). Citrus Genetic Resources of North Eastern Himalayan Region and their Utilization. *Indian J. Hill Farming* 10(1&2): 78-91
10. Singh, N. P., Kumar Pramod and Verma N. D. (2000), Agro-based Industry: A Boon for the Shifting Cultivators. *J. North Eastern Counc*[illegible] 20(4).

28

MANAGERIAL CHALLENGES OF SMALL SCALE INDUSTRIES

S. KESHORJIT SINGH
JIBON KUMAR L

"Small is beautiful"

India took on the path to liberalization in the year 1991. The economy has been freeing many a sectors that had been reserved for the small scale sectors. No organizations can afford to remain small beyond a time because in the globalize world, growth has become a way of life. The milieu has thrown up multivariate challenges for the small scale sectors. The emergence of outsourcing as a new and better way of doing the thing and further, dynamic development in technology, especially in information technology, that has been steadily lowering transaction cost, offer plethora of opportunities for the small scale industry. Today, products and services are benchmarked in terms of global standards. Time has come for the small scale firms to identify its core strength, be focused and grow. So the managerial challenges of small scale industries are immense.

Small scale industry occupies a significant place in India's economy. It accounts for 95 per cent of industrial units and employ about 18 million people. Indian economy is characterized by abundant and cheap labour. The economy offer great potential for labour intensive industry. Small scale sector accounts for 40 per cent of output in the manufacturing sector. So small scale sector has great employment potential. Moreover it is relatively easy to start, and start offering immediate employment. The question now is, will it be that easy or is it that easy. If so than India can solve its economic problem very easily. It may be easier said than done. In a liberalizing economy like India, it increasingly faces competition not only from big domestic organizations, but also from multinationals and global organizations.

What Exactly is SSI

Before going further, let us try to analyze what small scale industry is. The definition of SSI varies from one country to another and from one time to another in the same country depending upon the pattern and stage of development, government policy and administrative setup of the particular country. There are at least 50 different definitions of SSIs found and used in 75 countries. All these definitions either relate to capital or employment or both or any other criteria. An overview of the various definitions is given in table 1. In most countries, small- and medium-scale units are clubbed together for policy purposes and called SMEs.

What prevails in India is only the concept of small scale, and ancillary and tiny industry. There is no concrete definition. In other courtiers, small and medium enterprises are defined on the basis of both quantitive and qualitative elements, such as the number of workers employed and/or annual turnover or the level of fixed investment. However, employment is an ever present criterion for determining the size of the unit in these countries.

The Government of India set up Central SSI organization and Small-Scale Industries board in 1954-55. The SSI Board at its first meeting held on January 5th and 6th of 1955, defined SSI as a unit employing less than 50 employees if using power, and less that 100 employees without the use of power and with a capital asset not exceeding Rs. 5 lakh. (Table 1). Then as per the Abid Hussain Committee's recommendations on SSI, the Government of India has in March 1997, further raised the investment ceiling to Rs. 3 crores for SSI and Rs. 50 lakhs for tiny units. Further, the New Policy initiative in 1999-2000 for small scale sector has reduced the investment limit for small and ancillary undertaking from existing Rs 3 crores to Rs. 1 crore.

Table 1
Definitions of SSI: An Overview Table

Year	Investment Criterion		Employment Criterion
	SSI Unit	Ancillary Unit	
Upto 1958	Fixed capital investment upto 5 lakhs	Same as SSI unit	Employment upto 50 workers if using power or upto 100 if not using power.
1959	The value of machine was taken as the original price paid irrespective of new or old machinery	Same as SSI unit	Employment upto 50 workers if using power or upto 100 if not using power.
1960	Gross value of fixed asset upto Rs. 5 lakhs	Gross value of fixed asset upto Rs. 10 lakhs	Employment criterion dropped
1966	Rs. 7.5 lakhs	Rs. 10 lakhs	-do-
1975	Rs. 10 lakhs	Rs. 15 lakhs	-do-
1980	Rs. 20 lakhs	Rs. 25 lakhs	-do-
1985	Rs. 35 lakhs	Rs. 45 lakhs	-do-
1991	Rs. 60 lakhs	Rs. 75 lakhs	

Barriers to SSI

All our Five-Year Plans and Industrial Policy resolutions/statements have stressed the needs to accelerate and develop the small scale industries. It is estimated that the Total SSI sector comprises 1,05,21,190 units, in the country. About 55 per cent of these units are located in rural India. Over 44 lakhs (42.26 %) in the total SSI sector are SSIs and the remaining 61 lakhs (57.74 %) are SSSBEs. The number of ancillary units among SSIs is 2.98 per cent. The dominating presence of tiny units with original investment in plant and machinery up to Rs. 25 lakhs has been a continuous feature in the SSI sector. In the Third Census, it was found that 99.5 per cent of the SSIs were tiny units. So the sector generates employment for millions of people. Small business is the seed bed for entrepreneurship. So small scale industry has helped the economy bring forth entrepreneurship. Even many of the big and professional of today's organization started small. To name a few of the modern-day organizations – Wipro, Infosys, iflex, Hero Honda, Satyam. Many of such companies are worth billions of dollar in today's market value.

SSI sector occupy a crucial position in the economy. Of late, the SSI sector in India is not faring well. Many of the SSIs suffer from the problems of suboptimal scale of operation and technological obsolescence. The reasons of sickness/incipient sickness are given in Table 2. Percentage distribution of sick/incipient sick units in the total SSI sector state-wise is given in Table 3. Marketing, working capital and demand are the major reasons for industrial sickness. There are also other reasons that call for immediate attention. So what the industry needs today is not reservation and protection. Because reservation and protection don not solve many of the reasons for sickness cited in the Table 2.

Table 2
Reasons for Sickness/Incipient Sickness

Sl. No.	Reason for sickness/ incipient sickness	Proportion of sick/ incipient sick units*		
		Total SSI Sector	Regd. SSI sector	Unregd. SSI sector
1.	Lack of demand	66%	58%	69%
2.	Shortage of working capital	46%	57%	4%
3.	Non-availability of raw material	12%	12%	12%
4.	Power shortage	13%	17%	12%
5.	Labour problems	5%	6%	4%
6.	Marketing problems	36%	37%	36%
7	.Equipment problems	11%	9%	12%
8.	Management problems	4%	5%	3%

*The total in each column will exceed 100 %, as some units have reported more than one reason.

Source: smenetwork.net/economy/fcensus.htm.3

A new Ministry of Small-scale Industry and Agro and Rural Industries was created in 1999. It did not make any difference to the sector's plight. Soon after its creation, the new Ministry decided to do

Table 3

Percentage Distribution of Sick/incipient Sick Units in the Total SSI Sector, State-wise

Sl. No	Name of State/ UT	Sick units	Incipient sick units	Sick/incipient sick units	Sick units as per RBI criteria
1.	JAMMU & KASHMIR	0.26	0.06	0.08	0.27
2.	HIMACHAL PRADESH	0.61	1.13	1.0	90.68
3.	PUNJA	2.16	5.60	5.28	1.89
4.	CHANDIGARH	0.10	0.12	0.12	0.07
5	.UTTARANCHAL	0.15	0.96	0.89	0.11
6.	HARYANA	1.89	2.07	2.07	1.87
7.	DELHI	2.80	1.48	1.62	2.23
8.	RAJASTHAN	2.19	5.05	4.80	2.08
9.	UTTAR PRADESH	4.61	3.05	3.13	4.30
10.	BIHAR	1.85	2.50	2.50	1.89
11.	SIKKIM	0.02	0.01	0.01	0.01
12.	ARUNACHAL PRADESH	0.02	0.01	0.01	0.02
13.	NAGALAND	0.01	0.00	0.00	0.01
14.	MANIPUR	0.12	0.53	0.50	0.12

15.	MIZORAM	0.02	0.01	0.01	0.01
16.	TRIPURA	0.45	0.21	0.20	0.54
17.	MEGHALAYA	0.22	0.06	0.08	0.26
18.	ASSAM	1.23	1.01	1.02	0.98
19.	WEST BENGAL	15.96	5.71	6.92	18.28
20.	JHARKHAND	0.46	0.61	0.60	0.30
21.	ORISSA	4.11	2.33	2.42	4.04
22.	CHHATTISGARH	5.48	0.90	1.48	6.43
23.	MADHYA PRADESH	3.98	5.43	5.34	3.80
24.	GUJARAT	1.93	5.22	4.98	1.53
25.	DAMAN & DIU	0.07	0.02	0.02	0.05
26.	DADRA & NAGAR HAVELI	0.03	0.01	0.02	0.02
27.	MAHARASHTRA	13.70	6.62	7.31	14.17
28.	ANDHRA PRADESH	6.04	9.76	9.27	4.10
29.	KARNATAKA	9.20	9.03	9.07	9.90
30.	GOA	0.47	0.21	0.24	0.43
31.	LAKSHADWEEP	0.00	0.00	0.00	0.00

(Contd.)

Table 3 (*Contd.*)

Sl. No	Name of State/ UT	Sick units	Incipient sick units	Sick/incipient sick units	Sick units as per RBI criteria
32.	KERALA	14.64	18.61	17.80	15.28
33.	TAMIL NADU	4.93	11.40	10.84	4.02
34.	PONDICHERRY	0.25	0.24	0.24	0.27
35.	A. & N. ISLANDS	0.02	0.03	0.03	0.02
All India		100.00	100.00	100.00	100.00

Source: smenetwork.net/economy/fcensus.htm

a detailed sector-wise study of the impact of various WTO agreements on the SSI sector but nothing seems to have happened since. Not surprisingly, though the sector has grown at a rapid pace post-Independence, the incidence of sickness is also on the rise.

Challenges of Small Scale Industries

One of the major problems confronting the small industry is sickness/ incipient sickness. The range of problems faced by the small sector is multivariate. The problem needs to be seen through a wider context. It faces various challenges. In today's context the small enterprise need to be competitive. The success would depend upon its core competitiveness. It needs to explore opportunities that are increasingly global. Today the products and services are benchmarked in terms of global context. It can learn to become part of the global intellectual chain.

One of the advantages of being small is flexibility. So the small enterprise can tap the immense opportunities of customization. Customizing at low cost can be a strategic option. The outsourcing wave also offers tremendous potential. The small enterprise can readily adapt to the modern managerial practices, and also adopt the contemporary technology because the gestation time between implementation and practice will be less. The advantage of the enterprise is that it is more adaptive to change. This is an important property for today's dynamic business environment. The demand problem can be addressed by inherent scalability. Small enterprise can learn to manage work in high volatile environment political and otherwise, and to scale down or scale up operations according to needs. Instead of operating in much area the organization can be a niche player also. Today, knowledge is a resource; knowledge management is a domain where big and small can have symbiotic relationship. In the era of globalization growth matters and there is lot more opportunity for growth. Being small is transition phase. Small enterprise should have a strategic frame work for growth and size.

NOTES AND REFERENCES

1. Agrawal, A.N. (2001). *Indian Economy*, Wishwa Prakashan, New Delhi.
2. Cherunilam, Fancis (2003). *Business and Government*, Himalaya Publishing House, Mumbai.

3. *Observer Statistical Handbook*, 2003, Observer Research Foundation, New Delhi.
4. Dollinger, Mark J. (2003). *Entrepreneurship – Strategies and Resources*, Pearson Education.
5. Desai, Vasant (2003). *Small Scale Industries and Entrepreneurship*, Himalaya Publishing House, New Delhi.
6. smenetwork.net/economy/fcensus.htm

29

COOPERATIVE ENTREPRENEURSHIP IN NORTH EAST STATES: With Special Reference to Assam and Manipur

K.I. MEETEI

Introduction

Modern biologists believe that the cooperative forces are biologically more important and vital. Prince Peter Kropotkin in mutual aid asserts that "sociability is a much, a law of nature as mutual struggle". According to him human society itself could not be maintained for even so much as the lifetime for one single generation except by the practice of mutual aid. Montaque says that "Science points out the way to survival and happiness for all mankind through love and cooperation". According to E.R. Baven cooperation is the universal instrument of creation".

Socio-economic planners feel and confident that cooperation is the base of over all development in human society. Mutual help through group effort is the means of human development.

Cooperative societies are such organisations which create and facilitate in finding human needs and requirements for sustainability. The basic values of a cooperative are self help, self-responsibility, democracy, equality, equity and solidarity.

In the tradition of their founders, cooperative members believe in the ethical values of honesty, openness, social responsibility and caring of others.

An enterprise

A cooperative is an economic enterprise. It is a formal institution recognised by laws. Laws prevailing in different countries recognise cooperatives as distinct institutions, different from private and public ones.

Even from legal standpoint, what makes cooperative different from other forms of economic enterprises is their adherence to a set of principles guiding their organisational and business practices? These principles are clearly enunciated in the universally accepted ICA Cooperative Identity Statement (ICIS). They define what a cooperative is and on what conditions an enterprise is organised and carrying on business on a "Cooperative basis".

A cooperative enterprise has the following characteristics :

1. Associationship of homogeneous people.
2. An enterprise run by members themselves at their own expense and at their own risk.
3. A group under the governance of democracy and voluntarism.
4. A social institution and business organisation.

Principles

The enunciated principles of cooperation by the International Cooperative Alliance (ICA–1995) are –

1. Voluntary and Open Membership,
2. Democratic Member Control,
3. Member Economic Participation,
4. Autonomy and Independence,
5. Education, Training and Information,
6. Cooperation among Cooperatives,
7. Concern for Community.

New outlook

The cooperative movement in India has completed 100 years with commendable achievement.

Share of Agricultural Cooperatives in National Economic Development is shown below :

*	Rural Network (villages covered) :	100%
*	Agricultural Credit Disbursed by Cooperatives :	42.8%
*	Fertilizer Production:	25%
*	Capacity Utilisation of Sugar Mills :	99.8%
*	Sugar Produced(10.16 M.T.) :	50.5%
*	Wheat Procurement(6.9 M.T.) :	33.5%
*	Animal Feed Production/Supply :	50%
*	Storage Facility(Village level PACS) :	64.5%
*	Total Loan Advanced (Million) :	Rs.293,264.4
(a)	% of ST Loans :	80.28
(b)	% of MT Loans :	18.01
*	Agricultural Produce Marketed(Million) : Rs. 17513.5	

Source : National Resource Centre, NCUI, 2004

In the increasing tempo of competitiveness created by globalisation, liberalisation of markets and opening up of national economics, a new outlook to the fresh opportunities as well as new challenges to cooperatives in the country and in the specific region is called for.

Identification of fresh opportunities and pursue to new challenges are the tasks of cooperative enterprises through group entrepreneurship.

The Focus

This paper attempts to analyse the performance of cooperative enterprises in the North Eastern Region with special reference to agricultural cooperatives in Manipur and Assam.

This paper is intended to study the interaction between

A. Financial Institutions

B. Promoting Agencies

C. Cooperative Institutions

D. Individual – Members

Database

This academic exercise is based on both primary and secondary data. Primary data were collected through pre-tested interview schedule from cooperative members and officials. Secondary data were furnished from the internal records of the concerned selected cooperatives and reliable reports of various studies.

A. Findings

Major findings drawn out of specific study conducted in Assam (study on Viability of GPCS & LAMPS) are presented below :

A.1. In Assam most of the Primary Agricultural Cooperative Societies (PACS) are found weak and have lost basic spirit of cooperation.

A.2. Apparently, these societies have failed to generate the envisaged participation and involvement of members.

A.3. Agricultural credit flow has been blocked since 1991-92 due to dismal recovery performance of the societies.

A.4. Majority of the societies are fond having accumulated loss. Inadequate fund is also another emerging problem. As a result of having inadequate working fund and severe loss threaten to the financial viability of the societies (PACS).

A.5. The basic reasons of dismal recovery performance in Assam are:

- Improper selection of borrowers.
- Untimely disbursements
- Part of loan amounts pocketed by bank and PACS' personnel
- Diversion of funds
- Government's loan waiver scheme
- No technical guidance on proper utilisation of loan.
- Wilful defaulters
- Political interference
- Poor economic condition of borrowers
- Crop destruction due to floods, drought etc.

- Low productivity & profitability
- Lack of awareness of benefits of repayment for future dealings.

B.PACS in Manipur

B.1. In Manipur most of the PACS are found defunct. It accounts for 93.56% of the total PACS. Downfall in the business of PACS started since 1992-93. Credit flow was ceased since 1991-92.

B.2. Due to non-operationalisation of business, recovery performance was severely affected. Table 1 shows the districtwise recovery performance during the period from 1992-93 to 1997-98. Imphal East District recorded the highest recovery rate (23.7%), while Bishnupur District recorded the least recovery rate (2.21%) in 1997-98. Fluctuation in recovery and dismal picture of recovery performance are observed during the reference period (1992-93 to 1997-98).

Table 1

District-wise Trend of Recovery of Pacs in Manipur (1992-93 to 1997-98)

District	1992-93	1993-94	1994-95	1995-96	1996-97	1997-98
Imphal East	13.52	13.07	6.05	7.06	4.76	23.70
Imphal West	15.12	8.72	7.29	4.78	8.92	6.46
Bishnupur	10.40	2.82	7.03	2.57	2.59	2.21
Churachandpur	7.62	0.85	0.45	0.96	2.16	N.A.
Thoubal	14.16	7.21	4.31	1.82	0.88	N.A.
Ukhrul	32.47	0.60	0.52	0.13	0.24	2.27
Average	13.97	3.25	2.61	1.64	1.92	7.73

Source: Internal Records of the PACS.

B.3. Main responsible factors of dismal recovery performance are identified as below :

- Under - Finance
- Low incremental income

- Lack of proper documentation
- Misappropriation of recovered loan
- Loan waiving policy - ARDR Scheme -1991
- Misconception of loan.

B.4. Out of the 680 members surveyed, 66.62% did not receive financial assistance from their concerned PACS. Table 2 depicts the range of financial assistance in terms of loan received by the members.

Table 2
Distribution of Members According to the Financial Assistance Received

Amount (Rs.)	Districtwise No. of Members who Received Financial Assistance					
	Thoubal	Impahl West	Senapati	C.C. Pur	Total	(%)
0	109	175	80	89	453	66.62
100-500	17	9	6	10	42	6.18
501-1000	36	6	5	16	63	9.26
1001-2000	34	5	6	3	48	7.06
2001-3000	30	5	17	2	54	7.94
3001-4000	2	0	0	0	2	0.29
4001-5000	4	0	5	0	9	1.32
5001-6000	0	0	1	0	1	0.15
6001-7000	4	0	0	0	4	0.59
7001-8000	2	0	0	0	2	0.29
8001-9000	0	0	0	0	0	0.00
9001-10000	2	0	0	0	2	0.29
Total	240	200	120	120	680	100.00

Source: Field Data.

While providing credit facilities consumption loans are also to be made available - as shown in Table 3.

B.5. Members have the demand of loans for carrying on allied activities like poultry, piggery, weaving, sericulture, diary, fishery etc.

The surveyed members revealed their requirement of loans for agricultural allied loans as set out in Table 4.

Table 3
Range of Consumption Loan Demanded by the Farmer Members

Amount (Rs.)	Districtwise No. of Members who Received Financial Assistance					
	Thoubal	Impahl West	Senapati	C.C. Pur	Total	(%)
0	57	100	60	14	231	33.97
Upto-1000	10	0	0	9	19	2.79
1001-2000	8	4	0	9	21	3.09
2001-3000	16	13	7	4	40	5.88
3001-4000	4	13	0	2	19	2.79
4001-5000	50	23	7	36	116	17.06
5001-6000	15	20	21	6	62	9.12
6001-7000	20	0	0	4	24	3.53
7001-8000	4	7	7	9	27	3.97
8001-9000	0	0	0	0	0	0.00
9001-10000	56	20	18	27	121	17.79
Total	240	200	120	120	680	100.00

Source: Field Data.

B.6. None of the surveyed societies was found having paid secretary. The operational efficiency and business success essentially demand value-based professional management in PACS. The feature of not having paid manager implies ignorance of professional management.

B.7. Departmental Inspectors act as Managing Directors of PACS. One MD controls 3 to 4 PACS. Naturally, deficiency in the management of PACS happens.

B.8. The promotional roles of the State Cooperative Union and concerned department are found discouraging.

Table 4
Loan Required for Allied Activities

Amount (Rs.)	Districtwise No. of Members who Received Financial Assistance					
	Thoubal	Impahl West	Senapati	C.C. Pur	Total	(%)
0	10	8	0	0	18	2.65
Upto 15000	40	20	15	33	108	15.88
15001-20000	26	31	21	42	120	17.65
20001-25000	22	10	15	4	51	7.50
25001-30000	20	27	13	18	78	11.47
30001-35000	15	21	13	10	59	8.68
35001-50000	24	15	8	4	51	7.50
40001-50000	48	40	19	6	113	16.62
50001-60000	15	4	8	0	27	3.97
60001-70000	0	0	4	0	4	0.59
70001-80000	0	4	0	0	4	0.59
80001-90000	0	0	2	0	2	0.29
90001-10000	20	20	2	3	45	6.62
Total	240	200	120	120	680	100.00

Source: Field Data.

B.9. Proper nurturing and promotional guidelines for growth and development of PACS are not yet prepared by the concerned promoting agencies.

B.10. Necessary 'human capital' formulation trainings are not accessible to the members.

B.11. Demanded financial supports are not accessible to needy members who are looking to the entrepreneurial venture.

B.12. Members do not have new expectation from their PACS as economic enterprise.

C. Policy Options

In such situation having closet with multiple problems what short of remedial actions can be taken up ?

Being agriculture the mainstay of common people of N.E. States, strengthening and revitalising of PACS as active economic enterprise becomes the strategic need of the hour.

For ensuring effective operationalisation of PACS a sound interaction among and between –

1. Financing Agencies
2. Promotional Agencies
3. Cooperative Institutions
4. Individual Members

needs to be improved. Congenial conditions are to be made on:

- Autonomy and Independence,
- Legal Framework,
- Recognition,
- Fair Playing Field,
- Capitalisation,
- Networking

Autonomy and Independence

1. Autonomy and independence of cooperatives are to be legally guaranteed and recognised.
2. Cooperatives are to be empowerred and allowed to develop their own capacity.
3. Governments have to firm up and consistently pursue a strategy of disengagement from cooperatives.

Legal Framework

Necessary legal framework is to be constituted with the following aspects:

1. Recognition of cooperatives as defined in ICIS in law.
2. Setting ICIS as the minimum condition for legal definition and acceptance of cooperatives.

3. Acceptance of cooperatives as being equal to and equivalent with all other forms of social and economic organisations.
4. No government barriers to the principle of voluntary and open membership and the principle of democratic member control.
5. No specific barriers to the area or field of cooperative enterprise.
6. Recognition of new initiatives by cooperatives as legitimate.

Fair Playing Field

Governments can take advantage of the unique contribution of cooperatives to regional development by giving attention to the following considerations :

1. Recognition and acceptance by the government, of cooperatives as legitimate and involved in development, regional policy and social planning.
2. Assistance from government for the delivery of social and community service, on the basis of full equality with private or public enterprise.
3. Assistance in cooperative HRD including education and training for managerial, entrepreneurial and cooperative development.
4. Encouragement of new cooperative initiatives, such as the formation of new generation cooperatives.
5. Removal of all legal and other barriers which limit equal participation of men and women in membership, leadership, management and decision-making in cooperatives.

Capitalisation

1. Capital is central to the issue of ownership and control of an enterprise. In cooperatives, there is also a social purpose to capital. It is the means by which members gain access to needed services, not an instrument to realise economic returns, it has to be within reach of the least of all members so as to ensure equal opportunity for all.
2. Members participation in capital should be increased but individual share holdings should not exceed a certain percentage of total equity. Limited interest or dividend should

be paid on basic share; however, a market competitive rate of return may be paid on additional investments beyond the basic share.

3. When seeking to raise capital, cooperatives should be encouraged to adopt the strategies -
   (a) seek capital from members,
   (b) if further capital is required it should seek capital funds from other cooperative within the region or country, and
   (c) if further capital is required it should be sought from non-cooperative sources.
4. Investments from outside (non-member sources) can be accepted if these do not lead to loss of member control.
5. Cooperatives can promote their image and comparative advantage in the market by projecting their distinctiveness and cooperative character.

Networking

Networking is an important element in maximising business efficiency and scope. Networking may be promoted through the following programmes :

1. The establishment of a N.E. Cooperative Website.
2. Enhancing the regional database.
3. Networking in intra-State Business activities through cooperatives.

Conclusion

Cooperative societies in the N.E. Region are closet with multiple problems. As a change agent PACS should be re-strengthened for which possible action plans are to made jointly for serving the purpose of total development in the Region.

NOTES AND REFERENCES

1. Allen, P. (1993). *Connecting the Social and the Ecological Concerns in Sustainable Agriculture, in Food for the Future.*
2. Bilsborrow, R.E. (1987). *Population Pressures and Agricultural Development Countries : A Conceptual Framework and Recent Evidence, World Development, 15:2,PP.*

3. Conway, G.R(1997) *"The Properties of Agroecosystems" Agricultural Systems 24:95-117.*

4. FAO(1991) *Sustainable Agriculture and Rural Development in Latin America and the Carbbean, Regional Document., No. 3,- Rome:FAO.*

5. Markandya, A.(1992) *"Criteria of Sustainable Agricultural Development". In Environmental Economics : A Reader, eds, A. Markandya and J. Richardson, New York:St. Martin's Press.*

6. Meetei, K.I. (1999-2000) *"The Study on Viability of PACS(GPLMPCS & LAMPS) in Manipur. ICM, Imphal.*

7. Meetei, K.I.(2004) *"Institutional Arrangement for Agricultural Cooperatives for Agro-Business Development in N.E. India"*

8. Ministry of Finance Government of India New Delhi (2004). *"Economic Servey 2003-2004".*

9. NEC Secretariat,Shillong Govt. of India (2002) *"Basic Statistics of NER-2002".*

10. NCUI, New Delhi(2004) *"Indian Cooperative Movement – A Profile, 2004".*

11. Indian Institute of Bank Management (1988),Guwahati *"Study on Viability of GPSS & LAMS in Assam".*

12. Planning Commission Government of India, New Delhi, *"India, Vision 2020".*

13. Putnam, R.D. (1993) *"Making Democracy Work : Civic Traditions in Modern Italy". Princeton University Press, Princeton, N.J.*

30

PROSPECTS AND IMPEDIMENTS ON INDUSTRY IN MANIPUR

L. ORENKUMAR

Backdrop

Manipur was not known to the Indian mainlanders before two decades and it was due to the separation of the State by many big hill ranges. The climate of the State can not go beyond these high hills. By that time Manipur was introduced to the world by its rich-culture. In the recent decades Manipur is better known to the Indians and the world for its sports and culture and is taking a dominating role in the Indian Sports Arena. For a score of years Manipuris could not cross the great Bengal Sports barrier. It was due to the fact that there were no sufficient sport infrastructures and good coaches. By that time the sport persons were guided by the local elders. Now, time has brought a drastic change in the infrastructure and good foreign trained local coaches are employed to guide the sport persons. Such endeavour shows that in any discipline of sports infrastructure and guide are essential to produce/show optimum skills. The extraordinary talent and jell of the Manipuris in the field of sports shows that these indigenous people have an extraordinary quality of creative, intelligent, stamina, courage and vigilant. These precious qualities are highly essential for becoming a perfect man or an entrepreneur. In other view Manipuries can be determined as a dormant entrepreneur. When the time comes a blow of change shall surely weep-out the dormancy, but the question here is when and how such wind of change shall occur.

From the epic times Manipuri Women are better known for its

weaving and knitting skills, "Princess Thoibi" the daughter of Chingkhuba Yubraja in the "Moirang Kangleiron" or "Moirang Parba" was very skill in weaving. It was described that the Muga Inaphi or Muga Shawl she woven on the "Throw Shuttle Loom" for a present to her beloved hero "Khamba" was as fine as the clear water.

The Goddess Panthoibi is regarded as the Origin of Weaving Industry. The needle work of Manipur woman is well known for its skill artistic works. Mat making out of the kouna is the work of an ordinary village lady.

Likewise Manipuri men are known for its bamboo craft works. Bamboo baskets used in the marriage ceremony viz, *Phingairuk*, *Lukmai* etc. are worthy to mention. It has a unique skill in the manufacture of sword, spare and canon etc. for use in war times and brass metal works or crafts use at the royal entity. Manipur was self sufficient in the production of salt. Manipuris used spring salt, an extract from the spring before the coming of the so called "Kabow Salt" or "Common Salt". The Manipuris called the Mynmaries as "Kabo" and hence the salt first rooted through kabo was known as kabo salt. Many salt decantation plants were located in many places of the valley like-Shikhong, Ningel, Thangjao, Waikhong etc. The "Meitei Thum" or "Manipur Salt" are still used and available in the markets, has a unique quality and taste. This is the only salt found in the market which can be heated to a maroon red colour and the preheated salt is being issued to the newly delivered mothers with Lata Fish.

Manipuris have a good imitating quality. Once a Manipuri sees a sample of thing it can be made as the Original thing. This quality is called the innovative quality. The Manipuris are adorn with such inherent qualities but we can not see such beautiful qualities of us as we can not see the bright light of the sun in a cloudy day. Thus, the entrepreneurial skill of the Manipuris can not be shown due to the lack of proper nourishment.

Prospect of Industries in Manipur

Manipur has a vast industrial raw-material. Many small to large scale industries can be set-up based on such raw-materials. They can be grouped as follows:-

(a) Agro-based Industries

Manipur has a vast horticulture and agricultural raw-materials. Many citrus fruits (e.g., orange, lime, lemon, sweet orange etc), pineapple, passion fruit, banana, plumb, peach, pear and other agricultural products like ginger, turmeric, bird's chilli, Giant chilli, cho-cho, tomato etc. are available abundantly. These fruits and vegetable can be processed or packed in containers. Manipur orange has a very good peculiar taste. Concentrated fruit juice can be pasteurised and packed in tetra packs or tines. Such concentrated fruit juice is demanded in the international markets. Fruits can be processed in various forms such as squash, jam and jelly, pickles etc Lime and ginger can be made as Lime-Ginger Cordials. Such Lime-Ginger juice can be the substitution of the carbonated cold drinks like-limka, coca cola, thumbs-up etc. Carbonated drinks are harmful to health while such organic juice is good to health. They are rich in nutritic value and taste. Even the heart and BP patients can drink Lime Ginger Cordials for good health. It thrills in hot summer sun more than the carbonated drinks. Goose berry and soar apples can be made for swad or mouth freshers. Ginger, turmeric and other vegetables like cho-cho etc can be dehydrated. They have a good demand in the markets. Bird's chilli and gaint chillis also have a very good demand.

Orange is available in the entire Tamenglong District, eastern part of Ukhrul District and Tipaimuk Sub-Division of Churachandpur District. Chengpi and Damdei along the NH 150 and Taithu and Ferzol, 238 kms from Churachandpur along NH 150 are producing about 400 to 500 truck loads annually. However, due to the transport bottleneck these oranges can not be reached to the District Head Quarter and even information for huge production of oranges there due to great distance and worse road condition. Therefore, these oranges are marketed at Silchar and Aizwal. Purchasers from Jiribam and Silchar came by boat along the Barak river and purchased them. Lemon at throw away prices are available at all villages of Tamenglong District, like Khoupum' Nungba, Tamenglong etc, Kachai of Ukhrul District, Koide & Purul of Senapati District. They are not purchased by big purchasers, so they are wasted on the tree itself.

(b) Forest-based Industries

The world's largest bamboo reserve exists in India. As many as 136 species of bamboo have been reported from all over the country. Of these, more than 50% occur in the North Eastern Region and as many as 52 different species have been recorded from Manipur alone. Out of the total bamboo forest area of 2,0 4,39,000 ha in India, the growing stock of bamboos in Manipur is estimated to be 11,74,000 ha. Out of India's total growing stock of 3,10,04,000 metric tones, the highest value of 1,14,33,000 MT is obtained from Manipur constituting about 36.8% of the national product. The potential output of bamboo pulpwood at a glance is figured at 14.48 lakhs tones per year and available of extracts/ consumption at 390 tones per day. Paper Mill of a very large capacity can be set-up in the state. Bamboo shoot processing industries can also be set-up based on these bamboos. Bamboo shoot has a very big demand in the international as well as in the national markets.

Many types of wild mushrooms, brooms, Cinnamon, Bay leaf, Goose berry, Soar apple etc. are also available in the hilly forest. They can be collected cheaply, processed and marketed easily.

The ophiolite mineral belt which stretches from Ukhrul District to Chandel District has reported occurrence of many valuable rocks and minerals, such as - lime stone, surpentinite (Black marble), and chromites, nickel, platinum and copper etc. Lime stone is available in the entire Ukhrul District and also the places in and around Sugnu and Chakpikarong like-Berokhudam, Toupokpi, Nungpal, Mombi, Sunumol, Sajik Tampak etc. The Limestone available in these areas are almost of Cement grade. Very large scale cement factories and lime processing units can be established based on these raw-materials.

Surpentinite commercially known as black marble has a very big reserve area of 108 km x 16 km. Marble cutting and polishing units can be set up in the state and it has export potentials. It has also very good demand in the domestic markets.

Petroleum is found in the Imphal valley, Tamenglong, Churachandpur and Jiribam. However, deposit in the Imphal valley can not be exploited since the cape of this reserve had already been destroyed. The deposit of Jiribam is reported to be the largest followed by the Barrak basin of Churachandpur District.Thus, natural gas is present in the Imphal valley and Tamenglong.Above of all these valuable rocks and minerals, coal is reported to be available in the Churachandpur , Noney and Tamenglong. But they are not commercially viable.

Despite of all these scarce rocks and minerals the state Government is not taking-up any remarkable steps for exploration. The State Geology and Mining Department is still kept under the Department of Commerce and Industries, thereby, no fruitful steps has been taken-up so far. Therefore, the State has no record of the availability of such precious things that can be the valuable resources of the state. Many demand-based industries can also be set-up in the State.Industries based on the imported raw-materials.through Moreh such as Dal Mill, Spice Mill, Furniture houses can also be established in the State.

Impediments on Industry in the State

Entrepreneurship is crucial for the growth of a State or country. India is now emerging as a super power by the turn of 2020. It is becoming an economic giant in the Sub-continent. It is the leader of computer software in the world, a prominent leader of Super Computer and becoming a leader in the information technology. It has opened relationship with 10 ASEAN Countries for marketing of its huge industrial products. India has recognised Myanmar as a friend to establish congenial relations with the south Asian countries. Today, India and ASEAN Countries started construction of a Trans Asian Highway which will connect Hong Kong with the Arab countries, later it will extend upto Europe. These countries also started dreaming of an Asian Railway Project which will connect South Asia with the Asian Nations. Such a great change in the nation building is due to the development of Industries. Even though, India is dreaming of a Super Power in the near future the entire North Eastern Region particularly Manipur State is still under the curtail of underdevelopment because of the under development of Entrepreneurship or Industry. The underdevelopment of Industries in Manipur has many reasons. The impediment on the development of Industries in the State is discussed in detail as follows:-

(a) Lack of Financer

(i) Banks: Most of the Industries in the State has a chronic disease called the "shortage of working capital". The State has 10 nationalised Banks, State Bank has 16 Branches, UBI has 15 functioning Branches and 5 derated branches and most branches of UBI are now closed down, UCO has 2 functioning branches and 1 closed branch, Allababad Bank has 1 functioning branch and 1 closed branch, Bank of Baroda has 3 branches, Indian Over Seas Bank has only one branch, Vijaya Bank has 1 functioning branch and 1 closed branch, Punjab and Sind

Bank has 2 branches, Punjab National Bank has one functioning branch and 1 closed branch and Central Bank has 2 functioning branch and 1 closed branch.

The state is having altogether 44 functioning branches with and semi functioning or closed branches. This Bank branch has no fund in their annual budgets for Industrial loan for many years. A few units are getting loans from these banks only on advance appraisal subject to approval of their controlling offices located at Shillong, Guwahati and Silchar. This has caused a great negative impact on the growth of industries in the region.

The State has a financial institution called the "Manipur Industrial Development Financial Corporation" (MANIDCO). MANIDCO is working as the State Industrial Development Corporation as well as the State Financial Corporation. It is the only term loan lending institution in the State, therefore, it is the only hope of the Entrepreneurs in the State for availing financial assistance. MANIDCO had stopped lending of financial assistance from the last decade. The causes of sickness of MANIDCO are many. The main cause is: - this corporation is managing by unspecialised staffs and not adhere to the financing norms and ethics. Thus, many a number of entrepreneurs are the scapegoat of MANIDCO. It gives a serious blow to the development of Entrepreneurship in the State.

(ii) NEDFI: It is the only light at the end of the pipe for the industry loving people of the State. NEDFI has a small branch at Imphal. It is operating with funds from the Department of North East (Donor). Hence, it has equal right of all its constituent states. However, most of the loan of NEDFI goes to the bigger and influential states, thereby weak and smaller states like Manipur cannot get adequate share of loan. Their working in the State office is encouragable, means that the officials are doing at their own will, out of the General procedure. Such style of NEDFI hampers the growth of Entrepreneurship in the State. Therefore, Manipur can not get adequate finance from NEDFI

(b) Incentives

Since the state lies in a hillock and terrain region, any industrial unit needs support for a healthy survival. Moreover, the current law and order situation in the region forced for an exorbitant transportation cost e.g. the transportation charge from Imphal to Guwahati is almost

5 times the cost of transportation from Guwahati to Calcutta. Therefore, the transport subsidy currently provided in the State is not suitable and should be provided at actual from Calcutta or Shilliguri.

The Department of Commerce and Industries, Manipur has no proper fund for giving capital Investment subsidy to the industrial units. In such situation entrepreneurs can not get proper support from the Government, only the Central Capital Investment Subsidy to the tune of 25% of the cost is getting while receiving finance from NEDFI. Only industrial units set up in the identified industrial areas can avail the subsidy.

(c) Infrastructure

(i) Growth Centre/Industrial Estate

The State has no Growth Centre/ Industrial Estate/Industrial area/ Industrial land etc. while other states in the country are having. It is due to the poor financial position or mainly lack of Government willingness. Without the growth Centre regular and uninterrupted power supply, common facility, conducive atmosphere for industry, security etc. shall be a dream only. The only model Industrial Estate at Takyelpat cannot accommodate the need of the upcoming perspective entrepreneurs.

(ii) Road

Most parts of the State including the 3 National Highways have no good all weather metallic roads. The raw-materials from the high mountains can not reach to the factories and most of the fruits on the hill stop are perish on the plant itself or at the villages. Bandh, blockade, submersion of road, land slide, mud slide, threats, looting occupies most time in a year on the National High Ways. Such situation can not bring conducive atmosphere to the Industry.

(iii) Data based

The State has no proper record of any resource and they are accounted/assessed only on the office table. The State has not carried out any Horticultural survey till to-day, even-though, the Horticulture Department is maintaining record of the Horticultural products, based on the data supplied by revenue officer SDCs. Such datas are compiled at the Department, supplied it to the Central Govt. and published in the National Productivity Record.

For rocks and minerals, the Geological Survey of India conducted Geological Mapping in some parts of the State. It is the duty of the State Geology and Mining under the Commerce and Industries Department to explore and survey the size of the deposits and declare as the States resource. These are some of the examples, which the State Govt. is taking no care. The State should introduced a data base and enters all states resources to facilitate proper planning of projects.

(iv) Trainings

Most of the entrepreneurs in the State are not well equipped with technical qualifications. In the case of any technical failure or modification or up-gradation there is none to help them. In most of the trades, there is no expert in the Govt. Department/concerns to guide the entrepreneurs.

Entrepreneurship Development Programmes are conducted by different Government and Private Organization like Small Industries Service Institute, Indian Institute of Entrepreneurship, Institute of Co-Operative Management, All Manipur Entrepreneur's Assn., All Manipur Trained Entrepreneurs' Union, Rural Development Organization and Association of Food Scientist and Technologist and many other smaller organizations. Most of the trainings are conducted only in the name not for the result oriented. After the end of the training programme the trainees are set-off freely and the organizations who conducted the training did not care of their trainees or not taking even a single feed back. Follow-up actions in such EDPs will surely help the prospective entrepreneurs to their esteem venture.

Suggestions

The foregoing discussions expressed the prospects of industries in the State of Manipur and the problems faced by the entrepreneurs. The following suggestions will ease the problems of entrepreneurs to some extent:

(i) Banks be adviced to keep proper fund for industries in their annual budget;

(ii) Introduce pro-rata basis to the State in financing projects under NEDFI (pro rata basis means <u>Population + Unemployment</u> figure).

Budgetary Provision.

(iii) Introduce a data base of resources.

(iv) A Growth Centre be established at a proper place where entrepreneurs work freely and fearlessly and also to enjoy common facility.

(v) Provide adequate fund for Industrial Development in the annual budget of Commerce and Industries Department, Manipur.

(vi) Arrange EDP and Technical training programmes for entrepreneurs with follow up actions.

(vii) Give 30% capital Investment subsidy for new projects and also expansion of the existing units.

(viii) Give more emphasis on local products in all Government purchases.

(ix) Transport Subsidy be provided at actual from Calcutta/Silliguri.

SUMMARY OF RECOMMENDATIONS

1. In order to develop entrepreneurship there must be a multi-pronged approach - develop knowledge, skill and motivation of the individuals to take up entrepreneurial career, create positive family and social environment, create required infrastructure facilities for entrepreneurship to grow, and entrepreneur-friendly environment in the support organizations, including banks and financial institutions. In the strategies everybody will have a role- the government, the support organizations, training organizations, and the entrepreneurs themselves.
2. The government has several roles to play for the growth of entrepreneurship: develop infrastructure facilities, provide policy support, adopt promotional measures and also help in creation of entrepreneur-friendly environment. Infrastructure, particularly power and transport are crucial for growth of entrepreneurship and industry. Efforts are needed to improve power position and also roads and road transport.
3. Manipur and the entire North-Eastern Region has got vast potential for industrial development based on local resources, local potential and skills in particular. Further, it is also observed that women of the North Eastern Region are playing a significant role in the growth of small-scale and household industries. Hence, efforts should be made to divert the attention towards the development of women entrepreneurship and the provision of good and adequate support systems for the speedy growth of small-scale industries, household/cottage industries in Manipur and in the Region as well. This would no doubt boost the rural industrialization but also strengthen the economy of Manipur and of the entire North Eastern Region.

4. State agencies like the Manipur Industrial Development Corporation (MANIDCO),Directorate of Commerce and Industry, the nationalised banks and more particularly, the self-employment schemes initiated by the Government should be implemented honestly which may stimulate the desire of unemployed educated youths to jump into entrepreneurship.
5. Entrepreneurship is the lifeblood of any economy. It is now recognised both in the developed and in developing societies as an essential resources in the development process. The backwardness of the North Eastern Region and state may be attributed largely to the inadequacy of the supply of entrepreneurs in the state. If this deficiency were removed, the state would compete favourably with the rest of the country. The prospective entrepreneurs of the state should be dominated by a need for achievement and be driven by a high degree of motivation, in the absence of which even the highest degree of the opportunities may remain unexploited. To resolved this problems, entrepreneurs, state government, North Eastern Council, and central government's initiation, strong will and firm commitment is a need of the hour.
6. The challenges that lies ahead of the state is to find out the effective strategy for utilizing the materials, human, technological and social resources that we possess in the most rapid, efficient and organized manner. A totally new industrial policy is sought by the entrepreneurs for actual implementation in the most effective way in which main component consists of capital assistance, marketing assistance, power subsidies etc. More and above, it is also needed to bring into view the untapped potentials and unutilized opportunities that await exploitation in the state.
7. Entrepreneurship Development Programme (EDP) should emphasise more on specific target oriented programme for a longer period. Time-consuming process of financial institution/ commercial banks needs to be reviewed to encourage the young and potential entrepreneur. Identified EDP trained potential entrepreneurs should be provided handholding support system by the promotional institute. Technical institute should provide their support system at various level and plan according to its requirements. An effective production and marketing

network can alleviate economy & growth for the small-scale industrial units.

8. The planners and policy makers should be fully familiar with the problems and priorities of entrepreneurship development in the North-Eastern Region. It is therefore suggested that a road map requires to be planned for the promotion of local entrepreneurship with specific targets and all concerned authorities take due responsibility, be it in the area of training, finance, marketing, technology, infrastructure etc. with strict monitoring so that there is a vibrancy and visibility in the performance of the SSI sector.
9. Institutions and government agencies of the state can play a major role in bridging the information gap for the rural population of the state in this era of IT, using computer and internet, they can transmit locally relevant knowledge and information in all areas such as agriculture, small scale industries, live stock management, water management, waste management, health, career guidance etc. to different population segments in rural areas. All of this will contribute to reverse the current trend of urbanization, IT based E-commerce services and to reduce pollution.
10. India is projected to become an IT superpower by 2008. With a little effort, Manipur with all its various advantages, mainly the strong manpower can piggy-ride the country's success in this field. So, persons with suitable training and support should be encouraged to set up their ventures with minimum inputs in terms of investment both in rural and urban area of the state. Only then the State Governments vision of transforming Manipur into Information Technology driven economy and society can be fulfilled.
11. Rural women are empowered socially and economically after having become members of the Self Help Groups (SHGs). Hence, it is the duty of the Government, cooperative organizations, voluntary organization and allied agencies to assist the women in formation and management of many more SHGs covering all the rural areas in Manipur. What they need is encouragement and support from the family members, Government, Society, male counterpart. Greater and continuous

support for entrepreneurial activities is needed to further improve the lives of these women and the condition of their communities. Such a joint effort will help them to go for producing value added industrial products, which will fetch more income to the women entrepreneurs of such Self Help Groups (SHGs).

12. Government and non-Government organization should conduct elaborate training to women entrepreneurs. Government must give subsidies and concessions to women entrepreneurs. Government must make reservation of certain products to women entrepreneurs. Women entrepreneurs association for every state must be formed and should make arrangement for conducting exhibitions and conferences in collaboration with the concerned state Governments. The Government should provide special incentives to the women entrepreneurs.

13. Almost 98 percent of its borders form India's international boundaries- a veritable gateway to the South-East and, in turn, to the world. China to the North, Bangladesh in the South West, Myanmar in the East and Bhutan in the North West share borders with the North-Eastern Region (NER) of India. Thus, the NER possesses strong potential to be a future international trading hot spot and a strategic base for foreign and domestic investors to tap the vast contiguous markets of Myanmar, China, Malaysia, Thailand, Singapore, Philippines, Indonesia and other East and South East Asian Countries. It is this vast potential that the Government of India is giving increasing emphasis on its **" Look East Policy through North East"** Thus, it is clear and evident that the NER is a region in India waiting to things happen because vast opportunities are yet unexplored and unexploited which, in turn, means ample possibilities for entrepreneurship development and, in turn industrial / economic development of the region. Therefore, sooner it is created, better for the entrepreneurship development in the NER.

14. Creation of an environment for innovative tourism services is necessary. Exposure of local entrepreneurs to developed regions in different forms like inbound and outbound tours, exhibitions, fairs and festivals, competitions, symposium etc. may help in

this direction. The growth of tourism ancillary product units at a reachable distance of the major attraction should be encouraged. A special armed professional tourism protection force (non-voluntary) with sufficient calibre to prevent physical assaults to the tourists as well as to the tourism resources of the region should be formed.

15. The food and vegetable processing industry of region is still in its developing stage. Though there are enough potentialities within the region for development of this industry in terms of raw materials etc., yet the industry has to undergo a long process to establish itself in the national market. One of the major hurdles in the way of this potential industry is the lack of entrepreneurial spirit and adequate infrastructure that is a prerequisite for the development of entrepreneurship. The various problems faced by this industry are to be collectively solved by the government and private sector along with the semi government institution to make the food and vegetable industry a landmark in the industrial scenario of region and get the fruit of this 'Sunrise Industry.'

16. There is a need to create awareness about the importance of entrepreneurship in the region and make the farmers receptive to the new ideas, technology through farmer's participation in demonstrations and training programmes. Training facilities with respect to growing of horticultural crops and raising nursery has to be made available as per requirements. Therefore, there is a need for establishing a sound marketing system with forward and backward linkages so that vast potential of horticulture crops can be exploited through adoption of improved production technology. Transforming subsistence level farmers into entrepreneurs will go a long way in bringing about a complete turn around in the economy of North Eastern Region of India.

17. Cooperative societies in the North-Eastern Region are closet with multiple problems. As a change agent Primary Apex Cooperative Societies should be re-strengthened for which possible action plans are to make jointly for serving the purpose of total development in the Region.

18. Growth Centres should be established at proper places where entrepreneurs work freely and fearlessly and also enjoy common facility. Sufficient fund should be allocated in the annual budget of the Industry Department. Follow up actions and escort services should be provided to the EDP trained entrepreneurs. More emphasis should be given on local products in all purchases, and transport subsidy should be provided.

19. In order to develop entrepreneurship in Manipur, there should be a comprehensive plan that will incorporate measures for stimulating, supporting and sustaining entrepreneurship. For stimulating entrepreneurship Manipur should consider setting up of an Institute of Entrepreneurship Development, which will help in the development of entrepreneurship in the North East in general and Manipur in particular.

20. All the states of the region should identify type of industries having comparative advantage for development and exploiting the potential of border trade between North East India and its neighbouring countries and special emphasis should be given for export to the South East Asian countries.

INDEX

A

Academic exercise 382
Academic of Computer and Electronics Centre 208
Access to credit 253
Access to information 253
Active part 258
Adhyaksha 191
Advantages 377
Agriculture sector 155
Agro and Rural Industries 373
Agro-based 358, 361
Akhoiguri 156
All Manipur Entrepreneurs Association 234
All Manipur Trained Entrepreneurs Union 234
Ambani, Anil (of Reliance) 141
America Online 166
Area of health 155
Arunachal Pradesh 246, 301, 362
Assam Productivity Council (APC) 367
Assam Tourism Development Corporation (ATDC) 331
Association of Food Scientist Technologies (AFST) 123
Association of South East Asian Nations (ASEAN) 155
Audio and video 183
Awareness about the importance o entrepreneurship 404

B

Back-end data systems 162
Bamboo craft 208, 392
Banks 395
Bazar 256
Better facilities 280
Bhatia Committee 322
Bhuyan, S.K. 256
Bihar 293
Bill Botton 178
Bio-diversity 309, 310
Black marble 394
Board of Directors (BODs) 271
Border trade 155
Brown, R. 256
B-School graduates 187
Business plan 173
Business to customer (B2C) 198
Business Week 162
Business-to-business (B2B) 198
Buying and selling over digital media 162

C

Cantillon, Ricard 151
Centre for Entrepreneurship Development (CED) 295

Change in attitude 146
– – northeast 146
– – technology 146
Chicken Neck 291
China 310
Churachandpur 394
Clothes 263
Common Salt 392
Communication Skills 270
Community information 191
– Information Centres (CICs) 200
Computer infrastructure worldwide 179
Confederation of Indian Industry (CII) 323
Consortium Approach 135
Cooperative Education Field Project 268
– Identity Statement (ICIS) 380
– societies 379, 404
Cottage unit owners 246
Council of Scientific and Industrial Research (CSI 367
Creative Human Act 152
Credit 271
Critical Study of the Effectiveness of Entrepreneu 299
CSIR 368
Cultivation of off-season vegetables 362
Customary problems 280, 281
Customers 347

D

David, C. McClell 294
Decision-making 269
Declaration of Export House Status 323
Department of Development of North East Region (DO 136
Desk Top Publishing (DTP) 228
Development of Small Enterprises 340
Development of the civilization 141
Digital decade 163
Directorate of Industries & Commerce (DIC) 202
Directorate of Industries (DI) 207
District Industries Centres (DICs) 122 ,210
Dot Com 162
Draft Information Technology Policy 2001 237
Duties 364

E

Ebay 166
E-business 162
E-commerce 188, 191, 199, 201
Economic development and entrepreneurship 139
– Information Service 211
EDP 152, 214, 398
Educated youths 206
Education 154, 253
Educational system 146, 206
E-education 191
E-Entrepreneurs 180
E-entrepreneurship revolution 178
Eight Sister States 291
Electronic commerce 178
Electronic Data Interchange (EDI) 187
Electronics and Information Technology 231
E-mail to communicate 163

Embroidery sector 250
Emergency market 309
Employers 166
Encouragement of entrepreneurship development programme 248
Entrepreneur 151, 184
Entrepreneurial Motivation Training Centres (EMTCs 206, 296
Entrepreneurship 145, 186, 293, 395
Entrepreneurship development 142, 201
Entrepreneurship Development Programme (EDP) 124, 210, 293, 294
Entrepreneurship generation 334
Entrepreneurship in tourism 320
Eri variety 132
Export Packaging Training Programme (EPTP) 210

F

Finance 252, 363
Financial benefit 258
Financial institutions 365
Financial problems 281
Financing agencies 234
Flexibility of working hours 283
Food and Vegetable Processing Industry 404
Food Industry 354
Food processing units 363
Formal education 253
Four P's of Project Conception 172, 176
FPO (Food processing order) 364, 365
Fragile structure of the body 282
FRUIT AND VEGETABLE PROCESSING 354
Fruits and Vegetables (F&V) 355

G

Gates, Bill 163
Gates' 12 steps 163
General agreement 315
General problems 145
Geology 398
Globalisation 166, 340
Gross Domestic Product (GDP) 315
Gujarat 293
Gujarat Industrial Investment Corporation (GIIC) 295
Gupta study group 340

H

Handicap for women entrepreneurs 284
Handloom related enterprise 249
Handloom weaving 207
Handlooms (Reservations of Articles for Production) Act 132, 256
Handlooms and handicrafts industries 256
Haryana 293
Herbal medicines 155
Herlau 333
Higher Income Group 264
Hills, G. E. 133
Home furnishings 129
Home textiles 133
Horticulture 365

I

ICIS 387
Ima Keithel i.e. Mothers Market 259
India plunks 315
Indian economy 121
Indian Institute of Entrepreneurship

(IIE) 206, 208, 235, 297, 299
Indian Institute of Handloom Technology (IIHT) 135
Indian Tourism Development Corporation (ITDC) 321
Indonesia 310
Industrial activity 301
Industrial Development Bank of India (IDBI) 295
Industrial development in India 142
Industrial Policy 2003 304
Industrial Policy resolutions 372
Industrial Potential Survey 211
Information and Communication Technology (ICT) 161, 199
Information kiosks 228
Information Technology (IT) 151, 161, 190, 205
Information Technology awareness programmes 202
Information Technology capital (computer hardware), 165
Information Technology industry 237
Information Technology infrastructure 237
Information Technology literacy programme 219
Information Technology park 219
Information Technology policy 218
Infrastructure 147
Institute of Cooperative Management (ICM) 122, 268
Institute of Entrepreneurship, Guwahati 302
Insurgency problems 144
International Association of Scientific Experts 314
International Telecommunication Union (ITU) 202
Internet and Multimedia 161

K

Kabo 392
Kabow Salt 392
Kanglei Agro Business Services (KABS) 268
Kauna reed 132
Kerala 177
Khandah 156
Khudei 249
Khwairamb 256
Khwairamband Bazar 257
Koike, Sonny 188
Krishnabhai Patel 141

L

Lack of analytical EDP 146
Lack of availability of packing materials 363
Lack of consultancy organisation 146
Lack of infrastructural development 146
Large mineral resources 309
Laxmi bazar 263
Liberalisation 151, 166, 181, 370
Liberalization in the world-economy 314
Liberalized economic regime 323
Lime 356
Linghoinganbi Market 259, 262
Literacy skills 269
Local markets 362
Locality 268
Look East Policy 129
Lower Income Group 264
Lukmai 392

M

Madhya Pradesh 293
Maharashtra 293
Malaysia 310
Management Development Programme (MDP) 124, 210
Managerial Challenges of Small Scale Industries 370
Managerial problems 280, 281
Manipur 143, 144, 246, 301
Manipur Industrial Development Corporation (MANIDC) 122, 401
Manipur industrial policy, 2002 331
Manipur salt 392
Manipur State Cooperative Union (MSCU) 268
Manipur State Wide Area Network (MANNET) 219
Market place 257
Marketing problems 281, 286
McClelland 294
McCulloch 258
McKinsey 129
Middle income group 264
Million dollar 293
Ministry of small scale industries 351
Modern biologists 379
Mombi 394
Moori 156
Multi Fibre Agreement (MFA) 136
Multi-dimensional activity 323
Mynmar 310

N

Nagaland 246
NASA 347
National Bank for Agriculture and Rural Development (NABARD) 122, 207
National Cooperative Union of India (NCUI) 125
National Council of Applied Economic Research 236
National Council of Cooperative Training (NCCT) 125
National Handloom Development Corporation (NHDC) 132
National Institute of Rural Development (NIRD) 202
National Institute of Small Industry Extension 296
National Research Development Corporation (NRDC) 234
National Small Industries Corporation (NSIC) 206
National strategy for tourism development 322
National tourism policy 323
Natural barriers like climatic condition 144
NEDFI 396
Nehru, Jawaharlal 245
NER 291, 292
New Industrial Policy of Manipur 2002 235
New market 259, 262, 263
NGOs 156
NICNET 200
Nirma fame 141
Non-Governmental Organisations (NGOs) 125
North East Region (NER) 154, 206, 310, 355, 400
North Eastern Consultancy Organization (NECON) 208, 234
North Eastern Consultant Limited

(NECON) 206, 211
North Eastern Council (NEC) 296
North Eastern Handicrafts and Handlooms Development 136
North Eastern Industrial and Technical Consultancy 206 296
North Eastern Region (NER) 154, 206
North Eastern States 293
Nungpal 394

O

Observations 264
Oxford Encyclopaedic Dictionary 151

P

Paanwala 141
Packing 284
PACS 387
Panjab 293
People in handloom, handicraft and light food item 156
Periodic market surveys 365
Philippines 310
Phingairuk 392
Pickles of mango 356
Podons 261
Policy statement 332
Population 245
Porter, Michael E. 130
Potential and credit policy 284
Poverty amidst plenty 293
Power 271
Pradhan 191
Pricing place 284
Privatisation 151
Problem is scarcity of raw materials 252
Problems and prospects 139
Problems of government assistance 281
Problems of women entrepreneurs 280
Production of vegetable 367
Production problems 281
Production technologies in fruit crops 366
Productivity of vegetables per unit area 367
Prominent role 250
Promotional agencies 121
Purana bazar 258, 262, 263

Q

Quality Management System 234, 344, 345

R

Raw materials 364
Realizing 294
Reserve Bank of India (RBI) 122
Resource-based theory 178
Resources 147
Ricardo 140
Rupmahal tank 234
Rural Entrepreneurship Development Programme (REDP 122
Rural tourism 336

S

SAARC 310
Say, Jean Baptiste 140, 151
Schumpter, Joseph Alois 152
Self Help Group (SHG) 156, 267-270
women 246, 269-270
Self-propelling growth in rural tourism 336

Selling on the Net 162
Session Court 263
Shikhong, Ningel 392
SIDBI (Small Industries Development Bank of India) 233, 368
Sikkim 246
Singapore 310
Singh, Gambhir 257
Singh, N. Mohendro 236
SISI 124, 208
Six broad areas of tourism policy 330
Skill Development Programme (SDP) 210
Skill in handlooms and handicrafts 258
Skilled and semiskilled labour 363
Small Industries Development Bank of India (SIDBI) 367
Small Industries Development Organization (SIDO) 192, 208, 295, 343
Small Industries Service Institute (SISI) 122, 206, 295
Small Industry Development in Selected Asian Count 297
Small Industry Extension and Training Institute (SIETI) 294
Smith, Adam 140, 269
Social forestry 267
Socio-economic traditions 332
Soil conservation 267
State industrial profile 211
State informatics centre/districts 200
State information literacy policy 203
State Institutes of Rural Development (SIRD) 202
State policy of small scale industries 203
State Pollution Control Board 232
Statistical Handbook Assam, 2002 321
Strength 130
Successful SHGs in Imphal East District 270
Sunumol 394
Surveyed societies 385
Sweets 261

T

Tamenglong 394
Tampak, Sajik 394
Taxes 364
Technical Consultancy Organisations (TCOs) 248, 295
Technological innovation 166
Technopreneurship 164, 165*412*
Tetzschner 333
Thailand 310
Thangjao 392
Thompson, John 178
Thrust Areas 235
Tikendrajit, Bir road 257
Tools 358
Total population 320
Total Quality Management (TQM) 342, 347, 350
Tourism 155
Tourism and hotel industry 365
Tourism Business Incubator 334
Tourism services 337, 403
Trade in services (GATS, 1994) 315
Trade Unions 166
Traditional herbal medicines 155
Traditional university programme 165
Training programmes 207

Transact commerce 162
Traveller's Companion 322
Tripura 246
Typical global restructuring process 322

U

Unemployment 206
Unemployment problem 122
United Nations Conference on Environment and Development 317
University of texas 165
Up-Pradhan of Panchayat 191

V

Various constraints 280
Various obstacles 147
Vast natural resources 143
Velya Vahini 183
Voluntary organization 214

W

Waikhong 392
Warehousing 363
Warfare between Manipur and Burma 257
Watershed project 267
Weakness 130
Web technology 161
Whinston, Andrew 165
Williams 320
Women businessman of Chakrikom Bazar 263
Women businessman runs 263
Women Cooperative Education Project 268
Women Cooperatives 271
Women entrepreneurs 145, 245, 250, 256, 266
Women market 256, 258
Women walk miles 256
Womenfolk (*pungou phanek*) 261
World Bank Report (1991) 266
World Tourism Organisation (WTO) 136, 315, 316, 317
World Travel and Tourism Council (WTTC) 316
Woven Textiles 129

Y

Yahoo 166
Young women 263